Business
Plans
Handbook

Business Plans

A COMPILATION OF BUSINESS PLANS DEVELOPED BY INDIVIDUALS THROUGHOUT NORTH AMERICA

Handbook

VOLUME

33

**Kristin B. Mallegg,
Project Editor**

GALE
CENGAGE Learning·

Farmington Hills, Mich • San Francisco • New York • Waterville, Maine
Meriden, Conn • Mason, Ohio • Chicago

Business Plans Handbook, Volume 33

Project Editor: Kristin B. Mallegg

Content Developer: Michele P. LaMeau

Product Design: Jennifer Wahi

Composition and Electronic Prepress: Evi Seoud

Manufacturing: Rita Wimberley

For product information and technology assistance, contact us at
Gale Customer Support, 1-800-877-4253.
For permission to use material from this text or product,
submit all requests online at **www.cengage.com/permissions.**
Further permissions questions can be emailed to
permissionrequest@cengage.com

Gale, a part of Cengage Learning
27500 Drake Rd.
Farmington Hills, MI 48331-3535

ISBN-13: 978-1-56995-844-5
1084-4473

Printed in Mexico
1 2 3 4 5 6 7 19 18 17 16 15

Contents

CONTENTS

Highlights

Business Plans Handbook, Volume 33 (BPH-33) is a collection of business plans compiled by entrepreneurs seeking funding for small businesses throughout North America. For those looking for examples of how to approach, structure, and compose their own business plans, *BPH-33* presents 20 sample plans, including plans for the following businesses:

*   Academic Testing Improvement Service
*   Children's Party Planner
*   Custom Monogramming and Engraving Services
*   Custom Spiritwear Company
*   Estate Sale Organization
*   Internet Cafe
*   Lawn and Garden Equipment Repair Business
*   Library Systems Consultants
*   Medical Marijuana Clinic
*   Mobile Wood-Burning Pizza Oven Business
*   Nightclub
*   Nutritionist
*   Pediatric Special Needs Advocate Business
*   Real Estate Developer
*   Refreshment Stand
*   Senior Advocate Business
*   Tree Care and Trimming Business
*   Veterinary Practice
*   Video Game Studio
*   Winery

FEATURES AND BENEFITS

BPH-33 offers many features not provided by other business planning references including:

*   Twenty business plans, each of which represent an attempt at clarifying (for themselves and others) the reasons that the business should exist or expand and why a lender should fund the enterprise.
*   Two fictional plans that are used by business counselors at a prominent small business development organization as examples for their clients. (You will find these in the Business Plan Template Appendix.)

- A directory section that includes listings for venture capital and finance companies, which specialize in funding start-up and second-stage small business ventures, and a comprehensive listing of Service Corps of Retired Executives (SCORE) offices. In addition, the Appendix also contains updated listings of all Small Business Development Centers (SBDCs); associations of interest to entrepreneurs; Small Business Administration (SBA) Regional Offices; and consultants specializing in small business planning and advice. It is strongly advised that you consult supporting organizations while planning your business, as they can provide a wealth of useful information.

- A Small Business Term Glossary to help you decipher the sometimes confusing terminology used by lenders and others in the financial and small business communities.

- A cumulative index, outlining each plan profiled in the complete Business Plans Handbook series.

- A Business Plan Template which serves as a model to help you construct your own business plan. This generic outline lists all the essential elements of a complete business plan and their components, including the Summary, Business History and Industry Outlook, Market Examination, Competition, Marketing, Administration and Management, Financial Information, and other key sections. Use this guide as a starting point for compiling your plan.

- Extensive financial documentation required to solicit funding from small business lenders. You will find examples of Cash Flows, Balance Sheets, Income Projections, and other financial information included with the textual portions of the plan.

Introduction

Perhaps the most important aspect of business planning is simply doing it. More and more business owners are beginning to compile business plans even if they don't need a bank loan. Others discover the value of planning when they must provide a business plan for the bank. The sheer act of putting thoughts on paper seems to clarify priorities and provide focus. Sometimes business owners completely change strategies when compiling their plan, deciding on a different product mix or advertising scheme after finding that their assumptions were incorrect. This kind of healthy thinking and re-thinking via business planning is becoming the norm. The editors of *Business Plans Handbook, Volume 33 (BPH-33)* sincerely hope that this latest addition to the series is a helpful tool in the successful completion of your business plan, no matter what the reason for creating it.

This thirty-third volume, like each volume in the series, offers business plans created by real people. *BPH-33* provides 20 business plans. The business and personal names and addresses and general locations have been changed to protect the privacy of the plan authors.

NEW BUSINESS OPPORTUNITIES

As in other volumes in the series, *BPH-33* finds entrepreneurs engaged in a wide variety of creative endeavors. Examples include a custom spiritwear company, a nutritionist, and a pediatric special needs advocate business. In addition, several other plans are provided, including a medical marijuana clinic, a nightclub, and a refreshment stand, among others.

Comprehensive financial documentation has become increasingly important as today's entrepreneurs compete for the finite resources of business lenders. Our plans illustrate the financial data generally required of loan applicants, including Income Statements, Financial Projections, Cash Flows, and Balance Sheets.

ENHANCED APPENDIXES

In an effort to provide the most relevant and valuable information for our readers, we have updated the coverage of small business resources. For instance, you will find a directory section, which includes listings of all of the Service Corps of Retired Executives (SCORE) offices; an informative glossary, which includes small business terms; and a cumulative index, outlining each plan profiled in the complete *Business Plans Handbook* series. In addition we have updated the list of Small Business Development Centers (SBDCs); Small Business Administration Regional Offices; venture capital and finance companies, which specialize in funding start-up and second-stage small business enterprises; associations of interest to entrepreneurs; and consultants, specializing in small business advice and planning. For your reference, we have also reprinted the business plan template, which provides a comprehensive overview of the essential components of a business plan and two fictional plans used by small business counselors.

SERIES INFORMATION

If you already have the first thirty-two volumes of *BPH*, with this thirty-third volume, you will now have a collection of over 600 business plans (not including the updated plans); contact information for hundreds of organizations and agencies offering business expertise; a helpful business plan template; more than 1,500 citations to valuable small business development material; and a comprehensive glossary of terms to help the business planner navigate the sometimes confusing language of entrepreneurship.

ACKNOWLEDGEMENTS

The Editors wish to sincerely thank the contributors to *BPH-33*, including:

*   BizPlanDB.com
*   Fran Fletcher
*   Paul Greenland
*   Claire Moore
*   Zuzu Enterprises

COMMENTS WELCOME

Your comments on *Business Plans Handbook* are appreciated. Please direct all correspondence, suggestions for future volumes of *BPH*, and other recommendations to the following:

Managing Editor, Business Product
Business Plans Handbook
Gale, a part of Cengage Learning
27500 Drake Rd.
Farmington Hills, MI 48331-3535
Phone: (248)699-4253
Fax: (248)699-8052
Toll-Free: 800-347-GALE
E-mail: BusinessProducts@gale.com

Academic Testing Improvement Service

Academic Assistance

20 Elmstead Ln.
Madison, Wisconsin 53705

Juan C. Falquez, Sutton Lasater, Scott MacArthur, and Tracy Reynolds

Academic Assistance is a LLC created with the intention of helping students throughout school. Our mission is to foster the improvement of students' performance during test taking by means of tools that would help them perform more efficiently and effectively.

*This business plan appeared in a previous volume of **Business Plans Handbook**. It has been updated for this volume.*

EXECUTIVE SUMMARY

Business Overview

Academic Assistance is a LLC created with the intention of helping students throughout school. Our mission is to foster the improvement of students' performance during test taking by means of tools that would help them perform more efficiently and effectively. We decided to form a LLC to get all the benefits of forming a corporation and avoid drawbacks such as double taxation and excessive paperwork.

Our reason for existence is the constant need for students' academic improvement. Nowadays, advertisers would have you believe that through study techniques and/or nutritional supplements, students are able to study for a test within a night, take it in matter of minutes and still get an A or B grade. Unfortunately, the reality for many students is different. While many students can finish their test in an average of twenty minutes, others are not able to finish it within the time given. Some students would study really hard for days and still would not get a good grade, perhaps due to a failure to properly fill in the answer sheet. We felt that students within this segment were under-represented and not given the attention that they deserve. We feel that with the use of our inaugural product, the *Precise Pencil*, their needs will be more fully met and we would be solving the test-time problem as well as the problem of inaccurately filling out the answer sheet.

PRODUCTS & SERVICES

Precise Pencil

The *Precise Pencil* is the first product of our company. It intends to replace the No. 2 pencil, normally used on tests that require the use of a Scantron sheet. Eventually, we hope that the *Precise Pencil* will become the standard utensil for test taking. The *Precise Pencil* is very user friendly. When the student is ready to fill in the blank circles, all he/she needs to do is to place the pencil right on the circle he/she wishes to fill in and then push down. The mechanism inside the pencil will make the graphite lead twist down, applying enough pressure to leave a solid mark, simulating the action of a stamper.

The concept of the *Precise Pencil* is one that is a little difficult to create because it is the first one of its kind. In order to perfect and utilize the *Precise Pencil* to the fullest, the prototype works along the same concepts as the mechanical pencil. The *Precise Pencil* takes the traditional mechanical pencil model, and alters it so that instead of the user clicking on the top part of the base unit, there is another tubular base that fits within the original base, which makes it possible for the user to push down to activate the movement of the pencil lead out of the base. Additionally, one of the primary modifications made to the prototype is the twisting action as the pencil lead descends from the base unit, which accounts for the way the mark on the Scantron sheet is made. In order to make this possible, the *Precise Pencil* has a spring loaded twisting action that occurs when the inner base is pressed inward. One of the other key differences in this product is the 3 mm lead required to operate the device. This is the size needed to fill in the entire Scantron bubble. A common question that comes to the floor is if it will be possible to replace the lead within the *Precise Pencil*. At Academic Assistance, we have figured out a way around that. Each time the pencil deploys lead, the track holding the lead returns to approximately half of the original length of deployment. This will cause the lead to continue to move closer and closer to the bottom of the base, until the time is needed for a replacement of the lead.

After running several test–trials, we realized that the majority of students focus most of their time in the actual test and leave little time to fill in the blanks of the Scantron sheet. We also found that on average, a student takes between four to seven minutes to fill in the circles of a Scantron sheet of a fifty question test. Time is an important element during test taking and we hope that the *Precise Pencil* helps reduce this time down to one to two minutes.

In order to manufacture this product, any pencil manufacturer that makes mechanical pencils would suffice because of the similarities in the design. Some of the companies that have facilities already set up that could handle a product like this are: Kingways Stationary Company Ltd (China, Taiwan), Guangdong Genvana Stationary Company Ltd (China), Shenzhen Acme Pen Co Ltd (China), Blue Bond Technology Industry Co Ltd (Taiwan). Because there are more parts involved in the creation of the *Precise Pencil*, Academic Assistance has to charge a mildly higher price based on complexity of the prototype design.

This product is very revolutionary because it is the first one of its kind to do something this user–friendly. The *Precise Pencil* is so easy to use that all a user has to do is place the base over the desired Scantron bubble and push down to fill in the necessary bubble. The *Precise Pencil* is a practical and time saving solution to long Scantron tests, which could greatly benefit anyone.

A second, complimentary product will also be produced once the *Precise Pencil* is well established. This product will be the elctronic counterpart to the *Precise Pencil,* and will work with tests being administered via touch screen devices such as the iPad and Microsoft Surface Pro. The electronic pen or stylus will work in much the same way as the *Precise Pencil,* but it will help students clearly and quickly identify their answer in a way that is safe for the device and more accurate than their fingertip. As more and more school settings are moving towards this type of testing for state tests and college admissions tests, this product will only increase in need and demand. The success of the *Precise Pencil* will put us squarely in the lead to produce this offshoot product.

MARKET ANALYSIS

The pencil industry is comprised of numerous producers which include, but are not limited to: Paper Mate, BIC, Faber–Castell, Musgrave Pencil Company, General Pencil Company, Dixon Ticonderoga Pencil Company, Liberty Pencil Company Limited, and the American Pencil Company. Although all of these companies and more manufacture pencils as well as other writing utensils, there is not a single business in the industry that creates a *Precise Pencil* or similar product, which is a void in the market that we hope to fill.

Currently, the pencil industry is growing every year. Although more and more people are using word processors instead of using a wooden pencil (which dates back to over 400 years ago), the industry is still experiencing growth. The industry has about a $220 million dollar market, and some companies have been increasing production, some by up to 12 percent from 2013 to 2014. In 2014, it is estimated that over 15 billion pencils were sold worldwide. Some financial numbers in the industry are as follows:

- Industry Average Annual Sales: $6,263,945

- Cost of Sales: $3,679,442

- Gross Profit: $2,584,503

Clearly, the pencil industry is one that can offer high profits and large growth. At Academic Assistance, we feel that entrance into this large market, especially with our new product, will not be associated with high risk or threat of failure.

Customers

The market for our product is mainly focused on students at institutions that use Scantron exam sheets. We could market our product to students as well as schools, which may opt to buy our product to offer to their students for no cost. This would be especially beneficial to schools in low–income areas where students don't have the disposable income to buy our product. Across the United States, there are 54.8 million students in 129,200 public, private, and chartered primary and secondary schools. About $619 billion will be spent per year related to their education. As far as post–secondary schools, there are 21 million two- and four-year college students in private and public institutions and full-time and part-time programs. There are 4,599 post-secondary schools which includes private, public, two-year schools and four-year schools. The market for our product is clearly very large and, if properly marketed and manufactured, our product has the potential to help any of the aforementioned students with test taking.

Academic Assistance has the option of marketing the *Precise Pencil* to schools or to the students themselves. Marketing to schools may provide our business with more sales since schools may like to provide this product to all of their students, as to give all of them a better test–taking advantage. Marketing to students, however, may provide our company with the option to create a "hot trend" in the school supply market. When back–to–school shopping, many students race to get the hot new products, and we believe that our product has the potential to become one of the latest back–to–school trends.

Another potential market that Academic Assistance may have for the *Precise Pencil* is to sell to office supply stores. Some office supply stores that we may focus on selling our product to include, but are not limited to: Staples (1,621 stores), Office Depot/OfficeMax (2,000+ stores), Target (1,790 U.S. stores), and Wal–Mart (11,000 stores worldwide). The benefit of marketing our product to office supply stores is that Academic Assistance would not need to focus on direct sales to the consumer, but rather sell in bulk quantities.

At Academic Assistance, we have also been researching selling our product to Scantron, who would then be able to sell our product with their Scantron sheets. Approximately 96 percent of schools across the country at all levels use Scantron sheets, which is about 52 million students. If Academic Assistance can effectively market to these students and can earn sales from even one half of one percent of them, there is the potential to sell nearly 300,000 *Precise Pencils*. By selling our pencils to Scantron, they can use the market ties that they have already established and sell our product to supplement theirs.

Strengths and Weaknesses

A thorough analysis of the strengths, weaknesses, opportunities, and threats of our product can be seen below. This analysis demonstrates areas that are positive to our company as well as possible limitations or areas in which to improve.

Strengths

- No product like this on the market

- Potentially raises students' grades by giving them more time to focus on the test itself as well as eliminating errors when filling in the answer sheet

- Students are becoming more competitive with academics and want to have the best scores possible

Weaknesses

- Possible lack of need for product since it hasn't yet been developed

- Unsure about darkness of the lead mark left on Scantron sheet

- The No. 2 pencil has been around for over 400 years and has survived the introductions of ball point pens and computers

- Poor economy encourages people to be thrifty rather than frivolous (*Precise Pencil* may be considered a frivolous item)

- The move to electronic test taking via computer or online applications may eliminate the need for *Precise Pencil*

BUSINESS STRATEGY

In order to determine what we needed to do next in terms of our future action plan we turned to Stanley Rooke. Stanley Rooke is the Associate Director and head of Intellectual Property at Suburban University. We went to him to discuss how to keep our idea safe from being copied, what procedures we would need to go through, and any other information that he could give to us.

After meeting with Stanley Rooke, our next step is to apply for a utility patent (1.16A1). A utility patent protects any new invention or functional improvements on existing inventions. This can be to a product, machine, a process, or even composition of matter. The basic filing fee for a utility patent is $280.00. The process to be granted a utility patent takes anywhere from six months to one year. Once we are granted a utility patent it is good for twenty years.

Once we have filed for our utility patent, our next step will be to create non–disclosure agreements. These are extremely important to create because they ensure that, while our patent is being processed, nobody that works on this project can steal our idea. We will draft a document that anyone that has any interaction with this project will have to sign. These could be our engineers that we have physically creating the product, attorneys that are helping us with legal issues, or counterparts. We will make sure not to discuss this project and/or idea with anyone that has not signed or that refuses to sign our non–disclosure agreement.

In congruence with the non–disclosure agreement, we will be contracting a mechanical engineer. Once again, before the engineer begins working on this project and before we discuss it with him/her we will have them sign a non–disclosure agreement. We are contracting a mechanical engineer so that they will be able to design and build our initial prototype. We will then be able to take this prototype with us to explain how our product works, to help gain more funding, and for our sales pitches. Once we have a prototype it will be much more feasible for us to be able to gain investor interest and expand our product. This way we will allow people to see and use the prototype so that they are able to gain a better understanding of how it works.

Once we have our prototype, we will apply for a design patent (1.16B1). A design patent protects the ornamental design, configuration, improved decorative appearance, or shape of an invention. A design patent also grants the exclusive right to manufacture or sell your design. The basic filing fee for a design patent is $180.00. The process to be granted a design patent takes anywhere from six months to one year. Once we are granted a design patent it is good for fourteen years.

Once we have filed for all of our patents and we have our initial prototype completed, it will be time to conduct some market research. We want to conduct market research in order to gauge the response to our new pencil. We want to be able to make sure that consumers like it, that universities find it to be a beneficial tool, and that people would actually use it. In order to conduct this market research we are going to conduct focus groups. These focus groups will consist of eight to ten people. We will give them a questionnaire to answer on a Scantron sheet and also provide them with our new pencil. Once they are finished using it we will be able to talk to them and see what they thought of it. Throughout the time they take the test we will also be observing to make sure that the pencil is working properly and that nobody is having problems with it. We will also conduct surveys and hand out prototypes in classrooms since our main target market is universities and students.

FINANCIAL ANALYSIS

In order to fund our costly endeavor we have come up with various outlets. We plan to apply for United States' grants that are geared towards education advancement. We feel that our product can enhance the achievement of students across the nation with their education and, because of this, we feel that we would be the perfect candidates to receive a grant that is geared towards educational advancement.

We also plan on getting in contact with the Educational Testing Service. The Educational Testing Service is the organization that proctors tests such as the GRE and TOEFL. We hope to present our prototype to them to be able to form some type of a partnership. Many of the tests that this organization proctors are administered on Scantron sheets, which are what our new pencil is compatible with. We hope that the Educational Testing Service will be interested in a partnership in order to make their testing methods easier for those taking the test. Another possible alliance will be pursued with CollegeBoard, makers of the SAT and AP tests, and a good fit for the *Precise Pencil*.

Lastly, we would like to talk with university investors. With the help of the Educational Testing Service, high schools and universities will gain interest and invest in the product of their respective schools. All schools are interested in ways to advance their level of education and we feel that this would be an appropriate use of their funds. One set of university investors that we especially would like to get in contact with are the Investors of Suburban University (ISU). Seeing that we are all students at this university, we feel that we would have a good chance of gaining funds from them for a product that was not only developed by their own students but that will benefit their students for years to come.

CONCLUSION

In conclusion, once we have the funding that we need to cover the startup costs for the *Precise Pencil*, we will find a low–cost manufacturer to mass produce the prototype. Then we will find a distributor to distribute to the office supply store chains, such as Office Depot and Office Max. We also plan to market the *Precise Pencil* to universities in order to further the advancement of educational tools. We will market to Scantron as well, in hopes to create a bundle package. Anyone that would purchase the Scantron sheets and machines from the company would then be able to get the *Precise Pencil* as well.

Children's Party Planner
Party Pizzazz

16652-A Tomahawk Circle
Tallahassee, Florida 32307

Fran Fletcher

Party Pizzazz is a home-based party planning service for kids located in Tallahassee, Florida. It is owned and operated by Priscilla Young, a graduate student at Florida State.

BUSINESS OVERVIEW

Party Pizzazz is a home-based party planning service for kids located in Tallahassee, Florida. It is owned and operated by Priscilla Young, a graduate student at Florida State.

Starting a party planning service is a way that Ms. Young can work part time and offset her living expenses while attending school full time. The idea for Party Pizzazz was conceived after she helped plan birthday parties for several friends' children. Attendees were impressed with her creativity and told her that she should start a business.

Party Pizzazz will offer party ideas to clients or will take a client's idea and find all of the accessories and plan all of the details. Busy parents with limited time will be the target market of Party Pizzazz. Customers can choose from a list of themes or Party Pizzazz can help customers who have a unique or personalized theme in mind. Services include, but are not limited, to:

- Theme suggestions
- Custom party favors
- Custom decorations
- Decorating assistance
- Balloon filling
- Goody bags
- Character visits (10 Princesses available)
- Scheduling performers i.e. Clowns, other characters
- Ordering inflatables

The entertainment industry for kids is a multi-million dollar industry. Children's parties are big business and themed parties are all the rage, with parents forking over an average of $300 per party, as they try to make their children's parties fun and memorable.

7

There are approximately 19,410 children in Leon County, Florida under the age of 13. Ms. Young hopes to plan as many of these kids' parties as possible.

Social media and referrals will serve as the main ways of getting the word out about Party Pizzazz.

Ms. Young is seeking a small loan in the amount of $2,500 to cover upfront costs to get started. She is confident that the business will grow and that she will pay back this loan in 13 months.

COMPANY DESCRIPTION

Location
Ms. Young will perform business operations from her home and will meet clients at their homes or other agreed upon locations.

Hours of Operation

Consultation
Hours will depend upon Ms. Young's class schedule. Customers will be able to contact her by phone, email, or text at any hour and she will get back with them promptly.

Party Set-up
Ms. Young will be available for set-up two hours or more prior to an event. Most event set-up will occur on the weekend, but set-up is also available on weeknights.

Personnel

Priscilla Young
Priscilla has a B.S. in Chemistry from Georgia State College and is currently pursuing her MBA at Florida State.

Ms. Young will be the sole proprietor and will perform all duties associated with the business. If she needs help for any particular project, she will pay friends to help her as required. She will not personally make cookies, cupcakes, or other confections at this time, but will use Holly Cakes of Tallahassee, Florida.

Products and Services

Services
Party Pizzazz will make planning an awesome party as quick and easy as making a phone call. Customers can choose from a list of themes or Party Pizzazz can help customers who have a unique or personalized theme in mind. Party Pizzazz will order the appropriate decorations and party favors for one-of-a-kind parties. Services include, but are not limited, to:

- Theme suggestions
- Custom party favors
- Custom decorations
- Decorating
- Balloon filling
- Goody bags
- Character visits (10 Princesses available)
- Scheduling performers i.e. Clowns, other characters
- Ordering inflatables

Products

Party Pizzazz will not keep party supplies in stock due to inadequate storage facilities. Rather, supplies will be ordered as needed.

MARKET ANALYSIS

Industry Overview

The entertainment industry for kids is a multi-million dollar industry. According to the Bureau of Labor Statistics, the event planning industry is set to increase by 33% over the next ten years. Children's parties are big business and themed parties are all the rage, with parents forking over an average of $300 per party. Many middle to high-income families spend more than that, as they try to make their children's parties fun and memorable.

Target Market

The target market for Party Pizzazz will be busy parents of kids of all ages who need help with party planning in the Tallahassee, Florida area. The University of Florida estimates that in 2014, there were approximately 19,410 children in Leon County, Florida under the age of 13. The owners of Party Pizzazz hope to plan as many of these kids' parties as possible.

Competition

There are several party supply stores, wedding planners, and caterers in Tallahassee, but there are no other businesses that advertise exclusively as party planners for children's parties.

GROWTH STRATEGY

The overall strategy of Party Pizzazz is to be the premiere business for Tallahassee-area kids to call for all of their birthday party needs. Additionally, it is the goal of Party Pizzazz to obtain and retain a loyal customer base and to achieve strong financial growth during the first year of operation. The company will strive to come up with new and exciting party themes and ideas in order to make clients feel special and to make parties unique. The owner of Party Pizzazz will consider buying inflatables to rent after the business profits become stable.

Sales and Marketing

The owner has identified key tactics to support the business's growth strategy.

Advertising/marketing will include:

- Social media—party pictures from Party Pizzazz customers will be used to advertise services

- Referrals—referrals will be vital to the business, as satisfied customers suggest that their friends use Party Pizzazz

- Fliers—fliers will be posted around campus and at local party supply stores

Party Pizzazz plans to partner with other vendors in the party industry and its customers will benefit from those connections.

FINANCIAL ANALYSIS

Start-up Costs

Start-up costs will be minimal. Ms. Young only wants to borrow enough so that she will not have to request up-front payment from her customers.

Start-up costs

Cash on hand for supplies	$2,500
Total	**$2,500**

Estimated Monthly Expenses

Monthly expenses are going to be directly related to the number of customers. For parties with estimated expenses exceeding $500, one half of the payment will be required up-front.

Monthly expenses

Loan	$200
Phone/Internet	$150
Gas	$100
Total	**$450**

Estimated Monthly Income

The number of parties and related services will determine monthly income.

Price Schedule

Prices for services

Party set-up	$35 per hour
Party planning	$100 per party
Character dress-up	$100 per party
Goody bags	$20 per 10 bags
Balloon filling	$10 per 10 balloons

Profit/Loss

Party Pizzazz will offer party set-up services. If all parties occur within the Tallahassee perimeter, Ms. Young should be able to set up for four parties each day.

Conservative estimates show 2 parties booked in the first month. Subsequent months are estimated with an increasing number of parties each month and a variety of additional services added.

Profit/loss

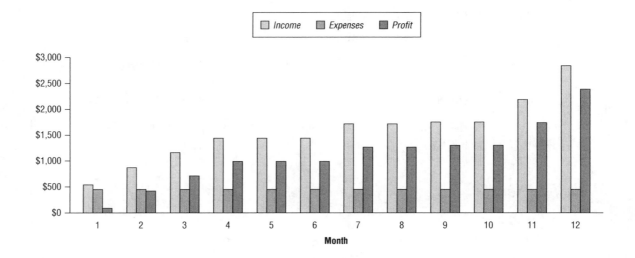

Annual profit/loss

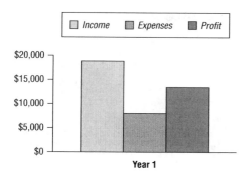

Financing

The owner of Party Pizzazz wishes to obtain financing in the form of a business loan or line of credit for the amount needed to cover the start up costs. This loan would be in the amount of $2,500. Party Pizzazz will be able to pay back the loan in 13 months.

Repayment plan

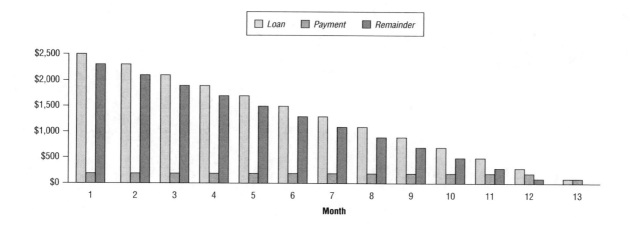

Custom Monogramming & Engraving Services

C h i c a d e e z

135 Tumbleweed Street
Clovis, New Mexico 88101

Fran Fletcher

Chicadeez is a monogramming and engraving service located in Clovis, New Mexico. Its owner, Isabella Morales, is a talented seamstress and she wants to expand her talents into personalizing items through embroidery and engraving. Chicadeez will be located at Ms. Morales's home and will provide services to local clients. Additionally, she will have an online store hosted by the website Crafty.com.

BUSINESS OVERVIEW

Chicadeez is a monogramming and engraving service located in Clovis, New Mexico. Its owner, Isabella Morales, is a talented seamstress and she wants to expand her talents into personalizing items through embroidery and engraving. Chicadeez will be located at Ms. Morales's home and will provide services to local clients. Additionally, she will have an online store hosted by the website Crafty.com.

Since Chicadeez will be a side job for Ms. Morales in the beginning, local customers can schedule a time to drop off and pick up items that they wish to have monogrammed. Chicadeez will ship items purchased in its online store on Monday and Thursday of each week.

Monogramming is very popular at the moment and there is a large demand for quality work at an affordable price with quick turn around time. According to the Bureau of Labor Statistics, jobs for craft and fine artists are expected to increase by 3% over the next ten years.

Chicadeez will have both an online and local market for its products and services. The local target market for Chicadeez will be businesses and schools in the surrounding area that wish to have their logos monogrammed onto various items. The target market for the Chicadeez online store will be customers from all over the country who want custom monogrammed products at an affordable price.

There are numerous online competitors that offer monogramming services. Chicadeez plans to set itself apart by offering competitive pricing and 3-day turn around on most items.

There is one competitor in Clovis offering similar services, but Chicadeez plans to set itself apart from this local competitor by offering volume discounts on monogramming services and by also offering laser-etching services.

The growth strategy for Chicadeez includes opening a web-based store on the widely visited online marketplace Crafty.com so that it will have a nationwide customer base. She will use SEO tactics to drive traffic to her Crafty.com store. The business strategy for sustaining and increasing local growth is to seek contracts with local businesses and schools.

Ms. Morales wishes to obtain financing in the form of a business loan or line of credit for $14,400. This will cover start-up costs and three months' expenses. According to conservative sales projections, Chicadeez should be able to pay back the loan in 36 months.

COMPANY DESCRIPTION

Location

Ms. Morales will perform business operations at her home.

Hours of Operation

Chicadeez will be open for local customers to drop off/pick up items by appointment only.

Chicadeez will ship items on Monday and Thursday of each week.

Personnel

Isabella Morales

Initially, Ms. Morales will perform all duties associated with the business. She is a talented seamstress and enjoys using her creative side to make various crafts.

Products and Services

Services

Chicadeez will personalize various items by monogramming and laser etching. Customers can drop off or ship their items to Chicadeez, or purchase items from the online store.

Products

Monogrammed and etched items will be available to purchase.

MARKET ANALYSIS

Industry Overview

According to the Bureau of Labor Statistics, jobs for craft and fine artists are expected to increase by 3% over the next ten years.

Monogramming is very popular at the moment and there is a large demand for quality work at an affordable price with quick turn around time. Clovis is home to more than 30,000 residents. This will provide a large local customer base.

Target Market

Chicadeez will have both an online and local market.

The online target market for Chicadeez will be customers from all over the country who want custom monogrammed products at an affordable price.

The local target market for Chicadeez will be individuals, businesses, and schools in the surrounding area that wish to have their logos monogrammed onto various items.

Competition

There are numerous online businesses that offer monogramming services. Chicadeez plans to set itself apart by offering competitive pricing and 3-day turn around on most items.

There is one local competitor in Clovis—The Embroidery Place, located at 1875 Old Hobbs Highway. They offer monogramming services on various cloth items.

Chicadeez plans to set itself apart from this local competitor by offering volume discounts on monogramming services and by also offering laser-etching services.

GROWTH STRATEGY

Ms. Morales plans to open a web-based store on the widely visited online marketplace Crafty.com so that she will have a nationwide customer base. She will use SEO tactics to drive traffic to her Crafty.com store.

The business strategy to sustain and increase local growth is to seek contracts with local businesses and schools.

Sales and Marketing

Chicadeez has identified key tactics to sustain its growth strategy.

Initial and ongoing advertising/marketing will include:

- Crafty.com—the notoriety of the online marketplace will bring potential customers to the online store.

- Promotional codes—Chicadeez will advertise promotional codes through social media that can be used at its online store.

- Newspaper—the Clovis newspaper will be used for local advertising. A coupon will be placed in the paper to celebrate the grand opening.

- Social media—pictures of Ms. Morales's creations will be posted to boost both online and local sales.

- Volume discounts—Ms. Morales will give samples to local businesses and school administrators in order to showcase her work and obtain their business. Businesses and schools may receive a volume discount for 10 or more of the same item.

- Fliers—Fliers for Chicadeez will be placed in several local children's clothing boutiques.

FINANCIAL ANALYSIS

Start-up Costs

The embroidery and laser etching machines make up the bulk of start-up costs.

Start-up costs

Advertising	$ 300
Business cards	$ 50
Crafty.com hosting/listing fees	$ 100
Embroidery machine	$ 5,000
Laser etching machine	$ 2,000
Products for online store	$ 3,000
Embroidery supplies	$ 800
Total	**$11,250**

Estimated Monthly Expenses

Monthly expenses

Loan	$ 400
Phone/Internet	$ 150
Advertising	$ 50
Payment services	$ 150
Supplies	$ 300
Total	**$1,050**

Estimated Monthly Income

The monthly profit will serve as Ms. Morales's income. Net sales will determine business income. Internet sales will be active 24 hours a day, 7 days a week.

Estimated prices for monogramming products provided by local customers:

Product	Price
Baby items	
Blankets	$ 6
Bibs	$ 6
Sleepers	$ 8
Onesies	$ 6
Towels	$ 8
Socks	$ 8
Hair accessories	$ 6
Toddler/kids clothing	
Girls tops	$10
Dresses	$10
Overalls	$10
Boys shirts	$10
Adult clothing	
Polo shirts	$ 8
Tee shirts	$ 8
Athletic apparel	$12–$20
Blankets	
Large	$10
Medium	$ 8
Small	$ 6
Towels	
Beach	$10
Kids	$ 8
Bath	$ 6
Hand	$ 6
Bath cloths	$ 4
Linens	
Pillowcases (1 pair)	$12
sheet sets	$12
Cloth napkins (set of 4)	$16
Placemats (set of 4)	$16
Accessories	
Umbrellas	$ 6
Scarves	$ 6
Hair bows	$ 6
Caps	$ 8
Hats	$ 8
Bags	
Make-up	$ 6
Small	$ 6
Medium	$ 8
Large	$10
Luggage	$8–$12

Estimated prices for monogrammed products sold through online store at Crafty.com:

Product	Price
Baby items	
Blankets	$ 20
Bibs	$ 10
Sleepers	$ 18
Onesies	$ 10
Towels	$ 20
Socks	$ 8
Hair accessories	$ 12
Blankets	
Large	$ 40
Medium	$ 30
Small	$ 20
Towels	
Beach	$ 30
Kids	$ 20
Bath	$ 16
Hand	$ 12
Bath cloths	$ 10
Linens	
Pillowcases (1 pair)	$ 20
sheet sets	$80–$100
Cloth napkins (set of 4)	$ 40
Placemats (set of 4)	$ 48
Accessories	
Umbrellas	$ 20
Scarves	$ 25
Hair bows	$ 12
Caps	$ 18
Hats	$ 25
Bags	
Make-up	$ 16
Small	$ 20
Medium	$ 30
Large	$ 40
Miscellaneous	
Bookmarks	$ 10
Pet tags	$ 12
Key chains	$ 12

Estimated prices for etched products sold through online store at Crafty.com:

Product	Price
Metal picture frames	
4 × 6	$20
5 × 7	$30
8 × 10	$35
11 × 14	$40
Wooden picture frames	
4 × 6	$15
5 × 7	$18
8 × 10	$20
11 × 14	$28
Acrylic picture frames	
4 × 6	$12
5 × 7	$15
8 × 10	$18
11 × 14	$20
Miscellaneous	
Key chains (metal, wood, acrylic)	$10

Profit/Loss

The chart titled "Monthly Profit/Loss" presents estimated monthly income data. Conservative estimates will be used to determine monthly income and profit. Ms. Morales expects the first two months to be slow, but then expects business to pick up as she gains local clients and as the holidays approach in Months 5 and 6. Months 7 and 8 are expected to see a decrease after Christmas but sales are expected to increase by 10% each month for the remaining months in the first year. Profits are expected to at least remain constant in subsequent years, and these conservative estimates will be used to estimate the loan repayment.

Monthly profit/loss

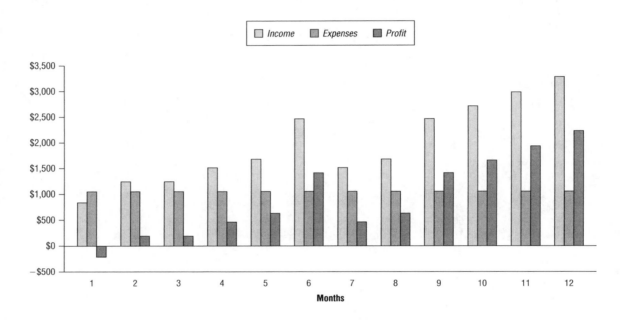

Annual profit/loss

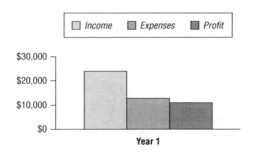

Financing

The owner of Chicadeez wishes to obtain financing in the form of a business loan or line of credit for the amount needed to cover the start up costs and three months' expenses. This loan would be in the amount of $14,400. According to the estimated expenses vs. income, Chicadeez should be able to pay back the loan in 36 months if the company meets or exceeds projected income.

Repayment plan

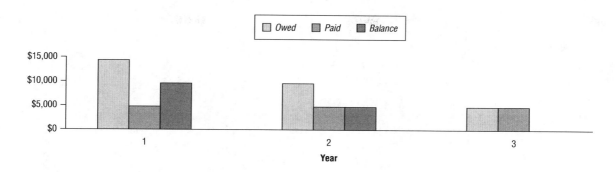

Custom Spiritwear Company

Richmond Athletic Apparel

4321 W. Main St.
Richmond, Minnesota 56368

Zuzu Enterprises

A customized T-shirt printing company that creates apparel and promotional products for schools, school groups, community organizations, and local businesses.

EXECUTIVE SUMMARY

Richmond Athletic Apparel is a customized t-shirt printing company that creates apparel and promotional products for schools, school groups, community organizations, and local businesses.

PRODUCTS

While t-shirts and sweatshirts comprise nearly 75% of the business, they are by no means the only items we offer. We offer a complete line of apparel and promotional products that can be customized with an organization's logo and/or mascot. A complete list of products includes:

Apparel
* T-shirts
* Sweatshirts/hoodies
* Sweatpants
* Jackets
* Letterman jackets
* Fleece jackets
* Warm-ups (jackets and pants)
* Uniforms
* Hats—baseball hats, visors, knit beanie caps
* Socks

Promotional Products
* Bags—tote bags, sports gear bags (bat bags, tennis racket bags, rolling equipment bags, team helmet bags, drawstring backpacks, etc.)
* Hanging sports gear organizers

- Mugs/travel cups

- Pens, pencils

- Automotive decals

All of our items are available in a rainbow of standard colors, and feature:

- Glitter designs, metallic designs

- Gildan brand apparel—long wearing, standard sizes, no fading or shrinkage, color matching

- Rainbow of apparel colors, including tie-dye

- Rainbow of ink colors

- Screen printing

- Embroidery

Our service will exceed customer expectations. Standout features of our superior service include:

- Quick turn-around

- Delayed billing

- Standard logos and mascots on hand that require no setup or design fees

- Order sorting and organization by team/player

- Local delivery

MARKET ANALYSIS

Richmond, Minnesota is a relatively small, rural community roughly 25 minutes from St. Cloud and an hour from Minneapolis. The population within city limits is a mere 1,425 but that number does not include the small, surrounding townships that travel to Richmond for shopping and services. Furthermore, the population of Richmond itself is growing; since 2000, the population has increased 17.5%, a number that is expected to increase.

Within a 25 mile radius of Richmond are 5 school districts, each with at one or two elementary schools, one middle school, and one high school. The smaller districts like this have the same mascot and colors for all of their schools, essentially making the school colors the town colors. You will not see just the kids in town sporting spiritwear, you will see nearly everyone wearing it, from the youngest residents to the oldest. This will be our biggest market.

Recreational sports and sports camps are another segment of the market in the Richmond area that will lead to significant sales. This includes little league, soccer, and softball as well as the yearly camps sponsored by the school teams to raise money and increase interest and expertise in the sports.

Clubs, musical groups, and the Regional Youth Initiative are another potential source of income for Richmond Athletic Apparel. The RYI sponsors 3-4 plays a year and serves 100-150 kids with each performance (split between multiple casts). T-shirts sporting the name and image of the play as well as performance dates are ordered early and worn as advertisement.

To a lesser extent, special events, festivals, and tournaments will offer opportunities for design work and sales, as will local businesses and organizations.

Below is a breakdown of potential clients.

Potential Clients

- Schools and school stores—generic school items including t-shirts, sweatshirts, sweatpants, and jackets

- Middle school/high schools sports teams—including track (boys and girls), cross country (boys and girls), football (boys), tennis (boys and girls), basketball (boys and girls), soccer (boys and girls), softball (girls), baseball (boys), volleyball (girls), wrestling (boys), power lifting (boys and girls), cheerleading (girls), rugby (boys), and swimming (boys and girls)

- Sports camps—volleyball, basketball, football, wrestling, cheerleading

- Richmond Area Little League (RALL) baseball—22 rec baseball teams and district teams within the league

- Richmond Girls' Fastpitch Association (RGFA)—12 rec softball teams and five travel teams (including warmups, practice shirts, and spiritwear)

- Richmond AYSO—16 teams at various levels within the league.

- Travel sports—including softball, baseball, basketball, hockey, and volleyball. Local teams include: Foster Oilers, Vengeance, Elite Lakers, Eastside Niners, Armada Tigers, MV Marysville, Anchor Bay Angels, Hurricanes, Great Lakes Volleyball, Vipers, Almont Rampage, St. Clair Shores Sharks, St. Clair Starz, Richmond Blues, Romeo Renegades, Marine City Heat, L'Anse Cruise Bandits, and Cross-Lex Fastpitch

- Richmond Area Football League (RAFL) football—football teams and cheerleaders

- Regional Youth Initiative (RYI)—plays, staff t-shirts, summer camps

- Clubs—programming club, Key Club, SADD, Student Council, WEB Leaders, NJHS/NHS

- Musical groups—choir, chorale, band

- Special events/spirit days—Cancer football game, rival football games, Winter Festival

- Good Old Days festival—staff shirts

- Parent spiritwear

- Tournament shirts—Friendship Games, CanAm Games, Blue Devil Tournament

- Local businesses—lawyers, doctors, dentists, orthodontists, insurance companies, real estate companies, churches, and fitness clubs

PERSONNEL

Owner/Operator

To begin, Richmond Athletic Apparel will be staffed by owner/operator Roger Debrantio and one part-time machine operator. Both Roger and the part-time operator will fill screenprint and embroidery orders. As business increases, the part-time machine operator will increase hours as needed to complete the work.

Roger will also staff the storefront, meet with clients, and take orders. He will be the point person for design and approvals.

The machine operator will serve as backup to Roger in these capacities as well as serve as a "second pair of eyes" when preparing and proofing designs.

Partner with business screenprinting/embroidery business in nearby St. Cloud to handle large jobs or serve as backup in case of mechanical issues.

Professional & Advisory Support

Roger incorporated his business with the assistance of an attorney, and has hired a local bookkeeper to assist him with financial record-keeping and tax preparation services. A commercial checking account has been established with First State Bank and equipment has been obtained that will allow him to process credit card payments on-site.

OPERATIONS

Location

The business will be housed at 4321 W. Main Street in Richmond, Minnesota. This location is at the center of town and is easily accessed by local thoroughfares for all surrounding communities. The building suits our needs by having a large storefront to display samples and take orders as well as a large backroom area for working on the machines and storing/organizing orders. It also contains a storage area off the workroom that is perfect for storing and organizing extra inventory. A small half bath and a kitchenette area complete the space. A lease was obtained for 3 years at the rate of $2,500 a month including utilities.

EQUIPMENT

Richmond Athletic Apparel will require an industrial embroidery machine and an industrial screen-printing machine in addition to two computers and design software. These items will be discussed below.

Embroidery Machine

The model of embroidery machine we have chosen is a state-of-the-art machine from Brother that will work equally well on small as well as large jobs. It is easily customizable and can accommodate complex, multi-color thread designs as well as embroidery areas up to 14x14 inches. It can operate at up to 1,000 stitches per minute, making large orders able to be completed in a short amount of time. The 10 needle design make multi-color designs faster, easier, and more precise than machines with 1 or even 6 needles. The complete details are noted below:

Brother Embroidery machine
- Model: PR-1000E Single Head 10 Needle Embroidery Machine (2014)
- Retail cost: $14,999
- Lease: $325/month
- Large Full Color 4.3"x7.2" HD LCD Touch Screen from Sharp Corporation
- Approx. 14"x14" Embroidery Area
- Automatic Needle Threading
- Automatic Color Changing and Thread Trimmer
- 3 USB Ports
- Number of Needles: 10
- Network Capabilities: Link up to four PR1000 series or upgraded PR650 series machines to one computer
- Maximum Embroidery Speed (Stitches Per Minute): Up to 1000spm

- Can accommodate wide area caps with optional cap frame

- Built-in Border Function and Designs

- Multimedia capability: Secure Digital (SD) Card, CompactFlash, Memory Stick, Smart Media, MultiMediaCard (MMC), xD-Picture Card, USB Flash Drive (USB Flash Memory), USB Floppy Disk Drive, USB CD-ROM, CD-R, CD-RW drives (reading only)

- Cap frame attachment to embroider caps quickly and easily

- InnovEye Technology and Snowman® Embroidery Positioning Marker

- InnovaChrome LED Thread Color System simplifies thread color setup and provides status cues

- 110 built-in designs; 28 size-adjustable fonts, plus frames and decorative frames and decorative alphabet designs

- Ability to rotate designs in 1-degree increments

- Ability to pre-program automatic color changes for the entire design

- Automatic upper and lower thread trimmers

- Compatible with Brother's award-winning PE-Design software and BE-100 digitizing software for use with popular home and commercial embroidery formats

- Uses L-size prewound bobbins

Optional accessories that we have chosen to include with our machine consist of:

- 14" x 14" Jumbo frame

- 4" x 14" Border frame

- 8" x 8" Quilting frame a Wide cap frame, driver and mounting jig

- Standard cap frame, driver and mounting jig

- Round frame kit (Includes Arm C Embroidery frame holder, Round 4", 5" and 6" frames)

- Cylinder frame

- 8" x 12" Flat frame

- Adjustable-height metal stand

- Upgrade kit (PRPUGK1)—Allows you to scan virtually anything in your frame with InnovEye Technology; change design color palette with Color Shuffling Function; features On-screen Auto Density Adjustment when designs are resized; includes Design Connection for alignment of repetitive designs; and contains 10 new designs and 2 new fonts

Screen Printing Machine

The screen printing machine we chose is also from Brother. It is a modular, direct-to-garment printer that features eight print heads which, coupled with single pass printing, allows for increased productivity. It has a convenient, built in user interface and a front loading ink cartridge that is designed to provide consistent print quality. The complete details are noted below:

Brother Screen Printing Machine

- Model: GT-381 Garment Printer

- Retail Cost: $24,999

- Lease: $525/month

- CMYK and white ink printing

- Up to 1200dpi printing

- One pass printing, with both CMYK and white ink printing simultaneously for higher productivity

- USB memory stick compatibility

- USB 2.0 or LAN/Ethernet Connectivity

- Front-loading ink cartridge system

- Compact size for greater versatility in many work environments, including storefront

- Simple user interface—No RIP required

- Inks certified by Oeko-Tex Standard 100, Class I

- 2 Year Limited Warranty, One Full Year Bumper-to-Bumper, Including Printheads

- Direct Inkjet Garment Printer

- Max printing area: 16" x 18"

- Ink Type: Water based pigment ink

- Ink volume: 180cc CMYK standard ink cartridges/ 380cc CMYK high yield ink cartridges / 380cc White high yield ink cartridges

- Number of Print Heads: 8

- Print Head Type: On demand piezo head

- Print Head Resolution: 600 dpi; 1200 dpi

- Print Mode: Single or double for CMYK; Underbase and highlight for white

- Printed Substrate: 100% cotton; 50/50% cotton/polyester blends

- Warranty: 2 Year Limited Warranty, One Full Year Bumper-to-Bumper, Including Printheads.

Optional accessories that we have chosen to include with our machine consist of:

- InkSoft Business Tools—Online software for designing artwork, facilitating communication and artwork approval with customers, and production tools for simplifying the whole process. It allows you to send web quotes & invoices; maintain job and task scheduling calendar; features real-time alerts and commenting; enables online approvals and payments; improves internal communication; manages customers and contacts; and utilizes cloud-based software.

- Ink Cartridges/Solutions

- Platens

- Cleaning Kits

Computers and Software

Two computers will be necessary for the operations. One will be utilized in the front storeroom for taking orders, ordering inventory and supplies, communicating with clients, monitoring the website and social media accounts, as well as some design work. This computer will be networked with the other placed in the back room that will be used with the screen printing and embroidery machines in addition to design work. Both computers will feature Windows 8 (32/64 bit); Microsoft Office applications (Word, Internet Explorer, Excel, Outlook, Publisher, etc.); Adobe Photoshop; Adobe Photoshop Elements (for bitmap editing); Adobe Illustrator; CorelDraw (for vector data editing), and Corel PaintShop Pro. An all-in-one printer/scanner/copier/fax machine will be purchased for printing orders, product approvals, invoices, and receipts as well as scanning designs and emailing/faxing approval forms. Other needed computer equipment includes a wireless router and large-screen monitors.

INVENTORY

A basic inventory will be stocked featuring t-shirts and sweatshirts in popular colors and sizes in order to maximize turn-around times. The local school system features the same mascot and three colors for all clothing items, including navy, Carolina blue, and white. These colors will be stocked at all times, as well as minimal number of red, yellow, orange, green, purple, and black (common colors of teams in the surrounding communities). When necessary, additional inventory can be ordered and delivered typically within3- 4 business days.

MARKETING & SALES

Owner Roger Debrantio has already approached the local school board and applied to be the contractor of choice for the school district. As a long-time resident and a graduate of the district, Roger is well-known and liked within the community and he was awarded the status of preferred business. All school sports and clubs are now highly encouraged to use Richmond Athletic Apparel and will receive delayed billing payable by school purchase order (rather than requiring upfront cash or credit payment) as well as free delivery to the school in return.

Roger will also approach local businesses and organizations will printed advertising materials and price sheets to talk about all of the available spiritwear and promotional products available. He is already scheduled to appear at the local Little League board meeting as well as the board meeting of the local AYSO and girls' softball association to make presentations and bids for their yearly uniform order.

GROWTH STRATEGY

During the first three years of operations, Roger will concentrate his efforts on establishing a reputation for quality and quick turnaround in Richmond and the surrounding communities. He will accomplish this by providing exceptional, reliable service and a superior product that exceeds the customers' expectations.

Start-up costs will be repaid over the three years, averaging $34,000 per year. After covering start-up and operational costs, we anticipate that Richmond Athletic Apparel will generate a net profit of about $15,000 during the first year. This will greatly increase over the next two year as word spreads and more and more businesses and clubs utilize Richmond Athletic Apparel for their spiritwear needs.

FINANCIAL ANALYSIS

Start Up Costs

Embroidery machine—$14,250 (15,000)*

Accessories—including thread, software, etc. —$7,725 ($8,300)*

Screen printing machine—$23,750 ($25,000)*

Accessories—including ink, software, etc. —$4,275 ($4,500)*

Computer, printer, business software—$11,250

Office furniture, phones, etc.—$4,000

Inventory of apparel (samples, popular colors)—$2,750

Salaries (first 6 months of operations)—$12,000

Rent (first 6 months of operations)—$15,000

Phone/wireless (first 6 months of operations)—$2,000

Marketing & Advertising—$1,500

Legal—$1,500

TOTAL: $100,000

*Roughly 5% discount when purchased together directly from Brother

Estate Sale Organization
Estate Sales by Emmy

12855 E. Adams Street
Ocala, FL 34471

Fran Fletcher

Estate Sales by Emmy is an estate sale service located in Ocala, Florida. Owner, Emmy Andrews, wants to provide estate sale assistance to clients who are downsizing and to those who need to liquidate the estate of a family member.

BUSINESS OVERVIEW

Estate Sales by Emmy is an estate sale service located in Ocala, Florida. Owner, Emmy Andrews, wants to provide estate sale assistance to clients who are downsizing and to those who need to liquidate the estate of a family member.

Clients will receive a free consultation, and after viewing the property, Ms. Andrews will recommend what type of sale she thinks will make the most profit. Estate Sales by Emmy will use any combination of tactics, including estate sales, auctions, online estate sales, and online auctions. She plans to showcase collectibles on the company website in order to reach clients from all over the world. As the estate sale organizer, Ms. Andrews will advertise the estate sale, clean items for the sale, conduct the estate sale, clean up after the sale, and donate any unsold items to charity.

According to the American Estate Sales Association, estate sales are a multi-million dollar industry. All over the country, approximately 12,300 estate sales are held each month with an estimated $102 million dollars worth of goods sold.

Reasons for estate sales can vary, but the top three reasons for estate sales are death, downsizing, and divorce. Thirty-three percent, or 16,500, of Ocala's residents are ages 55 and older. These older residents will serve as the target market for Estate Sales by Emmy, since this age group will most likely downsize after retirement, or liquidate the estate of a deceased parent or spouse.

Estate Sales by Emmy plans to set itself apart from the competition by offering online auctions/sales and using social media and the Internet to get her clients the best possible price for their possessions by pairing them with buyers and collectors from all over the country.

Estate Sales by Emmy will work to build a reputation for getting customers a fair price for their precious possessions. Ms. Andrews plans to create a website where she can showcase and sell items for clients. She envisions her business growing and her website becoming one of the most visited websites in the world for interesting antiques and one-of-a kind items. Estate Sales by Emmy will consider opening a store in the future if there is a need.

Ms. Andrews is seeking financing in the form of a business loan or line of credit for $5,750. This will cover start-up costs and 3 months' expenses. Profit projections show that the loan should be repaid by the end of the first year of operation.

COMPANY DESCRIPTION

Location

Ms. Andrews will perform business operations from her home and will meet clients at the location of the estate sale.

Hours of Operation

Consultation

Thursday 8:00 a.m. to 4:00 p.m. by appointment. Ms. Andrews will meet with clients and determine the best method for selling their belongings. Options include 1 to 3-day estate sales, online estate sales, and estate auctions.

Estate Sales

Estate sales will be mainly conducted on the weekend. Estate sale preparations will be made on Monday through Wednesday.

Personnel

Emmy Andrews

Ms. Andrews will perform all duties associated with the business. She has always enjoyed going to garage sales, flea markets, estate sales, and antique shops. She has performed extensive research into the value of antiques and will be able to help clients get the highest price for their items.

Estate Sale Helper

A helper will be hired as needed to help with estate sale activities.

Services

Estate Sales by Emmy will help people who wish to downsize and also will help the family of deceased individuals sell their property.

Services include, but are not limited, to:

- Advertising—newspaper, website, signs
- Pricing items
- Posting items for Internet sales
- Cataloging items
- Organizing items
- Coordinating the sale
- Cleaning up after the sale
- Donating remaining items
- Hiring an auctioneer
- Appraising items
- Washing dishes and items for the sale
- Arranging and setting up the sale

MARKET ANALYSIS

Industry Overview

According to the American Estate Sales Association, estate sales are a multi-million dollar industry. All over the country, approximately 12,300 estate sales are held each month with an estimated $102 million dollars' worth of goods sold.

Reasons for estate sales can vary, but the top three reasons for estate sales are death, downsizing, and divorce. Thirty-three percent, or 16,500, of Ocala's residents are ages 55 and older. This will give a large customer base for estate sales.

Target Market

The target market for Estate Sales by Emmy will be homeowners in the Ocala, Florida area who need to sell their personal property, whether downsizing in order to move to a retirement community or to liquidate the estate of a deceased loved one.

Competition

A1 Auctions

3556 Beech Avenue, Ocala, FL—Provides auctioneer services and advertising

Royal Estate Sales

10076 B Main St., Ocala, FL—Provides services related to estate sales and auctions, including advertising and managing estate sales

Estate Sales by Emmy plans to set itself apart from the competition by offering online auctions/sales and using social media and the Internet to get clients the best possible price for their possessions by pairing them with buyers and collectors from all over the country.

GROWTH STRATEGY

Estate Sales by Emmy will work to build a reputation for getting customers a fair price for their hard-earned possessions. Ms. Andrews plans to create a website where she can showcase and sell items for clients. She envisions her business growing and her website becoming one of the most visited websites in the world for interesting antiques and one-of-a-kind items. Estate Sales by Emmy will consider opening a store in the future if there is a need.

Sales and Marketing

Estate Sales by Emmy has identified key tactics to support its growth strategy.

Initial advertising/marketing will include:

- Newspaper—the Ocala newspaper will be the primary source for obtaining clients

- Social media—pictures of items for sale will be used to advertise estate sales

- Speaking engagements—Ms. Andrews will speak at the local Retirement Association as well as other local senior adult meetings to advertise her services

Ongoing advertising will include:

- Newspaper—the Ocala newspaper will be used to advertise estate sales

- Estatesalesbyemmy.com—will advertise estate sale dates, post preview pictures, and host online auctions

- Social media—will advertise sale dates and post preview pictures

- Referrals—referrals will be vital to the business, as satisfied customers suggest that their friends use Estate Sales by Emmy

- Speaking engagements—Ms. Andrews will ask to speak at the local Retirement Association as well as other local senior adult meetings

- Signs—signs will be placed at the estate site two weeks prior to the sale

FINANCIAL ANALYSIS

Start-up Costs

Estate Sales by Emmy will require minimal capital to get started. Ms. Andrews only wants to borrow enough for start-up costs and three months expenses.

Start-up costs

Advertising	$ 300
Business cards	$ 100
Business license	$ 300
Insurance	$ 500
Website	$ 500
Total	**$1,700**

Estimated Monthly Expenses

Monthly expenses are expected to remain constant until a helper is hired around Month 9. The monthly profit will serve as Ms. Andrew's income.

Monthly expenses

Loan	$ 500
Phone/Internet	$ 150
Advertising	$ 400
Payment services	$ 300
Total	**$1,350**
Helper (hired month 9)	**$2,400**
Total at month 9	**$3,750**

Estimated Monthly Income

The number of clients and gross sales will determine estimated income. Estate Sales by Emmy will receive 35% commission on sales. Estate Sales by Emmy has the potential to host one estate sale per weekend. Internet sales will be active 24 hours a day, 7 days a week.

Ms. Andrews will consult with potential clients and appraise items of the estate to determine what the profit potential may be. If she does not think that the homeowners have enough for a formal estate sale, she will advise them on what they should do. She will also work with these clients using a set rate of $50 per hour.

Profit/Loss

The chart titled "Monthly Profit/Loss" presents estimated monthly income, expenses, and profit data.

Conservative estimates will be used to determine business sustainability. The estimated income in the chart does not include Internet sales or estates that pay by the hour.

Statistics show that $8,500 is the average amount of money made for items sold at an estate sale. The chart shows monthly income starting off with one estate sale with sales totaling $4,250. Subsequent months show gradual increases in income and profits. Projections for Month 12 include 4 estate sales all with $8,500 in sales. Monthly expenses are expected to stay the same until month 9, at which time a helper will be hired to help prepare for estate sales. This person will be paid $25 per hour and will work an estimated 24 hours per week.

Monthly profit/loss

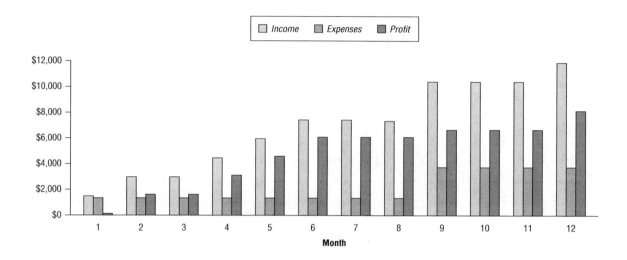

Financing

Ms. Andrews wishes to obtain financing in the form of a business loan or line of credit for the amount needed to cover the start up costs and three months' expenses. This loan would be in the amount of $5,750. According to the estimated expenses vs. income, Estate Sales by Emmy should be able to pay back the loan in 12 months.

Loan repayment plan

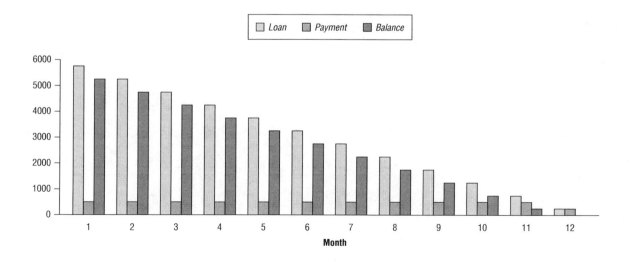

Internet Cafe Business

The Postal Cafe Inc.

5832 Main St.
Parkville Hills, MN 55692

Paul Greenland

The Postal Cafe is an Internet Cafe located in downtown Parkville Hills, Minnesota.

EXECUTIVE SUMMARY

Business Overview

The Postal Cafe is an Internet Cafe located in downtown Parkville Hills, Minnesota. Located within a former post office, the Cafe is situated in an inner-city area that is being revitalized. The following business plan has been developed by owners Brian and Melissa Abbott, who are seeking $50,000 in economic development funds from the City of Parkville Hills. The city has offered to provide matching funds (e.g., corresponding to their own personal investment) in the form of a three-year forgivable grant to cover facility renovations and capital purchases.

Business Philosophy

For those who live or work in downtown Parkville Hills, the Postal Cafe is the ideal destination for meetings and refreshment.

MARKET ANALYSIS

As with many other communities throughout the country, Parkville Hills, Minnesota, has been impacted by difficult economic conditions. Once a strong manufacturing town, many of the organizations that were long-time employers have been acquired and relocated, or moved manufacturing to offshore locations that offer lower labor costs. Downtown Parkville Hills was once home to the headquarters of several large fastener and furniture manufacturing companies. Until recently, these facilities were dormant for many years.

A pivotal development occurred in 2012 when Parkville Technologies, a local software development company, decided to expand its operations. Although relocating to other parts of the country was an option, this emerging employer, led by two Parkville Hills natives, decided to remain in the community. After renovating the former headquarters of Parkville Furniture Manufacturing Co., Parkville Technologies brought 250 new jobs to the downtown area. Subsequently, Parkville Community College established a downtown campus, mainly for its new science and technology department.

35

Building on this momentum, the city has been recruiting other technology companies in order to establish Parkville Hills as a Midwestern technology hub. The city has developed a compelling economic development strategy, which includes incentives and tax breaks for new businesses willing to establish and remain in the market.

In addition to industry and education, the City of Parkville Hills also has made recent government-related investments, including the construction of a new city hall building in the heart of downtown. In addition, the Parkville Hills School District has relocated its headquarters from an older structure on the north side of town to a newly renovated building in the downtown area. The downtown area also is witnessing a slow but steady comeback in residential growth.

The Postal Cafe is a prime example of a new small business that is being established to serve the growing downtown community. Although there are a combination of existing and new eating and drinking places, the Postal Cafe is the only business of its kind in the market, with the exception of a small coffee shop located directly on the campus of Parkville Community College.

INDUSTRY ANALYSIS

The Postal Cafe is part of the restaurant industry. According to the National Restaurant Association, industry revenues were expected to reach $683.4 billion in 2014, up significantly from $586.7 billion in 2010 and $379 million in 2000. The restaurant industry's share of the food dollar totals 47 percent, compared to only 25 percent in 1955. Eating places like The Postal Cafe account for the majority ($455.9 billion) of industry sales. Employment at the industry's 990,000 locations also is increasing, rising from 11.9 million in 2004 to a projected 13.5 million in 2014. By 2024, the restaurant industry is projected to employ 14.8 million people.

PERSONNEL

Ownership Summary

The Postal Cafe's owners are Brian and Melissa Abbott. Before taking early retirement at the age of 60, Brian enjoyed a 35-year career with the U.S. Postal Service. A large portion of his career was spent working in the main Parkville Hills Post Office. When the facility was closed and subsequently purchased by a local real estate developer, the Abbotts foresaw an opportunity to lease a portion of the space and establish a unique business that preserves the character and notoriety of the remarkable building. After retiring, Brian and Melissa took small business management courses at Parkville Hills Community College as part of a certificate program. This, coupled with Melissa's experience managing a local diner for 15 years, has positioned them for success as owners of their own business. Brian will work at the business full-time, mainly concentrating on growing and marketing the Postal Cafe, while Melissa will work part-time, assisting with daily operations.

Staff Employees

Including the owners, the Postal Cafe will employ an initial staff of nine employees, as outlined in the following table (with corresponding salary projections for the first three years):

Title	2015	2016	2017
Brian Abbott	$ 70,000	$ 71,750	$ 73,544
Melissa Abbott	$ 45,000	$ 46,125	$ 47,278
1 full-time cook	$ 40,000	$ 41,000	$ 42,025
1 part-time cook	$ 20,000	$ 20,500	$ 21,013
1 full-time dishwasher	$ 17,500	$ 17,938	$ 18,386
2 full-time counter/wait staff	$ 35,000	$ 35,875	$ 36,772
2 part-time counter/wait staff	$ 17,500	$ 17,938	$ 18,386
	$245,000	**$251,125**	**$257,403**

Professional and Advisory Support

The Abbotts have secured local accountant Martha Randolph to handle bookkeeping and provide tax advisory services. Additionally, commercial checking accounts have been established with Parkville Hills Community Bank, which also will provide merchant accounts needed for accepting credit card and debit card payments.

GROWTH STRATEGY

The Abbotts have established specific goals and targets for their business during its first three years of operations:

Year One: Concentrate on establishing The Postal Cafe in downtown Parkville Hills and developing a regular customer base. Become a member of the local Chamber of Commerce and demonstrate a commitment to being a good community partner. Book at least two meetings per month in the Postal Cafe's conference room meeting space and host one special event per month. Secure $30,000 business loan (term 6% for 36 months) and $50,000 economic development grant. Generate net sales of more than $430,000 and net income of $73,598.

Year Two: Continue building awareness about the business and establishing a regular customer base. Book at least two meetings per month in the Postal Cafe's conference room meeting space and host two special events per month. Increase net sales five percent, to nearly $453,000, and generate net income of $82,665.

Year Three: Book at least three meetings per month in the Postal Cafe's conference room meeting space and host three special events per month. Increase net sales five percent, to nearly $475,500, and generate net income of $91,837. Achieve repayment of $30,000 business loan.

SERVICES

Catering primarily to employees in downtown Parkville Hills, the Postal Cafe will offer the following food and beverage items. Generally speaking, beverages and baked goods will be available at any time, while soups and food items will be offered from 11 AM-1 PM, and from 4 PM-6 PM.

Menu

Beverages

- Coffee $1.49/$1.69

- Cafe Au Lait $1.99/$2.99

- Breve $2.99/$3.99

- Cappuccino $2.99/$3.99

- Macchiatto $2.99/$3.99

- Espresso $1.99/$2.99

- Cafe Latte $2.99/$3.99
- Chai Latte $2.99/$3.99
- Americano $1.99/$2.99
- Mocha $2.99/$3.99
- Hot Chocolate $1.99/$2.99
- Smoothies (various flavors) $3.99
- Frappes (various flavors) $3.99
- Milk
- Iced Coffee $2.99
- Iced Tea $1.99
- Iced Chai Tea $2.99
- Canned Soft Drinks $1.49
- Bottled Water $1.49

Food
- Soups $3.75
- Flatbread Pizzas (barbecue chicken, Baja, Thai chicken, margherita) $8.75
- Sandwiches (pot roast, chicken bruschetta, turkey, ham, roast beef, vegetarian) $6.50
- Wraps (buffalo chicken, turkey club, chicken salad, veggie, and grilled chicken) $6.50
- Burgers (signature Black Angus, turkey, and black bean)

Sandwiches, wraps, and burgers served with choice of french fries, potato chips, or fruit. A variety of breads and cheeses available.

Baked Goods (prices and selections will vary)
- Pastries
- Cookies
- Muffins
- Scones
- Pies

Live Entertainment

In addition to being known for its great coffee and food selections, the Postal Cafe occasionally will offer live entertainment on Friday nights and extended evening hours, providing customers with an opportunity to relax while listening to local acoustic and jazz musicians.

MARKETING & SALES

A marketing plan has been developed for the Postal Cafe that includes these main tactics:

1. Social Media: Guests will be able to follow the business on Facebook and Twitter, and take advantage of exclusive lunch and dinner specials.

2. Mobile Marketing: The Postal Cafe has identified a mobile marketing service, which will allow customers to receive text message alerts about special discounts and upcoming events.

3. Web Site: A site with key information about the Postal Cafe and its meeting facilities will be developed. The site will include menu information, location, hours, and special discounts. It also will include video and still photography, in order to showcase the unique environment at the Postal Cafe.

4. Direct-Mail: The Abbotts will send a color, glossy postcard to organizations located in and around the downtown area, in order to encourage meeting space rental, catering, and carryout orders.

5. Advertising: In order to generate buzz about the business, the Postal Cafe will run regular print ads in *The Parkville Post,* a monthly publication of the local Chamber of Commerce. In addition, the business will run a regular advertisement in *Parkville Hills Lifestyle Magazine.* A detailed advertising schedule is being developed for these publications, and can be provided upon request.

6. Incentives: To encourage prospective customers to visit the Postal Cafe, the Abbotts will distribute 500 coupons for one free cup of regular coffee, one half-price latte, and 15 percent off any sandwich during the business' first 60 days of operation. The coupons will be distributed personally to businesses and establishments throughout the downtown area.

7. Public Relations: The Abbotts will attempt to secure a story in the business section of the *Parkville Hills Times,* which typically profiles new businesses that have been established in the city. In addition, they will encourage the paper's food critic to write a review of their establishment.

8. Community Outreach: The Postal Cafe is committed to being a good neighbor in its community. With this in mind, the business will participate in and support downtown events, including the annual Memorial Day, Independence Day, and Labor Day parades, as well as the annual Holiday Stroll festival that is held on Main Street.

OPERATIONS

Hours
Catering primarily to employees in downtown Parkville Hills, the Postal Cafe will operate from 6 AM-6 PM Monday through Friday, and 6 AM-11 AM on Saturday. Exceptions will be made for special events/ live music. Generally speaking, beverages and baked goods will be available at any time, while soups and food items will be offered from 11 AM-1 PM, and from 4 PM-6 PM.

Suppliers
The Postal Cafe has identified several local, regional, and national food service distributors who will supply the business with food and beverage items. This list is available upon request.

Facility and Location
The Postal Cafe is located in leased space within a truly remarkable building. Built in the 1920s, it includes beautiful Art Deco design elements and features several marble countertops, including a long one in the main customer service area. Whenever possible, the Abbotts have retained the original features of the former post office, including walls with old post office boxes. In addition, they have procured a variety of postal memorabilia to decorate their new Cafe. Many of these items are from Brian Abbott's personal collection.

Features of The Postal Cafe include:

- A 750-square-foot coffee bar/dining area

- A 500-square-foot meeting room: this unique space includes perimeter walls that feature original post office boxes and can be sub-divided into two, 250-square-foot meeting rooms, providing ideal meeting space for medium- or small-sized business/group meetings.

- Comfortable seating/lighting

- Free Wi-Fi

- A free library that encourages patrons to donate and take used books/magazines

- A vintage shuffleboard table

- Both on- and off-street parking

- Men's and women's bathroom facilities

Start-up Costs

The Postal Cafe will require the following equipment prior to start-up:

Equipment	
Beverage dispensing equipment	
Soft drink dispenser with ice bin (provided by beverage supplier)	$ 0
Carbonator with double check valve (provided by beverage supplier)	$ 0
Wall mounted syrup pumps (provided by beverage supplier)	$ 0
CO-2 tanks (provided by beverage supplier)	$ 0
Automatic coffee maker	$ 656
Coffee grinder	$ 742
Cup dispensers – 10 units required	$ 539
Lid organizer	$ 79
Espresso machine 240V ($4,150)	$ 2,150
Commercial blender	$ 485
Medium capacity (1 phase-air cooled) ice machine	$ 1,874
Storage equipment units	
6 × 8 freezer storage shelving set	$ 873
18" × 36" storage shelf unit – 4 units required	$ 468
Commercial freezer	$ 1,076
Electric can opener	$ 65
Single door reach-in refrigerator	$ 2,214
Sales & display equipment	
Cash register	$ 1,678
Menu board	$ 1,156
Daily special panel	$ 125
Refrigerated pastry display case	$ 3,459
Miscellaneous equipment	
Work table	$ 1,108
File cabinet	$ 348
7-person locker	$ 242
Safe	$ 1,390
Tackboard	$ 209
Mop & broom holder	$ 22
Tablet computer, printer and software	$ 1,875
Silverware	$ 350
Dishes	$ 564
Low temperature undercounter commercial dishwasher	$ 3,416
Commercial grill	$ 2,046
Meat slicer	$ 410
Commercial microwave	$ 350
Total equipment costs	**$29,969**

LEGAL

The Postal Cafe is in full compliance with all legal and regulatory requirements pertaining to the operation of our business in the state of Minnesota. According to Minnesota statutes, an annual license ($150) is required for "every person, firm, or corporation engaged in the business of conducting a food and beverage service establishment." In addition to this fee, the state also charges $450 to review construction plans for medium-sized establishments like the Postal Cafe. This must be paid with the business' initial license application. The Abbotts also have obtained appropriate business and liability insurance coverage for their Cafe (policies available upon request).

FINANCIAL ANALYSIS

During the Postal Cafe's first year, the Abbotts anticipate that the business' gross revenues will break down by category as follows:

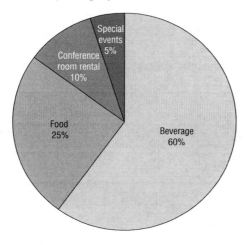

A complete set of pro forma financial statements is available upon request. The following table provides an overview of key projections for years one through three:

Funding

The Abbotts will invest $20,000 of their own money in the Postal Cafe. In addition, they have obtained a $30,000 business loan (term 6%, 36 months). The owners are applying for a $50,000 economic development grant from the City of Parkville Hills, to achieve total funding of $100,000.

	2015	2016	2017
Sales			
Beverage (60%)	$450,000	$472,500	$496,125
Food (25%)	$187,500	$196,875	$206,719
Conference room rental (10%)	$ 75,000	$ 78,750	$ 82,688
Special events (5%)	$ 37,500	$ 39,375	$ 41,344
Cost of goods sold	($318,750)	($334,689)	($351,423)
Net sales	**$431,250**	**$452,811**	**$475,452**
Expenses			
Advertising & marketing	$ 25,000	$ 30,000	$ 35,000
General/administrative	$ 1,500	$ 1,500	$ 1,500
Legal	$ 1,500	$ 750	$ 750
Accounting	$ 1,800	$ 2,000	$ 2,200
Office supplies	$ 1,500	$ 1,500	$ 1,500
Business insurance	$ 4,500	$ 5,000	$ 5,500
Payroll	$245,000	$251,125	$257,403
Payroll taxes	$ 36,750	$ 37,669	$ 38,610
Facility lease	$ 16,500	$ 16,500	$ 16,500
Postage	$ 450	$ 450	$ 450
Utilities	$ 4,700	$ 4,950	$ 5,250
Business-class internet	$ 2,500	$ 2,750	$ 3,000
Startup loan	$ 10,952	$ 10,952	$ 10,952
Repairs & maintenance	$ 5,000	$ 5,000	$ 5,000
Total expenses	**$357,652**	**$370,146**	**$383,615**
Net income	**$ 73,598**	**$ 82,665**	**$ 91,837**

Lawn & Garden Equipment Repair Business

Center City Repair Inc.

29 Andrews St.
Center City, MN 55740

Paul Greenland

Center City Repair Inc. is a new lawn and garden equipment repair business located in Center City, Minnesota. Unlike the majority of its competitors, Center City Repair adheres to a mobile business model, performing most equipment repairs on-site. This is a great convenience for both consumers and businesses alike. Instead of bringing equipment in for service or arranging/paying for pickup and delivery, Center City Repair comes to them. Services are provided directly by owner Jeff Dahlstrom via a 6 x 12 mobile trailer outfitted with tools, supplies, equipment, and a variety of basic parts.

EXECUTIVE SUMMARY

Center City Repair Inc. is a new lawn and garden equipment repair business located in Center City, Minnesota, along State Highways 27 and 29, near Interstate 94. Unlike the majority of its competitors, Center City Repair adheres to a mobile business model, performing most equipment repairs on-site. This is a great convenience for both consumers and businesses alike. Instead of bringing equipment in for service or arranging/paying for pickup and delivery, Center City Repair comes to them. Services are provided directly by owner Jeff Dahlstrom via a 6 x 12 mobile trailer outfitted with tools, supplies, equipment, and a variety of basic parts.

In addition to providing equipment service and repair, Center City Repair also buys and sells a limited inventory of used/reconditioned lawn and garden equipment, including lawn mowers, snow blowers, string trimmers, and lawn tractors. Jeff Dahlstrom picks up and hauls away equipment that residents wish to dispose of. He then "harvests" the equipment for usable parts, or repairs/resells the equipment if possible. This inventory is maintained in an outbuilding on Dahlstrom's property, where he also has a workspace for performing extensive repairs (e.g., services that cannot be provided on-site for the customer).

MARKET ANALYSIS

Center City Repair is located in Center City, Minnesota, along State Highways 27 and 29, near Interstate 94. The business will focus on two main target markets: property owners and landscaping businesses.

Property Owners

In 2014 Center City's population included about 171,000 people. At that time, 58 percent of the community's housing units were single-family homes, 40 percent were structures with two or more rental units, and 2 percent were mobile homes or trailers. Because all property owners, including landlords, are in need of property maintenance services (e.g., lawn mowing and snow removal), there is ample opportunity within this market segment.

Landscaping Companies

Significant opportunity also exists for exists for Center City Repair within the commercial sector. According to an analysis of local business data that Jeff Dahlstrom obtained from his library, the Center City area was home to 78 landscaping and lawn care businesses in 2014, the majority of which were sole proprietors.

Competition

Center City Repair's main competition will come from established lawn and garden repair services, including:

1. B & J Small Engine Repair

2. Bill's Small Engine Repair

3. Center City Hardware

4. Center City Outdoor Power

5. Express Lawn Repair

6. Mountain View Lawn & Power Equipment

7. Retail Home Services

8. Tractor Central

Among these competitors, Retail Home Services is the only competitor offering on-site maintenance and repair. Center City Repair still has a competitive edge against this well-known competitor, in that all services will be personally provided or overseen by Jeff Dahlstrom, who will take the time to develop relationships and build trust with customers. For example, unlike national home repair services offered by "big-box" retailers, Dahlstrom will go the extra mile by locating hard-to-find used parts when necessary.

SERVICES

Center City Repair will provide maintenance and repair services for all makes and models of lawn equipment (including 2- and 4-cycle engines, but not electric motors). Examples include:

- Lawn Mowers
- Lawn Tractors
- Power Rakes
- Aerators
- Commercial Sprayers
- Spreaders
- Garden Tractors
- Tractor Implements (e.g., plows, snow throwers, mower decks, dethatchers, sweepers, etc.)
- String Trimmers
- Chainsaws
- Leaf Blowers

Models include, but are not limited to:

- Agri-Fab
- Alpina
- ATCO
- Black & Decker
- Bosch
- Cub Cadet
- Deere & Company
- Earth wise
- Einhell Germany
- Enviromower
- Hayter
- Honda Motor Company
- Husqvarna
- Lawn Boy
- Lawnflite
- Makita
- Poulan
- Qualcast
- Recharge Ultralite
- Ryobi
- Simplicity
- Toro
- Troy-Bilt
- Victus
- Wolf Garten
- Worx
- Yard Man

Fees:

Center City Repair charges $75 per hour for labor. Customers are required to pay a one-hour minimum for all service calls. After the first hour, labor time is billed in 15-minute increments. In addition to an hourly labor rate, customers will be charged for all parts and supplies (e.g., oil, oil filters, spark plugs, etc.).

Service Packages

In addition to providing service and repair on an hourly basis, Center City Repair also offers a number of routine maintenance packages for lawn and garden equipment. These include:

Riding Lawn Mower Complete Package ($150 plus tax)

- Oil Change

- Battery Check

- New Spark Plugs

- Filter Replacement (if needed)

- Carburetor (basic adjustments/maintenance)

- Cooling System Check

- Mower Deck Cleaning/Leveling

- Blade Sharpening

- Tire Pressure Check

- General Inspection (chassis, etc.)

Riding Lawnmower Basic Package ($75 plus tax)

- Oil Change

- Mower Deck Cleaning/Leveling

- Blade Sharpening

- General Inspection (chassis, etc.)

Walk-behind Lawn Mower Package ($75 plus tax)

- Oil Change

- New Spark Plugs

- Filter Replacement (if needed)

- Carburetor (basic adjustments/maintenance)

- Mower Deck Cleaning

- Blade Sharpening

- General Inspection

Snow Blower Package ($75 plus tax)

- Oil Change

- New Spark Plugs

- Filter Replacement (if needed)

- Carburetor (basic adjustments/maintenance)

- Bearing Lubrication

- Auger Inspection

- Tire Inspection

- General Inspection (scraper blade, slide shoes, etc.)

OPERATIONS

Center City Repair is based in Center City, Minnesota, along State Highways 27 and 29, near Interstate 94. The business adheres to a mobile business model, performing most equipment repairs on-site.

Services are provided by owner Jeff Dahlstrom in a 6 x 12 mobile trailer outfitted with tools, supplies, equipment, and a variety of basic parts.

In addition to mobile operations, Center City Repair maintains physical space in an outbuilding on owner Jeff Dahlstrom's property. This includes a work area for performing extensive repairs (e.g., services that cannot be provided on-site for the customer), a selection of both used and new parts, and space for a limited inventory of used lawn and garden equipment that is in need of repair, or which has been repaired and is available for resale.

Seasonal Cycles:

- Fall/Winter: Focus on repairing and selling reconditioned snow removal equipment (e.g., snow-blowers, lawn tractor implements, etc.) and reconditioning used lawn care inventory for early spring/summer resale.

- Spring/Summer: Concentrate on repairing and selling reconditioned lawn care equipment (e.g., lawn mowers, tractors, string trimmers, etc.). Work on reconditioning used snow removal equipment for fall/winter resale.

Tools & Equipment

Jeff Dahlstrom will purchase a dedicated set of tools for Center City Repair, which he can utilize cost-effectively by sharing between his mobile unit and home-based workshop.

- Combination Wrenches
- Hex (Allen) Wrenches
- Screw Drivers (Phillips & Flat-Head)
- Torx Bits (Screwdriver & Sockets)
- 6" Slip Joint Pliers
- 6" Needle Nose Pliers
- 7" Diagonal Cutters
- 12" Channel Locks
- 10" Vice Grip Pliers
- Internal Retaining Ring Pliers
- External Retaining Ring Pliers
- Snap Ring Pliers
- Flat 10" Mill Bastard File
- Round 8"—10" File
- Three-cornered File
- 16oz Ball Peen Hammer
- 16oz Soft Faced Dead Blow Hammer
- Center Punch
- Safety Glasses
- Hearing Protectors
- Wire Stripper/Cutter Pliers 8"
- Pocket Flash Light

- Pocket Knife
- Spark Plug Gap Tool
- Feeler Gauge (Blade type)
- Tape Measure 12"
- Hack Saw
- Tubing Cutter
- Micrometer
- Pry Bar Screwdriver
- Compression Gauge
- Feeler Gauge
- Socket Set—1/2" Drive
- Torque Wrench—1/2" Drive
- 1/2" Drive Air Impact Gun
- Socket Set—1/4" Drive
- Brass Punch—3/4"
- Cold Chisels—3/8"—3/4"
- Socket Set—3/8" Drive
- 3/8" Drive Air Ratchet
- Taper Punch 3/8", 1/2", 5/8"
- Pin Punch—1/8", 3/16", 1/4", 5/16"
- Cape Chisel—5/16"
- Halogen Work Lights (2)
- Creeper
- Funnels
- Oil Disposal Containers (2)
- Air Compressor
- Portable Generator
- Gasoline Containers (2)
- Portable Grinder
- Rotary Tool
- Grease Gun
- Oil Can

Supplies & Parts

In addition, Center City Repair will maintain a limited inventory of supplies and parts, including:

- Grease
- Hardware (common standard and metric bolts, nuts, washers, etc.)

- Lubricants

- Degreaser

- Fuel Filters

- Spark Plugs

- Air Filters

- Gasoline

- Motor Oil

- Hand Cleaner

- Rags

- Tubing

- Zip Ties

- Razor Blades

- Sandpaper

Location

As a mobile equipment repair business, the majority of Center City Repair's operations occur on the road in a 6 x 12 cargo trailer. In addition to performing service and repair on a mobile basis, a variety of administrative tasks will be performed from the road as well. Center City Repair will engage in communications with customers (e.g., voice, text, and e-mail) via smartphone. In addition, a tablet computer and printer equipped with mobile Internet access will enable Jeff Dahlstrom to handle functions like appointment scheduling and invoicing from anywhere.

The trailer includes standard features such as:

- Spring-assisted Ramp Door with Bar Locks

- 3/4" Heavy Duty Plywood Floors

- 3/8" Plywood Walls

- Interior Roof Vents

- 12 Volt Interior Trailer Dome Lights w/ Wall Switch

In addition, Dahlstrom has made several custom modifications to the trailer, in order to make it suitable for business operations.

These include:

- Security System: A simple vehicle alarm has been installed to prevent theft.

- Promotional Graphics: Custom semi-permanent graphics have been produced by a local large-format printer, providing mobile advertising for the business.

- Generator: A quiet generator provides up to 20 hours of power (3,000 watts/25 amps at 120 volts) on 3.4 gallons of gas, providing enough energy for an RV air-conditioning unit, a space heater, and to meet other needs (recharging battery-powered tools, etc.). The generator features inverter technology that supplies safe power to sensitive equipment, including Jeff Dahlstrom's laptop computer and printer when needed.

PERSONNEL

Center City Repair is owned and operated by Center City native Jeff Dahlstrom. Prior to establishing his own business, Dahlstrom spent 10 years working for Center City Outdoor Power. In that role, he began as a repair technician, receiving hands-on training, as well as in-services on equipment repair offered by major manufacturers such as Briggs & Stratton, Tecumseh, and Toro. After five years, the owners of Center City Outdoor Power promoted Jeff to senior technician, and then service manager (a role he held for two years). Coupled with a small business management certificate received from Center City Community College, Jeff has obtained the technical and business management skills that will position him for success as the owner of Center City Repair.

Professional & Advisory Support

Jeff incorporated his business with the assistance of an attorney, and has hired a local bookkeeper to assist him with financial record-keeping and tax preparation services. In addition, Jeff has established a commercial checking account with Center City Bank, and has purchased technology that will allow him to process credit card payments on-site using a tablet computer.

MARKETING & SALES

Center City Repair will utilize the following tactics to market the business:

1. Printed collateral describing the business.

2. Marketing on social media channels, including Facebook and LinkedIn.

3. Magnetic business cards, which Jeff Dahlstrom will distribute around the community, especially to landscaping businesses he encounters on his mobile repair routes.

4. A Yellow Page listing.

5. Regular print advertisements in the *Center City Times*, a free weekly newspaper distributed throughout Center City.

6. A Web site with complete details about the business and a listing of its used lawn and garden equipment inventory.

7. Semi-annual (late winter/early spring and late fall/early winter) direct mail campaigns to residents with household incomes of $60,000 and more. The mailer will include printed collateral about Center City Repair, a lawn and garden equipment care tip sheet, and a 10 percent coupon for new customers.

8. A customer loyalty program that provides a 10 percent discount to those referring a friend or family member to our business.

9. Mobile marketing (displaying the business' name, Web site address, phone number, and tagline on the outside of our vehicle).

GROWTH STRATEGY

During the first three years of operations, Jeff Dahlstrom will concentrate his efforts on establishing a reputation for quality and trust in Center City. He will accomplish this by providing exceptional, reliable service. After covering start-up and operational costs, Jeff Dahlstrom anticipates that Center City Repair will generate a net profit of about $15,785 during the first year. He anticipates more substantial profits during the second and third years of operation, providing capital for the potential addition of a second technician and mobile service unit in year four.

FINANCIAL ANALYSIS

Start-up Budget

Jeff Dahlstrom is anticipating $24,824 in start-up costs for Center City Repair, which will be covered by a combination of cash savings and a family loan. These expenses include:

- Tools & Equipment ($2,500)

- 2004 Dodge Dakota SXT 2D Regular Cab with Tow Hitch ($9,599)

- Initial Supplies & Parts Inventory ($675)

- 6 x 12 Cargo Trailer ($6,000)

- Security System ($350)

- Promotional Vehicle/Trailer Graphics ($650)

- Generator ($1,550)

- Laptop Computers/Peripherals ($3,500)

In addition, Dahlstrom is anticipating $74,250 in operational costs during the first year:

- Advertising & Marketing ($10,500)

- Fuel ($8,000)

- Miscellaneous Items ($500)

- Legal ($1,500)

- Accounting ($750)

- Office Supplies ($500)

- Insurance ($2,500)

- Salary ($50,000)

By category, Center City Repair anticipates gross revenues will break down as follows during the business' first year of operations:

Lawn & garden repair—images

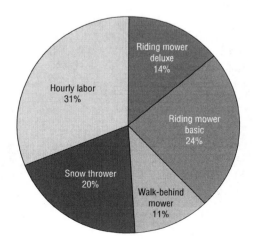

Gross Revenue Projections

The following gross revenue projections have been developed for Center City Repair's first three year of operations:

Year 1	Riding mower deluxe	Riding mower basic	Walk-behind mower	Snow thrower	Hourly labor	
January	$ 0	$ 0	$ 0	$ 1,301	$ 2,168	$ 3,468
February	$ 0	$ 0	$ 0	$ 650	$ 4,696	$ 5,347
March	$ 759	$ 1,301	$ 650	$ 325	$ 4,389	$ 7,424
April	$ 2,168	$ 3,902	$ 1,734	$ 5,202	$ 5,581	$ 18,586
May	$ 3,035	$ 5,202	$ 2,601	$ 2,601	$ 5,636	$ 19,074
June	$ 1,517	$ 2,601	$ 1,301	$ 0	$ 2,493	$ 7,911
July	$ 759	$ 1,301	$ 650	$ 0	$ 1,355	$ 4,064
August	$ 379	$ 650	$ 325	$ 0	$ 813	$ 2,168
September	$ 379	$ 650	$ 650	$ 650	$ 813	$ 3,143
October	$ 1,517	$ 2,601	$ 1,301	$ 2,601	$ 3,360	$ 11,379
November	$ 3,035	$ 5,202	$ 2,601	$ 5,202	$ 2,168	$ 18,207
December	$ 2,168	$ 3,902	$ 650	$ 5,202	$ 2,168	$ 14,089
	$15,714	**$27,311**	**$12,463**	**$23,734**	**$35,637**	**$114,859**

Year 2	Riding mower deluxe	Riding mower basic	Walk-behind mower	Snow thrower	Hourly labor	
January	$ 0	$ 0	$ 0	$ 1,530	$ 2,550	$ 4,080
February	$ 0	$ 0	$ 0	$ 765	$ 5,525	$ 6,290
March	$ 893	$ 1,530	$ 765	$ 383	$ 5,164	$ 8,734
April	$ 2,550	$ 4,590	$ 2,040	$ 6,120	$ 6,566	$ 21,866
May	$ 3,570	$ 6,120	$ 3,060	$ 3,060	$ 6,630	$ 22,440
June	$ 1,785	$ 3,060	$ 1,530	$ 0	$ 2,933	$ 9,308
July	$ 893	$ 1,530	$ 765	$ 0	$ 1,594	$ 4,781
August	$ 446	$ 765	$ 383	$ 0	$ 956	$ 2,550
September	$ 446	$ 765	$ 765	$ 765	$ 956	$ 3,698
October	$ 1,785	$ 3,060	$ 1,530	$ 3,060	$ 3,953	$ 13,388
November	$ 3,570	$ 6,120	$ 3,060	$ 6,120	$ 2,550	$ 21,420
December	$ 2,550	$ 4,590	$ 765	$ 6,120	$ 2,550	$ 16,575
	$18,488	**$32,130**	**$14,663**	**$27,923**	**$41,926**	**$135,129**

Year 3	Riding mower deluxe	Riding mower basic	Walk-behind mower	Snow thrower	Hourly labor	
January	$ 0	$ 0	$ 0	$ 1,800	$ 3,000	$ 4,800
February	$ 0	$ 0	$ 0	$ 900	$ 6,500	$ 7,400
March	$ 1,050	$ 1,800	$ 900	$ 450	$ 6,075	$ 10,275
April	$ 3,000	$ 5,400	$ 2,400	$ 7,200	$ 7,725	$ 25,725
May	$ 4,200	$ 7,200	$ 3,600	$ 3,600	$ 7,800	$ 26,400
June	$ 2,100	$ 3,600	$ 1,800	$ 0	$ 3,450	$ 10,950
July	$ 1,050	$ 1,800	$ 900	$ 0	$ 1,875	$ 5,625
August	$ 525	$ 900	$ 450	$ 0	$ 1,125	$ 3,000
September	$ 525	$ 900	$ 900	$ 900	$ 1,125	$ 4,350
October	$ 2,100	$ 3,600	$ 1,800	$ 3,600	$ 4,650	$ 15,750
November	$ 4,200	$ 7,200	$ 3,600	$ 7,200	$ 3,000	$ 25,200
December	$ 3,000	$ 5,400	$ 900	$ 7,200	$ 3,000	$ 19,500
	$21,750	**$37,800**	**$17,250**	**$32,850**	**$49,325**	**$158,975**

Library Systems Consultant

Library Solutions, LLC

PO Box 4401
Sterling Heights, MI 48311

Zuzu Enterprises

Library Solutions, LLC is a consulting firm specializing in systems and services for the library market. Services include product selection, customization, problem resolution, and staff training. The business was founded by Chris Miller.

EXECUTIVE SUMMARY

Library Solutions, LLC is a consulting firm specializing in systems and services for the library market. Services include product selection, customization, problem resolution, and staff training on general business hardware and software as well as library-specific products. The business was founded by Chris Miller, a librarian and IT specialist.

MARKET ANALYSIS

The market for consulting services within the library community is vast. In the southeastern Michigan area alone, there are more than 100 libraries of varying sizes and budgets. No matter the size or budget, though, all libraries utilize computer hardware and software as an integral part of their business processes. Libraries rely on computers and various software to serve the public and get their jobs done; when something goes wrong, most libraries are at a standstill. Time is of the essence in getting their systems back online and working so that they can continue to serve their patrons and retain their confidence.

Libraries realize the significance of their reliance on technology and have either employed dedicated technology staff or other staff that is at least tech-savvy. Most libraries also join a local cooperative that can assist in technology issues to varying degrees. Despite this, there still exists the opportunity of assisting organizations in special projects or emergency situations.

Competition

There is relatively little competition in the library technology consulting market. Listed below are the biggest competitors.

Hartzell-Mika Consulting, LLC located in East Lansing, Michigan is a consultant firm focused on libraries. However, they focus on strategic planning, building project management, and executive searches, not computer systems and solutions as Library Solutions does. They are not a direct competitor.

Library cooperatives such as the Suburban Library Cooperative and The Library Network are not consulting firms, but they do offer the same types of services as Library Solutions, LLC to their member organizations. There is an opportunity to work with the cooperatives as a services provider, or directly to their member organizations when a specific service isn't offered.

Other general services consultants may offer expertise in common applications such as Microsoft software, but these consultants lack the experience and expertise of working within the library world. Although it may not seem like it, the library environment is much different than traditional business environments and it is crucial to recognize this difference to be successful in this market.

SERVICES

The services of Library Solutions, LLC include consulting with library personnel on any and all systems used in the library environment. This includes product selection, customization, problem resolution, and training on any number of applications used in the library, including operating systems, general business and accounting software, wireless networks, and antivirus software as well as library-specific applications such as ILS software and session management software. Each service line is detailed below.

Product Selection

Product selection takes into account the unique business needs and challenges of each individual organization. It evaluate products based on cost, level of increased efficiency expected, appropriateness, and long-term feasibility and helps narrow down the choices to select the one product that will best meet the requirements of the organization.

Product selection consultation will be billed at the rate of $25 per hour.

Customization

Another service line is customization of current products. This may range from maximizing under-utilized features and benefits to designing and creating custom interfaces, reports, and the like. Cookie cutter products may serve most of our needs and would be "perfect" if only they had that one additional feature. Most products, however, can be customized to fit the unique needs and desires of the individual organization, if only they had the time and expertise to easily do so. Library Solutions, LLC has this knowledge and expertise and is more than willing to work with organizations to make the most out of their current products.

Customization consultation will be billed at the rate of $25 per hour.

Problem resolution

Problem resolution is another service line offered my Library Solutions, LLC. Problems may occur that are simply annoying or that are completely debilitating to a library. They may beyond the knowledge and scope of the IT specialist, or they may occur at a time when the specialist is busy with other tasks. No matter what the scenario, Library Solutions, LLC is able to step in, diagnose the problem, and identify the solutions in a timely manner.

Problem resolution will be billed at the rate of $35 per hour.

Training

Library Solutions, LLC also offers small- and large-group training on any of the hardware and software applications that a library offers. This training may be done for employees of the library on how to utilize their existing tools, or it may even be offered as classes to library patrons on how to use the resources and technology made available to them by the library. This latter case is especially useful in such cases as using e-readers and tablets to access e-books as well as such things accessing available databases, foreign language applications, and digital magazines.

Training sessions are offered on a per-person basis and will vary depending on the topic and time frame.

Hardware and Software

The service lines of product selection, customization, problem resolution, and training are available on any and all types of library applications, including:

- Operating systems
- General business software, including word processing, email, etc.
- Antivirus and anti-spyware software
- Accounting software
- Social media and websites
- Integrated Library System software
- Event calendars
- Room booking software
- Computer session management software
- Print management systems
- Security programs
- Wireless network access
- Electronic data available to patrons, including e-books, foreign language applications, digital magazines, online databases, music downloads, and the like
- Online homework helper applications
- Online chat applications
- System backups
- Computers, printers, scanners, copiers, and fax machines

PERSONNEL

Library Solutions, LLC is owned and operated by Chris Miller. Chris has a unique blend of education and experience, including:

- Bachelor's degree in Business Information Systems from Western Michigan University
- 5 years' experience as IT professional in the business world
- Master's Degree in Library and Information Science from Wayne State University
- 6 years' experience as an adult services librarian/IT specialist for the Warren Public Library system, which is made up of 4 branches and is part of the Suburban Library Cooperative

Chris is currently employed on a part-time basis as a library IT professional for the Warren Public Library system but wanted to use her considerable expertise to help other, local libraries to fully embrace and utilize the electronic tools at their disposal. She whole-heartedly believes that libraries that embrace technology and the fast-paced world of change that it requires will be able to not only survive but thrive in the future. Utilizing and maximizing the benefits of technology will only make us better serve library patrons and be an integral part of their information, media, and educational needs for years to come.

Professional & Advisory Support

Library Solutions, LLC has secured the tax advisory services of Durr & Durr Accounting. A business checking account has been established with Fifth Third Bank.

MARKETING & SALES

Two library cooperatives dominate the library market in the southeastern Michigan area. Each one is profiled below.

Suburban Library Cooperative

The Suburban Library Cooperative has 27 member libraries in the southeastern Michigan region, including libraries in the following communities: Armada, Center Line, Chesterfield, Clinton Township, Eastpointe, Fraser, Harper Woods, Lenox, Macomb Township, Mount Clemens, New Baltimore, Ray, Richmond, Romeo, Roseville, Shelby, St. Clair Shores, Sterling Heights, Troy, Utica, and Warren. It manages the SIRSI Unicorn online system for its members, allowing libraries throughout the cooperative to access the holdings of all of the participating libraries, check out items to patrons, place holds on items, process library materials, and access online databases. However, at least one member of the cooperative has elected to use a different system due to its functional limitations. Other member libraries may do the same, and those who stay with the system because of budget concerns may benefit from consulting services of customization and problem resolution. Marketing efforts will be made to both the Cooperative as well as all member libraries on both of these fronts.

The Library Network (TLN)

The Library Network is a public library cooperative serving 73 libraries in southeast Michigan, including such places as Canton, Rochester Hills, Chelsea, Oxford, Birmingham, West Bloomfield, Ypsilanti, and Royal Oak. Members pick and choose which of the TLN services they want to participate in; the services range from acquisitions and cataloging to delivery to shared technology services including such things as PC and network support. There is an opportunity to work directly with TLN as a service provider to their members at any of the service lines Library Solutions LLC offers including product selection, customization, problem resolution, and training. There is also an opportunity to provide services directly to those member libraries that opt not to participate in these offerings directly from TLN.

Marketing efforts will be made to both of these cooperatives as well as their 100 member organizations. Direct mailings detailing services offered as well as testimonials of excellent service will be sent with a follow-up phone call made approximately 1-2 weeks after they are received. A targeted list of libraries as well as the cooperative offices will be approached for a meeting and presentation.

OPERATIONS

Problem resolution and training services will be done on-site for the participating organization. Customers tend to feel more confident in the person and the results when they can actually see the person doing the work. Also, being onsite and talking one-on-one with the customer prevents miscommunication and allows for immediate results.

Product selection and customization services will be provided either onsite or offsite, depending on customer preference. These tasks are easily accomplished remotely and have the added bonus of not requiring time or resources to travel. However, some customers may still desire these tasks to be completed onsite.

A laptop computer/tablet will allow for the work to be completed anywhere and at any time of the day or night. No office space other than a small home office with a backup server, printer, and other various components is necessary.

LEGAL

Library Solutions, LLC complies with the American Library Association's Library Bill of Rights, which affirms that rights of privacy are necessary for intellectual freedom and are fundamental to the ethics and practice of librarianship. Confidentiality exists when a library is in possession of personally identifiable information about users and keeps that information private on their behalf; as a contractual employee of a library or a library cooperative on behalf of its member libraries, Library Solutions, LLC is bound to uphold this mission to protect user information in order to preserve free speech, free thought, and free association.

FINANCIAL ANALYSIS

It is expected that Library Solutions, LLC will make a profit in year one. Startup costs are minimal, merely consisting of a laptop/tablet, software applications, and marketing materials. Chris Miller has a dedicated office space in her home that will be utilized as the business headquarters and work space. Detailed receipts will be kept on all purchases as well as a record of all incurred travel-related expenses for tax purposes.

Medical Marijuana Clinic

M M J C l i n i c

32111 W. 103 rd Street
New York, NY 10012

BizPlanDB.com

MMJ Clinic is a New York-based corporation that will provide medical marijuana to customers in its targeted market. The Company was founded by John Applegate.

1.0 EXECUTIVE SUMMARY

The purpose of this business plan is to raise $160,000 for the development of a medical marijuana clinic and pharmacy while showcasing the expected financials and operations over the next three years. MMJ Clinic is a New York-based corporation that will provide medical marijuana to customers in its targeted market. The Company was founded by John Applegate.

1.1 The Products and Services

The primary operations of the business will be the distribution of medical marijuana to customers within the target market. The Company will earn gross margins of approximately 20% on all marijuana distributed by the business. At the onset of operations, the Company will have one full-time pharmacist and an assistant to manage the distribution of marijuana to customers in accordance with state laws.

MMJ Clinic will sell raw marijuana buds as well as candies, cakes, sodas, and other edibles that contain THC (the active ingredient in cannabis).

The third section of the business plan will further describe the services offered by MMJ Clinic.

1.2 Financing

Mr. Applegate is seeking to raise $160,000 from a bank loan. The interest rate and loan agreement are to be further discussed during negotiation. This business plan assumes that the business will receive a 10-year loan with a 9% fixed interest rate. The financing will be used for the following:

- Development of the Company's clinical location.

- Financing for the first six months of operation.

- Capital to purchase the Company's inventory of marijuana products.

Mr. Applegate will contribute $10,000 to the venture.

1.3 Mission Statement

MMJ Clinic's mission is to become the recognized leader in its targeted market for providing medical marijuana in accordance with state laws to the local general public.

1.4 Management Team

The Company was founded by John Applegate. Mr. Applegate has more than ten years of experience in the retail industry. Through his expertise, he will be able to bring the operations of the business to profitability within its first year of operations.

1.5 Sales Forecasts

Mr. Applegate expects a strong rate of growth at the start of operations. Below are the expected financials over the next three years.

Proforma profit and loss (yearly)

Year	1	2	3
Sales	$1,749,570	$2,099,484	$2,456,396
Operating costs	$ 388,745	$ 406,572	$ 424,954
EBITDA	$ 178,357	$ 273,951	$ 371,258
Taxes, interest, and depreciation	$ 90,685	$ 121,096	$ 157,415
Net profit	$ 87,673	$ 152,854	$ 213,843

Sales, operating costs, and profit forecast

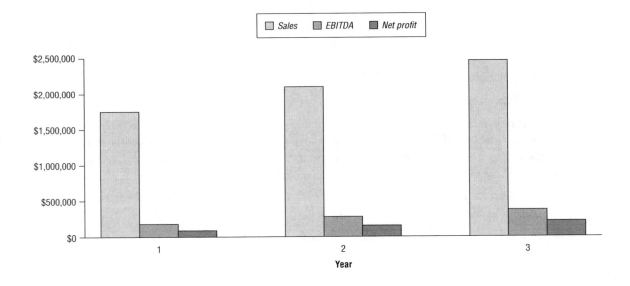

1.6 Expansion Plan

The Founder expects that the business will aggressively expand during the first three years of operation. Mr. Applegate intends to implement marketing campaigns that will effectively target individuals that have medical marijuana prescriptions within the target market.

2.0 COMPANY AND FINANCING SUMMARY

2.1 Registered Name and Corporate Structure

The Company is registered as a corporation in the State of New York.

2.2 Required Funds

At this time, MMJ Clinic requires $160,000 of debt funds. Below is a breakdown of how these funds will be used:

Projected startup costs

Initial lease payments and deposits	$ 10,000
Working capital	$ 35,000
FF&E	$ 25,000
Leasehold improvements	$ 5,000
Security deposits	$ 5,000
Insurance	$ 2,500
Marijuana inventories	$ 75,000
Marketing budget	$ 7,500
Miscellaneous and unforeseen costs	$ 5,000
Total startup costs	**$170,000**

Use of funds

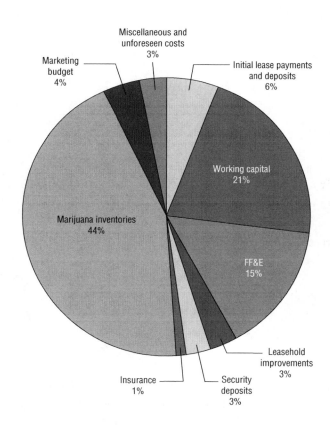

2.3 Investor Equity

Mr. Applegate is not seeking an investment from a third party at this time.

2.4 Management Equity

John Applegate owns 100% of MMJ Clinic.

2.5 Exit Strategy

If the business is very successful, Mr. Applegate may seek to sell the business to a third party for a significant earnings multiple. Most likely, the Company will hire a qualified business broker to sell the business on behalf of MMJ Clinic. Based on historical numbers, the business could fetch a sales premium of up to 4 times earnings.

3.0 PRODUCTS AND SERVICES

Below is a description of the products offered by MMJ Clinic.

3.1 Sales of Marijuana

As discussed in the executive summary, the business will be engaged in the legal sale of medical marijuana to patients that have an appropriate prescription for usage of medical marijuana in accordance with state law. The business will sell raw marijuana buds of many different types of strains. The business will acquire its inventories from licensed producers of marijuana within the state.

The business will also sell a large number of "edibles" which are cooked goods and confections that contain THC (again, the active ingredient within marijuana and cannabis).

Mr. Applegate is currently obtaining the proper licensure so that the business can distribute prescription medical marijuana from its retail location.

4.0 STRATEGIC AND MARKET ANALYSIS

4.1 Economic Outlook

This section of the analysis will detail the economic climate, the medical marijuana industry, the customer profile, and the competition that the business will face as it progresses through its business operations.

Currently, the economic market condition in the United States is in a state of moderate growth. Unemployment rates have declined while asset prices have risen substantially. The demand for medical cannabis continues to remain strong in states that allow for the sale of this product. As such, the business will be able to remain profitable and cash flow positive at all times.

Pharmacies and medical marijuana clinics operate with great economic stability as people will continue to require medications despite drawbacks in the general economy.

4.2 Industry Analysis

It is currently estimated that the sale of medical marijuana is a $900 million industry within the United States. The advent of this industry has occurred over the past seven years, and many more states are expected to continue to allow for sales of medical marijuana. The industry currently employs approximately 15,000 people (which includes dispensary workers as well as marijuana growers).

There are a number of legal issues that come with operating a medical marijuana clinic. At this time, marijuana remains an illegal substance (for any purpose) per federal government law. However, many states through their legislation and popular vote have allowed for the growth, distribution, and sale of marijuana for medical purposes. The landscape of this industry in regards to legal matters is expected to continue to change significantly over the next five to ten years.

4.3 Customer Profile

MMJ Clinic's average client will be a middle- to upper-middle-class man or woman living in the Company's target market. Common traits among clients will include:

- Annual household income exceeding $50,000

- Lives or works no more than 15 miles from the Company's location

- Will spend $100 per visit to the Company's medical marijuana dispensary

- Has a medical condition that will benefit from the use of medical marijuana and a valid New York Medical Marijuana Card

4.4 Competition

Medical marijuana is new to the New York area. As such, there are only a handful of licensed pharmacies that can provide this form of treatment to the general public. Once MMJ Clinic receives its state licensure, the Company will only have three to four competitors operating within the greater New York metropolitan area. However, it is imperative that the business establish a strong brand name from the onset of operations in order to have customers continue to fill their prescriptions with the clinic.

5.0 MARKETING PLAN

MMJ Clinic intends to maintain an extensive marketing campaign that will ensure maximum visibility for the business in its targeted market. Below is an overview of the marketing strategies and objectives of MMJ Clinic.

5.1 Marketing Objectives

- Establish relationships with referring physicians.

- Develop an online presence by developing a website and placing the Company's name and contact information with online directories.

- Remain within the letter of the law as it relates to advertising the medical marijuana fulfillment services offered by the business.

5.2 Marketing Strategies

Of most importance to the Company is Management's ability to developing ongoing referral relationships with physicians that see medical marijuana as an appropriate treatment for a number of different illnesses and ailments. Mr. Applegate will directly contact a number of doctors directly in order to develop these ongoing referral relationships.

Mr. Applegate intends on using a number of marketing strategies that will allow MMJ Clinic to easily target men and women within the target market. These strategies include traditional print advertisements and ads placed on search engines on the Internet. Below is a description of how the business intends to market its services to the general public.

The Pharmacy will also use an internet-based strategy. This is very important as many people seeking local services and products, such as medical marijuana clinics, now use the Internet to conduct their preliminary searches. Mr. Applegate will register MMJ Clinic with online portals so that potential customers can easily reach the business. The Company will also develop its own online website showcasing hours of operation, directions, applicable licensure, available marijuana strains, and applicable laws pertaining to obtaining medical marijuana.

5.3 Pricing

Management estimates that the Company will generate revenues of approximately $50 per gram of medical marijuana sold to an individual that has a valid license/prescription for acquiring this drug.

6.0 ORGANIZATIONAL PLAN AND PERSONNEL SUMMARY

6.1 Corporate Organization

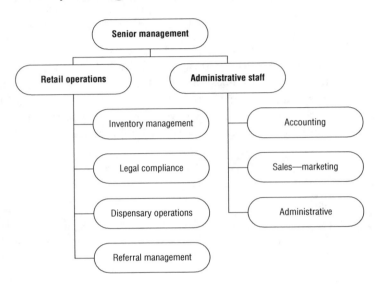

6.2 Organizational Budget

Personnel plan—yearly

Year	1	2	3
Owner	$ 80,000	$ 82,400	$ 84,872
Pharmacist	$ 75,000	$ 77,250	$ 79,568
Clinic employees	$ 63,000	$ 64,890	$ 66,837
Bookkeeper	$ 24,000	$ 24,720	$ 25,462
Administrative	$ 23,000	$ 23,690	$ 24,401
Total	**$265,000**	**$272,950**	**$281,139**

Numbers of personnel

Owner	1	1	1
Pharmacist	1	1	1
Clinic employees	3	3	3
Bookkeeper	1	1	1
Administrative	1	1	1
Totals	**7**	**7**	**7**

Personnel expense breakdown

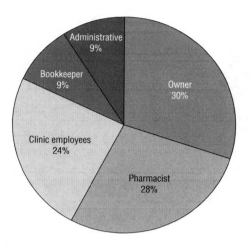

7.0 FINANCIAL PLAN

7.1 Underlying Assumptions

The Company has based its proforma financial statements on the following:

• MMJ Clinic will have an annual revenue growth rate of 16% per year.

• The Owner will acquire $160,000 of debt funds to develop the business.

• The loan will have a 10-year term with a 9% interest rate.

7.2 Sensitivity Analysis

The Company's revenues are not sensitive to changes in the general economy. As discussed earlier, the business provides marijuana medication to its customers and, as such, the business will not suffer any major declines in revenues despite deleterious changes in the economy.

7.3 Source of Funds

Financing

Equity contributions	
Management investment	$ 10,000.00
Total equity financing	**$ 10,000.00**
Banks and lenders	
Banks and lenders	$ 160,000.00
Total debt financing	**$160,000.00**
Total financing	**$170,000.00**

7.4 General Assumptions

General assumptions

Year	1	2	3
Short term interest rate	9.5%	9.5%	9.5%
Long term interest rate	10.0%	10.0%	10.0%
Federal tax rate	33.0%	33.0%	33.0%
State tax rate	5.0%	5.0%	5.0%
Personnel taxes	15.0%	15.0%	15.0%

7.5 Profit and Loss Statements

Proforma profit and loss (yearly)

Year	1	2	3
Sales	$1,749,570	$2,099,484	$2,456,396
Cost of goods sold	$1,182,468	$1,418,962	$1,660,185
Gross margin	32.41%	32.41%	32.41%
Operating income	$ 567,102	$ 680,522	$ 796,211
Expenses			
Payroll	$ 265,000	$ 272,950	$ 281,139
General and administrative	$ 25,200	$ 26,208	$ 27,256
Marketing expenses	$ 8,748	$ 10,497	$ 12,282
Professional fees and licensure	$ 5,219	$ 5,376	$ 5,537
Insurance costs	$ 1,987	$ 2,086	$ 2,191
Drug sourcing costs	$ 7,596	$ 8,356	$ 9,191
Rent and utilities	$ 14,250	$ 14,963	$ 15,711
Miscellaneous costs	$ 20,995	$ 25,194	$ 29,477
Payroll taxes	$ 39,750	$ 40,943	$ 42,171
Total operating costs	$ 388,745	$ 406,572	$ 424,954
EBITDA	$ 178,357	$ 273,951	$ 371,258
Federal income tax	$ 58,858	$ 86,110	$ 118,572
State income tax	$ 8,918	$ 13,047	$ 17,965
Interest expense	$ 13,980	$ 13,010	$ 11,949
Depreciation expenses	$ 8,929	$ 8,929	$ 8,929
Net profit	$ 87,673	$ 152,854	$ 213,843
Profit margin	5.01%	7.28%	8.71%

Sales, operating costs, and profit forecast

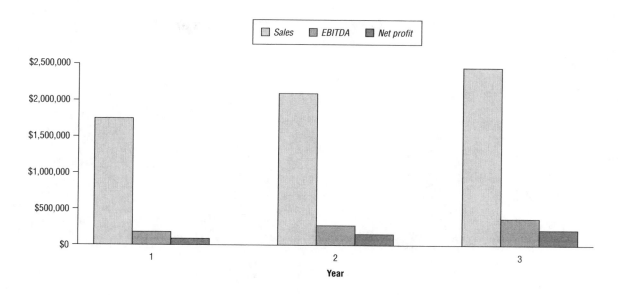

7.6 Cash Flow Analysis

Proforma cash flow analysis—yearly

Year	1	2	3
Cash from operations	$ 96,601	$161,783	$222,771
Cash from receivables	$ 0	$ 0	$ 0
Operating cash inflow	**$ 96,601**	**$161,783**	**$222,771**
Other cash inflows			
Equity investment	$ 10,000	$ 0	$ 0
Increased borrowings	$160,000	$ 0	$ 0
Sales of business assets	$ 0	$ 0	$ 0
A/P increases	$ 37,902	$ 43,587	$ 50,125
Total other cash inflows	**$207,902**	**$ 43,587**	**$ 50,125**
Total cash inflow	**$304,503**	**$205,370**	**$272,897**
Cash outflows			
Repayment of principal	$ 10,341	$ 11,312	$ 12,373
A/P decreases	$ 24,897	$ 29,876	$ 35,852
A/R increases	$ 0	$ 0	$ 0
Asset purchases	$125,000	$ 40,446	$ 55,693
Dividends	$ 86,941	$113,248	$155,940
Total cash outflows	**$247,180**	**$194,882**	**$259,857**
Net cash flow	**$ 57,324**	**$ 10,489**	**$ 13,040**
Cash balance	**$ 57,324**	**$ 67,812**	**$ 80,852**

Proforma cash flow (yearly)

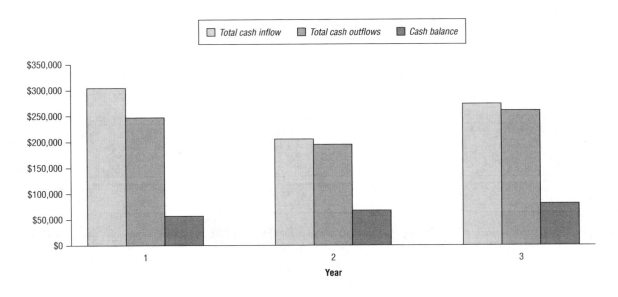

7.7 Balance Sheet

Proforma balance sheet—yearly

Year	1	2	3
Assets			
Cash	$ 57,324	$ 67,812	$ 80,852
Amortized development costs	$ 25,000	$ 29,045	$ 34,614
Inventories	$ 75,000	$105,334	$147,104
FF&E	$ 25,000	$ 31,067	$ 39,421
Accumulated depreciation	($ 8,929)	($ 17,857)	($ 26,786)
Total assets	**$173,395**	**$215,401**	**$275,205**
Liabilities and equity			
Accounts payable	$ 13,005	$ 26,716	$ 40,990
Long term liabilities	$149,659	$138,347	$127,036
Other liabilities	$ 0	$ 0	$ 0
Total liabilities	**$162,664**	**$165,063**	**$168,025**
Net worth	**$ 10,732**	**$ 50,338**	**$107,180**
Total liabilities and equity	**$173,395**	**$215,401**	**$275,205**

Proforma balance sheet

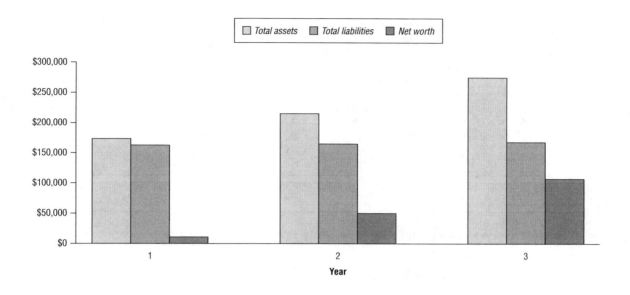

7.8 Breakeven Analysis

Monthly break even analysis

Year	1	2	3
Monthly revenue	$ 99,943	$ 104,526	$ 109,252
Yearly revenue	$1,199,319	$1,254,317	$1,311,027

Break even analysis

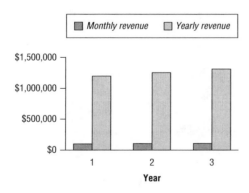

7.9 Business Ratios

Business ratios—yearly

Year	1	2	3
Sales			
Sales growth	0.00%	20.00%	17.00%
Gross margin	32.40%	32.40%	32.40%
Financials			
Profit margin	5.01%	7.28%	8.71%
Assets to liabilities	1.07	1.30	1.64
Equity to liabilities	0.07	0.30	0.64
Assets to equity	16.16	4.28	2.57
Liquidity			
Acid test	0.35	0.41	0.48
Cash to assets	0.33	0.31	0.29

7.10 Three Year Profit and Loss Statement

Profit and loss statement (first year)

Months	1	2	3	4	5	6	7
Sales	$145,000	$145,145	$145,290	$145,435	$145,580	$145,725	$145,870
Cost of goods sold	$ 98,000	$ 98,098	$ 98,196	$ 98,294	$ 98,392	$ 98,490	$ 98,588
Gross margin	32.4%	32.4%	32.4%	32.4%	32.4%	32.4%	32.4%
Operating income	$ 47,000	$ 47,047	$ 47,094	$ 47,141	$ 47,188	$ 47,235	$ 47,282
Expenses							
Payroll	$ 22,083	$ 22,083	$ 22,083	$ 22,083	$ 22,083	$ 22,083	$ 22,083
General and administrative	$ 2,100	$ 2,100	$ 2,100	$ 2,100	$ 2,100	$ 2,100	$ 2,100
Marketing expenses	$ 729	$ 729	$ 729	$ 729	$ 729	$ 729	$ 729
Professional fees and licensure	$ 435	$ 435	$ 435	$ 435	$ 435	$ 435	$ 435
Insurance costs	$ 166	$ 166	$ 166	$ 166	$ 166	$ 166	$ 166
Drug sourcing costs	$ 633	$ 633	$ 633	$ 633	$ 633	$ 633	$ 633
Rent and utilities	$ 1,188	$ 1,188	$ 1,188	$ 1,188	$ 1,188	$ 1,188	$ 1,188
Miscellaneous costs	$ 1,750	$ 1,750	$ 1,750	$ 1,750	$ 1,750	$ 1,750	$ 1,750
Payroll taxes	$ 3,313	$ 3,313	$ 3,313	$ 3,313	$ 3,313	$ 3,313	$ 3,313
Total operating costs	$ 32,395	$ 32,395	$ 32,395	$ 32,395	$ 32,395	$ 32,395	$ 32,395
EBITDA	$ 14,605	$ 14,652	$ 14,699	$ 14,746	$ 14,793	$ 14,840	$ 14,887
Federal income tax	$ 4,878	$ 4,883	$ 4,888	$ 4,893	$ 4,898	$ 4,902	$ 4,907
State income tax	$ 739	$ 740	$ 741	$ 741	$ 742	$ 743	$ 744
Interest expense	$ 1,200	$ 1,194	$ 1,188	$ 1,181	$ 1,175	$ 1,169	$ 1,162
Depreciation expense	$ 744	$ 744	$ 744	$ 744	$ 744	$ 744	$ 744
Net profit	$ 7,043	$ 7,091	$ 7,139	$ 7,186	$ 7,234	$ 7,282	$ 7,330

Profit and loss statement (first year cont.)

Month	8	9	10	11	12	1
Sales	$146,015	$146,160	$146,305	$146,450	$146,595	$1,749,570
Cost of goods sold	$ 98,686	$ 98,784	$ 98,882	$ 98,980	$ 99,078	$1,182,468
Gross margin	32.4%	32.4%	32.4%	32.4%	32.4%	32.4%
Operating income	$ 47,329	$ 47,376	$ 47,423	$ 47,470	$ 47,517	$ 567,102
Expenses						
Payroll	$ 22,083	$ 22,083	$ 22,083	$ 22,083	$ 22,083	$ 265,000
General and administrative	$ 2,100	$ 2,100	$ 2,100	$ 2,100	$ 2,100	$ 25,200
Marketing expenses	$ 729	$ 729	$ 729	$ 729	$ 729	$ 8,748
Professional fees and licensure	$ 435	$ 435	$ 435	$ 435	$ 435	$ 5,219
Insurance costs	$ 166	$ 166	$ 166	$ 166	$ 166	$ 1,987
Drug sourcing costs	$ 633	$ 633	$ 633	$ 633	$ 633	$ 7,596
Rent and utilities	$ 1,188	$ 1,188	$ 1,188	$ 1,188	$ 1,188	$ 14,250
Miscellaneous costs	$ 1,750	$ 1,750	$ 1,750	$ 1,750	$ 1,750	$ 20,995
Payroll taxes	$ 3,313	$ 3,313	$ 3,313	$ 3,313	$ 3,313	$ 39,750
Total operating costs	$ 32,395	$ 32,395	$ 32,395	$ 32,395	$ 32,395	$ 388,745
EBITDA	$ 14,934	$ 14,981	$ 15,028	$ 15,075	$ 15,122	$ 178,357
Federal income tax	$ 4,912	$ 4,917	$ 4,922	$ 4,927	$ 4,932	$ 58,858
State income tax	$ 744	$ 745	$ 746	$ 746	$ 747	$ 8,918
Interest expense	$ 1,156	$ 1,149	$ 1,142	$ 1,136	$ 1,129	$ 13,980
Depreciation expense	$ 744	$ 744	$ 744	$ 744	$ 744	$ 8,929
Net profit	$ 7,378	$ 7,425	$ 7,473	$ 7,521	$ 7,570	$ 87,673

Profit and loss statement (second year)

Quarter	Q1	2 Q2	Q3	Q4	2
Sales	$419,897	$524,871	$566,861	$587,856	$2,099,484
Cost of goods sold	$283,792	$354,740	$383,120	$397,309	$1,418,962
Gross margin	32.4%	32.4%	32.4%	32.4%	32.4%
Operating income	$136,104	$170,131	$183,741	$190,546	$ 680,522
Expenses					
Payroll	$ 54,590	$ 68,238	$ 73,697	$ 76,426	$ 272,950
General and administrative	$ 5,242	$ 6,552	$ 7,076	$ 7,338	$ 26,208
Marketing expenses	$ 2,099	$ 2,624	$ 2,834	$ 2,939	$ 10,497
Professional fees and licensure	$ 1,075	$ 1,344	$ 1,451	$ 1,505	$ 5,376
Insurance costs	$ 417	$ 522	$ 563	$ 584	$ 2,086
Drug sourcing costs	$ 1,671	$ 2,089	$ 2,256	$ 2,340	$ 8,356
Rent and utilities	$ 2,993	$ 3,741	$ 4,040	$ 4,190	$ 14,963
Miscellaneous costs	$ 5,039	$ 6,298	$ 6,802	$ 7,054	$ 25,194
Payroll taxes	$ 8,189	$ 10,236	$ 11,054	$ 11,464	$ 40,943
Total operating costs	$ 81,314	$101,643	$109,774	$113,840	$ 406,572
EBITDA	$ 54,790	$ 68,488	$ 73,967	$ 76,706	$ 273,951
Federal income tax	$ 17,222	$ 21,528	$ 23,250	$ 24,111	$ 86,110
State income tax	$ 2,609	$ 3,262	$ 3,523	$ 3,653	$ 13,047
Interest expense	$ 3,347	$ 3,285	$ 3,222	$ 3,157	$ 13,010
Depreciation expense	$ 2,232	$ 2,232	$ 2,232	$ 2,232	$ 8,929
Net profit	$ 29,380	$ 38,181	$ 41,740	$ 43,553	$ 152,854

Profit and loss statement (third year)

Quarter	Q1	3 Q2	Q3	Q4	3
Sales	$491,279	$614,099	$663,227	$687,791	$2,456,396
Cost of goods sold	$332,037	$415,046	$448,250	$464,852	$1,660,185
Gross margin	32.4%	32.4%	32.4%	32.4%	32.4%
Operating income	$159,242	$199,053	$214,977	$222,939	$ 796,211
Expenses					
Payroll	$ 56,228	$ 70,285	$ 75,907	$ 78,719	$ 281,139
General and administrative	$ 5,451	$ 6,814	$ 7,359	$ 7,632	$ 27,256
Marketing expenses	$ 2,456	$ 3,070	$ 3,316	$ 3,439	$ 12,282
Professional fees and licensure	$ 1,107	$ 1,384	$ 1,495	$ 1,550	$ 5,537
Insurance costs	$ 438	$ 548	$ 591	$ 613	$ 2,191
Drug sourcing costs	$ 1,838	$ 2,298	$ 2,482	$ 2,574	$ 9,191
Rent and utilities	$ 3,142	$ 3,928	$ 4,242	$ 4,399	$ 15,711
Miscellaneous costs	$ 5,895	$ 7,369	$ 7,959	$ 8,253	$ 29,477
Payroll taxes	$ 8,434	$ 10,543	$ 11,386	$ 11,808	$ 42,171
Total operating costs	$ 84,991	$106,238	$114,737	$118,987	$ 424,954
EBITDA	$ 74,252	$ 92,814	$100,240	$103,952	$ 371,258
Federal income tax	$ 23,714	$ 29,643	$ 32,014	$ 33,200	$ 118,572
State income tax	$ 3,593	$ 4,491	$ 4,851	$ 5,030	$ 17,965
Interest expense	$ 3,090	$ 3,023	$ 2,953	$ 2,883	$ 11,949
Depreciation expense	$ 2,232	$ 2,232	$ 2,232	$ 2,232	$ 8,929
Net profit	$ 41,621	$ 53,425	$ 58,189	$ 60,607	$ 213,843

7.11 Three Year Cash Flow Analysis

Cash flow analysis (first year)

Month	1	2	3	4	5	6	7
Cash from operations	$ 7,788	$ 7,835	$ 7,883	$ 7,930	$ 7,978	$ 8,026	$ 8,074
Cash from receivables	$ 0	$ 0	$ 0	$ 0	$ 0	$ 0	$ 0
Operating cash inflow	$ 7,788	$ 7,835	$ 7,883	$ 7,930	$ 7,978	$ 8,026	$ 8,074
Other cash inflows							
Equity investment	$ 10,000	$ 0	$ 0	$ 0	$ 0	$ 0	$ 0
Increased borrowings	$160,000	$ 0	$ 0	$ 0	$ 0	$ 0	$ 0
Sales of business assets	$ 0	$ 0	$ 0	$ 0	$ 0	$ 0	$ 0
A/P increases	$ 3,159	$ 3,159	$ 3,159	$ 3,159	$ 3,159	$ 3,159	$ 3,159
Total other cash inflows	$173,159	$ 3,159	$ 3,159	$ 3,159	$ 3,159	$ 3,159	$ 3,159
Total cash inflow	$180,946	$10,994	$11,041	$11,089	$11,137	$11,184	$ 11,232
Cash outflows							
Repayment of principal	$ 827	$ 833	$ 839	$ 846	$ 852	$ 858	$ 865
A/P decreases	$ 2,075	$ 2,075	$ 2,075	$ 2,075	$ 2,075	$ 2,075	$ 2,075
A/R increases	$ 0	$ 0	$ 0	$ 0	$ 0	$ 0	$ 0
Asset purchases	$125,000	$ 0	$ 0	$ 0	$ 0	$ 0	$ 0
Dividends	$ 0	$ 0	$ 0	$ 0	$ 0	$ 0	$ 0
Total cash outflows	$127,902	$ 2,908	$ 2,914	$ 2,920	$ 2,927	$ 2,933	$ 2,939
Net cash flow	$ 53,044	$ 8,086	$ 8,127	$ 8,169	$ 8,210	$ 8,251	$ 8,293
Cash balance	$ 53,044	$61,130	$69,258	$77,426	$85,636	$93,887	$102,180

Cash flow analysis (first year cont.)

Month	8	9	10	11	12	1
Cash from operations	$ 8,122	$ 8,170	$ 8,217	$ 8,265	$ 8,314	$ 96,601
Cash from receivables	$ 0	$ 0	$ 0	$ 0	$ 0	$ 0
Operating cash inflow	**$ 8,122**	**$ 8,170**	**$ 8,217**	**$ 8,265**	**$ 8,314**	**$ 96,601**
Other cash inflows						
Equity investment	$ 0	$ 0	$ 0	$ 0	$ 0	$ 10,000
Increased borrowings	$ 0	$ 0	$ 0	$ 0	$ 0	$160,000
Sales of business assets	$ 0	$ 0	$ 0	$ 0	$ 0	$ 0
A/P increases	$ 3,159	$ 3,159	$ 3,159	$ 3,159	$ 3,159	$ 37,902
Total other cash inflows	**$ 3,159**	**$ 3,159**	**$ 3,159**	**$ 3,159**	**$ 3,159**	**$207,902**
Total cash inflow	**$ 11,280**	**$ 11,328**	**$ 11,376**	**$ 11,424**	**$11,472**	**$304,503**
Cash outflows						
Repayment of principal	$ 871	$ 878	$ 884	$ 891	$ 898	$ 10,341
A/P decreases	$ 2,075	$ 2,075	$ 2,075	$ 2,075	$ 2,075	$ 24,897
A/R increases	$ 0	$ 0	$ 0	$ 0	$ 0	$ 0
Asset purchases	$ 0	$ 0	$ 0	$ 0	$ 0	$125,000
Dividends	$ 0	$ 0	$ 0	$ 0	$86,941	$ 86,941
Total cash outflows	**$ 2,946**	**$ 2,952**	**$ 2,959**	**$ 2,966**	**$89,913**	**$247,180**
Net cash flow	**$ 8,334**	**$ 8,376**	**$ 8,417**	**$ 8,458**	**−$78,441**	**$ 57,324**
Cash balance	**$110,514**	**$118,890**	**$127,307**	**$135,765**	**$57,324**	**$ 57,324**

Cash flow analysis (second year)

Quarter	Q1	2 Q2	Q3	Q4	2
Cash from operations	$32,357	$40,446	$43,681	$45,299	$161,783
Cash from receivables	$ 0	$ 0	$ 0	$ 0	$ 0
Operating cash inflow	**$32,357**	**$40,446**	**$43,681**	**$45,299**	**$161,783**
Other cash inflows					
Equity investment	$ 0	$ 0	$ 0	$ 0	$ 0
Increased borrowings	$ 0	$ 0	$ 0	$ 0	$ 0
Sales of business assets	$ 0	$ 0	$ 0	$ 0	$ 0
A/P increases	$ 8,717	$10,897	$11,769	$12,204	$ 43,587
Total other cash inflows	**$ 8,717**	**$10,897**	**$11,769**	**$12,204**	**$ 43,587**
Total cash inflow	**$41,074**	**$51,343**	**$55,450**	**$57,504**	**$205,370**
Cash outflows					
Repayment of principal	$ 2,734	$ 2,795	$ 2,859	$ 2,924	$ 11,312
A/P decreases	$ 5,975	$ 7,469	$ 8,067	$ 8,365	$ 29,876
A/R increases	$ 0	$ 0	$ 0	$ 0	$ 0
Asset purchases	$ 8,089	$10,111	$10,920	$11,325	$ 40,446
Dividends	$22,650	$28,312	$30,577	$31,709	$113,248
Total cash outflows	**$39,448**	**$48,688**	**$52,423**	**$54,323**	**$194,882**
Net cash flow	**$ 1,626**	**$ 2,655**	**$ 3,027**	**$ 3,180**	**$ 10,489**
Cash balance	**$58,950**	**$61,605**	**$64,632**	**$67,812**	**$ 67,812**

Cash flow analysis (third year)

Quarter	Q1	Q2	Q3	Q4	3
		3			
Cash from operations	$44,554	$55,693	$60,148	$62,376	$222,771
Cash from receivables	$ 0	$ 0	$ 0	$ 0	$ 0
Operating cash inflow	**$44,554**	**$55,693**	**$60,148**	**$62,376**	**$222,771**
Other cash inflows					
Equity investment	$ 0	$ 0	$ 0	$ 0	$ 0
Increased borrowings	$ 0	$ 0	$ 0	$ 0	$ 0
Sales of business assets	$ 0	$ 0	$ 0	$ 0	$ 0
A/P increases	$10,025	$12,531	$13,534	$14,035	$ 50,125
Total other cash inflows	**$10,025**	**$12,531**	**$13,534**	**$14,035**	**$ 50,125**
Total cash inflow	**$54,579**	**$68,224**	**$73,682**	**$76,411**	**$272,897**
Cash outflows					
Repayment of principal	$ 2,990	$ 3,058	$ 3,127	$ 3,198	$ 12,373
A/P decreases	$ 7,170	$ 8,963	$ 9,680	$10,038	$ 35,852
A/R increases	$ 0	$ 0	$ 0	$ 0	$ 0
Asset purchases	$11,139	$13,923	$15,037	$15,594	$ 55,693
Dividends	$31,188	$38,985	$42,104	$43,663	$155,940
Total cash outflows	**$52,487**	**$64,929**	**$69,948**	**$72,494**	**$259,857**
Net cash flow	**$ 2,093**	**$ 3,295**	**$ 3,734**	**$ 3,918**	**$ 13,040**
Cash balance	**$69,905**	**$73,200**	**$76,934**	**$80,852**	**$ 80,852**

Mobile Wood-Burning Pizza Oven Business

Italy to You Inc.

562 30th St.
Amber Ridge, GA 37777

Paul Greenland

Italy to You Inc. is a mobile wood-burning pizza oven business that uses organic and locally-grown ingredients.

EXECUTIVE SUMMARY

Business Overview

Almost everyone loves pizza, and more than ever before, consumers are interested in eating healthy and knowing more about the food they eat. Italy to You Inc. is a mobile wood-burning pizza oven business that uses organic and locally-grown ingredients. The business focuses on catering and special events, providing guests with a wide range of delicious handmade pizzas under the guidance of owner Joe Stanton, who spent seven years working at a traditional pizzeria before deciding to establish his own business.

According to *Pizza Restaurants in the US*, a market research report from IBISWorld, by 2014 the pizza industry was generating annual revenues of approximately $39 billion on the strength of more than 38,000 businesses. The larger restaurant industry generated sales of $624.3 billion in 2014, according to data from the National Restaurant Association. Of that total, mobile operations were part of a category with $66.4 billion in sales. In its *2014 Restaurant Industry Pocket Factbook*, the association reported that 64 percent of consumers indicated they would be more likely to visit a restaurant offering locally-produced food items.

In addition to being a unique concept, a mobile wood-burning pizza oven provides owner Joe Stanton with a number of distinct advantages over brick-and-mortar businesses. Specifically, Italy to You has the ability to bring its offerings anywhere the target market desires. Furthermore, as a mobile operation, Italy to You avoids the need to pay property taxes and utilities.

MARKET ANALYSIS

Summary

According to market data that Joe Stanton obtained from his local library, the community of Amber Ridge was home to about 69,532 people in 2014. This figure essentially was expected to remain steady through 2019, with nominal growth projected. Italy to You will concentrate its consumer marketing efforts (e.g., catering for functions such as weddings, anniversaries, wedding showers, etc.) on households with income of $50,000 or more. In 2014 nearly 20 percent of Amber Ridge households fell within the $50,000 to $74,999 category. Next were households with income between $75,000 and $99,999 (15.3%), $100,000 to $149,999 (12.7%), and more than $150,000 (6%).

Beyond the consumer market, services will be marketed to organizations. These include, but are not limited to:

- Colleges & Universities (3 establishments)
- Large Companies (7 establishments)
- Mid-Sized Companies (85 establishments)
- Hospitals (3 establishments)
- Health & Medical Services (165 establishments)
- Membership Organizations (86 establishments)
- Museums & Zoos (4 establishments)
- Churches & Religious Organizations (78 establishments)
- Entertainment & Recreation Services (50 establishments)
- Amber Ridge School District

Special/Public Event Opportunities

Italy to You's delicious wood-burning pizza is an ideal choice for a variety of private and public functions, including:

- Anniversary Parties
- Baby Showers
- Birthday Parties
- Carnivals and Fairs
- Church Functions
- College Sporting Events
- Company Picnics
- Concerts
- Corporate Events
- Family Reunions
- Festivals
- Fun Fairs
- Fundraisers
- Golf Outings
- Graduation Parties
- High School Sporting Events
- PTA Events
- Retirement Parties
- Scouting Events
- Special Events
- Sporting Events
- Tailgating Parties

- Wedding Showers

- Weddings

Specific annual event opportunities exist for Italy to You in the Amber Ridge market, including:

- Amber Ridge 10K

- Amber Ridge Fashion Show

- Amber Ridge Harvest Festival

- Amber Ridge High School (Multiple Sporting/School Events)

- Amber Ridge Junior High (Multiple Sporting/School Events)

- Amber Ridge Wine & Food Weekend

- Annual Cheese Days

- Annual Festival of Historic Houses

- Annual Fishing Derby

- Annual Holiday Parade

- Autumn on Parade

- Breast Cancer Awareness Walk

- Chili Cookoff

- Festival of Lights

- Festival on the Square

- Fourth of July Parade

- Hot Air Balloon, Crafts & Music Festival

- Labor Day Parade

- Memorial Day Parade

- Midcity Car & Motorcycle Show

- Old House & Garden Festival

- Riverfront Fest

- Something About Crafts

- Strawberry Fest

- Summer On the Green

Competition

Although Italy to You competes with traditional brick-and-mortar restaurants, its main competition comes from other mobile food businesses, as well as traditional catering operations.

In 2014 the following two Amber Ridge-area businesses were considered to be Italy to You's primary mobile food competitors:

1. Tacos by Tim (a mobile taco stand, which primarily focuses on catering to the lunch crowd in downtown, but also is available for special events and catering functions).

2. Dave's Dogs (a mobile gourmet hotdog and Italian sausage vendor that, in addition to focusing on the lunch crowd like Tacos by Tim, is heavily involved with school fundraisers/athletic events).

In addition, the business also faces strong competition from traditional caterers, as well as restaurants that offer catering services, such as:

- Carlisle Catering

- Red Flame Restaurant

- Jim's Bistro

- Fontana Catering Services

- Best Banquets

- Second Avenue Meats

- Urban Grill

- Pappa Primo's

Fortunately, Italy to You is among the first mobile food operations in Amber Ridge, which provides the business with the opportunity to corner a share of the local market. In addition, the business is the only mobile operation that uses only organic and locally grown ingredients, providing it with a strong differential.

INDUSTRY ANALYSIS

According to *Pizza Restaurants in the US*, a market research report from IBISWorld, by 2014 the pizza industry was generating annual revenues of approximately $39 billion on the strength of more than 38,000 businesses. The larger restaurant industry generated sales of $624.3 billion in 2014, according to data from the National Restaurant Association. Of that total, mobile operations were part of a category with $66.4 billion in sales. In its *2014 Restaurant Industry Pocket Factbook*, the association reported that 64 percent of consumers indicated they would be more likely to visit a restaurant offering locally-produced food items.

In fact, as Hudson Riehle, senior vice president of the National Restaurant Association's research and knowledge group, explained: "Today's consumers are more interested than ever in what they eat and where their food comes from, and that is reflected in our menu trends research."

PERSONNEL

Italy to You is owned by Joe Stanton, who spent seven years working at Rick's on Broadway, a traditional pizzeria, before deciding to establish his own business. While working at Rick's, Joe learned the ins and outs of the pizza business, including how to make delicious pizza; manage inventory; work with suppliers, staff, and customers; perform basic bookkeeping; and adhere to health and sanitation regulations. As owner of Italy to You, Joe will have sole responsibility for the business' daily operations and management. He has enhanced this experience by taking a small business management course at Amber Ridge Community College and attending small business ownership training offered by the Small Business Association.

According to the National Restaurant Association, about 90 percent of restaurants have fewer than 50 employees. Italy to You fits this profile, with Joe Stanton serving as the business' only full-time worker. Joe will be assisted in the business by three part-time employees (his wife and two teenage sons). Temporary staff will be hired when needed for especially large events.

Professional & Advisory Support

Italy to You has established a business banking account with Amber Ridge Community Bank. Additionally, Stanton will utilize a service that enables him to accept mobile payments via his phone or tablet computer. Tax advisement is provided by Amber Ridge Financial Services LLC.

GROWTH STRATEGY

Year One: Focus on generating awareness about Italy to You in the local market and strong "word of mouth" buzz. Achieve a nominal net profit of $1,450 on gross revenue of $144,000.

Year Two: Continue to emphasize word-of-mouth promotion and build awareness about Italy to You in the local market. Achieve a net profit of $7,400 on gross revenue of $180,000.

Year Three: Achieve a net profit of $13,850 on gross revenue of $216,000. Recoup personal investment in the business, including start-up costs of $12,655 and $10,000 for operations. Develop expansion plans based on local demand/opportunity, including the possible addition of a second mobile unit and hiring additional staff in year four or five.

SERVICES

As opposed to traditional street vending, Italy to You initially will concentrate on catering and special events, offering hand-made pizzas with organic and locally-grown ingredients, made fresh in its mobile wood-burning pizza oven.

Catering

Joe Stanton will meet with customers prior to their function or special event to develop a catering package designed especially for their unique situation. During the meeting, he will define the timeframe that services are desired, the anticipated number of guests (in order to determine the amount of staff and ingredients required), and specific menu selections.

Stanton will provide an estimate to the customer. If accepted, the customer will be provided with a catering services agreement. Stanton will require customers to pay a 50 percent deposit prior to the event. The deposit is refundable as long as service is canceled at least 14 days prior to the event. Italy to You accepts payment by check, credit card, debit card, or PayPal. In addition, Stanton requires customers to provide a firm number of anticipated attendees no later than 48 hours before the event date. At private parties, Italy to You typically will serve a selection of traditional and specialty pizzas buffet style, providing guests with the opportunity to enjoy a variety of choices.

Public Events & Festivals

When Italy to You is chosen to provide services at public events and festivals, Joe Stanton will attempt to gauge the projected attendance (using figures from past years if it is an existing event). After agreeing upon any terms with the event organizer (especially in the case of a fundraiser), the contract will be developed specifying expectations of Italy to You (e.g., service dates, time frames, menu selections, etc.). At the event, pizzas will be sold individually, typically for $10 apiece.

When providing service for private parties or public events, Italy to You requires a 12' x 12' outdoor space for its wood-burning pizza oven, clear of obstructions and fire hazards.

Menu

Italy to You will provide guests with a wide range of delicious selections, ranging from classics to specialty pizzas. These include, but are not limited to:

- Barbecue Chicken
- Buffalo Chicken
- Cheese
- Hawaiian
- Margherita
- Mediterranean
- Mushroom & Gorgonzola
- Pepperoni
- Sausage
- Veggie

The business will offer beverage products from Pepsico, including:

- Bottled Water
- Diet Pepsi
- Mug Root Beer
- Pepsi
- Pepsi Lime
- Pepsi Max
- Sierra Mist

MARKETING & SALES

The Italy to You marketing plan includes the following main tactics:

1. Online Advertising: Italy to You will advertise regularly on popular social media sites, such as Facebook. Compared to traditional print advertising, this is a cost effective tactic that will allow us to reach prospects in a highly targeted way (e.g., based on criteria such as age, gender, geography, etc.).

2. Web Site: Italy to You will develop a Web site where customers can find details about our menu, link to our social media channels, view items in our online photo gallery (e.g., photos from past events), read special announcements, and inquire about bookings and availability.

3. Promotional Fliers: With the help of a local graphic designer, Joe Stanton has developed two four-color fliers. One addresses the consumer market, while another addresses organizations. These fliers can be left behind following sales calls, used in direct mailings, and more.

4. Print Advertising: Italy to You will maintain a regular advertising presence in *The Chamber Gazette*, a newspaper published by the Amber Ridge Chamber of Commerce, enabling the business to stay visible within the business community. In addition, Joe Stanton will run a regular ad in *Amber Ridge Life & Style*, an upscale, quarterly business and lifestyle magazine.

5. Wedding & Event Planners: Joe Stanton will build and maintain relationships with area wedding and event planners, in order to generate a steady stream of referrals.

6. Direct Marketing: A monthly direct-marketing campaign will concentrate on the corporate event market. A local mailing list broker has been identified, and arrangements have been made with a local mail house to handle mailings.

7. Sales Promotion: Each month, Joe Stanton will make at least six lunch presentations to key decision-makers at local groups and organizations promoting Italy to You. These will include free samples of Stanton's pizza, prepared on-site.

OPERATIONS

Hours

As a mobile operation, Italy to You will maintain variable hours, depending on the needs of its customers.

Suppliers

Joe Stanton has established supply agreements with several local farmers and food distributors to assure a steady supply of ingredients that are organic and locally grown. Regional and national suppliers will be utilized when necessary. Italy to You's supply partners include:

- Amber Ridge Meats

- Planet Produce

- Tremblay Foods Inc.

- Ridgway Dairy Distributors

Other suppliers include:

- Provenza Italian Foods Co.

- Ronald Swanson (firewood)

- Mancuso Beverage Distribution Inc.

- Sysco Corp.

Equipment

Mobile Brick Oven ($8,500)

The centerpiece of Italy to You's operations is its combination brick oven/trailer, the Chicago Brick Oven CBO-750. The oven/wagon combination's features include:

- 40" x 27" cooking surface/17" wide opening

- Diamond plate finish

- Highway-ready tires

- Infrared thermometer gun

- Insulation blanket (to increase heat retention)

- Stone brush

- Storage compartments (for wood, etc.)

- Temperature capabilities < 1,000 degrees F

Stanton well utilize his personal pickup truck to haul the trailer and related equipment and supplies.

Refrigerated Pizza Table ($1,655)

Joe Stanton will purchase a 48"Arctic Air APP48R One Door Pizza Prep Table with the following features:

- 17 3/4" deep cutting board (slicing fresh toppings/keeping dough)

- 6 (1/3 size food pans) for ingredients

- Refrigerated cabinet

- 1/2 hp compressor

- Electronic thermostat with external LED display

Oven Accessories ($500)
- Ash Shovel

- Fire Poker

- Large Pizza Peel

- Small Pizza Peel

- Wire Cleaning Brush

Miscellaneous ($2,000)
- 7,000-Watt Generator

- Portable Sink

- 3 Fold-up Awnings

- Menu Board

- Aprons

Supplies

As part of regular operations, an inventory of basic supplies will be required. Items include:

- Cleaning Rags

- Disposable Cups

- Disposable Plates

- Disposable Silverware

- Firewood (hardwoods)

- Garbage Bags

- Hand Sanitizer

- Kitchen Utensils

- Paper Towels

- Plastic Wrap

- Tinfoil

Preparation Process

Joe Stanton will utilize his home kitchen for dough preparation. He will use a commercial dough mixer to prepare and weigh dough balls (for the pizza crust) in advance for events. After placing the dough in containers and allowing it to rise in the refrigerator (Stanton has a second refrigerator in his garage that he will use for this purpose), it can be transferred and stored in the aforementioned refrigerated pizza table, making it easy to prepare pizzas on the day of the event. Stanton also will prepare pizza sauce and ingredients ahead of time.

LEGAL

Italy to You adheres to all local, state, and federal regulations pertaining to food handling and safety. Specifically, Joe Stanton has obtained a permit from the Georgia Department of Community Health to operate a food service establishment. Additionally, he has obtained all local and county permits needed to operate a business, as well as an adequate level of liability coverage for the business. Copies of these documents are available upon request.

FINANCIAL ANALYSIS

According to some industry reports, on average, traditional pizzerias achieve profit margins of only 7 percent, with more successful operators realizing profit margins of 20 percent. As a mobile operation with lower overhead than a traditional pizzeria, Joe Stanton is confident that Italy to You can achieve a profit margin of at least 20 percent, and he will use this figure as the basis of his financial projections.

Stanton estimates that he will achieve gross revenues of $10 per pizza, resulting in a net profit of $2 per unit. On average, Stanton anticipates that he will make 150 pizzas per event, resulting in per-event gross revenues of $1,500 and net revenues of $300.

Following is the Italy to You projected balance sheet for its first three years of operations. Joe Stanton will contribute approximately $23,000 of his own money to cover the initial startup costs outlined in this plan, and to provide cash flow for initial operations. He expects to recover this amount at the end of 2017. Beginning in 2018, all net profits can be reinvested into the business for expansion purposes.

	2015	2016	2017
Total sales	$144,000	$180,000	$216,000
Cost of goods sold	$ 50,400	$ 63,000	$ 75,600
Labor cost	$ 64,800	$ 81,000	$ 97,200
Total cost of goods sold	$115,200	$144,000	$172,800
Gross profit	$ 28,800	$ 36,000	$ 43,200
Marketing & advertising	$ 8,500	$ 8,500	$ 8,500
General/administrative	$ 500	$ 500	$ 500
Accounting/legal	$ 1,500	$ 1,500	$ 1,500
Office supplies	$ 350	$ 350	$ 350
Insurance	$ 2,500	$ 2,750	$ 3,000
Supplies	$ 3,500	$ 4,000	$ 4,000
Vendor permits & licenses	$ 500	$ 500	$ 500
Gasoline	$ 7,500	$ 8,000	$ 8,500
Maintenance & repairs	$ 500	$ 500	$ 500
Wireless telecommunications	$ 2,000	$ 2,000	$ 2,000
Total expenses	$ 27,350	$ 28,600	$ 29,350
Net income	$ 1,450	$ 7,400	$ 13,850

Nightclub

Club NY

PO Box 12221
New York, NY 10047

BizPlanDB.com

The purpose of this business plan is to raise $125,000 for the development of a nightclub while showcasing the expected financials and operations over the next three years. Club NY is a New York-based corporation that will provide an exciting dancing and music-oriented venue that will also provide alcoholic beverages to its customers in its targeted market. The Company was founded by Liam Christensen.

1.0 EXECUTIVE SUMMARY

The purpose of this business plan is to raise $125,000 for the development of a nightclub while showcasing the expected financials and operations over the next three years. Club NY is a New York-based corporation that will provide an exciting dancing and music-oriented venue that will also provide alcoholic beverages to its customers in its targeted market. The Company was founded by Liam Christensen.

1.1 The Services

Management is committed to developing Club NY into a premier nighttime entertainment location. This venue will feature alcohol beverage services in additional to musical entertainment. Other services offered by Club NY include:

- Full food and beverage services

- Music (DJ and live music)

- Event planning services

The third section of the business plan will further describe the services offered by Club NY.

1.2 Financing

Mr. Christensen is seeking to raise $125,000 from a bank loan. The interest rate and loan agreement are to be further discussed during negotiation. This business plan assumes that the business will receive a 10-year loan with a 9% fixed interest rate. The financing will be used for the following:

- Development of the nightclub.

- Financing for the first six months of operation.

- Capital to purchase sound equipment and an inventory of alcohol.

Mr. Christensen will contribute $25,000 to the venture.

1.3 Mission Statement

Management's mission is to have Club NY become one of the premier nighttime entertainment locations in its targeted market.

1.4 Management Team

The Company was founded by Liam Christensen. Mr. Christensen has more than ten years' experience in the nightclub industry. Through his expertise, he will be able to bring the operations of the business to profitability within its first year of operations.

1.5 Sales Forecasts

Mr. Christensen expects a strong rate of growth at the start of operations. Below are the expected financials over the next three years.

Proforma profit and loss (yearly)

Year	1	2	3
Sales	$601,260	$721,512	$844,169
Operating costs	$337,646	$371,560	$407,073
EBITDA	$ 88,702	$140,058	$191,520
Taxes, interest, and depreciation	$ 52,307	$ 67,202	$ 86,244
Net profit	$ 36,394	$ 72,855	$105,276

Sales, operating costs, and profit forecast

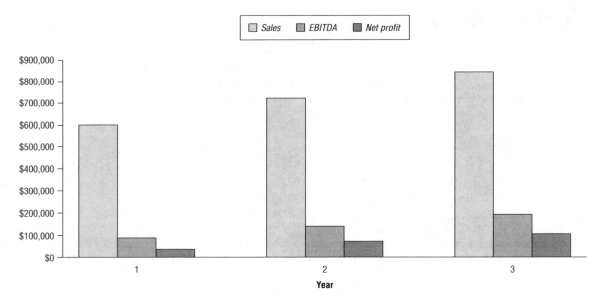

1.6 Expansion Plan

The Founder expects that the business will aggressively expand during the first three years of operation. Mr. Christensen intends to implement marketing campaigns that will effectively target individuals within the target market.

2.0 COMPANY AND FINANCING SUMMARY

2.1 Registered Name and Corporate Structure

Club NY is registered as a corporation in the State of New York.

2.2 Required Funds

At this time, Club NY requires $125,000 of debt funds. Below is a breakdown of how these funds will be used:

Projected startup costs

Initial lease payments and deposits	$ 30,000
Working capital	$ 35,000
FF&E	$ 15,000
Leasehold improvements	$ 5,000
Security deposits	$ 5,000
Inventory	$ 2,500
DJ and sound equipment	$ 45,000
Marketing budget	$ 7,500
Miscellaneous and unforeseen costs	$ 5,000
Total startup costs	**$150,000**

Use of funds

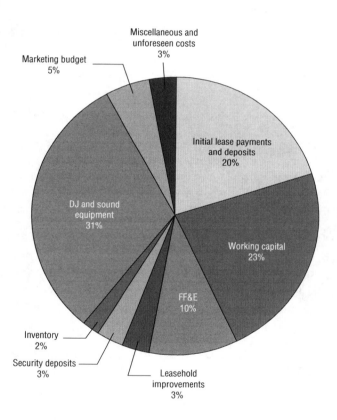

2.3 Investor Equity

Mr. Christensen is not seeking an investment from a third party at this time.

2.4 Management Equity

Liam Christensen owns 100% of Club NY.

2.5 Exit Strategy

If the business is very successful, Mr. Christensen may seek to sell the business to a third party for a significant earnings multiple. Most likely, the Company will hire a qualified business broker to sell the business on behalf of Club NY. Based on historical numbers, the business could fetch a sales premium of up to 4 times earnings.

3.0 PRODUCTS AND SERVICES

Below is a description of the entertainment services offered by Club NY.

3.1 Venue and Sales of Alcohol

The Company is committed to providing a true club atmosphere. The club will include amenities such as:

- Large, flat screen TVs that feature a variety of channels
- Pool tables
- Darts

Club patrons will experience may enjoyable features about the club, including, but not limited to:

- The development of a unique, innovative, entertaining, atmosphere that will differentiate us from the competition.
- Hiring the best people available, training, motivating and encouraging them, and thereby retaining the friendliest, most efficient staff possible.
- Implement a successful advertisement and marketing campaign to inform the existing clientele and the public of Club NY's image.
- Retain the services of a reputable bartender.

A substantial portion of the revenues generated by the business (approximately 85%) will come from the direct sale of alcoholic beverages. Mr. Christensen intends to hire several bouncers and door attendants to ensure that only people over the age of 21 will be allowed to enter the club. A state or federally issued ID will be required for everyone to enter the location.

3.2 Cover Charges

The Company will also generate secondary revenues from cover charges on busy weekend nights or when a popular DJ/artist is at the location. This is an important secondary revenue stream for the business as it will defray the costs of hiring a well known DJ or artist to perform for the evening.

4.0 STRATEGIC AND MARKET ANALYSIS

4.1 Economic Outlook

This section of the analysis will detail the economic climate, the nightclub industry, the customer profile, and the competition that the business will face as it progresses through its business operations.

Currently, the economic market condition in the United States is moderate. The economy has rebounded substantially since the end of the recession. Unemployment has declined and individuals' income has risen moderately. However, it should be noted that nightclubs are generally able to remain profitable and cash flow positive at all times due to the fact that there is a strong demand nighttime entertainment.

4.2 Industry Analysis

There are many nightclub entertainment venues in the United States. A U.S. Economic census report indicates that there are over 53,000 individual establishments in the country. This number is expected to increase as nightclubs remain a popular form of entertainment among people under forty. Each year the industry generates more than $12 billion dollars of revenue and provides gross annual payrolls of $3 billion dollars. The industry also employs more than 250,000 people nationwide.

As the trend continues, Management expects that the business may incur price warring among neighboring nightclubs. However, the atmosphere of club will be geared towards a higher-end client that is willing to spend extra money to enjoy the many additional value-added amenities at the facility.

4.3 Customer Profile

Club NY's average client will be a middle income person between the ages of 21 and 40 living in the Company's target market. Common traits among clients will include:

- Annual household income exceeding $30,000

- Lives or works no more than 15 miles from the Company's location

- Will spend $25 to $100 per visit to Club NY

4.4 Competition

There are a tremendous number of nightclubs within the greater New York metropolitan area. It will be of the utmost importance that Club NY develops a relationship with a well-established club promoter in order to promote patronage to the venue. The business will also need to place highly prominent advertisements in New York-based magazines so that the launch of the nightclub is met with a large audience of club goers.

5.0 MARKETING PLAN

Club NY intends to maintain an extensive marketing campaign that will ensure maximum visibility for the business in its targeted market. Below is an overview of the marketing strategies and objectives of Club NY.

5.1 Marketing Objectives

- Establish relationships with club promoters in the target market.

- Place large-scale advertisements in magazines and circulars that target the Company's demographics (as outlined in the fourth section of the business plan).

- Attract celebrity club goers in order to promote the brand name of Club NY.

5.2 Marketing Strategies

Mr. Christensen intends on using a number of marketing strategies that will allow Club NY to easily target younger men and women within the target market. These strategies will include paying minor celebrities to come to the club frequently, working with club promoters on a commission basis, and hiring a public relations firm that will promote the brand name of the club from the onset of operations.

Initially, the business intends to hire a public relations firm that has substantial experience developing the brand names of nightclubs within the New York metropolitan area. Management anticipates that these fees will run approximately $5,000 per month for the first three months of operation.

Mr. Christensen also intends to partner with local club promoters that will be paid for each person that they attract to the venue. They will distribute discount coupons to potential patrons, which will be redeemable for free admission or discounts on drinks. These coupons will then be tallied, and a fee (based on the number of coupons collected) will be paid to the local promoter.

Finally, the business will maintain a highly interactive website that showcases Club NY, its location, hours of operation, and prominent DJs that will be invited to the club on a regular basis. The business will also maintain a large social media presence on Facebook and Twitter in order to promote discounts and the grand opening of the club.

5.3 Pricing

The average cover charge for a customer will be $20 to $25 depending on whether it is a weeknight or weekend evening. Beverage pricing will range from $8 to $15 per unit.

6.0 ORGANIZATIONAL PLAN AND PERSONNEL SUMMARY

6.1 Corporate Organization

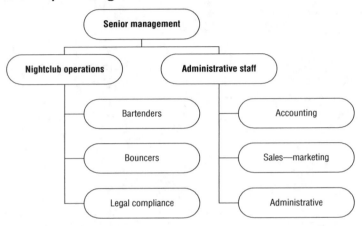

6.2 Organizational Budget

Personnel plan—yearly

Year	1	2	3
Owner	$ 45,000	$ 46,350	$ 47,741
General manager	$ 39,000	$ 40,170	$ 41,375
Bouncers and bartenders	$ 85,000	$105,060	$126,247
Administrative	$ 54,000	$ 55,620	$ 57,289
Accounting (P/T)	$ 22,000	$ 22,660	$ 23,340
Total	**$245,000**	**$269,860**	**$295,991**

Numbers of personnel

Owner	1	1	1
General manager	1	1	1
Bouncers and bartenders	5	6	7
Administrative	2	2	2
Accounting (P/T)	1	1	1
Totals	**10**	**11**	**12**

Personnel expense breakdown

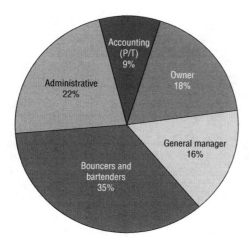

7.0 FINANCIAL PLAN

7.1 Underlying Assumptions

The Company has based its proforma financial statements on the following:

* Club NY will have an annual revenue growth rate of 16% per year.

* The Owner will acquire $125,000 of debt funds to develop the business.

* The loan will have a 10-year term with a 9% interest rate.

7.2 Sensitivity Analysis

In the event of an economic downturn, the business may have a decline in its revenues. However, nighttime entertainment venues, like nightclubs, remain a popular and relatively inexpensive form of entertainment. As such, only a severe economic downturn would result in a decline in top-line revenues for the business.

7.3 Source of Funds

Financing

Equity contributions	
Management investment	$ 25,000.00
Total equity financing	**$ 25,000.00**
Banks and lenders	
Banks and lenders	$ 125,000.00
Total debt financing	**$125,000.00**
Total financing	**$150,000.00**

7.4 General Assumptions

General assumptions

Year	1	2	3
Short term interest rate	9.5%	9.5%	9.5%
Long term interest rate	10.0%	10.0%	10.0%
Federal tax rate	33.0%	33.0%	33.0%
State tax rate	5.0%	5.0%	5.0%
Personnel taxes	15.0%	15.0%	15.0%

7.5 Profit and Loss Statements

Proforma profit and loss (yearly)

Year	1	2	3
Sales	**$601,260**	**$721,512**	**$844,169**
Cost of goods sold	$174,912	$209,894	$245,576
Gross margin	70.91%	70.91%	70.91%
Operating income	**$426,348**	**$511,618**	**$598,593**
Expenses			
Payroll	$245,000	$269,860	$295,991
General and administrative	$ 25,200	$ 26,208	$ 27,256
Marketing expenses	$ 3,006	$ 3,608	$ 4,221
Professional fees and licensure	$ 5,219	$ 5,376	$ 5,537
Insurance costs	$ 1,987	$ 2,086	$ 2,191
Laboratory expenses	$ 9,019	$ 10,823	$ 12,663
Rent and utilities	$ 4,250	$ 4,463	$ 4,686
Miscellaneous costs	$ 7,215	$ 8,658	$ 10,130
Payroll taxes	$ 36,750	$ 40,479	$ 44,399
Total operating costs	**$337,646**	**$371,560**	**$407,073**
EBITDA	**$ 88,702**	**$140,058**	**$191,520**
Federal income tax	$ 29,272	$ 42,865	$ 60,121
State income tax	$ 4,435	$ 6,495	$ 9,109
Interest expense	$ 10,922	$ 10,164	$ 9,335
Depreciation expenses	$ 7,679	$ 7,679	$ 7,679
Net profit	**$ 36,394**	**$ 72,855**	**$105,276**
Profit margin	**6.05%**	**10.10%**	**12.47%**

Sales, operating costs, and profit forecast

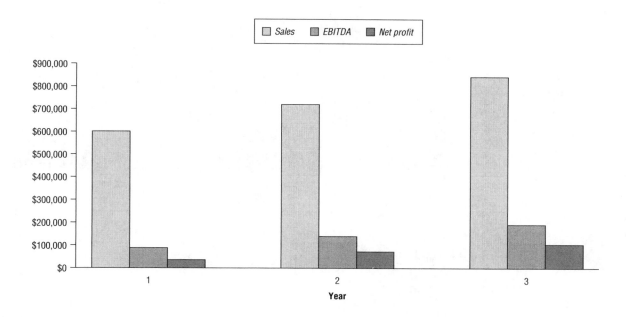

7.6 Cash Flow Analysis

Proforma cash flow analysis—yearly

Year	1	2	3
Cash from operations	$ 44,073	$ 80,534	$112,955
Cash from receivables	$ 0	$ 0	$ 0
Operating cash inflow	**$ 44,073**	**$ 80,534**	**$112,955**
Other cash inflows			
Equity investment	$ 25,000	$ 0	$ 0
Increased borrowings	$125,000	$ 0	$ 0
Sales of business assets	$ 0	$ 0	$ 0
A/P increases	$ 37,902	$ 43,587	$ 50,125
Total other cash inflows	**$187,902**	**$ 43,587**	**$ 50,125**
Total cash inflow	**$231,975**	**$124,121**	**$163,080**
Cash outflows			
Repayment of principal	$ 8,079	$ 8,837	$ 9,666
A/P decreases	$ 24,897	$ 29,876	$ 35,852
A/R increases	$ 0	$ 0	$ 0
Asset purchases	$108,000	$ 20,134	$ 28,239
Dividends	$ 30,851	$ 56,374	$ 79,068
Total cash outflows	**$171,827**	**$115,221**	**$152,825**
Net cash flow	**$ 60,148**	**$ 8,900**	**$ 10,255**
Cash balance	**$ 60,148**	**$ 69,048**	**$ 79,303**

Proforma cash flow (yearly)

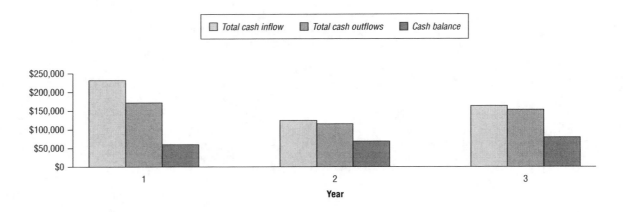

7.7 Balance Sheet

Proforma balance sheet—yearly

Year	1	2	3
Assets			
Cash	$ 60,148	$ 69,048	$ 79,303
Amortized development costs	$ 45,000	$ 47,013	$ 49,837
DJ and sound equipment	$ 45,000	$ 60,100	$ 81,279
FF&E	$ 15,000	$ 18,020	$ 22,256
Inventory	$ 2,500	$ 2,500	$ 2,500
Accumulated depreciation	($ 7,679)	($ 15,357)	($ 23,036)
Total assets	**$159,969**	**$181,324**	**$212,140**
Liabilities and equity			
Accounts payable	$ 13,005	$ 26,716	$ 40,990
Long term liabilities	$116,921	$108,084	$ 99,247
Other liabilities	$ 0	$ 0	$ 0
Total liabilities	**$129,926**	**$134,800**	**$140,236**
Net worth	**$ 30,043**	**$ 46,525**	**$ 71,904**
Total liabilities and equity	**$159,969**	**$181,324**	**$212,140**

Proforma balance sheet

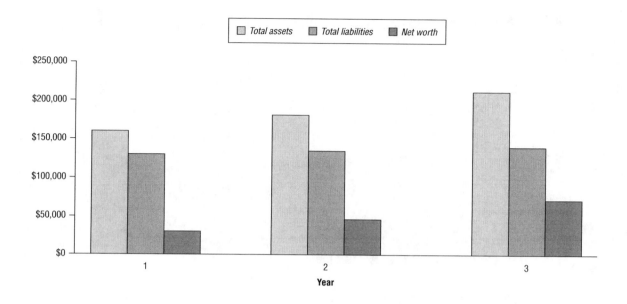

7.8 Breakeven Analysis

Monthly break even analysis

Year	1	2	3
Monthly revenue	$ 39,681	$ 43,666	$ 47,840
Yearly revenue	$476,168	$523,995	$574,077

Break even analysis

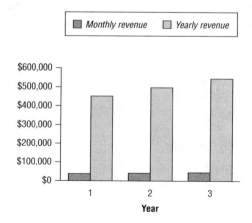

7.9 Business Ratios

Business ratios—yearly

Year	1	2	3
Sales			
Sales growth	0.00%	20.00%	17.00%
Gross margin	70.90%	70.90%	70.90%
Financials			
Profit margin	6.05%	10.10%	12.47%
Assets to liabilities	1.23	1.35	1.51
Equity to liabilities	0.23	0.35	0.51
Assets to equity	5.32	3.90	2.95
Liquidity			
Acid test	0.46	0.51	0.57
Cash to assets	0.38	0.38	0.37

7.10 Three Year Profit and Loss Statement

Profit and loss statement (first year)

Months	1	2	3	4	5	6	7
Sales	**$49,500**	**$49,610**	**$49,720**	**$49,830**	**$49,940**	**$50,050**	**$50,160**
Cost of goods sold	$14,400	$14,432	$14,464	$14,496	$14,528	$14,560	$14,592
Gross margin	70.9%	70.9%	70.9%	70.9%	70.9%	70.9%	70.9%
Operating income	**$35,100**	**$35,178**	**$35,256**	**$35,334**	**$35,412**	**$35,490**	**$35,568**
Expenses							
Payroll	$20,417	$20,417	$20,417	$20,417	$20,417	$20,417	$20,417
General and administrative	$ 2,100	$ 2,100	$ 2,100	$ 2,100	$ 2,100	$ 2,100	$ 2,100
Marketing expenses	$ 251	$ 251	$ 251	$ 251	$ 251	$ 251	$ 251
Professional fees and licensure	$ 435	$ 435	$ 435	$ 435	$ 435	$ 435	$ 435
Insurance costs	$ 166	$ 166	$ 166	$ 166	$ 166	$ 166	$ 166
Laboratory expenses	$ 752	$ 752	$ 752	$ 752	$ 752	$ 752	$ 752
Rent and utilities	$ 354	$ 354	$ 354	$ 354	$ 354	$ 354	$ 354
Miscellaneous costs	$ 601	$ 601	$ 601	$ 601	$ 601	$ 601	$ 601
Payroll taxes	$ 3,063	$ 3,063	$ 3,063	$ 3,063	$ 3,063	$ 3,063	$ 3,063
Total operating costs	**$28,137**	**$28,137**	**$28,137**	**$28,137**	**$28,137**	**$28,137**	**$28,137**
EBITDA	**$ 6,963**	**$ 7,041**	**$ 7,119**	**$ 7,197**	**$ 7,275**	**$ 7,353**	**$ 7,431**
Federal income tax	$ 2,410	$ 2,415	$ 2,421	$ 2,426	$ 2,431	$ 2,437	$ 2,442
State income tax	$ 365	$ 366	$ 367	$ 368	$ 368	$ 369	$ 370
Interest expense	$ 938	$ 933	$ 928	$ 923	$ 918	$ 913	$ 908
Depreciation expense	$ 640	$ 640	$ 640	$ 640	$ 640	$ 640	$ 640
Net profit	**$ 2,610**	**$ 2,687**	**$ 2,764**	**$ 2,841**	**$ 2,917**	**$ 2,994**	**$ 3,071**

Profit and loss statement (first year cont.)

Month	8	9	10	11	12	1
Sales	$50,270	$50,380	$50,490	$50,600	$50,710	$601,260
Cost of goods sold	$14,624	$14,656	$14,688	$14,720	$14,752	$174,912
Gross margin	70.9%	70.9%	70.9%	70.9%	70.9%	70.9%
Operating income	$35,646	$35,724	$35,802	$35,880	$35,958	$426,348
Expenses						
Payroll	$20,417	$20,417	$20,417	$20,417	$20,417	$245,000
General and administrative	$ 2,100	$ 2,100	$ 2,100	$ 2,100	$ 2,100	$ 25,200
Marketing expenses	$ 251	$ 251	$ 251	$ 251	$ 251	$ 3,006
Professional fees and licensure	$ 435	$ 435	$ 435	$ 435	$ 435	$ 5,219
Insurance costs	$ 166	$ 166	$ 166	$ 166	$ 166	$ 1,987
Laboratory expenses	$ 752	$ 752	$ 752	$ 752	$ 752	$ 9,019
Rent and utilities	$ 354	$ 354	$ 354	$ 354	$ 354	$ 4,250
Miscellaneous costs	$ 601	$ 601	$ 601	$ 601	$ 601	$ 7,215
Payroll taxes	$ 3,063	$ 3,063	$ 3,063	$ 3,063	$ 3,063	$ 36,750
Total operating costs	$28,137	$28,137	$28,137	$28,137	$28,137	$337,646
EBITDA	$ 7,509	$ 7,587	$ 7,665	$ 7,743	$ 7,821	$ 88,702
Federal income tax	$ 2,447	$ 2,453	$ 2,458	$ 2,463	$ 2,469	$ 29,272
State income tax	$ 371	$ 372	$ 372	$ 373	$ 374	$ 4,435
Interest expense	$ 903	$ 898	$ 893	$ 887	$ 882	$ 10,922
Depreciation expense	$ 640	$ 640	$ 640	$ 640	$ 640	$ 7,679
Net profit	$ 3,148	$ 3,225	$ 3,302	$ 3,379	$ 3,456	$ 36,394

Profit and loss statement (second year)

Quarter	Q1	2 Q2	Q3	Q4	2
Sales	$144,302	$180,378	$194,808	$202,023	$721,512
Cost of goods sold	$ 41,979	$ 52,474	$ 56,671	$ 58,770	$209,894
Gross margin	70.9%	70.9%	70.9%	70.9%	70.9%
Operating income	$102,324	$127,904	$138,137	$143,253	$511,618
Expenses					
Payroll	$ 53,972	$ 67,465	$ 72,862	$ 75,561	$269,860
General and administrative	$ 5,242	$ 6,552	$ 7,076	$ 7,338	$ 26,208
Marketing expenses	$ 722	$ 902	$ 974	$ 1,010	$ 3,608
Professional fees and licensure	$ 1,075	$ 1,344	$ 1,451	$ 1,505	$ 5,376
Insurance costs	$ 417	$ 522	$ 563	$ 584	$ 2,086
Laboratory expenses	$ 2,165	$ 2,706	$ 2,922	$ 3,030	$ 10,823
Rent and utilities	$ 893	$ 1,116	$ 1,205	$ 1,250	$ 4,463
Miscellaneous costs	$ 1,732	$ 2,165	$ 2,338	$ 2,424	$ 8,658
Payroll taxes	$ 8,096	$ 10,120	$ 10,929	$ 11,334	$ 40,479
Total operating costs	$ 74,312	$ 92,890	$100,321	$104,037	$371,560
EBITDA	$ 28,012	$ 35,014	$ 37,816	$ 39,216	$140,058
Federal income tax	$ 8,573	$ 10,716	$ 11,574	$ 12,002	$ 42,865
State income tax	$ 1,299	$ 1,624	$ 1,754	$ 1,819	$ 6,495
Interest expense	$ 2,615	$ 2,566	$ 2,517	$ 2,466	$ 10,164
Depreciation expense	$ 1,920	$ 1,920	$ 1,920	$ 1,920	$ 7,679
Net profit	$ 13,605	$ 18,189	$ 20,052	$ 21,010	$ 72,855

Profit and loss statement (third year)

Quarter	Q1	3 Q2	Q3	Q4	3
Sales	$168,834	$211,042	$227,926	$236,367	$844,169
Cost of goods sold	$ 49,115	$ 61,394	$ 66,306	$ 68,761	$245,576
Gross margin	70.9%	70.9%	70.9%	70.9%	70.9%
Operating income	$119,719	$149,648	$161,620	$167,606	$598,593
Expenses					
Payroll	$ 59,198	$ 73,998	$ 79,918	$ 82,878	$295,991
General and administrative	$ 5,451	$ 6,814	$ 7,359	$ 7,632	$ 27,256
Marketing expenses	$ 844	$ 1,055	$ 1,140	$ 1,182	$ 4,221
Professional fees and licensure	$ 1,107	$ 1,384	$ 1,495	$ 1,550	$ 5,537
Insurance costs	$ 438	$ 548	$ 591	$ 613	$ 2,191
Laboratory expenses	$ 2,533	$ 3,166	$ 3,419	$ 3,546	$ 12,663
Rent and utilities	$ 937	$ 1,171	$ 1,265	$ 1,312	$ 4,686
Miscellaneous costs	$ 2,026	$ 2,533	$ 2,735	$ 2,836	$ 10,130
Payroll taxes	$ 8,880	$ 11,100	$ 11,988	$ 12,432	$ 44,399
Total operating costs	$ 81,415	$101,768	$109,910	$113,980	$407,073
EBITDA	$ 38,304	$ 47,880	$ 51,710	$ 53,626	$191,520
Federal income tax	$ 12,024	$ 15,030	$ 16,233	$ 16,834	$ 60,121
State income tax	$ 1,822	$ 2,277	$ 2,459	$ 2,551	$ 9,109
Interest expense	$ 2,414	$ 2,361	$ 2,307	$ 2,252	$ 9,335
Depreciation expense	$ 1,920	$ 1,920	$ 1,920	$ 1,920	$ 7,679
Net profit	$ 20,124	$ 26,291	$ 28,791	$ 30,070	$105,276

7.11 Three Year Cash Flow Analysis

Cash flow analysis (first year)

Month	1	2	3	4	5	6	7
Cash from operations	$ 3,250	$ 3,327	$ 3,404	$ 3,480	$ 3,557	$ 3,634	$ 3,711
Cash from receivables	$ 0	$ 0	$ 0	$ 0	$ 0	$ 0	$ 0
Operating cash inflow	$ 3,250	$ 3,327	$ 3,404	$ 3,480	$ 3,557	$ 3,634	$ 3,711
Other cash inflows							
Equity investment	$ 25,000	$ 0	$ 0	$ 0	$ 0	$ 0	$ 0
Increased borrowings	$125,000	$ 0	$ 0	$ 0	$ 0	$ 0	$ 0
Sales of business assets	$ 0	$ 0	$ 0	$ 0	$ 0	$ 0	$ 0
A/P increases	$ 3,159	$ 3,159	$ 3,159	$ 3,159	$ 3,159	$ 3,159	$ 3,159
Total other cash inflows	$153,159	$ 3,159	$ 3,159	$ 3,159	$ 3,159	$ 3,159	$ 3,159
Total cash inflow	$156,409	$ 6,486	$ 6,562	$ 6,639	$ 6,716	$ 6,793	$ 6,869
Cash outflows							
Repayment of principal	$ 646	$ 651	$ 656	$ 661	$ 666	$ 671	$ 676
A/P decreases	$ 2,075	$ 2,075	$ 2,075	$ 2,075	$ 2,075	$ 2,075	$ 2,075
A/R increases	$ 0	$ 0	$ 0	$ 0	$ 0	$ 0	$ 0
Asset purchases	$108,000	$ 0	$ 0	$ 0	$ 0	$ 0	$ 0
Dividends	$ 0	$ 0	$ 0	$ 0	$ 0	$ 0	$ 0
Total cash outflows	$110,721	$ 2,726	$ 2,730	$ 2,735	$ 2,740	$ 2,745	$ 2,750
Net cash flow	$ 45,688	$ 3,760	$ 3,832	$ 3,904	$ 3,975	$ 4,047	$ 4,119
Cash balance	$ 45,688	$49,448	$53,280	$57,184	$61,159	$65,206	$69,325

Cash flow analysis (first year cont.)

Month	8	9	10	11	12	1
Cash from operations	$ 3,788	$ 3,865	$ 3,942	$ 4,019	$ 4,096	$ 44,073
Cash from receivables	$ 0	$ 0	$ 0	$ 0	$ 0	$ 0
Operating cash inflow	**$ 3,788**	**$ 3,865**	**$ 3,942**	**$ 4,019**	**$ 4,096**	**$ 44,073**
Other cash inflows						
Equity investment	$ 0	$ 0	$ 0	$ 0	$ 0	$ 25,000
Increased borrowings	$ 0	$ 0	$ 0	$ 0	$ 0	$125,000
Sales of business assets	$ 0	$ 0	$ 0	$ 0	$ 0	$ 0
A/P increases	$ 3,159	$ 3,159	$ 3,159	$ 3,159	$ 3,159	$ 37,902
Total other cash inflows	**$ 3,159**	**$ 3,159**	**$ 3,159**	**$ 3,159**	**$ 3,159**	**$187,902**
Total cash inflow	**$ 6,946**	**$ 7,023**	**$ 7,100**	**$ 7,177**	**$ 7,254**	**$231,975**
Cash outflows						
Repayment of principal	$ 681	$ 686	$ 691	$ 696	$ 701	$ 8,079
A/P decreases	$ 2,075	$ 2,075	$ 2,075	$ 2,075	$ 2,075	$ 24,897
A/R increases	$ 0	$ 0	$ 0	$ 0	$ 0	$ 0
Asset purchases	$ 0	$ 0	$ 0	$ 0	$ 0	$108,000
Dividends	$ 0	$ 0	$ 0	$ 0	$30,851	$ 30,851
Total cash outflows	**$ 2,755**	**$ 2,760**	**$ 2,766**	**$ 2,771**	**$33,627**	**$171,827**
Net cash flow	**$ 4,191**	**$ 4,263**	**$ 4,335**	**$ 4,406**	**−$26,373**	**$ 60,148**
Cash balance	**$73,516**	**$77,779**	**$82,114**	**$86,520**	**$60,148**	**$ 60,148**

Cash flow analysis (second year)

Quarter	Q1	2 Q2	Q3	Q4	2
Cash from operations	$16,107	$20,134	$21,744	$22,550	$ 80,534
Cash from receivables	$ 0	$ 0	$ 0	$ 0	$ 0
Operating cash inflow	**$16,107**	**$20,134**	**$21,744**	**$22,550**	**$ 80,534**
Other cash inflows					
Equity investment	$ 0	$ 0	$ 0	$ 0	$ 0
Increased borrowings	$ 0	$ 0	$ 0	$ 0	$ 0
Sales of business assets	$ 0	$ 0	$ 0	$ 0	$ 0
A/P increases	$ 8,717	$10,897	$11,769	$12,204	$ 43,587
Total other cash inflows	**$ 8,717**	**$10,897**	**$11,769**	**$12,204**	**$ 43,587**
Total cash inflow	**$24,824**	**$31,030**	**$33,513**	**$34,754**	**$124,121**
Cash outflows					
Repayment of principal	$ 2,136	$ 2,184	$ 2,233	$ 2,284	$ 8,837
A/P decreases	$ 5,975	$ 7,469	$ 8,067	$ 8,365	$ 29,876
A/R increases	$ 0	$ 0	$ 0	$ 0	$ 0
Asset purchases	$ 4,027	$ 5,033	$ 5,436	$ 5,637	$ 20,134
Dividends	$11,275	$14,093	$15,221	$15,785	$ 56,374
Total cash outflows	**$23,412**	**$28,780**	**$30,957**	**$32,072**	**$115,221**
Net cash flow	**$ 1,412**	**$ 2,250**	**$ 2,556**	**$ 2,682**	**$ 8,900**
Cash balance	**$61,560**	**$63,810**	**$66,366**	**$69,048**	**$ 69,048**

Cash flow analysis (third year)

Quarter	Q1	3 Q2	Q3	Q4	3
Cash from operations	$22,591	$28,239	$30,498	$31,627	$112,955
Cash from receivables	$ 0	$ 0	$ 0	$ 0	$ 0
Operating cash inflow	**$22,591**	**$28,239**	**$30,498**	**$31,627**	**$112,955**
Other cash inflows					
Equity investment	$ 0	$ 0	$ 0	$ 0	$ 0
Increased borrowings	$ 0	$ 0	$ 0	$ 0	$ 0
Sales of business assets	$ 0	$ 0	$ 0	$ 0	$ 0
A/P increases	$10,025	$12,531	$13,534	$14,035	$ 50,125
Total other cash inflows	**$10,025**	**$12,531**	**$13,534**	**$14,035**	**$ 50,125**
Total cash inflow	**$32,616**	**$40,770**	**$44,032**	**$45,662**	**$163,080**
Cash outflows					
Repayment of principal	$ 2,336	$ 2,389	$ 2,443	$ 2,498	$ 9,666
A/P decreases	$ 7,170	$ 8,963	$ 9,680	$10,038	$ 35,852
A/R increases	$ 0	$ 0	$ 0	$ 0	$ 0
Asset purchases	$ 5,648	$ 7,060	$ 7,624	$ 7,907	$ 28,239
Dividends	$15,814	$19,767	$21,348	$22,139	$ 79,068
Total cash outflows	**$30,968**	**$38,178**	**$41,096**	**$42,583**	**$152,825**
Net cash flow	**$ 1,648**	**$ 2,592**	**$ 2,936**	**$ 3,080**	**$ 10,255**
Cash balance	**$70,697**	**$73,288**	**$76,224**	**$79,303**	**$ 79,303**

Nutritionist

Right Way Nutrition Inc.

58 Lemont Pkwy. NE
Parker Ridge, TN 37240

Paul Greenland

Led by Registered Dietitian Mary Wilson, Right Way Nutrition Inc. is an independent nutrition consulting practice focused on children and young adults, with a special emphasis on childhood obesity.

EXECUTIVE SUMMARY

According to the National Conference of State Legislatures (NCSL), in the United States roughly 13 million children are considered to be obese, and many more are overweight. Obesity and weight problems ultimately lead to major health risks for children, including high blood pressure, cancer, stroke, heart disease, and type II diabetes. The NCSL reports that adolescents who are obese have an 80 percent likelihood of becoming obese during adulthood.

Based in Parker Ridge, Tennessee, Right Way Nutrition Inc. is an independent nutrition consulting practice focused on children and young adults, with a special emphasis on childhood obesity. The practice is led by Registered Dietitian Mary Wilson, whose professional background includes extensive experience working as a clinical dietitian for a leading children's hospital. In addition to offering individual consultations, Right Way Nutrition provides families with other reasonably priced options for improving their eating habits. These range from nutritional analyses and healthy shopping trips to premium subscription-based nutritional information, including recipes.

INDUSTRY ANALYSIS

According to the U.S. Bureau of Labor Statistics, in 2012 the nation employed approximately 67,400 dietitians and nutritionists. By 2022 this figure is expected to reach 81,600, a 21 percent increase that is much greater than the average for all occupations. The key driver of this growth will be an increased focus on preventing and caring for individuals with chronic conditions, such as diabetes. Approximately 11 percent of dietitians were self-employed in 2012, providing significant opportunity for entrepreneurs like Mary Wilson. Most states require dietitians to be licensed, and many dietitians hold the Registered Dietitian Nutritionist (RDN) credential, which is administered by the Academy of Nutrition and Dietetics' credentialing agency, the Commission on Dietetic Registration.

MARKET ANALYSIS

Right Way Nutrition focuses on children and young adults, from birth to age 24, with an objective of preventing or reversing weight problems before they develop into serious chronic health conditions.

According to the National Conference of State Legislatures (NCSL), in the United States roughly 13 million children are considered to be obese, and many more are overweight. Related health expenses total approximately $14 billion each year. Obesity and weight problems in children often lead to major health risks, including high blood pressure, cancer, stroke, heart disease, and type II diabetes. Shockingly, obesity rates for children between the ages of six and 11 have skyrocketed from five percent to 14 percent over the past 40 years. During that same timeframe, obesity levels among those aged 12 to 19 have increased from five percent to 17.1 percent.

Right Way Nutrition is based in Parker Ridge, Tennessee. In 2014 Parker Ridge had a population of 29,945 people. Approximately 30 percent of residents were in the practice's target age range:

0–4:	1,647	(6.5%)
5–14:	3,092	(12.3%)
15–19:	1,515	(6.0%)
20–24:	1,518	(6.0%)

Consulting services provided by licensed dietitians are often covered by private insurance plans. In 2013 per capita expenditures in Parker Ridge for private insurance totaled approximately $1,750. Per capita expenditures on healthcare services were about $850 that year.

In addition to individuals, Right Way Nutrition will market its services via outreach initiatives to the Parker Ridge Consolidated School District (PRCSD). The PRCSD was home to 4,150 students who attended a total of 10 different schools, including six elementary schools, two middle schools, an alternative school, and one high school. Additionally, significant opportunities will exist among the many different private schools located throughout the Parker Ridge Region.

Health professionals represent an important referral source for Right Way Nutrition. Specifically, the practice will focus on outreach to family medicine physicians, family nurse practitioners, pediatricians, and mental health practitioners. A detailed list of providers has been developed and is available upon request.

SERVICES

Right Way Nutrition will offer a number of different services to clients. These include, but are not limited to:

1. Private Consultations: Registered Dietitian Mary Wilson will meet with customers where it is convenient for them (typically at their home). In this role, she will assess the dietary and health needs of her clients; provide them with healthy eating and nutritional guidance; and develop, evaluate, and adjust customized meal plans. Right Way Nutrition typically bills consultation services at a rate of $75 per hour, which may be discounted based on contracts with different insurance plan networks (consulting services provided by licensed dietitians are often covered by private insurance plans). This service is offered on an hourly basis (one hour minimum charge with additional time billed in 15-minute increments).

2. Dietary Assessments: Right Way Nutrition will offer a special dietary assessment package for $150. This includes an initial consultation with Mary to discuss a child or young adult's situation, eating habits, food preferences, food allergies, etc. Also included is a nutritional analysis, which involves parents or young adults keeping a food diary of everything they eat and drink for a period of three days. Using special computer software, the food diary is used to provide the family with information such as caloric intake and nutrient values, along with specific recommendations and suggestions for improvement.

3. Contract Services: Right Way Nutrition is fortunate to have a three-year contract for the provision of services to Parker Ridge Pediatrics, the community's largest group of independent pediatricians. Per the agreement, which allows the business to receive referrals from other local physicians and pediatricians not affiliated with Parker Ridge Pediatrics, Mary Wilson will provide 15 hours of service to the practice per week for $25,000 annually.

4. Seminars/Special Events: Right Way Nutrition will host periodic seminars in the community, which typically will be funded by a sponsoring organization (allowing participants to attend for free), or on an individual fee basis (typically $25 per person). Seminars will include topics such as Healthy Eating 101, Introduction to Organics & Natural Foods, and Sensational Snacks. Additionally, Mary also will sponsor healthy shopping trips, which involve "field trips" to local grocery stores, delis, farmers markets, and health food stores.

5. Subscriptions: Right Way Nutrition will offer affordable subscriptions to premium content on its Web site. Mary Wilson has produced a database of approximately 150 original healthy recipes, along with articles and short videos that provide guidance to those who wish to improve the health of their families through better nutrition. Subscriptions are offered on a monthly basis for $5, with annual subscriptions offered at a discounted rate of $50.

MARKETING & SALES

Right Way Nutrition has developed a marketing plan that includes a number of tactics to grow the practice:

1. A four-color, bi-fold brochure describing the business.

2. A Web site with complete details about Right Way Nutrition and the services it offers, as well as subscription-based premium content, including information about nutrition basics, food allergies, organic and natural foods, and healthy recipes.

3. The use of social media outlets such as Facebook (to stay connected with individuals and families) and LinkedIn (to reach the professional community, including referral sources). Social media channels also will be useful in driving subscriptions to Right Way Nutrition's premium Web content.

4. Online advertising and search engine optimization (SEO) strategies, with the assistance of a local Web developer, to generate referrals and link prospective customers to the practice's premium online content.

5. A quarterly e-mail newsletter for key prospects (e.g., parents, pediatricians, school counselors, school nurses, and teachers.)

6. A public relations campaign that involves the submission of healthy eating articles to local and regional print media, as well as guest appearances on morning news shows of local network affiliates to discuss topics such as childhood obesity, healthy eating, cooking/recipes, etc. Mary Wilson will take advantage of seasonal opportunities, such as holidays, providing advice at times when overeating can be more problematic.

7. Presentations at local churches, PTOs, parent groups, and service clubs to generate referrals and overall awareness about childhood obesity and healthy eating.

8. Presentations at local/regional medical professional meetings to generate referrals from the medical community.

PERSONNEL

Mary Wilson, RD (owner)

The practice is led by Registered Dietitian Mary Wilson, whose professional background includes extensive experience working as a clinical dietitian for a leading children's hospital. In that role, Mary developed nutritional programs for both individuals and groups, and worked closely with other professionals, including pediatricians. Mary earned her undergraduate degree in dietetics from Tennessee Hill University. She is a member of the Tennessee Dietetic Association and is licensed in Tennessee by the Board of Dietitians/Nutritionists Examiners.

Professional & Advisory Support

Right Way Nutrition has established a commercial checking account with Parker Ridge Community Bank, along with a merchant account for accepting credit card payments. Tax advisory services are provided by Lauren Thompson Accounting Services. Finally, Right Way Nutrition works with Mary Ellen Smith for ongoing Web site development and hosting, as well as assistance with online advertising and search engine optimization services.

BUSINESS STRATEGY

Right Way Nutrition is fortunate to begin operations with a three-year contract to provide part-time nutritional counseling services to Parker Ridge Pediatrics. This will provide Mary Wilson with an immediate income stream as she builds the other components of her practice. Her objective is to establish Right Way Nutrition in the local marketplace, building trust with area families and generating strong growth through word-of-mouth referrals.

Mary will pursue measured growth, steadily increasing the five revenue-generating components of her business (as outlined in the table below). By year three, Mary will be devoting more than 40 hours of work to her business each week. By year five she projects that the business will be at full capacity, requiring the addition of a second dietitian in order to achieve continued growth and expansion. At that time, Mary will consider securing separate office space for Right Way Nutrition in a local office building.

Revenue source	2015	2016	2017	2018	2019
Private consultations (hours)	500	750	1,000	1,250	1,500
Dietary assessments (number of assessments)	350	400	450	500	550
Parker ridge pediatrics service contract (consulting hours)	750	750	750	750	750
Seminars/special events (number of events)	12	18	24	32	40
Content subscriptions (number of annual subscriptions)	100	200	300	400	500

OPERATIONS

Right Way Nutrition initially will be based in a home office to minimize expenses. Mary Wilson has an ideal home office space in her basement, which is adjacent to a small kitchenette that can be used for producing brief cooking videos and trialing new recipes. Wilson's home office already is equipped with broadband Internet service, and she has purchased a smart phone for business use.

Start-up Costs

Mary Wilson will need to purchase several items to establish the business. She will use her own personal savings to purchase these items, which include:

- Dietary Analysis Software ($595): Right Way Nutrition has purchased a license for Nutritionist Pro software for analyzing diets, menus, and recipes. According to the manufacturer, the application includes a database of more than 75,000 foods and ingredients. In addition to more than 500 brands from 700 different manufacturers, the database includes ethnic foods and fast foods, and provides Mary Wilson with the ability to enter an unlimited number of her own foods and recipes. Additionally, the application will store information about her clients and allows her to generate a variety of different reports.

- Billable Hours App: Mary Wilson has identified a free mobile application that will allow her to track billable hours on her smart phone.

- Tablet Computer ($800)

- Portable Printer ($300)

- Educational Food Props ($350)

LEGAL

Right Way Nutrition complies with the Health Insurance Portability & Accountability Act of 1996 (HIPAA), a public law passed by Congress that protects the privacy of health information. The business signs legal agreements with clients, obligating it to maintain strict confidentiality standards. In addition, the business will sign all appropriate medical release forms from healthcare providers and other professionals when necessary. Finally, Mary Wilson has secured an appropriate level of business and malpractice coverage, based upon the recommendations of a local business attorney.

FINANCIAL ANALYSIS

During Right Way Nutrition's first year of operations, Mary Wilson anticipates that the business' gross revenues will break down by category as follows:

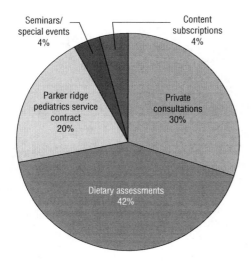

Mary has prepared a complete set of pro forma financial statements, which are available upon request. The following table provides an overview of key projections for years one through five:

	2015	2016	2017	2018	2019
Revenue					
Private consultations	$ 37,500	$ 56,250	$ 75,000	$ 93,750	$112,500
Dietary assessments	$ 52,500	$ 60,000	$ 67,500	$ 75,000	$ 82,500
Parker ridge pediatrics service contract	$ 25,000	$ 25,000	$ 25,000	$ 26,250	$ 26,250
Seminars/special events	$ 4,500	$ 6,750	$ 9,000	$ 12,000	$ 15,000
Content subscriptions	$ 5,000	$ 10,000	$ 15,000	$ 20,000	$ 25,000
Total gross revenue	**$124,500**	**$158,000**	**$191,500**	**$200,750**	**$235,000**
Expenses					
Salaries	$ 75,000	$ 85,000	$ 95,000	$105,000	$115,000
Payroll taxes	$ 11,250	$ 12,750	$ 14,250	$ 15,750	$ 17,250
Insurance	$ 6,500	$ 7,000	$ 7,500	$ 8,000	$ 8,500
Office supplies	$ 950	$ 1,000	$ 1,050	$ 1,100	$ 1,150
Web site hosting & development	$ 3,500	$ 4,000	$ 4,500	$ 5,000	$ 5,500
Equipment	$ 500	$ 500	$ 500	$ 500	$ 500
Marketing & advertising	$ 8,500	$ 9,500	$ 10,500	$ 11,500	$ 12,500
Telecommunications & internet	$ 2,250	$ 2,500	$ 2,750	$ 3,000	$ 3,250
Professional development	$ 2,000	$ 2,000	$ 2,000	$ 2,000	$ 2,000
Travel & entertainment	$ 3,000	$ 3,000	$ 3,000	$ 3,000	$ 3,000
Subscriptions & dues	$ 250	$ 250	$ 250	$ 250	$ 250
Licensure & fees	$ 327	$ 327	$ 327	$ 327	$ 327
Total expenses	**$114,027**	**$127,827**	**$141,627**	**$155,427**	**$169,227**
Net income	**$ 10,473**	**$ 30,173**	**$ 49,873**	**$ 45,323**	**$ 65,773**

Pediatric Special Needs Advocate Business

Kids First Advocacy LLC

59 Timber Ridge Trail
Peterborough, MO 63009

Paul Greenland

Kids First Advocacy is a private, fee-based patient advocacy business specializing in children with special needs.

EXECUTIVE SUMMARY

Business Overview

Every day, thousands of children are born with special needs, ranging from mild developmental delays to profound physical or mental disabilities. Kids First Advocacy is a private, fee-based patient advocacy business specializing in this important population. The practice is led by Kate Harris, a registered nurse and mother of an adult child with Down syndrome, and Lisa Malone, a social worker with an autistic teenage daughter. In addition to experience in their respective professions, the business partners benefit clients with their first-hand perspectives as parents of special needs children.

While Harris and Malone will work with children impacted by a variety of conditions, Kids First Advocacy specializes in several key areas. Specifically, the practice is mainly focused on serving children with autism spectrum disorder (ASD), which encompasses a series of disorders that until mid-2013 were diagnosed distinctly. These include Asperger syndrome, autistic disorder, pervasive developmental disorder not otherwise specified, and childhood disintegrative disorder. Additionally, Kids First Advocacy specializes in genetic disorders such as Down syndrome, which affects approximately 400,000 people in the United States, and 22q11.2 deletion syndrome (also known as DiGeorge syndrome), the second-most-common genetic disorder behind Down syndrome.

MARKET ANALYSIS

Summary

Kids First Advocacy works with clients throughout the United States. According to the organization, Autism Speaks, autism spectrum disorder (ASD) affects approximately 2 million people, with an occurrence rate of one in every 88 births. Down syndrome is estimated to affect some 400,000 people in the United States, according to the National Down Syndrome Society, with an occurrence rate of one in every 691 births. Finally, the U.S. National Library of Medicine reports that 22q11.2 deletion syndrome, has an occurrence rate of approximately one in every 4,000 births.

After analyzing U.S. population data, Harris and Malone estimate that the total population impacted by the aforementioned conditions totals about 2.5 million individuals, or 950,000 households. Approximately 650,000 of these individuals are under the age of 18, representing about 247,000 households. After applying a household income filter of at least $50,000 annually, Harris and Malone estimate that the target market for Kids First Advocacy represents roughly 325,000 individuals or 123,500 households.

Competition

In addition to other private special-needs advocates, Kids First Advocacy will face competition from associations and non-profit service organizations that provide assistance to families impacted by disabilities. Although these services are often provided at no charge, Kids First Advocacy will differentiate itself by providing client families with a much deeper level of support, analysis, and individualized attention.

INDUSTRY ANALYSIS

Patient advocacy is a growing, but by no means new, profession. Patient advocates work in many different capacities. While Kids First Advocacy is a private firm that works only for individuals and families, other advocates work for social service organizations, government agencies, insurance companies, and healthcare organizations, sometimes with titles such as case manager, disability advisor, health insurance advisor, care manager, and patient navigator. Compared to advocates who work for an organization, private advocates concentrate only on their clients' specific needs, and not those of their employer. Private advocates benefit from access to professional organizations, such as the Alliance of Professional Health Advocates, which provide benefits such as a provider directory, educational opportunities, business forms, and more.

PERSONNEL

Kids First Advocacy is led by two dynamic business partners who each bring something unique to the practice.

Kate Harris, RN, MSN

Kate Harris is a registered nurse and mother of an adult child with Down syndrome. She has nearly 30 years of experience as a registered nurse. The majority of Kate's career was spent as a staff nurse on the pediatric unit at Peterborough Community Hospital. After working as the unit manager for five years, she spent an additional seven years as the hospital's nursing supervisor, giving her experience in a wide range of different patient care situations. Additionally, Kate was a founding member of the Peterborough Community Hospital Patient Advisory Council, the goal of which was to ensure the highest level of quality and safety for patients. Kate earned Master of Science in Nursing and Business Administration Degrees from Missouri Central University, and her Bachelor Degree in Nursing from Harold Brantley College.

Lisa Malone, LCSW, MSW

Lisa Malone is a Licensed Clinical Social Worker (LCSW) with an autistic teenage daughter. She has more than 25 years of professional experience, especially in the area of case management. Lisa has worked with a wide variety of individuals during her time as a counselor at Worchester Children's Home and a member of the social work staff at Oaklawn Health System, where she most recently served as director of case management. She is a Certified Advanced Social Work Case Manager (C-ASWCM). In addition, Lisa is a member of the National Association of Social Workers, and is on the boards of several nonprofit organizations that benefit special needs children.

Professional & Advisory Support

Kids First Advocacy has established a business banking account with Peterborough Community Bank, including a merchant account for accepting credit card payments. Tax advisement is provided by Lewinsky & Associates LLC. Finally, the owners engaged the services of business attorney Stan Bowman for assistance in drafting service agreements, and providing guidance in the areas of risk management and liability.

GROWTH STRATEGY

Kids First Advocacy has developed the following strategy for growing the business during its first five years:

Year One: Begin Kids First Advocacy as a part-time "virtual" business. Focus on securing an initial client base and growing the business through strong word-of-mouth referrals and marketing.

Year Two: Secure enough clients to operate Kids First Advocacy as a full-time "virtual" business. Continue to grow the practice's client base through word-of-mouth recommendations and marketing.

Year Three: Expand the offerings of Kids First Advocacy by adding a full-time educational consultant to help families develop individualized education plans (IEPs) for their children and serve as a liaison with public and private schools. Continue to employ a "virtual" business model.

Year Four: Continue to increase the scope of services provided to clients via the addition of an advocate who specializes in billing and insurance issues, in order to help families navigate the often confusing process of working with healthcare providers, medical facilities, and insurance companies with respect to matters of payment and reimbursement.

Year Five: Consider leasing physical office space for Kids First Advocacy and adding additional advocates (specialties to be determined based upon prior client demand).

SERVICES

Healthcare advocates come in many shapes and sizes, and provide a number of different services on behalf of clients. For example, some advocates attend appointments with patients, serve as a patient's family "spokesperson," and stay in regular communication with healthcare providers in matters pertaining to a patient's healthcare. Others may specialize in dealing with matters related to billing and insurance.

Kids First Advocacy specializes in helping parents develop sound health, wellness, and social strategies for their special-needs children. This especially is the case with new parents, who may be overwhelmed by their situation and the amount of information provided to them by medical professionals, friends, and family members. Kate Harris and Lisa Malone work closely with clients to develop a firm, objective understanding of their unique situation. From there, they identify specific needs and objectives, drawing from information about the child (age, type of disability, severity of disability, developmental milestones, placement, etc.), as well as their professional and personal experience. Finally, Harris and Malone prioritize these needs and objectives and put them into a plan that is easy for parents to easily understand.

Some clients may only turn to Kids First Advocacy for the development of an initial plan for their child. However, other clients may need more in-depth assistance, in terms of researching medical centers, healthcare providers, support groups, funding sources, social programs, educational options (although education will not be a detailed focus of the practice initially), and occupational opportunities. In this regard, Harris and Malone provide assistance to families in identifying resources and programs to meet their child's needs. With the appropriate privacy agreements in place, Harris and Malone also will communicate directly with healthcare providers and other resources on behalf of their clients.

Process

Generally speaking, Kids First Advocacy will take the following approach with clients:

1. Initial Consultation: Harris and Malone will provide prospective clients with a free 30-minute telephone consultation to explain the range of services that are provided by Kids First Advocacy and determine if those services would be beneficial.

2. Agreement: If Kids First Advocacy is retained, Harris and Malone will work with the client to identify the scope of services needed. These will be summarized in a formal agreement outlining the expectations of Kids First Advocacy and the client and specifying payment arrangements. Typically, Harris and Malone will charge a flat fee for client assessment and plan development, after which time an hourly rate will be charged for ongoing research and service coordination. Clients will be required to pay half of the assessment/plan development fee in advance, with the remainder due upon conclusion.

3. Client Assessment: If Kids First Advocacy is retained, Harris and Malone will perform an initial assessment to determine the client/family's situation, evaluating medical, social, emotional, financial, and other needs.

4. Resource Identification: After assessing a client's needs, Kids First Advocacy will then identify general types of appropriate medical, social, and financial resources.

5. Plan Development: Harris and Malone will summarize the client's situation in a detailed report that also will include the aforementioned general resources and specific recommendations for the child.

6. Research & Coordination: For families who desire assistance in identifying and/or pursuing specific resources, Kids First Advocacy will offer services in this area. This may entail detailed research about specific medical centers, healthcare providers, support groups, funding sources, social programs, educational options, and occupational opportunities at the local, regional, and national levels. As part of this process, Harris and Malone also may communicate directly with medical professionals and other organizations on behalf of their clients.

7. Second Opinion Guidance: When parents are at a crossroads, in terms of trying to make the best decision for their child regarding medical treatment and related services, Kids First Advocacy will provide an objective third-party perspective after evaluating all of the pertinent facts. Additionally, Harris and Malone will help to connect families with healthcare professionals who can offer a second opinion.

Fees

Kids First Advocacy typically will charge a fee of $100 per hour for advocacy services. However, Harris and Malone will offer the aforementioned assessment, resource identification, and plan development services as part of one bundled package named "Smart Start," offered for a flat fee of $750.

MARKETING & SALES

Kids First Advocacy's marketing plan will focus heavily on direct marketing, relationship building, and word-of-mouth promotion. By 2014 support groups for children with autism spectrum disorder, autism, Asperger syndrome, Down syndrome, 22q11.2 deletion syndrome, developmental disabilities, and other conditions could be found at the local, state, regional, national levels. Some support groups were mainly online communities. Harris and Malone will make a concerted effort to reach out to these support groups via e-mail, social media, U.S. mail, and phone. Other marketing tactics will include:

1. Community Presentations: Harris and Malone will give presentations about special-needs advocacy in larger cities nationwide, beginning with St. Louis, Columbia and Kansas City, Missouri; Nashville,

Tennessee; and Louisville, Kentucky, which are within easy driving distance. When possible, they will attempt to notify various support groups about upcoming presentations and customize their talks to the needs of attendees.

2. Web Site: Kids First Advocacy will develop a Web site offering complete details regarding the advocacy practice, the services it offers, and Harris and Malone. The site will include contact information, as well as a calendar of upcoming presentations.

3. Brochure: A four-color brochure will be developed, providing information about Kids First Advocacy to prospective clients.

OPERATIONS

As a virtual operation, Harris and Malone will maintain home offices dedicated specifically to the business. A single phone number will be established for Kids First Advocacy, and the business partners initially will handle all frontline communications with prospective and existing customers. They also will provide their mobile phone numbers and e-mail addresses to established clients for easy access. If assistance is needed with frontline communications, the partners have agreed to hire a virtual assistant to answer initial service inquiries, schedule conference calls and meetings, etc. In addition to voice calls, Kids First Advocacy will use video chat services for clients who wish to do so.

LEGAL

Kids First Advocacy complies with the Health Insurance Portability & Accountability Act of 1996 (HIPAA), a public law passed by Congress that protects the privacy of health information. The business signs legal agreements with clients, obligating it to maintain strict confidentiality standards. In addition, Kids First Advocacy provides medical release forms to healthcare providers and other professionals when it is necessary to obtain medical records. Finally, Harris and Malone have secured an appropriate level of business and malpractice coverage, based upon the recommendations of their attorney.

Financial analysis

Revenue	2015	2016	2017
Smart start packages	$ 37,500	$ 75,000	$112,500
Hourly service	$104,000	$156,000	$208,000
Total revenue	**$141,500**	**$231,000**	**$320,500**
Expenses			
Salaries	$ 85,000	$150,000	$215,000
Payroll taxes	$ 15,000	$ 22,500	$ 33,250
Insurance	$ 7,500	$ 8,000	$ 8,500
Office supplies	$ 1,950	$ 2,080	$ 2,210
Equipment	$ 6,500	$ 2,600	$ 2,600
Marketing & advertising	$ 8,500	$ 10,000	$ 10,000
Telecommunications & internet	$ 3,200	$ 3,500	$ 3,750
Professional development	$ 2,000	$ 2,500	$ 3,000
Travel & entertainment	$ 3,000	$ 3,500	$ 4,500
Subscriptions & dues	$ 500	$ 500	$ 500
Permits & fees	$ 2,500	$ 3,000	$ 3,500
Total expenses	**$135,650**	**$208,180**	**$286,810**
Net income	**$ 5,850**	**$ 22,820**	**$ 33,690**

Real Estate Developer
Premium Real Estate Services, Inc.

12338 W. Washington Ave.
Bellerose, NY 11426

BizPlanDB.com

Premium Real Estate Services, Inc. is a New York-based corporation that will provide real estate development and rental services to customers in its targeted market. The Company was founded by Tim Sayre.

1.0 EXECUTIVE SUMMARY

The purpose of this business plan is to raise $900,000 for the development of a real estate development firm that specializes in residential properties while showcasing the expected financials and operations over the next three years. Premium Real Estate Services, Inc. is a New York-based corporation that will provide real estate development and rental services to customers in its targeted market. The Company was founded by Tim Sayre.

1.1 The Services

The primary revenue center for the business is acquiring land with the intent to develop new residential units that in turn will be to resold or rented to the general public. This is a strategy that is popular in any economic climate as profits come from the sale of the property after it is completed.

Immediate wealth is created from the moment that the property is complete. The primary focus of the Company's marketing strategies will be the sale of properties, but the business may rent its completed units in the event that the property does not sell within 90 days of placing the property on the market.

The third section of the business plan will further document the residential development services offered by the business.

1.2 Financing

Mr. Sayre is seeking to raise $900,000 from an investor. The terms, dividend payouts, and aspects of the deal are to be determined at negotiation. This business plan assumes that an investor will receive 50% of the Company's stock, a regular stream of dividends, and a seat on the board of directors. The financing will be used for the following:

- Financing to acquire the initial property for development.

- Financing for the first six months of operation.

- Capital for the development of residential units.

1.3 Mission Statement

Mr. Sayre's mission is to develop Premium Real Estate Services, Inc. into a premier regional development firm that will develop and sell houses profitably.

1.4 Management Team

The Company was founded by Tim Sayre. Mr. Sayre has more than 15 years' experience in the real estate industry. Through his expertise, he will be able to bring the operations of the business to profitability within its first year of operations.

1.5 Sales Forecasts

Mr. Sayre expects a strong rate of growth at the start of operations. Below are the expected financials over the next three years.

Proforma profit and loss (yearly)

Year	1	2	3
Sales	$1,212,000	$1,454,400	$1,701,648
Operating costs	$ 365,581	$ 395,766	$ 466,980
EBITDA	$ 365,219	$ 481,194	$ 559,063
Taxes, interest, and depreciation	$ 201,640	$ 245,711	$ 275,301
Net profit	$ 163,579	$ 235,483	$ 283,762

Sales, operating costs, and profit forecast

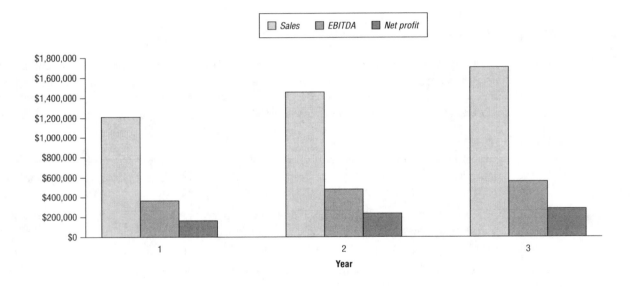

1.6 Expansion Plan

The Founder expects that the business will aggressively expand during the first three years of operation. As the real estate market returns to normal conditions, Premium Real Estate Services, Inc. will be in an excellent position to recognize profits from the sale of completed properties. In the future, the business may also develop mortgage brokering operations to assist homebuyers with financing their purchases from the business.

2.0 COMPANY AND FINANCING SUMMARY

2.1 Registered Name and Corporate Structure

Premium Real Estate Services, Inc. is registered as a corporation in the State of New York.

2.2 Required Funds

At this time, Premium Real Estate Services, Inc. requires $900,000 of investor funds. Below is a breakdown of how these funds will be used:

Projected startup costs

Working capital	$ 15,000
FF&E	$ 10,000
Leasehold improvements	$ 5,000
Security deposits	$ 5,000
Insurance	$ 2,500
Property acquisitions	$850,000
Marketing budget	$ 7,500
Miscellaneous and unforeseen costs	$ 5,000
Total startup costs	**$900,000**

2.3 Investor Equity

Tim Sayre intends to sell 50% of Premium Real Estate Services in exchange for the capital.

2.4 Management Equity

Tim Sayre will retain 50% of the business once the capital is raised.

2.5 Exit Strategy

If Premium Real Estate Services is very successful, Mr. Sayre may seek to sell the business to a third party for a significant earnings multiple. Most likely, the Company will hire a qualified business broker to sell the business on behalf of the Company. Based on historical numbers, the business could fetch a sales premium of up to 4 times earnings.

2.6 Investor Divestiture

This will be discussed during negotiations.

3.0 REAL ESTATE SERVICES

Below is a description of the real estate services offered by Premium Real Estate Services, Inc.

3.1 Developer of Residential Real Estate

Premium Real Estate Services will primarily engage the business of developing residential properties with the intent to sell or rent the property once the project is completed. If the real estate market does not provide a fair and reasonable market value for the property, then Management will aggressively rent the units until such time when the building can be divested at a fair market value.

After the development process is complete, the Company can quickly divest these assets to a real estate investor for a significant profit. There are several considerations that the Company must deal with before purchasing land for development purposes.

Once the property is competed the business will then seek to divest the property or rent the units in order to generate income to satisfy the debt obligations of the business.

3.2 Rental of Completed Properties

The direct finance and purchase of residential property is the secondary business of Premium Real Estate Services. Residential real estate will provide a continuous stream of rental income that the Management will use for reinvestment and profit stability for the Company. Management is developing a complex economic pricing strategy that will determine the fair market rate of a property based on its capitalization rate in conjunction with the market values of residential property. Residential real estate is the least risky form of real estate investing because the service offered is a necessity.

4.0 STRATEGIC AND MARKET ANALYSIS

4.1 Economic Outlook

Premium Real Estate Services, Inc. will be actively engaged in two primary business units that will seek to generate revenue in any real estate market. These strategies include developing residential properties and the rental of completed properties.

Management is developing a very complex pricing method to ensure that the Company can continue to provide its units at profit despite possible drawbacks in the overall economic market. The Company's two-prong approach to real estate will allow the business to grow successfully in the rapidly changing real estate market. More importantly, this strategy will allow the Company to offset the risks from each business unit so that there is a diversified balance in the Company's real estate portfolio. This is especially important as the business uses leverage to finance the acquisition of its properties.

4.2 Industry Analysis

The U.S. Economic Census estimates that there are 21,300 companies that specialize in the construction of new residential units in the United States. On an annualized basis, these companies generate fees of $43.9 billion dollars while concurrently providing jobs to more than 520,000 people. In each of the last five years, aggregate payrolls have exceeded $20 billion dollars.

The number of real estate sales has increased significantly within the last year. This is one of the primary signals of an overvalued real estate market. As stated earlier, the Bureau of Economic Analysis estimates that homes on the market have increased more than 9% over last year's figures.

4.3 Customer Profile

As the Company intends to operate among several different investment and operating units, it is hard to characterize any specific tenant that will occupy the Company's properties. However, Management will enact strict tenant quality and credit review procedures to ensure the Company's revenues will not be interrupted by tenant default.

4.4 Competition

Since real estate is effactually one of the most free-market-oriented businesses in the country, competition can not be accurately categorized. The Company anticipates that there will be a sizable amount of competition from both single owner investment firms to large construction companies that are seeking to gain from the real estate prices throughout the target market.

5.0 MARKETING PLAN

Premium Real Estate Services, Inc. intends to maintain an extensive marketing campaign that will ensure maximum visibility for the completed units in its targeted market. Below is an overview of the marketing strategies and objectives of Premium Real Estate Services.

5.1 Marketing Objectives

- Develop an online presence by acquiring accounts for major online real estate portals.

- Implement a local campaign with the Company's targeted market via the use of flyers, local newspaper advertisements, and word-of-mouth.

- Establish relationships with other real estate brokers and agents within the targeted market.

5.2 Marketing Strategies

Property and home buyer marketing will be the most difficult portion of the marketing strategy. This task will be accomplished through the business's broad marketing campaign throughout its targeted market. Foremost, the business will retain a qualified real estate brokerage to list and market the Company's developed units for sale or rent within the target market. Management expects to pay commissions of 4% to 6% on each sale conducted through the use of a real estate brokerage. In regards to rentals, the business will pay a fee equal to two months of a single year rent contract with a tenant.

The Company will also use an internet-based strategy. This is very important as many people seeking real estate for purchase or rent use the Internet to conduct their preliminary searches.

Mr. Sayre will register Premium Real Estate Services, Inc. and its properties with these online portals so that potential buyers/renters can easily reach the Company. The Company will also develop its own online website.

The Company will maintain a sizable amount of print and traditional advertising methods within local markets to promote the homes and properties that the Company is selling.

5.3 Pricing

The Company expects that each house will sell for approximately $100,000 of revenue. Expected margins from sales will reach 60%. Rental income is to be determined based on market conditions.

6.0 ORGANIZATIONAL PLAN AND PERSONNEL SUMMARY

6.1 Corporate Organization

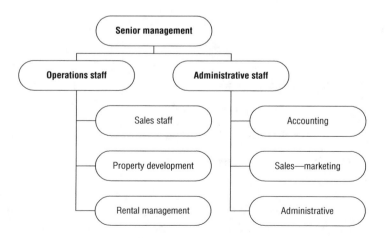

6.2 Organizational Budget

Personnel plan—yearly

Year	1	2	3
Owners	$ 80,000	$ 82,400	$ 84,872
Development manager	$ 35,000	$ 36,050	$ 37,132
Marketing staff	$ 65,000	$ 66,950	$103,438
Sales staff	$ 37,500	$ 51,500	$ 66,306
Administrative staff	$ 44,000	$ 45,320	$ 46,680
Total	**$261,500**	**$282,220**	**$338,427**

Numbers of personnel

Owners	2	2	2
Development manager	1	1	1
Marketing staff	2	2	3
Sales staff	3	4	5
Administrative staff	2	2	2
Totals	**10**	**11**	**13**

Personnel expense breakdown

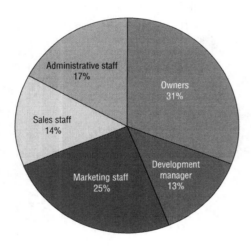

7.0 FINANCIAL PLAN

7.1 Underlying Assumptions

The Company has based its proforma financial statements on the following:

- Premium Real Estate Services, Inc. will have an annual revenue growth rate of 16% per year.

- The Owner will acquire $900,000 of investor funds to develop the business.

- The Company will not seek debt financing in the first three years of operations.

7.2 Sensitivity Analysis

The Company's revenues can change depending on the general economic climate of the real estate industry. In times of economic recession, Premium Real Estate Services, Inc. may have issues with its top line income as fewer sales will be made. However, the Company will generate income from its rental business, which will reduce the risks associated with this business.

7.3 Source of Funds

Financing

Equity contributions	
Investor(s)	$ 900,000.00
Total equity financing	**$900,000.00**
Banks and lenders	
Total debt financing	**$ 0.00**
Total financing	**$900,000.00**

7.4 General Assumptions

General assumptions

Year	1	2	3
Short term interest rate	9.5%	9.5%	9.5%
Long term interest rate	10.0%	10.0%	10.0%
Federal tax rate	33.0%	33.0%	33.0%
State tax rate	5.0%	5.0%	5.0%
Personnel taxes	15.0%	15.0%	15.0%

7.5 Profit and Loss Statements

Proforma profit and loss (yearly)

Year	1	2	3
Sales	**$1,212,000**	**$1,454,400**	**$1,701,648**
Cost of goods sold	$ 481,200	$ 577,440	$ 675,605
Gross margin	60.30%	60.30%	60.30%
Operating income	**$ 730,800**	**$ 876,960**	**$1,026,043**
Expenses			
Payroll	$ 261,500	$ 282,220	$ 338,427
General and administrative	$ 25,200	$ 26,208	$ 27,256
Marketing expenses	$ 6,060	$ 7,272	$ 8,508
Professional fees and licensure	$ 5,219	$ 5,376	$ 5,537
Insurance costs	$ 1,987	$ 2,086	$ 2,191
Travel and vehicle costs	$ 7,596	$ 8,356	$ 9,191
Rent and utilities	$ 4,250	$ 4,463	$ 4,686
Miscellaneous costs	$ 14,544	$ 17,453	$ 20,420
Payroll taxes	$ 39,225	$ 42,333	$ 50,764
Total operating costs	**$ 365,581**	**$ 395,766**	**$ 466,980**
EBITDA	**$ 365,219**	**$ 481,194**	**$ 559,063**
Federal income tax	$ 120,522	$ 158,794	$ 184,491
State income tax	$ 18,261	$ 24,060	$ 27,953
Interest expense	$ 0	$ 0	$ 0
Depreciation expenses	$ 62,857	$ 62,857	$ 62,857
Net profit	**$ 163,579**	**$ 235,483**	**$ 283,762**
Profit margin	**13.50%**	**16.19%**	**16.68%**

Sales, operating costs, and profit forecast

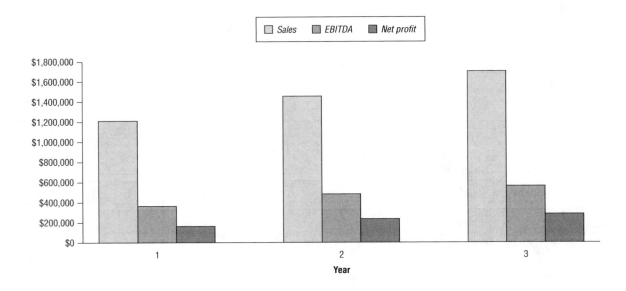

7.6 Cash Flow Analysis

Proforma cash flow analysis—yearly

Year	1	2	3
Cash from operations	$ 226,436	$298,340	$346,619
Cash from receivables	$ 0	$ 0	$ 0
Operating cash inflow	**$ 226,436**	**$298,340**	**$346,619**
Other cash inflows			
Equity investment	$ 900,000	$ 0	$ 0
Increased borrowings	$ 0	$ 0	$ 0
Sales of business assets	$ 0	$ 0	$ 0
A/P increases	$ 37,902	$ 43,587	$ 50,125
Total other cash inflows	**$ 937,902**	**$ 43,587**	**$ 50,125**
Total cash inflow	**$1,164,338**	**$341,928**	**$396,745**
Cash outflows			
Repayment of principal	$ 0	$ 0	$ 0
A/P decreases	$ 24,897	$ 29,876	$ 35,852
A/R increases	$ 0	$ 0	$ 0
Asset purchases	$ 850,000	$ 74,585	$ 86,655
Dividends	$ 158,505	$208,838	$242,634
Total cash outflows	**$1,033,402**	**$313,300**	**$365,140**
Net cash flow	**$ 130,936**	**$ 28,628**	**$ 31,605**
Cash balance	**$ 130,936**	**$159,564**	**$191,168**

Proforma cash flow (yearly)

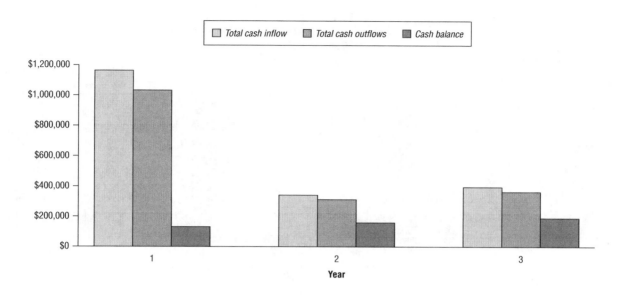

7.7 Balance Sheet

Proforma balance sheet—yearly

Year	1	2	3
Assets			
Cash	$130,936	$159,564	$ 191,168
Amortized development/expansion costs	$ 15,000	$ 22,459	$ 31,124
Property	$850,000	$905,939	$ 970,930
FF&E	$ 15,000	$ 26,188	$ 39,186
Accumulated depreciation	($ 62,857)	($125,714)	($ 188,571)
Total assets	**$948,079**	**$988,434**	**$1,043,837**
Liabilities and equity			
Accounts payable	$ 13,005	$ 26,716	$ 40,990
Long term liabilities	$ 0	$ 0	$ 0
Other liabilities	$ 0	$ 0	$ 0
Total liabilities	**$ 13,005**	**$ 26,716**	**$ 40,990**
Net worth	**$935,074**	**$961,719**	**$1,002,847**
Total liabilities and equity	**$948,079**	**$988,434**	**$1,043,837**

Proforma balance sheet

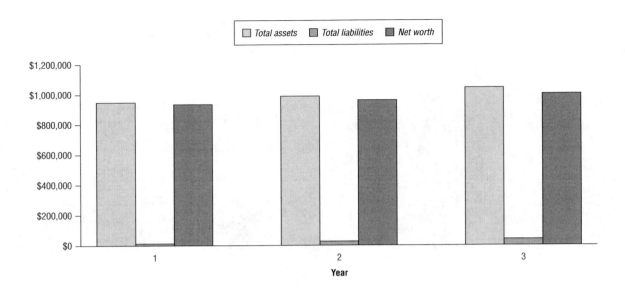

7.8 Breakeven Analysis

Monthly break even analysis

Year	1	2	3
Monthly revenue	$ 50,525	$ 54,697	$ 64,539
Yearly revenue	$606,300	$656,360	$774,466

Break even analysis

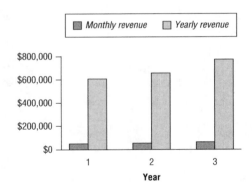

7.9 Business Ratios

Business ratios—yearly

Year	1	2	3
Sales			
Sales growth	0.00%	20.00%	17.00%
Gross margin	60.30%	60.30%	60.30%
Financials			
Profit margin	13.50%	16.19%	16.68%
Assets to liabilities	72.90	37.00	25.47
Equity to liabilities	71.90	36.00	24.47
Assets to equity	1.01	1.03	1.04
Liquidity			
Acid test	10.07	5.97	4.66
Cash to assets	0.14	0.16	0.18

7.10 Three Year Profit and Loss Statement

Profit and loss statement (first year)

Months	1	2	3	4	5	6	7
Sales	$101,000	$101,000	$101,000	$ 0	$ 0	$101,000	$202,000
Cost of goods sold	$ 40,100	$ 40,100	$ 40,100	$ 0	$ 0	$ 40,100	$ 80,200
Gross margin	60.3%	60.3%	60.3%	0.0%	0.0%	60.3%	60.3%
Operating income	$ 60,900	$ 60,900	$ 60,900	$ 0	$ 0	$ 60,900	$121,800
Expenses							
Payroll	$ 21,792	$ 21,792	$ 21,792	$21,792	$21,792	$ 21,792	$ 21,792
General and administrative	$ 2,100	$ 2,100	$ 2,100	$ 2,100	$ 2,100	$ 2,100	$ 2,100
Marketing expenses	$ 505	$ 505	$ 505	$ 505	$ 505	$ 505	$ 505
Professional fees and licensure	$ 435	$ 435	$ 435	$ 435	$ 435	$ 435	$ 435
Insurance costs	$ 166	$ 166	$ 166	$ 166	$ 166	$ 166	$ 166
Travel and vehicle costs	$ 633	$ 633	$ 633	$ 633	$ 633	$ 633	$ 633
Rent and utilities	$ 354	$ 354	$ 354	$ 354	$ 354	$ 354	$ 354
Miscellaneous costs	$ 1,212	$ 1,212	$ 1,212	$ 1,212	$ 1,212	$ 1,212	$ 1,212
Payroll taxes	$ 3,269	$ 3,269	$ 3,269	$ 3,269	$ 3,269	$ 3,269	$ 3,269
Total operating costs	$ 30,465	$ 30,465	$ 30,465	$30,465	$30,465	$ 30,465	$ 30,465
EBITDA	$ 30,435	$ 30,435	$ 30,435	−$30,465	−$30,465	$ 30,435	$ 91,335
Federal income tax	$ 10,044	$ 10,044	$ 10,044	$ 0	$ 0	$ 10,044	$ 20,087
State income tax	$ 1,522	$ 1,522	$ 1,522	$ 0	$ 0	$ 1,522	$ 3,043
Interest expense	$ 0	$ 0	$ 0	$ 0	$ 0	$ 0	$ 0
Depreciation expense	$ 5,238	$ 5,238	$ 5,238	$ 5,238	$ 5,238	$ 5,238	$ 5,238
Net profit	$ 13,632	$ 13,632	$ 13,632	−$35,703	−$35,703	$ 13,632	$ 62,966

Profit and loss statement (first year cont.)

Month	8	9	10	11	12	1
Sales	$ 0	$101,000	$101,000	$202,000	$202,000	$1,212,000
Cost of goods sold	$ 0	$ 40,100	$ 40,100	$ 80,200	$ 80,200	$ 481,200
Gross margin	0.0%	60.3%	60.3%	60.3%	60.3%	60.3%
Operating income	$ 0	$ 60,900	$ 60,900	$121,800	$121,800	$ 730,800
Expenses						
Payroll	$21,792	$ 21,792	$ 21,792	$ 21,792	$ 21,792	$ 261,500
General and administrative	$ 2,100	$ 2,100	$ 2,100	$ 2,100	$ 2,100	$ 25,200
Marketing expenses	$ 505	$ 505	$ 505	$ 505	$ 505	$ 6,060
Professional fees and licensure	$ 435	$ 435	$ 435	$ 435	$ 435	$ 5,219
Insurance costs	$ 166	$ 166	$ 166	$ 166	$ 166	$ 1,987
Travel and vehicle costs	$ 633	$ 633	$ 633	$ 633	$ 633	$ 7,596
Rent and utilities	$ 354	$ 354	$ 354	$ 354	$ 354	$ 4,250
Miscellaneous costs	$ 1,212	$ 1,212	$ 1,212	$ 1,212	$ 1,212	$ 14,544
Payroll taxes	$ 3,269	$ 3,269	$ 3,269	$ 3,269	$ 3,269	$ 39,225
Total operating costs	$30,465	$ 30,465	$ 30,465	$ 30,465	$ 30,465	$ 365,581
EBITDA	−$30,465	$ 30,435	$ 30,435	$ 91,335	$ 91,335	$ 365,219
Federal income tax	$ 0	$ 10,044	$ 10,044	$ 20,087	$ 20,087	$ 120,522
State income tax	$ 0	$ 1,522	$ 1,522	$ 3,043	$ 3,043	$ 18,261
Interest expense	$ 0	$ 0	$ 0	$ 0	$ 0	$ 0
Depreciation expense	$ 5,238	$ 5,238	$ 5,238	$ 5,238	$ 5,238	$ 62,857
Net profit	−$35,703	$ 13,632	$ 13,632	$ 62,966	$ 62,966	$ 163,579

Profit and loss statement (second year)

Quarter	Q1	2 Q2	Q3	Q4	2
Sales	$290,880	$363,600	$392,688	$407,232	$1,454,400
Cost of goods sold	$115,488	$144,360	$155,909	$161,683	$ 577,440
Gross margin	60.3%	60.3%	60.3%	60.3%	60.3%
Operating income	$175,392	$219,240	$236,779	$245,549	$ 876,960
Expenses					
Payroll	$ 56,444	$ 70,555	$ 76,199	$ 79,022	$ 282,220
General and administrative	$ 5,242	$ 6,552	$ 7,076	$ 7,338	$ 26,208
Marketing expenses	$ 1,454	$ 1,818	$ 1,963	$ 2,036	$ 7,272
Professional fees and licensure	$ 1,075	$ 1,344	$ 1,451	$ 1,505	$ 5,376
Insurance costs	$ 417	$ 522	$ 563	$ 584	$ 2,086
Travel and vehicle costs	$ 1,671	$ 2,089	$ 2,256	$ 2,340	$ 8,356
Rent and utilities	$ 893	$ 1,116	$ 1,205	$ 1,250	$ 4,463
Miscellaneous costs	$ 3,491	$ 4,363	$ 4,712	$ 4,887	$ 17,453
Payroll taxes	$ 8,467	$ 10,583	$ 11,430	$ 11,853	$ 42,333
Total operating costs	$ 79,153	$ 98,941	$106,857	$110,814	$ 395,766
EBITDA	$ 96,239	$120,299	$129,922	$134,734	$ 481,194
Federal income tax	$ 31,759	$ 39,699	$ 42,874	$ 44,462	$ 158,794
State income tax	$ 4,812	$ 6,015	$ 6,496	$ 6,737	$ 24,060
Interest expense	$ 0	$ 0	$ 0	$ 0	$ 0
Depreciation expense	$ 15,714	$ 15,714	$ 15,714	$ 15,714	$ 62,857
Net profit	$ 43,954	$ 58,871	$ 64,838	$ 67,821	$ 235,483

Profit and loss statement (third year)

Quarter	Q1	3 Q2	Q3	Q4	3
Sales	$340,330	$425,412	$459,445	$476,461	$1,701,648
Cost of goods sold	$135,121	$168,901	$182,413	$189,169	$ 675,605
Gross margin	60.3%	60.3%	60.3%	60.3%	60.3%
Operating income	$205,209	$256,511	$277,032	$287,292	$1,026,043
Expenses					
Payroll	$ 67,685	$ 84,607	$ 91,375	$ 94,760	$ 338,427
General and administrative	$ 5,451	$ 6,814	$ 7,359	$ 7,632	$ 27,256
Marketing expenses	$ 1,702	$ 2,127	$ 2,297	$ 2,382	$ 8,508
Professional fees and licensure	$ 1,107	$ 1,384	$ 1,495	$ 1,550	$ 5,537
Insurance costs	$ 438	$ 548	$ 591	$ 613	$ 2,191
Travel and vehicle costs	$ 1,838	$ 2,298	$ 2,482	$ 2,574	$ 9,191
Rent and utilities	$ 937	$ 1,171	$ 1,265	$ 1,312	$ 4,686
Miscellaneous costs	$ 4,084	$ 5,105	$ 5,513	$ 5,718	$ 20,420
Payroll taxes	$ 10,153	$ 12,691	$ 13,706	$ 14,214	$ 50,764
Total operating costs	$ 93,396	$116,745	$126,085	$130,754	$ 466,980
EBITDA	$111,813	$139,766	$150,947	$156,538	$ 559,063
Federal income tax	$ 36,898	$ 46,123	$ 49,813	$ 51,657	$ 184,491
State income tax	$ 5,591	$ 6,988	$ 7,547	$ 7,827	$ 27,953
Interest expense	$ 0	$ 0	$ 0	$ 0	$ 0
Depreciation expense	$ 15,714	$ 15,714	$ 15,714	$ 15,714	$ 62,857
Net profit	$ 53,610	$ 70,941	$ 77,873	$ 81,339	$ 283,762

7.11 Three Year Cash Flow Analysis

Cash flow analysis (first year)

Month	1	2	3	4	5	6	7
Cash from operations	$ 18,870	$18,870	$ 18,870	−$30,465	−$30,465	$18,870	$ 68,204
Cash from receivables	$ 0	$ 0	$ 0	$ 0	$ 0	$ 0	$ 0
Operating cash inflow	$ 18,870	$18,870	$ 18,870	−$30,465	−$30,465	$18,870	$ 68,204
Other cash inflows							
Equity investment	$900,000	$ 0	$ 0	$ 0	$ 0	$ 0	$ 0
Increased borrowings	$ 0	$ 0	$ 0	$ 0	$ 0	$ 0	$ 0
Sales of business assets	$ 0	$ 0	$ 0	$ 0	$ 0	$ 0	$ 0
A/P increases	$ 3,159	$ 3,159	$ 3,159	$ 3,159	$ 3,159	$ 3,159	$ 3,159
Total other cash inflows	$903,159	$ 3,159	$ 3,159	$ 3,159	$ 3,159	$ 3,159	$ 3,159
Total cash inflow	$922,028	$22,028	$ 22,028	−$27,307	−$27,307	$22,028	$ 71,363
Cash outflows							
Repayment of principal	$ 0	$ 0	$ 0	$ 0	$ 0	$ 0	$ 0
A/P decreases	$ 2,075	$ 2,075	$ 2,075	$ 2,075	$ 2,075	$ 2,075	$ 2,075
A/R increases	$ 0	$ 0	$ 0	$ 0	$ 0	$ 0	$ 0
Asset purchases	$850,000	$ 0	$ 0	$ 0	$ 0	$ 0	$ 0
Dividends	$ 0	$ 0	$ 0	$ 0	$ 0	$ 0	$ 0
Total cash outflows	$852,075	$ 2,075	$ 2,075	$ 2,075	$ 2,075	$ 2,075	$ 2,075
Net cash flow	$ 69,953	$19,953	$ 19,953	−$29,381	−$29,381	$19,953	$ 69,288
Cash balance	$ 69,953	$89,907	$109,860	$80,479	$51,098	$71,051	$140,339

Cash flow analysis (first year cont.)

Month	8	9	10	11	12	1
Cash from operations	−$ 30,465	$ 18,870	$ 18,870	$ 68,204	$ 68,204	$ 226,436
Cash from receivables	$ 0	$ 0	$ 0	$ 0	$ 0	$ 0
Operating cash inflow	**−$ 30,465**	**$ 18,870**	**$ 18,870**	**$ 68,204**	**$ 68,204**	**$ 226,436**
Other cash inflows						
Equity investment	$ 0	$ 0	$ 0	$ 0	$ 0	$ 900,000
Increased borrowings	$ 0	$ 0	$ 0	$ 0	$ 0	$ 0
Sales of business assets	$ 0	$ 0	$ 0	$ 0	$ 0	$ 0
A/P increases	$ 3,159	$ 3,159	$ 3,159	$ 3,159	$ 3,159	$ 37,902
Total other cash inflows	**$ 3,159**	**$ 3,159**	**$ 3,159**	**$ 3,159**	**$ 3,159**	**$ 937,902**
Total cash inflow	**−$ 27,307**	**$ 22,028**	**$ 22,028**	**$ 71,363**	**$ 71,363**	**$1,164,338**
Cash outflows						
Repayment of principal	$ 0	$ 0	$ 0	$ 0	$ 0	$ 0
A/P decreases	$ 2,075	$ 2,075	$ 2,075	$ 2,075	$ 2,075	$ 24,897
A/R increases	$ 0	$ 0	$ 0	$ 0	$ 0	$ 0
Asset purchases	$ 0	$ 0	$ 0	$ 0	$ 0	$ 850,000
Dividends	$ 0	$ 0	$ 0	$ 0	$158,505	$ 158,505
Total cash outflows	**$ 2,075**	**$ 2,075**	**$ 2,075**	**$ 2,075**	**$160,580**	**$1,033,402**
Net cash flow	**−$ 29,381**	**$ 19,953**	**$ 19,953**	**$ 69,288**	**−$ 89,217**	**$ 130,936**
Cash balance	**$110,958**	**$130,911**	**$150,865**	**$220,153**	**$130,936**	**$ 130,936**

Cash flow analysis (second year)

Quarter	Q1	2 Q2	Q3	Q4	2
Cash from operations	$ 59,668	$ 74,585	$ 80,552	$ 83,535	$298,340
Cash from receivables	$ 0	$ 0	$ 0	$ 0	$ 0
Operating cash inflow	**$ 59,668**	**$ 74,585**	**$ 80,552**	**$ 83,535**	**$298,340**
Other cash inflows					
Equity investment	$ 0	$ 0	$ 0	$ 0	$ 0
Increased borrowings	$ 0	$ 0	$ 0	$ 0	$ 0
Sales of business assets	$ 0	$ 0	$ 0	$ 0	$ 0
A/P increases	$ 8,717	$ 10,897	$ 11,769	$ 12,204	$ 43,587
Total other cash inflows	**$ 8,717**	**$ 10,897**	**$ 11,769**	**$ 12,204**	**$ 43,587**
Total cash inflow	**$ 68,386**	**$ 85,482**	**$ 92,320**	**$ 95,740**	**$341,928**
Cash outflows					
Repayment of principal	$ 0	$ 0	$ 0	$ 0	$ 0
A/P decreases	$ 5,975	$ 7,469	$ 8,067	$ 8,365	$ 29,876
A/R increases	$ 0	$ 0	$ 0	$ 0	$ 0
Asset purchases	$ 14,917	$ 18,646	$ 20,138	$ 20,884	$ 74,585
Dividends	$ 41,768	$ 52,210	$ 56,386	$ 58,475	$208,838
Total cash outflows	**$ 62,660**	**$ 78,325**	**$ 84,591**	**$ 87,724**	**$313,300**
Net cash flow	**$ 5,726**	**$ 7,157**	**$ 7,730**	**$ 8,016**	**$ 28,628**
Cash balance	**$136,661**	**$143,818**	**$151,548**	**$159,564**	**$159,564**

Cash flow analysis (third year)

Quarter	Q1	3 Q2	Q3	Q4	3
Cash from operations	$ 69,324	$ 86,655	$ 93,587	$ 97,053	$346,619
Cash from receivables	$ 0	$ 0	$ 0	$ 0	$ 0
Operating cash inflow	**$ 69,324**	**$ 86,655**	**$ 93,587**	**$ 97,053**	**$346,619**
Other cash inflows					
Equity investment	$ 0	$ 0	$ 0	$ 0	$ 0
Increased borrowings	$ 0	$ 0	$ 0	$ 0	$ 0
Sales of business assets	$ 0	$ 0	$ 0	$ 0	$ 0
A/P increases	$ 10,025	$ 12,531	$ 13,534	$ 14,035	$ 50,125
Total other cash inflows	**$ 10,025**	**$ 12,531**	**$ 13,534**	**$ 14,035**	**$ 50,125**
Total cash inflow	**$ 79,349**	**$ 99,186**	**$107,121**	**$111,089**	**$396,745**
Cash outflows					
Repayment of principal	$ 0	$ 0	$ 0	$ 0	$ 0
A/P decreases	$ 7,170	$ 8,963	$ 9,680	$ 10,038	$ 35,852
A/R increases	$ 0	$ 0	$ 0	$ 0	$ 0
Asset purchases	$ 17,331	$ 21,664	$ 23,397	$ 24,263	$ 86,655
Dividends	$ 48,527	$ 60,658	$ 65,511	$ 67,937	$242,634
Total cash outflows	**$ 73,028**	**$ 91,285**	**$ 98,588**	**$102,239**	**$365,140**
Net cash flow	**$ 6,321**	**$ 7,901**	**$ 8,533**	**$ 8,849**	**$ 31,605**
Cash balance	**$165,885**	**$173,786**	**$182,319**	**$191,168**	**$191,168**

Refreshment Stand

The Sno Cone Shack

8990 Bulldog Boulevard
Starkville, Mississippi 39759

Fran Fletcher

The Sno Cone Shack is a refreshment stand located in the heart of the M State University campus in Starkville, Mississippi. It is owned by John Callahan.

EXECUTIVE SUMMARY

The Sno Cone Shack is a refreshment stand located in the heart of the M State University campus in Starkville, Mississippi.

The idea for the Sno Cone Shack was born on a sweltering August day when college roommates John Callahan and Chris Moore longed for any snack that would cool them off. There were no businesses offering such refreshments on the campus and therefore they would have to travel to the other side of Starkville in order to find what they were looking for. Mr. Callahan thought it would be a good idea to bring such a business to the campus. After graduating with a business degree, he decided that he would make the Sno Cone Shack a reality and provide this refreshing service for M State University students.

The Sno Cone Shack will be open 7 days a week and will be managed by Mr. Callahan with the help of five part-time employees. The business will be open for the months of May through October, but may open during special on-campus events.

The Sno Cone Shack will offer 24 unique sno cone flavors and 12 fountain drink flavors which is sure to please anyone's taste. The business will also offer sno cone machine rental for various parties and functions.

According to the Bureau of Labor Statistics, jobs in the food and snack industry are expected to remain constant over the next five years. The target market for the Sno Cone Shack are students attending M State University. There are currently 15,000 students enrolled at the university, which will lend a large potential customer base.

The Sno Cone Shack has one competitor on the other side of Starkville; however, the business's prime location and two dozen flavors will set it apart and make it the premier place to enjoy a sno cone.

The overall strategy of the company is to attract college students by offering a convenient location to purchase inexpensive icy treats during Mississippi's hot summer months. The Sno Cone Shack projects profits from the start, and plans to remain profitable through the summer months.

The majority of customers will be reached via various social media platforms. In order to keep the business exciting and fresh, the owner will offer a variety of promotions that can be used to boost visibility and sales.

- The Sno Cone Shack will host a grand opening and will offer $2 sno cones and various giveaways.

- The Sno Cone Shack will offer daily specials.

- The Sno Cone Shack will offer surprise sales events and promotions via social media platforms.

Mr. Callahan wants to secure a business line of credit in the amount of $43,876. This will cover start-up costs and the first month's expenses. Conservative estimates show the business making a profit each month and even though the business will be closed during the off-season, the summer months make up for this loss and will allow Mr. Callahan to repay the loan by the end of the second year of operation.

COMPANY DESCRIPTION

Location
The Sno Cone Shack will be located on a small but prime piece of real estate on the M State College campus. It will be highly visible to campus traffic and easily accessed by students and faculty.

Hours of Operations
Initially, The Sno Cone Shack will only be open during the months of May through October. Operations may be extended depending upon the weather.

Sunday—Thursday, 10 AM—9 PM

Friday—Saturday, 10 AM—midnight

Personnel

John Callahan (Owner)
Mr. Callahan is a recent business graduate of M State University. He will manage all business operations.

Employees
Five M State University students will be hired as part-time employees to run the Sno Cone Shack.

Products and Services

Products
- Sno cones

- Fountain drinks

- The Sno Cone Shack tee shirts

Sno cones and drinks will be sold in the following flavors:

Sno cone flavors		Drinks
Grape	Tutti fruitti	Bottled water
Strawberry	Blue raspberry	Cola
Cherry	Banana	Diet cola
Lime	Bubble gum	Root beer
Peach	Candy apple	Diet root beer
Fruit punch	Bahama mama	Lemon lime
Blueberry	Orange	Lemonade
Watermelon	Cola	Cherry cola
Lemonade	Root beer	Orange soda
Sour apple	Cherry cola	Grape soda
Cotton candy	Lemon lime	Diet cherry cola
Piña colada	Tropical fruit	Cherry lemon lime

Services

The Sno Cone Shack will offer sno cone machine rental for parties, school fundraisers, etc.

MARKET ANALYSIS

Industry Overview

According to the Bureau of Labor Statistics, jobs in the food and snack industry are expected to remain constant over the next five years.

M State University's current enrollment is approximately 15,000 students. Twenty percent of these students live on campus and will provide a large customer base for the business.

Target Market

The target market for the Sno Cone Shack are M State University students, faculty, and staff who need a frozen snack to cool off during the hot summer months.

Competition

There is currently one other similar business in Starkville.

Sno Cone Central, 2567-C East First Street, Starkville, Mississippi—Offers 12 sno cone flavors

The Sno Cone Shack's prime location and two dozen flavors will set it apart and make it the premier place for sno cones.

GROWTH STRATEGY

The overall strategy of the company is to attract college students by offering a convenient location to purchase inexpensive icy treats during Mississippi's hot summer months. The Sno Cone Shack hopes to be profitable from the start, and to remain profitable through the summer months.

During the off-season, Mr. Callahan may choose to open up the business and sell sno cones or drinks during campus special events or home football games.

Mr. Callahan is already thinking about future endeavors. Possibilities include adding a smaller sno cone cart to the other side of the campus, setting up a booth at sports events, or transforming the business into Java Junction during the cooler months; offering coffee, hot chocolate, espresso, etc. to M State University students and staff.

Profits projection year 1

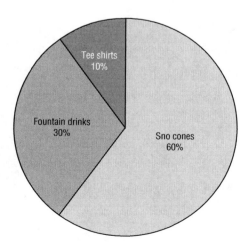

Sales and Marketing

The Sno Cone Shack will be highly visible to university students on the north side of the campus. However, the campus encompasses an expansive 14,000 acres, so it will be necessary to advertise in order to raise student awareness. The majority of students will be reached using various social media platforms.

In order to keep the business exciting and fresh, the owner will implement several promotions that will be used to boost visibility and sales.

- The Sno Cone Shack will host a grand opening and will offer $2 sno cones and various giveaways.

- The Sno Cone Shack will offer the following weekly promotions and discounts on sno cone products:

Promotions	Mon	Tues	Wed	Thurs	Fri	Sat	Sun
½ price kids						All day	
Greek $2 discount	All day						
$2 any small size							10–4
Graduate students $2 discount		All day					
Freshman Friday $2 discount					All day		
Sophomore Thursday $2 discount				All day			
Junior Wednesday $2 discount			All day				
Senior Saturday $2 discount						All day	
Faculty appreciation $2 discount	All day		All day		All day		

In addition to weekly specials, The Sno Cone Shack plans to offer surprise sales and specials to its followers on social media. Examples include:

- $2 sno cones for the first twenty customers to show The Sno Cone Shack's social media ad

- Free small sno cone for any customer wearing a Sno Cone Shack tee shirt

- $2 discount for any customer wearing a M State University tee shirt

Advertising

The Sno Cone Shack will advertise through:

- Social Media

- Fliers

- The University Newspaper

- Tee shirts

FINANCIAL ANALYSIS

Start-up costs

Estimated start-up costs

Building construction	$20,000
Ice machine	$ 3,500
Fountain drink system	$ 1,000
Supplies/flavors	$ 6,000
Picnic tables	$ 1,000
Business license	$ 500
Initial advertising/grand opening	$ 500
Tee shirts	$ 500
Mobile sno cone machine	$ 2,500
Total	**$35,500**

Estimated Monthly Income

Conservative estimates reveal that Mr. Callahan will sell at least 100 regular priced sno cones, 100 discounted sno cones, and 50 fountain drinks per day. If all of the products sold were small sizes, Mr. Callahan can expect an income of $4,550 per week or $18,200 per month.

Product prices

Sno cone—small	$ 4
Sno cone—medium	$ 5
Sno cone—large	$ 6
Fountain drink—small	$ 1
Fountain drink—medium	$ 2
Fountain drink—large	$ 3
Tee shirts (all sizes)	$15

Estimated monthly expenses

Rent (includes water and electricity)	$ 800
Bank loan	$2,000
Fountain drink machine rental	$ 200
Insurance	$ 100
Phone/Internet	$ 100
Advertising	$ 100
Supplies	$ 500
Wages for employees ($8/hour)	$2,656
Wages for Mr. Jackson ($12/hour)	$1,920
Total	**$8,376**

Profit/Loss

Mr. Callahan takes a conservative approach and estimates $9,800 profit each month for the first six months. Monthly expenses are expected to remain constant during months of operation. Mr. Callahan plans to pay himself a salary during the off-season and will also be responsible for paying rent and the bank loan during this time.

Estimated profit/loss months 1–6

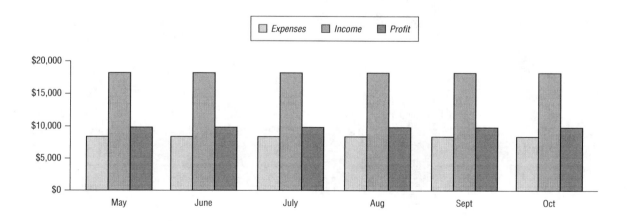

Estimated profit/loss months 7–12

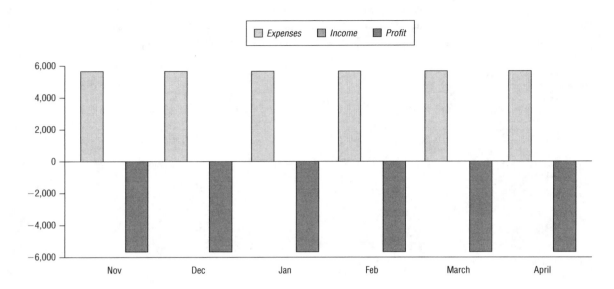

Estimated profits year 1

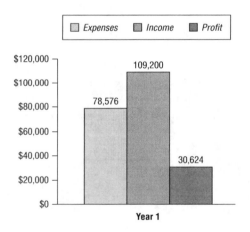

Financing

Mr. Callahan would like secure a business line of credit for the amount needed to cover the start-up costs and the first month's operating expenses. This loan would be in the amount of $43,876. Mr. Callahan plans to repay the line of credit after two years of operation.

Repayment plan

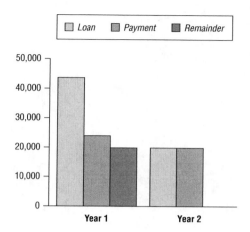

Senior Advocate Business

Stephen Fielding & Associates LLC

27 Piedmont St.
Maryvale, NC 28500

Paul Greenland

Stephen Fielding & Associates LLC is a new provider of advocacy services for senior citizens that specializes in health, housing, transportation, and finance.

EXECUTIVE SUMMARY

Based in Maryvale, North Carolina, Stephen Fielding & Associates LLC is a new provider of advocacy services for senior citizens that specializes in health, housing, transportation, and finance. In addition to advocating directly on behalf of a limited number of clients, the practice mainly focuses on aging-related planning and self-advocacy promotion for older adults and their children. In addition, Stephen Fielding & Associates produces self-advocacy training videos, which are available on DVD and online.

The business has been established by Stephen Fielding, a former project manager with Twin Way Logistics who was inspired to become a senior advocate following a personal experience with his own aging parents. Fielding used his skills as a project manager to help his parents address health concerns and navigate a series of other major life challenges and changes. He is joined in the practice by his wife, Mary, a worker's compensations nurse who initially will work for Stephen Fielding & Associates on a part-time basis.

MARKET ANALYSIS

National & State Outlook

According to *The State of Aging and Health in America 2013*, a report developed by the Centers for Disease Control and Prevention, U.S. Department of Health and Human Services, the population of older adults in the United States is experiencing unprecedented growth. Key drivers for this growth include the aging baby boomer population, as well as longer life spans in general.

Based on data from the U.S. Census Bureau, the number of individuals over the age of 65 totaled 40.2 million in 2010 (13% of the population). This figure is projected to reach 54.8 million (16.1%) by 2020 and 72.1 million (19.3%) by 2030. In North Carolina, specifically, adults over age 65 accounted for 12.4 percent of the population in 2010. Consistent with national trends, this figure is projected to increase, reaching 13.7 percent by 2015, 15.1 percent by 2020, 16.6 percent by 2025, and 17.8 percent by 2030.

Local Outlook

The population of Maryvale, North Carolina, included 99,599 people in 2014. Individuals over the age of 55 accounted for 34.3 percent of the population (much higher than the national average of 25.4 percent). By 2019 the population is projected to reach 132,712, at which time individuals over 55 will account for 34.5 percent of the population (compared to 27.3 percent nationally).

Beyond Maryvale, significant senior populations also exist in the nearby communities of Stackridge, Millville, Petersburg, and Rochelle Hills, offering opportunities for growth beyond the business' initial primary market.

SERVICES

In addition to advocating directly on behalf of a limited number of clients, Stephen Fielding & Associates mainly focuses on aging-related planning and self-advocacy promotion for older adults and their children.

Advocacy Services ($65/hour)

Stephen Fielding & Associates will work directly with a limited number of clients, providing direct advocacy services on their behalf. The business will limit this service mainly to senior citizens whose adult children do not live nearby, or who do not have an adequate level of family support. In this capacity, Stephen Fielding will serve as an advisor to older adults and a liaison with healthcare providers, social service agencies, and family members.

After conducting a life quality assessment (see Aging-Related Planning below) that considers the client's status in regard to health, housing, transportation, and finance, Fielding will offer recommendations in key areas where support or improvement is needed. In addition, he will attend related appointments with clients when desired, helping them to navigate the healthcare system, work through billing/insurance issues, arrange services, or obtain other resources.

When desired, Fielding will offer video chat/conferencing services to facilitate communications with his clients and their adult children or family members who live out of town.

This service is limited to a 30-mile radius around Maryvale.

Aging-Related Planning ($850)

Many older adults are frustrated with life situations pertaining to their health, housing arrangements, transportation options, or finances. Aging-related planning is a key service offered by Stephen Fielding & Associates in which a life quality assessment is conducted to determine how well a client is doing in significant life categories.

Fielding has developed specific benchmarks related to key areas listed in *The National Report Card on Healthy Aging*. He will use these to assess his clients' status and offer specific recommendations for improvement in the form of a written plan that families can follow independently. Fielding's report, based on paper- and computer-based assessment tools, record reviews, and client interviews, will concentrate on the following categories:

- Physical Health Status

- Mental Health Status

- Oral Health Status (assessed because poor oral health may impact food choices, social options, nutrition, and ultimately overall physical health)

- Financial Status/Resource Access

- Mobility/Transportation Access

- Housing Arrangements
- Disability (physical/mental/emotional impairments that require accommodations)
- Physical Activity Level
- Diet & Nutrition
- Obesity
- Smoking Status & History
- Vaccinations (flu, pneumonia, shingles)
- Prevention (e.g., annual physicals, screenings for breast/prostate/colon cancers)
- Fall Risk (preventing unnecessary injury and death)

As with individual advocacy services, during the planning process Fielding will offer video chat/conferencing services to facilitate communications with his clients and their adult children or family members who live out of town.

Self-Advocacy Promotion

Stephen Fielding & Associates also offers self-advocacy training for older adults and their families. In this regard, Fielding has developed presentations and training materials that offer helpful tips and guidelines families can use to navigate a variety of life challenges. One example is a Senior Finances 101 seminar, developed in partnership with a financial planner. The seminar not only covers topics such as budgeting and investments, but also security-related topics to help seniors avoid becoming victims of fraud. Other seminars include Aging in Place (e.g., modifying homes and apartments for senior living), Exercise & Nutrition, and Communicating with Healthcare Providers.

In some cases, organizations or groups will sponsor a seminar, while in other cases Stephen Fielding & Associates will charge an individual registration fee. These will vary based on the size and scope of the seminar. In addition to offering live seminars in a 100-mile radius around Maryvale, Fielding also will develop a series of DVDs and online videos, along with accompanying printed resources, and make them available for purchase. DVDs will retail for $19.95, and online videos for $14.95.

MARKETING & SALES

Stephen Fielding & Associates has developed a marketing strategy that includes the following tactics:

- A four-color, bi-fold brochure describing the business and services offered.

- Relationship building with area retirement communities and senior apartment facilities. In particular, special emphasis will be placed on Maryvale Center, Rosewood Tower, Greenview Terrace, Timberline Estates, Ridgewood High Point, and Parkview Plaza. These retirement communities and apartment complexes are home to nearly 875 senior citizen residents.

- A regular schedule of presentations to retirement groups, churches, and service clubs throughout the Maryvale region.

- Word-of-mouth marketing to drive referrals and grow the business. Stephen Fielding will give existing customers a $15 gift certificate to a local family restaurant for all referrals made to families and friends. In addition, a 15% discount will be provided to the new customer.

- A media relations strategy that involves guest appearances/columns focused on advocacy-related topics of interest to seniors and their families. Efforts initially will center on a popular AM radio station in Maryvale, which many senior citizens listen to. Additionally, Fielding will submit occasional articles to

The Maryvale Senior Times, a publication serving older readers in the market, and also online and regional publications.

- A Web site with complete details about our business and the services offered, as well as a related search engine optimization (SEO) strategy to stay visible with those seeking senior advocacy-related services.

- A presence on Facebook and LinkedIn, in order to connect with the adult children of senior citizens.

- Promotional premiums, such as back scratchers, pens, notepads, and refrigerator magnets, which can be distributed during presentations and also left behind with customers.

- A listing in the Maryvale Yellow Pages.

This marketing plan will be reviewed annually.

PERSONNEL

Stephen Fielding is a lifelong resident of Maryvale, North Carolina. Prior to establishing his own senior advocacy business, Fielding worked in the field of project management for several large companies, including Twin Way Logistics. In that capacity, he was responsible for developing and managing plans ranging from the simplest projects to large-scale corporate initiatives, overseeing factors such as project scope, costs, and objectives.

As a project manager, Fielding honed a number of skills that translate well to his role as a senior advocate, such as facilitating meetings, issue and risk management, status reporting, schedule management, documentation, task management, conflict management, and resource allocation. In particular, he skillfully worked with a wide range of project contributors, providing the strong leadership needed to move team members toward a common goal. What's more, Fielding applied these same skills to multiple projects, managing them simultaneously in a fast-paced, deadline-driven environment.

Although Fielding is not a financial specialist, he has strong analytical skills and a solid understanding of financial principles, modeling/forecasting, and technology. He earned an undergraduate business administration degree from the University of North Carolina.

Several unique circumstances preceded the formation of Stephen Fielding & Associates. In 2011 Fielding lost his job when Twin Way Logistics was acquired by one of its competitors. At the same time, his aging parents began experiencing serious health problems. As an only child, Fielding had no choice but to help his parents navigate the challenges they were facing. In addition to health concerns, these also extended to areas such as housing, transportation, and finances. With assistance from his wife, Mary, a registered nurse, Fielding was able to significantly improve his parents' quality of life by helping them through several major transitions.

Unable to find work as a full-time project manager in Maryvale, and unable to leave the local market due to his parents' needs, Fielding began working as an independent project management consultant. However, he found the advocacy and planning experience with his parents to be very meaningful. This, coupled with a rapidly aging population and strong demand for advocacy services, led to the formation of Stephen Fielding & Associates. Fielding is joined in the business by his wife, Mary, on a part-time basis, who has decided to reduce her hours as a worker's compensation nurse and ultimately transition to employment with Stephen Fielding & Associates on a full-time basis.

GROWTH STRATEGY

Year One: Focus on establishing Stephen Fielding & Associates as a trusted source of senior advocacy services and information. Secure a $25,000 business loan, with a term of 36 months at 6% interest. Achieve gross revenues of $86,461.

Year Two: Achieve gross revenues of $151,535. Welcome Mary Fielding as a full-time employee, providing the additional capacity needed to take on new business.

Year Three: Achieve gross revenues of $181,028. Break even during the early part of the year, ending 2017 with accumulated net profits of $46,658 that can be used as capital to scale up video production/DVD duplication in year four.

During Stephen Fielding & Associates' first year of operations, the business anticipates that revenues will break down by category as follows:

	2015	2016	2017
Planning (plans)	25	50	75
Advocacy (hours)	520	780	1,040
Seminars	24	36	48
DVD sales (units)	600	1,200	2,400
Online video sales (units)	900	1,500	2,700

OPERATIONS

Stephen Fielding & Associates will operate from a home office to keep overhead low. As the business grows, Fielding will consider establishing separate physical operations. However, he anticipates that the majority of his interaction with clients will occur either via phone, video chat, or (in the case of direct advocacy services) in the offices of local healthcare providers or agencies.

Fielding will equip his home office with broadband Internet service and will purchase a smart phone for business use. He will utilize a free software application, which comes with a corresponding mobile application, for tracking billable hours when providing direct advocacy services. Fielding also will purchase a laptop computer and a mobile hotspot, which will allow him to provide videoconferencing services in any location throughout Maryvale.

To keep expenses low, Fielding worked with students in a video production class at Maryvale Community College to produce videos of his advocacy-related seminars. He then posted the files on the Stephen Fielding & Associates Web site and made them available for sale with technical assistance from a local Web developer. Finally, Fielding is utilizing Maryvale Video Specialists to reproduce copies of his seminars on DVD, complete with plastic sleeves. Corresponding printed materials are being produced at a local printer that offers a digital press, enabling Fielding to take advantage of smaller print runs so that significant inventory investments are not needed.

LEGAL

Stephen Fielding & Associates complies with the Health Insurance Portability & Accountability Act of 1996 (HIPAA), a public law passed by Congress that protects the privacy of health information. The business signs legal agreements with clients, obligating it to maintain strict confidentiality standards. In addition, the business will sign all appropriate medical release forms to healthcare providers and other professionals when it is necessary to obtain medical records on behalf of clients. Finally, Stephen Fielding & Associates has secured an appropriate level of business and malpractice coverage, based upon the recommendations of a local business attorney.

FINANCIAL ANALYSIS

During its first year of operations, Stephen Fielding & Associates anticipates gross revenues will break down by category as follows:

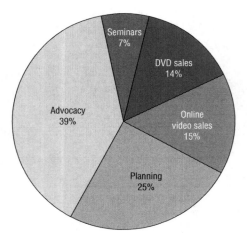

The business has prepared a complete set of pro forma financial statements, which are available upon request. The following table provides an overview of key projections for years one through three:

Revenue	2015	2016	2017
Planning	$ 21,250	$ 42,500	$ 63,750
Advocacy	$ 33,800	$ 50,700	$ 67,600
Seminars	$ 5,986	$ 11,970	$ 17,956
Dvd sales	$ 11,970	$ 23,940	$ 47,880
Online video sales	$ 13,455	$ 22,425	$ 40,365
Total revenue	**$ 86,461**	**$151,535**	**$237,551**
Expenses			
Salaries	$ 55,000	$ 80,000	$100,000
Business loan	$ 9,127	$ 9,127	$ 9,127
Payroll taxes	$ 8,250	$ 12,000	$ 15,000
Insurance	$ 6,500	$ 7,000	$ 7,500
Office supplies	$ 1,150	$ 1,475	$ 1,725
Video production	$ 3,500	$ 7,000	$ 15,000
Dvd duplication	$ 2,394	$ 4,788	$ 9,576
Equipment	$ 3,500	$ 1,500	$ 1,500
Marketing & advertising	$ 8,500	$ 10,000	$ 10,000
Telecommunications & internet	$ 2,250	$ 2,500	$ 3,000
Professional development	$ 1,500	$ 2,000	$ 2,500
Travel & entertainment	$ 3,000	$ 3,500	$ 4,500
Subscriptions & dues	$ 250	$ 300	$ 350
Permits & fees	$ 750	$ 1,000	$ 1,250
Total expenses	**$105,670**	**$142,190**	**$181,028**
Net income	**($ 19,210)**	**$ 9,345**	**$ 56,523**

Tree Care and Trimming Business
Placer Tree Care, Inc.

1130 Melody Avenue
Roseville, CA 95661

Claire Moore

Placer Tree Care, Inc. (PTCI) offers a variety of tree care services to residential and commercial customers in Sacramento, Placer, Sutter and El Dorado counties. A major factor in planned growth of the business is the use of software to map, analyze and create plans for long-term tree care services.

EXECUTIVE SUMMARY

Placer Tree Care, Inc. (PTCI) located at 1130 Melody Avenue in Roseville, California has been in operation since April 5, 2014. PTCI offers a variety of tree care services to residential and commercial customers in Sacramento, Placer, Sutter and El Dorado counties. A major factor in planned growth of the business is the use of software to map, analyze and create plans for long-term tree care services.

Mission

Placer Tree Care's mission is to provide superior arborist services to its clientele through education and tree care. We believe that our customers benefit from an understanding of how trees function and grow. With this understanding our clientele will be able to choose those services that are most appropriate for the needs of their trees.

Objectives

The objectives for the next three years of operation include:

- To expand service contracts with current clientele to build a base of regular, repeat business
- To develop additional contracts with commercial customers
- To increase gross sales by at least 10% per year
- To achieve a reputation for superior service above the usual trim, cut and removal services

Keys to Success

The keys to success for PTCI are:

- Prompt response to customer inquiries
- Staff comprised of ISA certified members
- Commitment to providing an outdoor space that is safe and visually appealing
- Continuous improvement through staff education and training

- Availability to customers through phone, email and social media

- Use of computer and Internet to map sites and create a long-term plan for tree maintenance

Operations

PCTI provides services six days a week. We provide free estimates for our services and upon request we will provide a Certified Arborist Report. Our services include: diagnosis, mapping and identification, tree planting, pruning and shaping, tree removal, power line and solar panel clearance.

Management

Placer Tree Care, Inc. is organized as a corporation in the state of California. It is owned and managed by Andrew Price, a certified arborist who earned his bachelor's degree in business in 2013. Corporate officers include Frank Langhorn, attorney at law, John Meyer, owner of Meyer's Landscaping, and Ashley Price who will serve as office manager and bookkeeper.

Marketing

PCTI will use its web site, social media and direct mail to reach its target market.

Financial

PCTI has been in operation since April 2014. Startup funding required was $57,065. The owners contributed $30,000 cash and obtained a bank loan for $30,000 to purchase the truck and chipper which serve as collateral for the loan.

COMPANY SUMMARY

PCTI will offer tree care services for residential and commercial customers in the Sacramento valley and Sierra foothills of Placer County.

While the Northern California counties of Sacramento, Placer, Sutter and El Dorado are home to numerous large farms and parcels, there are also millions of commercial locations and single family homes where trees are an important part of the landscape. Residents are proud of their trees and the State of California seeks to protect and preserve its many native species of trees such as Blue Oak, the California Buckeye and the Western Redbud.

Trees are not only beautiful, they add value to the landscape. Research conducted in 2010 by the Pacific Northwest (PNW) Research Station showed that street trees increased home prices in Portland, Oregon by as much as $8,870 and that shade trees in Sacramento, California reduced household energy use by an average of $25.16.

In a continuing effort to reduce energy usage during the hottest summer months, the Sacramento Municipal Utility District (SMUD) has given free shade trees to homeowners who agree to plant and care for them. Since 1990 the utility and its customers have planted nearly half a million trees. With the assistance of the nonprofit Sacramento Tree Foundation, the trees are delivered to the site and planted in a location that will maximize direct shading.

Because healthy trees and shrubs add value and contribute to a healthy environment, there will be a continuing need to choose, plant and maintain healthy trees in all landscapes.

Placer Tree Care, Inc. was established in April 2014 by Army veteran Andrew Price. After serving his country for five years, Price returned home in 2010 and completed his degree in business at California

State University, Sacramento. While maintaining a 3.5 grade point average in his studies, Price worked part-time for his uncle's tree and lawn care business.

Price found that his passion was tree care. Realizing that he had more to learn, Price studied and passed the ISA Certified Arborist exam in the fall of 2013. Using money that had been earned during his tenure in the Army, Price established Placer Tree Care, Inc. By the end of 2014 PCTI had grown to a staff of three certified tree workers, including Price and two assistant workers.

PTCI is located in Roseville, California between Sacramento and the Sierra foothills. Tree care services are offered to residents in Sacramento, Placer, El Dorado and Sutter counties. Areas that we serve include: Roseville, Rocklin, Citrus Heights, Antelope, Granite Bay, Sacramento, Orangevale, Fair Oaks, Loomis, Lincoln, Newcastle and Auburn.

Our staff includes members who have been certified by the International Society of Arboriculture (ISA). Services offered include: tree pruning, tree removal, cabling and bracing, tree fertilization, planting of trees and shrubs, tree disease diagnosis and treatment, and tree insect treatment. After tree removal is completed we can provide our customers stump grinding service as well.

Company Ownership

Placer Tree Care, Inc. is registered as corporation in the state of California under the same name. The corporate structure was chosen because it offers the benefits of liability protection for owners and should make the company more attractive for potential investors. There have been 500 shares of stock applied for and 200 shares issued to the sole shareholder and President Andrew Price at the time of incorporation.

Corporate Officers:

Andrew Price, President

Frank Langhorn, Vice President and Legal Counsel

John Meyer, Treasurer

Ashley Price, Secretary and bookkeeper

The officers of the company are charged with providing direction for the corporation. To that end regular board meetings will be held and minutes will be taken.

Strategy

The company's growth strategy is to establish long-term relationships with customers by offering to map, identify and create a plan for long-term care of the shrubs and trees in the landscape. Our primary focus will be on commercial accounts and residential customers who have more than five acres of land. Commercial establishments must maintain the health of trees and shrubs for reasons of cost savings as well as for liability protection. Residential customers who live on acreage are most likely to have a continuing need for tree care services.

Facility

The company currently leases storage and parking space with a large garage for the truck, chipper and equipment.

Start up Summary

Start up costs for PTCI include:

Office furniture	$ 750
Computer	$ 500
Software	$ 450
Tablet computer	$ 600
Printer/fax/Copier	$ 400
File cabinet	$ 50
Cell phone	$ 350
Truck 2000 GMC chip truck	$17,500
Chipper 2003 Woodsmen	$24,000
Chain saws various	$ 2,400
Ropes and gear	$ 1,650
Boots/apparel	$ 1,500
Misc equipment	$ 300
Chains, bars & files	$ 500
Hand saws & blades	$ 120
Pulleys, hooks, split tails, prusiks, carabiners	$ 200
Legal	$ 2,500
Accounting	$ 1,000
Stationery and business cards	$ 125
Brochures	$ 200
Logo design	$ 500
Insurance	$ 750
Web site development	$ 500
Licenses/fees	$ 220
Total startup costs	**$57,065**

MANAGEMENT AND PERSONNEL

Management

Currently, Andrew Price is the President and sole shareholder in PCTI. Andrew has four years experience working in the landscaping business and is a certified arborist. In 2013 Andrew earned his bachelor's degree in business from California State University, Sacramento. Andrew's managerial experience was gained during his service in the U.S. Army where he earned the rank of sergeant.

James Langhorn, vice president, is an attorney who specializes in business. Langhorn has been instrumental in creating the corporate structure for PCTI and ensuring compliance in corporate filing and tax matters. Langhorn is also responsible for review of customer contracts in order to minimize liability exposure.

John Meyer, treasurer, is also the owner of Meyer's Landscaping. Meyer is also Andrew Price's uncle. Meyer was Andrew's employer for four years and taught him the basics of landscaping and tree care. PCTI has been incorporated for nine months. During that time John Meyer has helped PCTI to acquire several contracts for tree maintenance. John Meyer continues to assist in the company's growth by providing the benefit of his 30 years of business experience in the Sacramento area and his numerous contacts.

Ashley Price is the office manager and bookkeeper for PCTI. She maintains the work schedule, handles customer inquiries, oversees marketing efforts and works with the freelance bookkeeper in keeping company records up to date.

PCTI also employs two certified arborists and two assistant landscape workers. As the business grows, more personnel will be hired.

Personnel plan

	Year 1	Year 2	Year 3
Manager	$ 40,000	$ 45,000	$ 52,000
Arborists	$ 72,000	$130,000	$170,000
Landscape workers	$ 42,000	$ 55,000	$ 65,000
Administrative	$ 36,000	$ 36,000	$ 42,000
Total people	**6**	**8**	**10**
Total payroll	**$190,000**	**$266,000**	**$329,000**

MARKET ANALYSIS SUMMARY

PTCI will target residential and commercial customers who wish to maintain and increase the safety, beauty and value of their properties. The greater Sacramento area is rich with trees and shrubs. Because of the mild Mediterranean-style climate the growing season extends for most of the year. However challenges present themselves in the form of hot, dry summers and wet, windy winters.

For this reason, even the heartiest species require regular monitoring and maintenance in order to maintain safety and health. Area residents appreciate the many virtues of healthy trees and shrubs and are willing to pay for expert care to maintain these green assets.

As an example of the ability of area residents to pay for expert tree care, the 2013 Placer County Economic and Demographic Profile explained that "in 2011, Placer County's median household income was around $71,000, the highest income among the counties within the Sacramento Region and much higher than California."

The year 2015 promises to see greater expansion in building of both commercial and residential properties as the effects of the 2008 recession fade away. Major projects that had been placed on hold have recently re-emerged into development. Two such projects broke ground in September 2012 due to strong leasing activity. Retail projects along the Interstate 80 and Sierra College Boulevard interchange in Rocklin opened in 2014. Major tenants included Walmart and Target. More retail shops are slated to open in 2015 in this location alone.

As for residential properties, Placer County offers a variety of housing types in various geographic areas: urban, suburban and rural. In addition to commonly found housing subdivisions and planned developments, Placer County offers the opportunity to live by rivers, lakes, streams, the foothills, and the Sierra Nevada Mountains. It is possible to find homes with significant acreage a short distance from major employment centers.

In all of these property types, trees and shrubs figure highly in the visual and economic value of the property. According to the Council of Tree and Landscape Appraisers, a mature tree can often have an appraised value of between $1,000 and $10,000.

Not only do trees add value to property, they contribute significant savings when it comes to heating and cooling the home. The USDA Forest Service estimates that trees properly placed around buildings can reduce air conditioning needs by 30 percent and can save 20 to 50 percent in energy used for heating.

In fact, Placer County Code, Article 12.16 specifically addresses tree preservation. According to the code, "It is acknowledged that the preservation of trees enhances the natural scenic beauty, improves air quality, water quality, reduces soil erosion, preserves significant natural heritage values, preserves wildlife habitat, and helps to reduce energy consumption for air cooling by providing shade. Trees in a community or neighborhood also provide a sense of identity and tradition, and they enhance property values which encourages higher quality development."

Our primary marketing focus will be on commercial accounts and residential customers who have more than five acres of land. Commercial establishments must maintain the health of trees and shrubs for reasons of cost savings as well as for liability protection. Residential customers who live on acreage are most likely to have a continuing need for tree care services.

Marketing strategies for PTCI will include the use of technologies ranging from flyers and brochures to digital marketing on social media and web sites. Centered in the city of Roseville in Placer County, PCTI's marketing efforts will extend to Sacramento, Yolo, El Dorado and Sutter counties.

Customer Profiles

The following descriptions of the types of customers and services that we intend to pursue are:

Residential customers: Many residences in the greater Sacramento area include homes located on acreage. For the average homeowner, the presence of multiple trees and shrubs presents a challenge regarding the upkeep of these green assets. Typical services that would be required include: pruning, removal, pest control, feeding, and planting. These services would likely be needed to one extent or another year-round. It is our intention to market our services to these customers by offering an initial free consultation where we would provide an explanation of the importance of an annual maintenance plan. The next step would be for the customer to order a site analysis and the creation of a long-term plan.

Corporate accounts: Residential communities such as the Dell Webb developments in Lincoln and Roseville have many common areas that require regular maintenance. While they will contract with a landscaping company for mowing, watering and weeding, they will need expert services when it comes to tree planting and maintenance. We will work with these and other communities to develop maintenance plans and provide long-term services.

Small business parks: Strip malls and small business parks will require periodic inspection and maintenance of trees. In the event of damage they will require immediate response to remove any dangerous debris. Because of liability exposure, we think that we will be able to develop contracts where we supply periodic inspection and maintenance with the proviso to provide emergency service as needed.

Competition

There are several tree care companies that service the same geographic area that is the target area for PCTI. Each offers similar services and is staffed by trained and certified personnel. In order to gain recognition among a field of qualified competitors it will be critical that PCTI build a brand identity that makes it stand out from the crowd.

We believe that the key factors in building our brand include:

- Creating a relationship with prospects: to this end we will respond promptly to every customer inquiry and ensure that their needs have been met even if it means that they are referred to a competitor.

- Providing value-added service: in addition to diagnosis and tree care we will offer customers a mapping of their property that includes tree identification and a long-term plan for tree care.

- Establishing our company as an expert in the care of trees: we will present informational seminars to the public on topics related to tree care and the benefits of trees. Our web site and Facebook page will include a calendar of events where we will be participating. These events include the annual home and garden show. Andrew Price is currently presenting a three-hour workshop on landscaping with trees for two adult schools in the greater Sacramento area.

The typical relationship between an arborist and a residential client is a one-time service initiated by the customer because of some need or event. After services are provided, it is rare that the customer will interact with the arborist again.

Our marketing plan is based on the commitment to create a relationship with customers that keeps us top-of-mind when tree-related needs arise. To this end we plan on maintaining regular contact with current and potential customers through print and digital means.

Our education efforts also include presenting customers with information on the importance of long-term, regular tree care. We also offer an affordable site analysis where we will create a written plan for regular tree care that is specific to their property.

As far as we can tell, very few of our competitors provide a service that includes mapping, identification and planning for continuing care. With the use of apps, computer software and GPS technology, we can gather information on site that can be used to create a comprehensive customized plan for each customer.

MARKETING PLAN

We will use both print and digital media to reach our intended clientele. These media will include:

- Web site

- Facebook page

- Sacramento County Certified Arborist List online

- Listing on the Arborist Search site of the ISA

- Listing on the Placer County Commerce site listing for Tree Services

Within the next year Andrew Price will qualify for membership in the American Society of Consulting Arborists (ASCA). At the time he will be listed in the ASCA referral directory where property owners and industry professionals can find Consulting Arborists. Membership in ASCA will also open new resources for education, collaboration and networking as well as the ability to compete for contracts with city and county agencies.

Andrew Price will continue to develop relationships with members of local organizations that are involved in the housing industry including:

- California Building Industry Association

- Placer County Association of Realtors

- Sacramento Association of Realtors

- Associated Builders and Contractors, Inc. Northern California Chapter

Andrew will present information at association meetings as a guest speaker where he will discuss issues related to tree health and its relationship to property values.

Direct mail is still an effective form of marketing. Bulk mailing allows the marketer to send information to a targeted group on a regular basis at an affordable cost. Because households need arborist services at various and unpredictable times, a regular mailing is important in order to maintain visibility with prospective and current customers.

A simple 8.5 x 11 flyer can be easily created and reproduced, folded and stamped with the bulk mail identification number. Because flyers are addressed to "resident" a specific database is not required. Mailings can be accomplished multiple times per year for a cost that much less than that of other venues.

PCTI will engage a regular mailing campaign by sending informational flyers to residences located in the geographic areas most likely to house profitable customers. With the help of list brokers, we will be able to identify target area zip codes to mail to by filtering for acreage size and for income levels.

Mailing list brokers can also assist PCTI in developing a direct marketing campaign aimed at real estate developers, commercial property owners, apartment building owners and property managers, among others.

FINANCIAL PROJECTIONS

Income statement

	Actual 2014	Projected 2015	Projected 2016	Projected 2017
Sales	$140,000	$301,000	$337,120	$370,832
Cost of sales				
Gross profit	$140,000	$301,000	$337,120	$370,832
Expenses				
Licenses & permits	$ 220	$ 200	$ 200	$ 200
Insurance: liability & business interruption	$ 2,500	$ 2,500	$ 2,500	$ 2,500
Insurance: commercial auto	$ 2,000	$ 3,600	$ 3,600	$ 3,600
Insurance: workman's compensation	$ 6,000	$ 12,000	$ 15,000	$ 20,000
Salaries: managerial	$ 20,000	$ 40,000	$ 45,000	$ 52,000
Salaries: administrative	$ 15,000	$ 28,000	$ 32,000	$ 32,000
Wages	$ 46,000	$128,000	$161,000	$166,000
Payroll taxes	$ 8,100	$ 19,600	$ 23,800	$ 25,000
Workers comp ins	$ 550	$ 850	$ 1,050	$ 1,200
Advertising	$ 2,700	$ 3,000	$ 3,500	$ 4,100
Accounting	$ 1,000	$ 2,400	$ 2,400	$ 2,400
Truck fuel	$ 4,000	$ 4,400	$ 5,000	$ 5,500
Truck repairs & maintenance	$ 1,520	$ 1,500	$ 1,500	$ 1,650
Truck storage	$ 1,400	$ 2,800	$ 2,800	$ 2,800
Supplies	$ 500	$ 300	$ 400	$ 500
Office supplies	$ 400	$ 350	$ 350	$ 350
Internet	$ 700	$ 700	$ 700	$ 700
Web site	$ 500	$ 360	$ 360	$ 360
Telephone	$ 900	$ 900	$ 900	$ 900
Auto and travel	$ 250	$ 300	$ 350	$ 400
Repairs & maintenance	$ 650	$ 750	$ 900	$ 800
Equipment rental	$ 2,400	$ 2,500	$ 2,500	$ 2,600
Depreciation	$ 11,824	$ 12,052	$ 8,296	$ 5,738
Total expenses	**$129,114**	**$267,062**	**$314,106**	**$331,298**
Interest expense	$ 1,523	$ 1,939	$ 1,494	$ 1,012
Profit before taxes	$ 9,363	$ 31,999	$ 21,520	$ 38,522
Taxes	$ 1,404	$ 4,800	$ 3,228	$ 5,778
Net income	**$ 7,959**	**$ 27,199**	**$ 18,292**	**$ 32,744**

Assumptions	12/31/2014	12/31/2015	12/31/2016	12/31/2017
Interest rate on loan	8.00%	8.00%	8.00%	8.00%
Tax rate	15%	15%	15%	15%
Growth in sales		15%	12%	10%

Balance sheet

Assets	12/31/2014	12/31/2015	12/31/2016	12/31/2017
Cash in bank	$28,009	$61,864	$ 82,608	$114,760
Other current assets				
Total current assets	**$28,009**	**$61,864**	**$ 82,608**	**$114,760**
Fixed assets				
Office furniture	$ 800	$ 800	$ 800	$ 800
Office equipment	$ 2,300	$ 2,300	$ 2,300	$ 2,300
Chipper	$24,000	$24,000	$ 24,000	$ 24,000
Truck	$17,500	$17,500	$ 17,500	$ 17,500
Misc equipment	$ 6,670	$ 6,670	$ 6,670	$ 6,670
Less: depreciation	($11,824)	($23,877)	($ 32,172)	($ 37,910)
Total assets	**$67,455**	**$89,257**	**$101,706**	**$128,120**
Liabilities				
Accounts payable	$ —	$ —	$ —	$ —
Current maturities loan	$ 5,396	$ 5,844	$ 6,329	$ 6,854
Total current liabilities	**$ 5,396**	**$ 5,844**	**$ 6,329**	**$ 6,854**
Long term liabilities loan	$20,830	$14,985	$ 8,656	$ 1,802
Total liabilities	**$26,226**	**$20,829**	**$ 14,985**	**$ 8,656**
Member investment	$33,270	$33,270	$ 33,270	$ 33,270
Retained earnings	$ 7,959	$35,158	$ 53,450	$ 86,193
Total owner's equity	**$41,229**	**$68,428**	**$ 86,720**	**$119,463**
Total liabilities & equity	**$67,455**	**$89,257**	**$101,705**	**$128,119**

Sources & uses of cash December 2014

December 2014	Total	Owner	Loan
Current assets			
Cash	$36,509	$36,509	
Total current	**$36,509**	**$36,509**	
Fixed assets			
Office furniture	$ 800	$ 800	
Office equipment	$ 2,300	$ 2,300	
Chipper	$24,000	$12,000	$12,000
Truck	$17,500		$17,500
Misc equipment	$ 6,670		
Total fixed	**$44,600**	**$15,100**	**$29,500**
Total assets	**$81,109**	**$51,609**	**$29,500**
Percent	100.0%	63.6%	36.4%

Cash flow

	2014	2015	2016	2017
Begin cash	12,000	28,009	61,864	82,608
Net profit after tax	7,959	27,199	18,292	32,744
Plus: depr	11,824	12,052	8,296	5,738
LT debt incr (decr)	(3,774)	(5,396)	(5,844)	(6,329)
End cash	28,009	61,864	82,608	114,760

Veterinary Practice

FOUR LEGGED FRIENDS CLINIC

900 Timkin Rd.
Arlington Heights, IL 60005

Gerald Rekve

Four Legged Friends Clinic (FLFC) is a new veterinary practice in Arlington Heights, Illinois. FLFC will be distinguished from other veterinary practices by its focus on farm animals and house pet issues as well as expertise in alternative treatments.

*This business plan appeared in a previous volume of **Business Plans Handbook**. It has been updated for this volume.*

EXECUTIVE SUMMARY

Four Legged Friends Clinic (FLFC) is a new veterinary practice in Arlington Heights, Illinois. FLFC will be distinguished from other veterinary practices by its focus on farm animals and house pet issues as well as expertise in alternative treatments.

It aims to be the first choice for farm animals and house pet owners in Arlington Heights that want the best for their farm animal or pet.

Veterinary care in the greater Chicago area is a $200 million market and it's growing. Positioned as a good choice for Arlington Heights farmers and pet owners, FLFC will offer owners care of older farm animals and house pets. These customers are likely to visit the veterinarian more than once a year and make veterinary care decisions based on quality rather than price. We will have promotional efforts set up to attract customers.

Company History

Born and raised in Arlington Heights, I studied veterinary science at Northwestern University. After my education I worked for the college for two years, and then went off to work at a large local veterinarian in Chicago. During this time I noticed a need for more veterinary clinics in Arlington Heights for several different reasons. Over the past five years, there has been about a 36 percent increase in the number of farm animals in a 60 mile radius of Arlington Heights. In addition to this increase, the population of Arlington Heights has increased by 2 percent, therefore increasing the amount of potential pet owners. The final reason is that the existing vet clinics cannot keep up with the business.

Growth Strategy

Four Legged Friends Clinic will be profitable by the end first of its year. By the end of its fourth year, it will likely grow to include another veterinarian. I am currently investing $50,000 in start–up funding to supplement my father's $25,000 investment in the business. These additional funds will primarily be used to buy veterinary equipment.

Management Summary

Patricia Pugh: After working with a successful veterinary practice in Chicago, I decided to return to my hometown of Arlington Heights to establish a veterinary practice to serve both the region's farm animals and house pets.

OBJECTIVES

Personal Objectives

- Re–establish myself in my hometown of Arlington Heights.

- Undertake the challenge of creating a profitable and respected practice.

- Achieve balance between my work and personal life as I hope to have children in the next few years.

- Earn sufficient income to pay off my personal debt within two years.

Company's Short–Term Objectives

- Obtain start–up financing of $200,000 by July 2015.

- Secure office and kennel space by September 2015.

- Hire a technician and an assistant by October 2015.

- Open for business by October 2015.

- Volunteer with the local zoo in order to make contacts.

- Talk with the local newspaper to see if they would print a weekly pets column that I write.

- Offer a pets tips series for the local radio station to play.

- Have 200 active patients by the end of the first year of operations.

- Be profitable by the end of the first year of operations.

Company's Long–Term Objectives

- Have 500 active patients by the end of the second year of operations.

- Have 700 active patients by the end of the third year of operations.

- Hire a second veterinarian by the end of the fourth year of operations.

Mission

Offer the best service as well as both conventional and non–traditional veterinary services in a way that stresses compassion and quality–of–life for farm animals, pets, and their owners.

SERVICES

General treatment for pets and farm animals, preventative vaccination, diagnosis, treatment, surgery and kennel facilities for domestic pets. The kennel portion of our business will be larger than traditional veterinarian offices. We will have a year round service open 7 days a week. This will allow for clients to drop off their pets for either a day or a week. We feel this kennel will add extra revenue to our office and allow for clients to become comfortable with us while we build long-term clients.

By focusing on farm animals and house pets, the Four Legged Friends Clinic will offer a variety of expertise, experience, and high–quality operations unmatched by other traditional veterinary clinics located in Arlington Heights. Also, no other area veterinarian has the well-rounded training that we will offer to our clients.

MARKET ANALYSIS

Demographic Factors and Trends

- The dog pet population is in a slow down over the past few years; this, however, is being offset by higher growth in the number of farm animals and other household pets.

- Baby Boomers are getting older and tend to have more disposable income to spend on their pets, therefore we will see more visits by boomer clients with money to spend.

- According to the Arlington Heights Economic Department, Arlington Heights has been the third fastest growing city in Illinois since 2010 and Arlington Heights has now over 76,000 residents.

Social Factors and Trends

- Pet owners are embracing veterinary service like preventative dental care.

- The city recently passed a bylaw stating all cats must be neutered and licensed. This has greatly increased the amount of cat neutering that is required.

Such products and services will be offered if interest continues to increase.

Economic Factors and Trends

- The current economic market has positively affected the market for essential veterinary services.

- The market for "non–traditional" veterinary products and services may grow even more quickly as the economy continues to grow.

- The Arlington Heights economy continues to grow.

Technological Factors and Trends

- New veterinary technologies are constantly emerging. For instance, using laser therapy to treat tissue disorders in small animals is gaining acceptance. As technologies continue to be designed, I anticipate upgrading my practice's equipment and skills.

- Many veterinarians are using practice management software to help run their businesses. We will want to invest in this specialized software.

Regulatory Factors and Trends

- Veterinarians must study for at least two years at a university and then graduate from a 4–year program at an accredited college of veterinary medicine. To qualify for a state license, veterinarians must pass the North American Veterinary Licensing Exam.

- According to the American Veterinary Medical Association, American veterinary colleges only graduate 2,900 new veterinarians each year and there are shortages of veterinarians in most rural communities.

Environmental Factors and Trends

- Veterinary medicine involves handling chemicals that could potentially harm humans. Special steps must be taken in the administration, storage, and disposal of medicines, vaccine needles, and blood samples, resulting in additional costs.

- With the spread of West Nile and similar viruses, veterinarians today must adhere to strict guidelines for reporting any infection that is listed in the federal government database. These controls are in place for the betterment of humans as well as protection for the animals.

The Arlington Heights population and the Baby Boomers' disposable income are causing an increase in the amount of money spent on pet care in Arlington Heights that will probably continue to increase in the coming years. At this time, the number of veterinarians remains restricted by the number of veterinary colleges. As a result, the demand may exceed the supply, and practicing veterinarians will likely enjoy a steady rise in business. Specialty treatments like preventative dental care will become more popular and will represent significant sources of income for veterinarians.

Arlington Heights, Illinois Demographic Profile 2013

[Primary trade area]

July 1, 2013 population (primary)	75,994
% change 2010–2013	3.6%
Average annual growth rate	1.2%
Median household income	$77,195
Retail sales	42% above national avg.
Per capita income	$40,189
Private households	29,798
Family size	2.5

Market Size

According to the Humane Society of the United States, 62 percent of American households have at least one pet. Based on the most recent American census data, this suggests that about 47,000 pet owners live in the greater Arlington Heights area. The average pet owner spends about $142 per year on pet health care. As a result, the market for veterinary services in the Arlington Heights area is estimated to be over $6 million.

Competition

Goodland Animal Clinic:

- Strengths: Large staff (at least 12 full–time veterinarians); strong relationships with area kennels

- Weaknesses: Aging equipment and higher-than-average pricing

Arlington Heights Pet Palace:

- Strength: Reasonable prices

- Weaknesses: Young staff; small, crowded kennel facility

Lakefront Vet Clinic:

- Strength: In business in Arlington Heights since 1947

- Weaknesses: Limited parking; expensive vaccines

Windy City Clinic:

- Strengths: Excellent reputation for dog–specific care; services include preventative dental care; also sells dog food and other products

- Weaknesses: Higher-than-average pricing

CUSTOMERS

At FLFC, my primary target customers are farm animals and house pet owners, specifically owners of older farm animals and house pets. Owners of older farm animals and house pets tend to:

- Visit the veterinarian more than once a year, due to the age of their pet.

- Make veterinary care decisions based on quality of care, rather than on price.

- Encounter more pet health problems that can be treated using alternative methods in conjunction with conventional treatment.

These customers will choose FLFC because as their farm animals and house pets' age, my clinic can offer an unparalleled range of animal–focused expertise in treating both the common and rare ailments that afflict farm animals and house pets.

Sales & Market Position

FLFC Client Benefits

- The sense of community and the comfort that comes with using a veterinarian that specializes in treating the species they love.

- The exclusivity that comes with knowing that their pet is being cared for by the only veterinarian in the area with alternative pet care expertise.

- The security that comes with knowing that everything is being done to prolong and improve the quality of their pets' lives.

BUSINESS STRATEGY

Customers will be required to pay immediately by cash, check, debit card, VISA or MasterCard.

Except in the case of checkups, farm animals and house pet owners will receive follow–up calls from my assistant within 24 hours after their appointment to check on their pet's well–being. Premises permitting, kennel facilities will also be offered. Existing customers will be able to leave healthy pets in the overnight facility for a small fee.

As the Veterinarian and owner of FLFC, I will be responsible for running the business and providing veterinary care to customers' pets.

Advertising

Planned promotional efforts are in keeping with the American Veterinary Medical Association Advertising Guidelines.

- A free workshop for farm animals and house pets owners in "Feline Health and Happiness" to be conducted at a busy local bookstore, Professor's Books, several weeks before the opening of the practice. Attendees' names will be collected, and I will send them an announcement of the practice's opening.

- A listing in the Yellow Pages as well as online search engines and directories.

- Meetings with area veterinarians to build relationships and channels for referrals.

- An article about the practice in the Lifestyles section of Arlington Heights' local newspaper.

- Social media accounts with contact information, pricing, and educational tidbits.

- Birthday cards sent to customers' pets.

New clients will either be referred by other veterinarians and pet businesses, or they will choose my practice based on promotional efforts. All services will be rendered in FLFC offices.

Alliances

Our business and strategic alliances include:

- Grooming Gods, a high–end grooming company

- Arlington Animal Hospital, which has agreed to help offer me 2–hour on–call veterinary service clinic, will be the only "Approved Referral"

When I'm away from my practice for short periods of time, Dr. Alfred Benito at the Arlington Animal Hospital has agreed to care for my patients.

Operations

1. *Premises:* I am looking to buy a free–standing building close to major streets in a residential neighborhood that is appropriately zoned and can be easily converted into a veterinary practice and kennel space. To maximize exposure to the under–served community, I am specifically looking in neighborhoods. Cost: $1,500–$ 2,500 per month, paid for initially from the equity investment I've made from the business.

2. *Renovation of space:* I expect I will have to convert the premises into a more suitable veterinary practice. Cost: Approximately $25,000, including furniture.

3. *Veterinary start–up package:* I will order this package from Animal Supplies Inc. It includes digital walk–on scale, treatment tub, hydraulic table, machine, feline spay pack, x–ray machine, film and supplies, a blood chemistry unit, used kennel cages, and other equipment. Cost: Approximately $73,000; financing is required.

4. *Computer hardware and software:* To manage the practice's front office, I intend to buy a computer from Computer Associates and management software from Veterinary PDM Inc. Cost: Approximately $2,000.

I am seeking $75,000 in bank loans to finance the purchase of veterinary equipment and computer hardware/software. The $75,000 in start-up equity will be used to cover rent, renovation of the space, furniture, and salaries until income cash flow is steady.

Risk Factors

I already have life and disability insurance and need to obtain critical illness insurance. My employees will be covered by workers' compensation insurance.

I have a will. While I don't have anybody in mind to take over my practice if I become unable to work, I have given my parents' contact information for competitors who would be potential buyers if something should happen to me.

If my supplier fails to deliver a shipment, suddenly raises its prices, or goes for business out-of-town, I have established a relationship with a back–up supplier of animal and house pets equipment in Chicago.

If I am unable to find a full–time assistant with practice experience, I will consider part–timers with only administrative experience.

If I need legal advice, I will retain the services of Robert Smith, a partner at the law firm of Smith and Smith Law Firm and one of the leading law firms in Arlington Heights. I will arrange a small line of credit or overdraft protection to cover any unforeseen expenses or to accommodate slow payment by a client.

Management Summary

Advisors

- Fred Brown, a chartered accountant
- Cindy Blum, Manager of a consulting firm

Administrative Assistant

- Responsibilities: Making appointments, ordering supplies, managing files, processing bills and payment, other clerical duties.
- Required experience: At least three years of employment at another veterinarian clinic or health care practice.
- Salary: $30,000
- Start date: October 2015

Veterinary Technician

- Responsibilities: Assisting with physical examinations, surgery, immunizations, extracting teeth, and caring for the farm animals and house pets.

- Required experience: A Veterinary Technician or Health Technician diploma from a nationally–recognized college, plus at least four years working with companion animals (preferably farm animals and house pets) at another veterinarian practice.

- Start date: October 2015

Through referrals, I already have leads on a number of qualified candidates for both positions.

I will also use the following methods to acquire potential employees:

- Place want ads in the Arlington Heights shopper

- Post listings at online job sites

- Contact employment agencies

Staff training will be ongoing.

By the end of my fourth year of operation, I expect to hire a second veterinarian to grow the clinic and give me more flexibility to be away from the clinic when necessary. The new hire's areas of expertise will depend upon the needs of the practice at that time, but I expect to pay them around $60,000 per year.

PRODUCTS & SERVICES

Services

In general, FLFC's prices for conventional diagnostics and treatment will be relatively high, in line with its exclusive positioning. Here are the clinic's intended prices for representative veterinary services.

For non–traditional treatments like acupuncture, FLFC will charge $65 per forty–minute session. Kennel services will cost $25 per night.

We will offer the following services in our clinic:

- Walk–in service

- Overnight care

- Seven days a week, 24 hours a day, call–in service

- Off–site service (the Vet will go to your farm)

- Routine animal care services

- Surgeries

- Neutering

- GPS Tagging for tracking animals

Veterinary On–Call Services

A veterinarian is on call 24 hours a day, 365 days a year (366 in a leap year) to provide veterinary services to all animals. The on-call service time will be shared and coordinated with other local veterinarians that are willing and able to participate. This service will better serve the community and provide all practitioners with the ability to take needed time off.

Drugs and Supplies

The veterinary practice will keep a small inventory of commonly used veterinary drugs and supplies. Drugs are only sold and used in strict compliance with all local, state, and federal regulations. Restricted drugs are only dispensed in small amounts. Accurate record keeping and suitable storage facilities are prerequisites.

Items are sold on a cost plus basis and are charged directly to the client.

FINANCIAL ANALYSIS

Throughout the first twelve months of business, FLFC will have a steady cash flow.

In its first year of business, FLFC is projected to do $377,000 in sales, with $54,000 profit.

Start-up requirements

Start-up expenses

Legal	$ 3,000
Stationery, etc.	$ 2,000
Brochures	$ 1,500
Consultants	$ 3,500
Insurance	$ 5,000
Rent	$ 12,000
Equipment	$ 73,000
Other	$ 50,000
Total start-up expenses	**$150,000**

Start-up assets needed

Cash balance on starting date	$ 75,000
Other current assets	$ 0
Total current assets	**$ 75,000**

Funding

Investment	$ 0
Current liabilities	$ 0
Accounts payable	$ 0
Current borrowing	$ 0
Other current liabilities	$ 0
Current liabilities	$ 0
Long-term liabilities	$ 75,000
Total liabilities	**$ 75,000**

Market analysis

Potential customers	Growth	2015	2016	2017	2018	2019	CAGR
Commercial 5%	12,000	14,500	15,000	17,000	19,005	5.00%	
Residential 5%	160,000	170,500	180,000	190,000	199,500	5.00%	

Video Game Studio

VideoGirl

6512 W. Elm St.
Staten Island, NY 10301

BizPlanDB.com

The purpose of this business plan is to raise $150,000 for the development of a video game development company that will sell applications specific for desktop/laptops, Apple tablet/phone devices, and Android devices. VideoGirl, Inc. is a New York-based corporation that will generate revenues through the sale of games via app stores (Google Play and Apple iTunes) and through the Company's website (for desktop/laptop based games). As the business expands, the Company may develop large-scale games that can be played on popular consoles including Xbox and Playstation.

1.0 EXECUTIVE SUMMARY

The purpose of this business plan is to raise $150,000 for the development of a video game development company that will sell applications specific for desktop/laptops, Apple tablet/phone devices, and Android devices. This business plan will also showcase the expected financials and operations over the next three years. VideoGirl, Inc. is a New York-based corporation that will generate revenues through the sale of games via app stores (Google Play and Apple iTunes) and through the Company's website (for desktop/laptop based games). As the business expands, the Company may develop large-scale games that can be played on popular consoles including Xbox and Playstation.

The Company was founded by Olivia Peacrey.

1.1 The Applications

The primary revenue center for the business will come from the ongoing development of games for the desktops/laptops (Apple and PC), iPad, iPhone, Android, and Windows-based devices that will be sold through app stores and through the Company's website.

The business will also generate revenues from developing gaming applications on an outsourced basis on behalf of third parties.

The third section of the business plan will further discuss the operations of VideoGirl, Inc.

1.2 Financing

Ms. Peacrey is seeking to raise $150,000 from a bank loan. The interest rate and loan agreement are to be further discussed during negotiation. This business plan assumes that the business will receive a 10-year loan with a 9% fixed interest rate. The financing will be used for the following:

- Development of the Company's gaming development platform.

- Financing for the first six months of operation.

- Capital to purchase servers, computers, and related technology.

Ms. Peacrey will contribute $25,000 to the venture.

1.3 Mission Statement

VideoGirl's mission is to develop high-quality games for consumer electronic devices.

1.4 Management Team

The Company was founded by Olivia Peacrey. Ms. Peacrey has more than nine years of experience in the software programming industry. Through her expertise, she will be able to bring the operations of the business to profitability within its first year of operations.

1.5 Sales Forecasts

Ms. Peacrey expects a strong rate of growth at the start of operations. Below are the expected financials over the next three years.

Proforma profit and loss (yearly)

Year	1	2	3
Sales	$990,450	$1,436,153	$1,938,806
Operating costs	$429,373	$ 480,774	$ 536,571
EBITDA	$462,033	$ 811,763	$1,208,354
Taxes, interest, and depreciation	$197,607	$ 324,961	$ 475,048
Net profit	$264,425	$ 486,802	$ 733,305

Sales, operating costs, and profit forecast

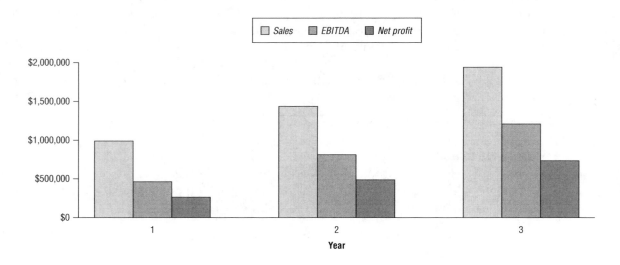

1.6 Expansion Plan

The Founder expects that the business will aggressively expand during the first three years of operation. Ms. Peacrey intends to implement marketing campaigns that will effectively target individuals that are interested in video games. Additionally, once the business develops and distributes its initial games, the Company may expand into developing video games for Playstation and Xbox.

2.0 COMPANY AND FINANCING SUMMARY

2.1 Registered Name and Corporate Structure

VideoGirl, Inc. is registered as a corporation in the State of New York.

2.2 Required Funds

At this time, VideoGirl requires $150,000 of debt funds. Below is a breakdown of how these funds will be used:

Projected startup costs

Initial lease payments and deposits	$ 15,000
Working capital	$ 25,000
FF&E	$ 30,000
Website development	$ 42,500
Security deposits	$ 5,000
Insurance	$ 2,500
Servers and technology equipment	$ 25,000
Marketing budget	$ 25,000
Miscellaneous and unforeseen costs	$ 5,000
Total startup costs	**$175,000**

Use of funds

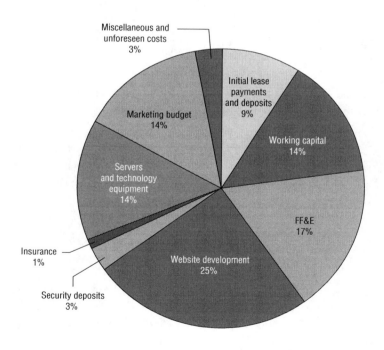

2.3 Investor Equity

Ms. Peacrey is not seeking an investment from a third party at this time.

2.4 Management Equity

Olivia Peacrey owns 100% of VideoGirl, Inc.

2.5 Exit Strategy

If the business is very successful, Ms. Peacrey may seek to sell the business to a third party for a significant earnings multiple. Most likely, the Company will hire a qualified business broker to sell the business on behalf of VideoGirl. Based on historical numbers, the business could fetch a sales premium of up to 10 times earnings.

3.0 PRODUCTS AND SERVICES

Below is a description of the services offered by VideoGirl, Inc.

3.1 Game Development and Distribution

As stated in the executive summary, the business intends to develop a large library of produced video games that will be primarily used on desktops, laptops, Apple devices, Android devices, and Windows Mobile devices. The business will initially focus on simple games that will be in demand within application stores including Google Play and Apple iTunes. As time progresses and the business expands, the Company will acquire licenses from Microsoft and Sony in order to produce large-scale games for Xbox and Playstation.

The business will generate a substantial amount of secondary revenues from the ongoing third party programming and development of Android, Windows, iPhone, iPod, and iPad applications. The business will not earn ongoing royalties from the ongoing sale of these video games as they will be built to customer specifications. This is an important way for the business to earn large-scale revenues.

4.0 STRATEGIC AND MARKET ANALYSIS

4.1 Economic Outlook

This section of the analysis will detail the economic climate, the software development industry, the customer profile, and the competition that the business will face as it progresses through its business operations.

Currently, the economic market condition in the United States is moderate. Unemployment rates have declined while asset prices have risen substantially. However, the pricing point of the Company's video games and related applications are low. As such, VideoGirl will be profitable and cash flow positive at all times.

4.2 Industry Analysis

Below is an overview of the industries that VideoGirl will operate within:

Video Game Sales

Analysts from Forrester Research show that the video game industry has surpassed the growth rate of the film industry. According to market research firm NPD Group, 2013 sales of video game hardware, software and accessories in the U.S. were $12.5 billion, the industry's highest-ever returns. 2014 end-of-year revenues are expected to increase by 20% over the previous year.

This is a mature industry, and the future expected growth rate is expected to equal that of the general economy.

E-Commerce Transactions

Online retailers are expected to generate $350 billion dollars this year. The United States Economic Census indicates that over the next five years, 60% of the businesses in the United States will have an internet presence. In early 2013, industry reports estimate that 210 million people will have access to the internet with approximately 65% of these people having direct high-speed internet access within the United States. Management expects that the e-commerce industry will grow steadily as more people obtain high-speed internet access. By 2014, e-commerce transactions will reach $450 billion.

Application Downloads

Currently, there are approximately 200,000 gaming applications that are available through the Google Play and Apple App Store. Many industry experts anticipate that there will be more than 2 million applications available by the end of 2014. The average sales price of a gaming application is $5.50.

4.3 Customer Profile

VideoGirl's average client will be a young middle- to upper-middle class male or female that owns an Android device or an Apple consumer product. Common traits among end users will include:

- Annual household income exceeding $50,000

- Between the ages of 25 to 50

- Has high-speed internet access

- Has an interest in gaming on tablet and desktop devices

4.4 Competition

With the advent of application development programs and platforms, the competition in the video game production industry has increased substantially over the past five years. In previous years, the development of video games (for any console or device) required a large staff and millions of dollars in development capital. However, now video games can be produced for as little as $10,000 (for commercial quality games). As such, it will be imperative that VideoGirl produces games that can be used among a number of different devices. Additionally, the business must have a strong marketing team in place in order to promote games developed and distributed by VideoGirl.

5.0 MARKETING PLAN

VideoGirl intends to maintain an extensive marketing campaign that will ensure maximum visibility for the business in its targeted market. Below is an overview of the marketing strategies and objectives of VideoGirl.

5.1 Marketing Objectives

- Develop an expansive online presence through the use of pay-per-click marketing and search engine optimization.

- Establish relationships with software professionals that need outsourced game development services.

- Develop a high-impact marketing campaign to inform businesses regarding the Company's newly developed game and related gaming applications.

5.2 Marketing Strategies

Ms. Peacrey intends to use a high-impact marketing campaign that will generate a substantial amount of traffic to the website that will feature descriptions showcasing the Company's produced videogames for Windows, Android, iPhone, iPod, and iPad platforms. These strategies include the use of search engine optimization and pay-per-click marketing to drive traffic to the Company's website.

The Company's web development firm will place large amounts of linking text on the Company's website. For instance, when a person does a Google search for a specialized type of game (or the brand name of the developer), the Company will appear on the first page of the search. This strategy is technically complicated, and VideoGirl will use a search engine optimization firm to develop the Company's visibility on a non-paid basis. Management expects that a SEO firm will place large amounts of linking data and text specific keywords into the business's website, which will allow the Company to appear more frequently among search engines. A majority of web portal and search engine companies use very complicated algorithms to determine a website's relevance in relation to a specific keyword. SEO firms place text and tags on the website to increase the rank of a specific website.

Additionally, VideoGirl, Inc. will develop ongoing relationships with software development companies that will outsource the development of gaming applications (either in whole or in part) to the Company in exchange for per project and per hour fees relating to the development of the applications.

5.3 Pricing

The average game purchase will net $5 to $10 for the business. Gross margins will be approximately 90%.

6.0 ORGANIZATIONAL PLAN AND PERSONNEL SUMMARY

6.1 Corporate Organization

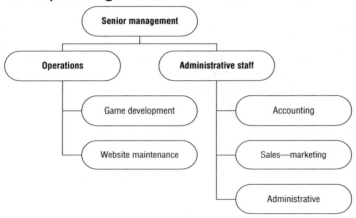

6.2 Organizational Budget

Personnel plan—yearly

Year	1	2	3
Owners	$ 80,000	$ 82,400	$ 84,872
Sales manager	$ 35,000	$ 36,050	$ 37,132
Assistant	$ 32,500	$ 33,475	$ 34,479
Game coders/ developers	$ 37,500	$ 51,500	$ 66,306
Administrative	$ 44,000	$ 45,320	$ 46,680
Total	**$229,000**	**$248,745**	**$269,469**

Numbers of personnel

Owners	2	2	2
Sales manager	1	1	1
Assistant	1	1	1
Game coders/ developers	3	4	5
Administrative	2	2	2
Totals	**9**	**10**	**11**

Personnel expense breakdown

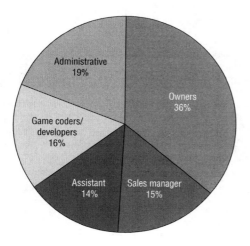

7.0 FINANCIAL PLAN

7.1 Underlying Assumptions

The Company has based its proforma financial statements on the following:

- VideoGirl, Inc. will have an annual revenue growth rate of 31% per year.

- The Owner will acquire $150,000 of debt funds to develop the business.

- The loan will have a 10-year term with a 9% interest rate.

7.2 Sensitivity Analysis

In the event of a severe economic decline, the revenues of VideoGirl should not decrease as the business will continue to generate revenues on a monthly basis from the Company's sales of games and gaming applications. This is primarily due to the fact that the costs related to these applications are relatively low.

7.3 Source of Funds

Financing

Equity contributions

Management investment	$ 25,000.00
Total equity financing	**$ 25,000.00**
Banks and lenders	
Banks and lenders	$ 150,000.00
Total debt financing	**$150,000.00**
Total financing	**$175,000.00**

7.4 General Assumptions

General assumptions

Year	1	2	3
Short term interest rate	9.5%	9.5%	9.5%
Long term interest rate	10.0%	10.0%	10.0%
Federal tax rate	33.0%	33.0%	33.0%
State tax rate	5.0%	5.0%	5.0%
Personnel taxes	15.0%	15.0%	15.0%

7.5 Profit and Loss Statements

Proforma profit and loss (yearly)

Year	1	2	3
Sales	**$990,450**	**$1,436,153**	**$1,938,806**
Cost of goods sold	$ 99,045	$ 143,615	$ 193,881
Gross margin	90.00%	90.00%	90.00%
Operating income	**$891,405**	**$1,292,537**	**$1,744,925**
Expenses			
Payroll	$229,000	$ 248,745	$ 269,469
General and administrative	$ 32,500	$ 33,800	$ 35,152
Marketing expenses	$ 39,618	$ 57,446	$ 77,552
Professional fees and licensure	$ 17,000	$ 17,510	$ 18,035
Insurance costs	$ 12,000	$ 12,600	$ 13,230
Server and technology costs	$ 25,000	$ 27,500	$ 30,250
Rent and utilities	$ 30,000	$ 31,500	$ 33,075
Miscellaneous costs	$ 9,905	$ 14,362	$ 19,388
Payroll taxes	$ 34,350	$ 37,312	$ 40,420
Total operating costs	**$429,373**	**$ 480,774**	**$ 536,571**
EBITDA	**$462,033**	**$ 811,763**	**$1,208,354**
Federal income tax	$152,471	$ 263,857	$ 395,060
State income tax	$ 23,102	$ 39,978	$ 59,858
Interest expense	$ 13,107	$ 12,197	$ 11,202
Depreciation expenses	$ 8,929	$ 8,929	$ 8,929
Net profit	**$264,425**	**$ 486,802**	**$ 733,305**
Profit margin	**26.70%**	**33.90%**	**37.82%**

Sales, operating costs, and profit forecast

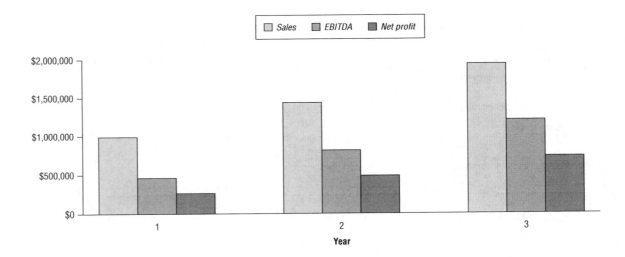

7.6 Cash Flow Analysis

Proforma cash flow analysis—yearly

Year	1	2	3
Cash from operations	$273,354	$495,731	$742,234
Cash from receivables	$ 0	$ 0	$ 0
Operating cash inflow	**$273,354**	**$495,731**	**$742,234**
Other cash inflows			
Equity investment	$ 25,000	$ 0	$ 0
Increased borrowings	$150,000	$ 0	$ 0
Sales of business assets	$ 0	$ 0	$ 0
A/P increases	$ 37,902	$ 43,587	$ 50,125
Total other cash inflows	**$212,902**	**$ 43,587**	**$ 50,125**
Total cash inflow	**$486,256**	**$539,318**	**$792,359**
Cash outflows			
Repayment of principal	$ 9,695	$ 10,605	$ 11,599
A/P decreases	$ 24,897	$ 29,876	$ 35,852
A/R increases	$ 0	$ 0	$ 0
Asset purchases	$125,000	$123,933	$185,558
Dividends	$191,348	$347,012	$519,564
Total cash outflows	**$350,940**	**$511,425**	**$752,573**
Net cash flow	**$135,316**	**$ 27,893**	**$ 39,786**
Cash balance	**$135,316**	**$163,209**	**$202,995**

Proforma cash flow (yearly)

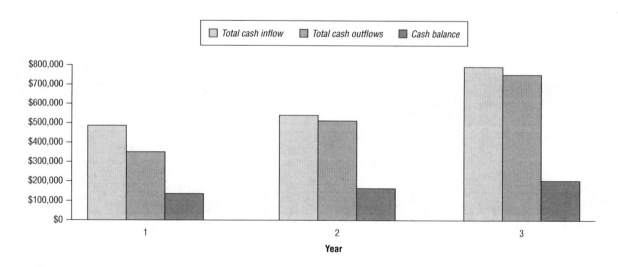

7.7 Balance Sheet

Proforma balance sheet—yearly

Year	1	2	3
Assets			
Cash	$135,316	$163,209	$202,995
Amortized development costs	$ 70,000	$ 82,393	$100,949
Servers and technology equipment	$ 25,000	$117,950	$257,118
FF&E	$ 30,000	$ 48,590	$ 76,424
Accumulated depreciation	($ 8,929)	($ 17,857)	($ 26,786)
Total assets	**$251,387**	**$394,284**	**$610,700**
Liabilities and equity			
Accounts payable	$ 13,005	$ 26,716	$ 40,990
Long term liabilities	$140,305	$129,700	$119,096
Other liabilities	$ 0	$ 0	$ 0
Total liabilities	**$153,310**	**$156,416**	**$160,085**
Net worth	**$ 98,078**	**$237,868**	**$450,615**
Total liabilities and equity	**$251,387**	**$394,284**	**$610,700**

Proforma balance sheet

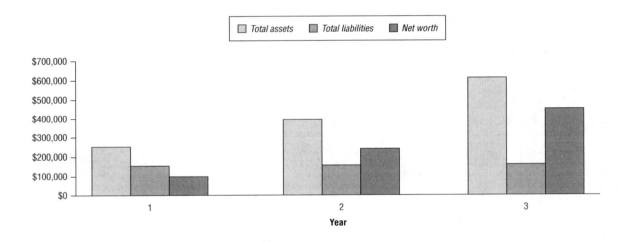

7.8 Breakeven Analysis

Monthly break even analysis

Year	1	2	3
Monthly revenue	$ 39,757	$ 44,516	$ 49,683
Yearly revenue	$477,081	$534,194	$596,191

Break even analysis

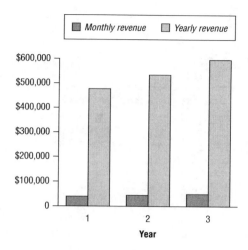

7.9 Business Ratios

Business ratios—yearly

Year	1	2	3
Sales			
Sales growth	0.00%	45.00%	35.00%
Gross margin	90.00%	90.00%	90.00%
Financials			
Profit margin	26.70%	33.90%	37.82%
Assets to liabilities	1.64	2.52	3.81
Equity to liabilities	0.64	1.52	2.81
Assets to equity	2.56	1.66	1.36
Liquidity			
Acid test	0.88	1.04	1.27
Cash to assets	0.54	0.41	0.33

7.10 Three Year Profit and Loss Statement

Profit and loss statement (first year)

Months	1	2	3	4	5	6	7
Sales	$69,750	$72,075	$74,400	$76,725	$79,050	$81,375	$83,700
Cost of goods sold	$ 6,975	$ 7,208	$ 7,440	$ 7,673	$ 7,905	$ 8,138	$ 8,370
Gross margin	90.0%	90.0%	90.0%	90.0%	90.0%	90.0%	90.0%
Operating income	$62,775	$64,868	$66,960	$69,053	$71,145	$73,238	$75,330
Expenses							
Payroll	$19,083	$19,083	$19,083	$19,083	$19,083	$19,083	$19,083
General and administrative	$ 2,708	$ 2,708	$ 2,708	$ 2,708	$ 2,708	$ 2,708	$ 2,708
Marketing expenses	$ 3,302	$ 3,302	$ 3,302	$ 3,302	$ 3,302	$ 3,302	$ 3,302
Professional fees and licensure	$ 1,417	$ 1,417	$ 1,417	$ 1,417	$ 1,417	$ 1,417	$ 1,417
Insurance costs	$ 1,000	$ 1,000	$ 1,000	$ 1,000	$ 1,000	$ 1,000	$ 1,000
Server and technology costs	$ 2,083	$ 2,083	$ 2,083	$ 2,083	$ 2,083	$ 2,083	$ 2,083
Rent and utilities	$ 2,500	$ 2,500	$ 2,500	$ 2,500	$ 2,500	$ 2,500	$ 2,500
Miscellaneous costs	$ 825	$ 825	$ 825	$ 825	$ 825	$ 825	$ 825
Payroll taxes	$ 2,863	$ 2,863	$ 2,863	$ 2,863	$ 2,863	$ 2,863	$ 2,863
Total operating costs	$35,781	$35,781	$35,781	$35,781	$35,781	$35,781	$35,781
EBITDA	$26,994	$29,086	$31,179	$33,271	$35,364	$37,456	$39,549
Federal income tax	$10,737	$11,095	$11,453	$11,811	$12,169	$12,527	$12,885
State income tax	$ 1,627	$ 1,681	$ 1,735	$ 1,790	$ 1,844	$ 1,898	$ 1,952
Interest expense	$ 1,125	$ 1,119	$ 1,113	$ 1,107	$ 1,101	$ 1,095	$ 1,089
Depreciation expense	$ 744	$ 744	$ 744	$ 744	$ 744	$ 744	$ 744
Net profit	$12,761	$14,447	$16,133	$17,819	$19,506	$21,192	$22,878

Profit and loss statement (first year cont.)

Month	8	9	10	11	12	1
Sales	$86,025	$88,350	$90,675	$93,000	$95,325	$990,450
Cost of goods sold	$ 8,603	$ 8,835	$ 9,068	$ 9,300	$ 9,533	$ 99,045
Gross margin	90.0%	90.0%	90.0%	90.0%	90.0%	90.0%
Operating income	$77,423	$79,515	$81,608	$83,700	$85,793	$891,405
Expenses						
Payroll	$19,083	$19,083	$19,083	$19,083	$19,083	$229,000
General and administrative	$ 2,708	$ 2,708	$ 2,708	$ 2,708	$ 2,708	$ 32,500
Marketing expenses	$ 3,302	$ 3,302	$ 3,302	$ 3,302	$ 3,302	$ 39,618
Professional fees and licensure	$ 1,417	$ 1,417	$ 1,417	$ 1,417	$ 1,417	$ 17,000
Insurance costs	$ 1,000	$ 1,000	$ 1,000	$ 1,000	$ 1,000	$ 12,000
Server and technology costs	$ 2,083	$ 2,083	$ 2,083	$ 2,083	$ 2,083	$ 25,000
Rent and utilities	$ 2,500	$ 2,500	$ 2,500	$ 2,500	$ 2,500	$ 30,000
Miscellaneous costs	$ 825	$ 825	$ 825	$ 825	$ 825	$ 9,905
Payroll taxes	$ 2,863	$ 2,863	$ 2,863	$ 2,863	$ 2,863	$ 34,350
Total operating costs	$35,781	$35,781	$35,781	$35,781	$35,781	$429,373
EBITDA	$41,641	$43,734	$45,826	$47,919	$50,011	$462,033
Federal income tax	$13,243	$13,601	$13,959	$14,317	$14,674	$152,471
State income tax	$ 2,006	$ 2,061	$ 2,115	$ 2,169	$ 2,223	$ 23,102
Interest expense	$ 1,083	$ 1,077	$ 1,071	$ 1,065	$ 1,059	$ 13,107
Depreciation expense	$ 744	$ 744	$ 744	$ 744	$ 744	$ 8,929
Net profit	$24,565	$26,251	$27,938	$29,624	$31,311	$264,425

Profit and loss statement (second year)

Quarter	Q1	2			2
		Q2	Q3	Q4	
Sales	$287,231	$359,038	$387,761	$402,123	$1,436,153
Cost of goods sold	$ 28,723	$ 35,904	$ 38,776	$ 40,212	$ 143,615
Gross margin	90.0%	90.0%	90.0%	90.0%	90.0%
Operating income	$258,507	$323,134	$348,985	$361,910	$1,292,537
Expenses					
Payroll	$ 49,749	$ 62,186	$ 67,161	$ 69,649	$ 248,745
General and administrative	$ 6,760	$ 8,450	$ 9,126	$ 9,464	$ 33,800
Marketing expenses	$ 11,489	$ 14,362	$ 15,510	$ 16,085	$ 57,446
Professional fees and licensure	$ 3,502	$ 4,378	$ 4,728	$ 4,903	$ 17,510
Insurance costs	$ 2,520	$ 3,150	$ 3,402	$ 3,528	$ 12,600
Server and technology costs	$ 5,500	$ 6,875	$ 7,425	$ 7,700	$ 27,500
Rent and utilities	$ 6,300	$ 7,875	$ 8,505	$ 8,820	$ 31,500
Miscellaneous costs	$ 2,872	$ 3,590	$ 3,878	$ 4,021	$ 14,362
Payroll taxes	$ 7,462	$ 9,328	$ 10,074	$ 10,447	$ 37,312
Total operating costs	$ 96,155	$120,194	$129,809	$134,617	$ 480,774
EBITDA	$162,353	$202,941	$219,176	$227,294	$ 811,763
Federal income tax	$ 52,771	$ 65,964	$ 71,241	$ 73,880	$ 263,857
State income tax	$ 7,996	$ 9,995	$ 10,794	$ 11,194	$ 39,978
Interest expense	$ 3,138	$ 3,080	$ 3,020	$ 2,959	$ 12,197
Depreciation expense	$ 2,232	$ 2,232	$ 2,232	$ 2,232	$ 8,929
Net profit	$ 96,216	$121,670	$131,888	$137,028	$ 486,802

Profit and loss statement (third year)

Quarter	Q1	3			3
		Q2	Q3	Q4	
Sales	$387,761	$484,701	$523,478	$542,866	$1,938,806
Cost of goods sold	$ 38,776	$ 48,470	$ 52,348	$ 54,287	$ 193,881
Gross margin	90.0%	90.0%	90.0%	90.0%	90.0%
Operating income	$348,985	$436,231	$471,130	$488,579	$1,744,925
Expenses					
Payroll	$ 53,894	$ 67,367	$ 72,757	$ 75,451	$ 269,469
General and administrative	$ 7,030	$ 8,788	$ 9,491	$ 9,843	$ 35,152
Marketing expenses	$ 15,510	$ 19,388	$ 20,939	$ 21,715	$ 77,552
Professional fees and licensure	$ 3,607	$ 4,509	$ 4,870	$ 5,050	$ 18,035
Insurance costs	$ 2,646	$ 3,308	$ 3,572	$ 3,704	$ 13,230
Server and technology costs	$ 6,050	$ 7,563	$ 8,168	$ 8,470	$ 30,250
Rent and utilities	$ 6,615	$ 8,269	$ 8,930	$ 9,261	$ 33,075
Miscellaneous costs	$ 3,878	$ 4,847	$ 5,235	$ 5,429	$ 19,388
Payroll taxes	$ 8,084	$ 10,105	$ 10,913	$ 11,318	$ 40,420
Total operating costs	$107,314	$134,143	$144,874	$150,240	$ 536,571
EBITDA	$241,671	$302,088	$326,256	$338,339	$1,208,354
Federal income tax	$ 79,012	$ 98,765	$106,666	$110,617	$ 395,060
State income tax	$ 11,972	$ 14,964	$ 16,162	$ 16,760	$ 59,858
Interest expense	$ 2,897	$ 2,834	$ 2,769	$ 2,702	$ 11,202
Depreciation expense	$ 2,232	$ 2,232	$ 2,232	$ 2,232	$ 8,929
Net profit	$145,558	$183,293	$198,427	$206,028	$ 733,305

7.11 Three Year Cash Flow Analysis

Cash flow analysis (first year)

Month	1	2	3	4	5	6	7
Cash from operations	$ 13,505	$15,191	$16,877	$ 18,563	$ 20,250	$ 21,936	$ 23,622
Cash from receivables	$ 0	$ 0	$ 0	$ 0	$ 0	$ 0	$ 0
Operating cash inflow	**$ 13,505**	**$15,191**	**$16,877**	**$ 18,563**	**$ 20,250**	**$ 21,936**	**$ 23,622**
Other cash inflows							
Equity investment	$ 25,000	$ 0	$ 0	$ 0	$ 0	$ 0	$ 0
Increased borrowings	$150,000	$ 0	$ 0	$ 0	$ 0	$ 0	$ 0
Sales of business assets	$ 0	$ 0	$ 0	$ 0	$ 0	$ 0	$ 0
A/P increases	$ 3,159	$ 3,159	$ 3,159	$ 3,159	$ 3,159	$ 3,159	$ 3,159
Total other cash inflows	**$178,159**	**$ 3,159**	**$ 3,159**	**$ 3,159**	**$ 3,159**	**$ 3,159**	**$ 3,159**
Total cash inflow	**$191,663**	**$18,349**	**$20,036**	**$ 21,722**	**$ 23,408**	**$ 25,095**	**$ 26,781**
Cash outflows							
Repayment of principal	$ 775	$ 781	$ 787	$ 793	$ 799	$ 805	$ 811
A/P decreases	$ 2,075	$ 2,075	$ 2,075	$ 2,075	$ 2,075	$ 2,075	$ 2,075
A/R increases	$ 0	$ 0	$ 0	$ 0	$ 0	$ 0	$ 0
Asset purchases	$125,000	$ 0	$ 0	$ 0	$ 0	$ 0	$ 0
Dividends	$ 0	$ 0	$ 0	$ 0	$ 0	$ 0	$ 0
Total cash outflows	**$127,850**	**$ 2,856**	**$ 2,862**	**$ 2,867**	**$ 2,873**	**$ 2,879**	**$ 2,885**
Net cash flow	**$ 63,813**	**$15,494**	**$17,174**	**$ 18,854**	**$ 20,535**	**$ 22,215**	**$ 23,895**
Cash balance	**$ 63,813**	**$79,307**	**$96,481**	**$115,335**	**$135,870**	**$158,085**	**$181,981**

Cash flow analysis (first year cont.)

Month	8	9	10	11	12	1
Cash from operations	$ 25,309	$ 26,995	$ 28,682	$ 30,368	$ 32,055	$273,354
Cash from receivables	$ 0	$ 0	$ 0	$ 0	$ 0	$ 0
Operating cash inflow	**$ 25,309**	**$ 26,995**	**$ 28,682**	**$ 30,368**	**$ 32,055**	**$273,354**
Other cash inflows						
Equity investment	$ 0	$ 0	$ 0	$ 0	$ 0	$ 25,000
Increased borrowings	$ 0	$ 0	$ 0	$ 0	$ 0	$150,000
Sales of business assets	$ 0	$ 0	$ 0	$ 0	$ 0	$ 0
A/P increases	$ 3,159	$ 3,159	$ 3,159	$ 3,159	$ 3,159	$ 37,902
Total other cash inflows	**$ 3,159**	**$ 3,159**	**$ 3,159**	**$ 3,159**	**$ 3,159**	**$212,902**
Total cash inflow	**$ 28,467**	**$ 30,154**	**$ 31,840**	**$ 33,527**	**$ 35,214**	**$486,256**
Cash outflows						
Repayment of principal	$ 817	$ 823	$ 829	$ 835	$ 842	$ 9,695
A/P decreases	$ 2,075	$ 2,075	$ 2,075	$ 2,075	$ 2,075	$ 24,897
A/R increases	$ 0	$ 0	$ 0	$ 0	$ 0	$ 0
Asset purchases	$ 0	$ 0	$ 0	$ 0	$ 0	$125,000
Dividends	$ 0	$ 0	$ 0	$ 0	$191,348	$191,348
Total cash outflows	**$ 2,892**	**$ 2,898**	**$ 2,904**	**$ 2,910**	**$194,264**	**$350,940**
Net cash flow	**$ 25,576**	**$ 27,256**	**$ 28,937**	**$ 30,617**	**−$159,051**	**$135,316**
Cash balance	**$207,557**	**$234,813**	**$263,749**	**$294,366**	**$135,316**	**$135,316**

Cash flow analysis (second year)

Quarter	Q1	2 Q2	Q3	Q4	2
Cash from operations	$ 99,146	$123,933	$133,847	$138,805	$495,731
Cash from receivables	$ 0	$ 0	$ 0	$ 0	$ 0
Operating cash inflow	**$ 99,146**	**$123,933**	**$133,847**	**$138,805**	**$495,731**
Other cash inflows					
Equity investment	$ 0	$ 0	$ 0	$ 0	$ 0
Increased borrowings	$ 0	$ 0	$ 0	$ 0	$ 0
Sales of business assets	$ 0	$ 0	$ 0	$ 0	$ 0
A/P increases	$ 8,717	$ 10,897	$ 11,769	$ 12,204	$ 43,587
Total other cash inflows	**$ 8,717**	**$ 10,897**	**$ 11,769**	**$ 12,204**	**$ 43,587**
Total cash inflow	**$107,864**	**$134,830**	**$145,616**	**$151,009**	**$539,318**
Cash outflows					
Repayment of principal	$ 2,563	$ 2,621	$ 2,680	$ 2,741	$ 10,605
A/P decreases	$ 5,975	$ 7,469	$ 8,067	$ 8,365	$ 29,876
A/R increases	$ 0	$ 0	$ 0	$ 0	$ 0
Asset purchases	$ 24,787	$ 30,983	$ 33,462	$ 34,701	$123,933
Dividends	$ 69,402	$ 86,753	$ 93,693	$ 97,163	$347,012
Total cash outflows	**$102,727**	**$127,826**	**$137,902**	**$142,971**	**$511,425**
Net cash flow	**$ 5,137**	**$ 7,004**	**$ 7,714**	**$ 8,038**	**$ 27,893**
Cash balance	**$140,453**	**$147,456**	**$155,171**	**$163,209**	**$163,209**

Cash flow analysis (third year)

Quarter	Q1	3 Q2	Q3	Q4	3
Cash from operations	$148,447	$185,558	$200,403	$207,826	$742,234
Cash from receivables	$ 0	$ 0	$ 0	$ 0	$ 0
Operating cash inflow	**$148,447**	**$185,558**	**$200,403**	**$207,826**	**$742,234**
Other cash inflows					
Equity investment	$ 0	$ 0	$ 0	$ 0	$ 0
Increased borrowings	$ 0	$ 0	$ 0	$ 0	$ 0
Sales of business assets	$ 0	$ 0	$ 0	$ 0	$ 0
A/P increases	$ 10,025	$ 12,531	$ 13,534	$ 14,035	$ 50,125
Total other cash inflows	**$ 10,025**	**$ 12,531**	**$ 13,534**	**$ 14,035**	**$ 50,125**
Total cash inflow	**$158,472**	**$198,090**	**$213,937**	**$221,861**	**$792,359**
Cash outflows					
Repayment of principal	$ 2,803	$ 2,867	$ 2,932	$ 2,998	$ 11,599
A/P decreases	$ 7,170	$ 8,963	$ 9,680	$ 10,038	$ 35,852
A/R increases	$ 0	$ 0	$ 0	$ 0	$ 0
Asset purchases	$ 37,112	$ 46,390	$ 50,101	$ 51,956	$185,558
Dividends	$103,913	$129,891	$140,282	$145,478	$519,564
Total cash outflows	**$150,998**	**$188,110**	**$202,995**	**$210,471**	**$752,573**
Net cash flow	**$ 7,474**	**$ 9,980**	**$ 10,942**	**$ 11,390**	**$ 39,786**
Cash balance	**$170,683**	**$180,663**	**$191,605**	**$202,995**	**$202,995**

Winery

North Coast Wines

7612 S. Redwood Hwy.
Ukiah, CA 95482

BizPlanDB.com

North Coast Wines is a California-based corporation that will produce and sell a number of varieties of wines via retail and wholesale distribution channels. The Company was founded by Pete Denapole.

1.0 EXECUTIVE SUMMARY

The purpose of this business plan is to raise $5,000,000 for the development of a winery and vineyard while showcasing the expected financials and operations over the next three years. North Coast Wines is a California-based corporation that will produce and sell a number of varieties of wines via retail and wholesale distribution channels. The Company was founded by Pete Denapole.

1.1 The Products

As stated above, North Coast Wines will specialize in providing a number of wine products which will be distributed on both a wholesale and retail level. Management expects that 75% of the Company's revenues will come from wholesale distribution of the Company's products. The business will produce a number of different vintages including merlots, cabernets, and shiraz-style wines. Mr. Denapole expects that the business will aggregately generate gross margins of 62% on each dollar of revenue produced.

The business will engage a substantial marketing campaign to brand the Company's products as premium wine products.

The third section of the business plan will further describe the services offered by North Coast Wines.

1.2 Financing

Mr. Denapole is seeking to raise $5,000,000 from an equity investment. The terms, equity covenants, and equity percentages are to be determined at the time of negotiation. Tentatively, Mr. Denapole anticipates that the Company will sell a 40% equity interest in the business in exchange for the capital sought in this business plan. The financing will be used for the following:

- Development of the Company's winery.

- Financing for the first six months of operation.

- Capital to purchase FF&E, irrigation systems, and other equipment needed to produce wine.

1.3 Mission Statement

The mission of North Coast Wines is to develop, produce, and distribute a number of wines on a nationwide basis while concurrently increasing the visibility of the business as a premier winery.

Additionally, Management will always abide by all state and federal laws regarding the production and distribution of alcohol products.

1.4 Management Team

The Company was founded by Pete Denapole. Mr. Denapole has more than eleven years of experience in the wine producing industry. Through his expertise, he will be able to bring the operations of the business to profitability within its first year of operations.

1.5 Sales Forecasts

Mr. Denapole expects a strong rate of growth at the start of operations. Below are the expected financials over the next three years.

Proforma profit and loss (yearly)

Year	1	2	3
Sales	$4,586,400	$5,503,680	$6,439,306
Operating costs	$1,817,457	$1,931,246	$2,048,793
EBITDA	$1,049,043	$1,508,554	$1,975,773
Taxes, interest, and depreciation	$ 666,315	$ 840,929	$1,018,472
Net profit	$ 382,728	$ 667,625	$ 957,300

Sales, operating costs, and profit forecast

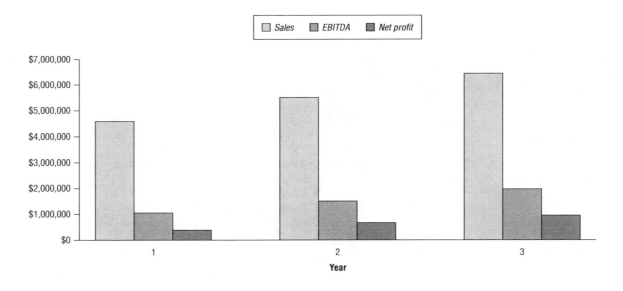

1.6 Expansion Plan

The Founder expects that the business will aggressively expand during the first three years of operation. Mr. Denapole intends to implement marketing campaigns that will effectively target individuals (and wholesale distributors) that will enjoy the Company's wine products.

2.0 COMPANY AND FINANCING SUMMARY

2.1 Registered Name and Corporate Structure

The Company is registered as a corporation in the State of California.

2.2 Required Funds

At this time, North Coast Wines requires $5,000,000 of equity funds. Below is a breakdown of how these funds will be used:

Projected startup costs

Facility acquisition	$ 1,625,000
Working capital	$ 1,350,000
FF&E	$ 750,000
Facility improvements	$ 350,000
Irrigation systems	$ 500,000
Insurance	$ 50,000
Initial inventories	$ 175,000
Marketing budget	$ 175,000
Miscellaneous and unforeseen costs	$ 25,000
Total startup costs	**$5,000,000**

Use of funds

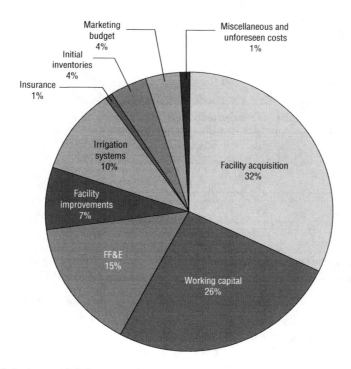

2.3 Investor Equity

At this time, Mr. Denapole is seeking to sell a 40% interest in North Coast Wines in exchange for the capital sought in this business plan. The investor will also receive a seat on the board of directors and a regular stream of dividends starting in the first year of operations.

2.4 Management Equity

Pete Denapole owns 100% of North Coast Wines. This capital structure will change once the business receives its capital infusion.

2.5 Exit Strategy

If the business is very successful, Mr. Denapole may seek to sell the business to a third party for a significant earnings multiple. Most likely, the Company will hire a qualified business broker to sell the business on behalf of North Coast Wines. Based on historical numbers, the business could fetch a sales premium of up to 8 to 10 times earnings.

3.0 WINERY PRODUCTS

Below is a description of the wine products offered by the Company.

3.1 Wholesale Distribution of Wine Products

Prior to the onset of operations, the business will develop a number of relationships with wine distributors throughout the United States. This will ensure that the Company will be able to immediately divest its inventories of wines once the Company begins distribution. Management expects that it will be able to begin distribution of completed products by the end of the 2015 fiscal year. North Coast Wines will feature a number of different grapes that will allow the business to produce a number of different wines including merlots, cabernets, shiraz wines, and blended wines.

At all times, the business will remain within the letter of the law regarding the production, distribution, and sale of wine both on a state and federal level.

3.2 Retail Distribution of Wine

The Company's secondary distribution channel will come from direct sales of wine to customers that visit North Coast Wines. The business will sell wines both by the bottle and by the case directly from its location as well as an online ordering website that will be developed prior to launching the operations of North Coast Wines. North Coast Wines will feature an extensive tasting room and wine store where customers can directly purchase the Company's products. The Company will employ four zymurgists (wine producing experts) that will provide insightful information about the Company's products and the wine producing operations of the business.

4.0 STRATEGIC AND MARKET ANALYSIS

4.1 Economic Outlook

This section of the analysis will detail the economic climate, the winery industry, the customer profile, and the competition that the business will face as it progresses through its business operations.

Currently, the economic market condition in the United States is moderate. Unemployment rates have declined while asset prices have risen substantially. However, it should be noted that as wine is a luxury product, by most standards, the business may have some issues with top line income during economic recessions. However, the targeted end user of North Coast Wines' products will tend to be upper middle income individuals, which are less swayed by deleterious economic conditions.

4.2 Industry Analysis

The sale of wine is a $43 billion dollar industry that provides jobs to more than 100,000 Americans. Within this industry, there are more than 2,000 individual wineries and vineyards that provide more than 22 cases of wine bottles to the general public. However, many of these companies deal in small volumes of alcohol sales. This is evident within the United States, where small wineries and vineyards dominate the American market. A significant amount of the wine consumed in America is imported from France, Italy, Australia, and other markets that have climates that are acceptable for grape growth.

South American sparking wines have also become prominent members of the market with new blends coming from Chile, Argentina, and Uruguay.

The companies within this market all face similar performance and economic issues. The supply and demand curves found within this industry are uniform as they all face the same interest rate, economic, and agricultural issues.

One of the primary shifts in the industry over the last ten years is the marketing approach that these companies have collectively used to promote their respective brands. The focus many new and established wines, cognacs, and liquors is to partner with major celebrities. Over the last five years, the celebrity aspect of the media has propagated throughout the world with the advent of the internet and streaming media communications.

As such, the interest among the general public concerning celebrity lifestyles has grown significantly, and there are many television shows that are dedicated to showcasing their luxurious lives. Alcoholic beverage companies, apparel businesses, and high-end automotive manufacturers have all begun to develop co-branding and marketing relationships due to this shift in media attention.

4.3 Customer Profile
North Coast Wines' average end user client will be an upper-middle class man or woman that enjoys premium wines. Common traits among clients will include:

* Consumer between the age of 35 and 55
* Has an annual income of $75,000 per year or more
* Became aware of the North Coast Wines brand name through a traditional media channel
* Will purchase North Coast Wines' products from a liquor/wine retailer or from a high-end restaurant

Within the United States, there are more than 60 million people that fall into the above demographic profile.

4.4 Competition
As stated above, there are more than 2,000 wineries that produce and distribute their wine products within the United States. The most important aspect to operating the winery is that the Company must create a strong branded image regarding the quality of its wine from the onset of operations. The business intends to hire a third party marketing firm that will actively assist the business in positioning its brand before the Company begins to distribute its line of produced wines.

5.0 MARKETING PLAN

North Coast Wines intends to maintain an extensive marketing campaign that will ensure maximum visibility for the business in its targeted market. Below is an overview of the marketing strategies and objectives of the Company.

5.1 Marketing Objectives
* Establish relationships with national wine distributors.
* Develop a relationship with a major marketing firm that will properly brand the Company's wine products within the market.
* Develop an independent sales force that will solicit purchase orders on behalf of North Coast Wines.

5.2 Marketing Strategies

North Coast Wines' products will be marketed with a broad spectrum of sales and marketing strategies that will promote its high-end brand name. This is the crux of the Company's operations, as wine has become somewhat of a commodity within its economic market. The key to succeeding within the alcoholic beverage industry is to develop a brand and an image associated with the wine product. To that end, Management has developed an extensive marketing campaign that will place North Coast Wines' products within the same market as other premium alcoholic beverage manufacturers.

Second, repetition of product is another very commonly used technique to promote a product. A recently published study indicates that the average consumer must be exposed to a product approximately 100 times before they become familiar with the brand name. As such, the business will engage an extensive print marketing campaign that will focus on high-end lifestyle magazines so that the Company's target audience becomes familiar with the Company's brand name.

In order to develop North Coast Wines' products as premium products, Mr. Denapole intends to hire a national level marketing and advertising firm that will properly implement marketing campaigns and targeted advertisements. Within the first year of operations, Management expects to spend $250,000 to promote the North Coast Wines brand.

Additional publicity activities designed to generate interest in North Coast Wines' products will include news articles, lifestyle articles, and product reviews that will further increase the visibility of the North Coast Wines brand name. Management intends to use public relations as one of its primary tools for increasing visibility.

5.3 Pricing

Management expects pricing of approximately $120 per case of wine sold on a wholesaler/distributor level. Gross margins on each sale will be approximately 62 cents per dollar of income generated.

6.0 ORGANIZATIONAL PLAN AND PERSONNEL SUMMARY

6.1 Corporate Organization

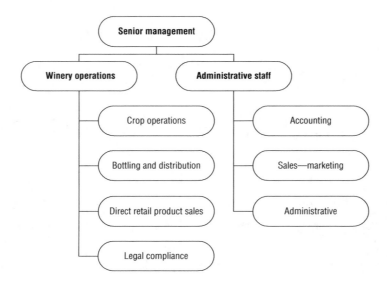

6.2 Organizational Budget

Personnel plan—yearly

Year	1	2	3
Owner	$ 200,000	$ 206,000	$ 212,180
Facility manager	$ 95,000	$ 97,850	$ 100,786
Zymurgist	$ 300,000	$ 309,000	$ 318,270
Winery staff	$ 360,000	$ 370,800	$ 381,924
Accountant	$ 55,000	$ 56,650	$ 58,350
Total	**$1,010,000**	**$1,040,300**	**$1,071,509**

Numbers of personnel

Owner	2	2	2
Facility manager	1	1	1
Zymurgist	4	4	4
Winery staff	12	12	12
Accountant	1	1	1
Totals	**20**	**20**	**20**

Personnel expense breakdown

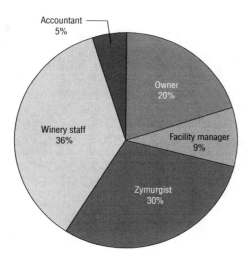

7.0 FINANCIAL PLAN

7.1 Underlying Assumptions

The Company has based its proforma financial statements on the following:

- North Coast Wines will have an annual revenue growth rate of 16% per year.

- Mr. Denapole will acquire $5,000,000 of equity funds to launch the operations of North Coast Wines.

- Management will settle most short-term payables on a monthly basis.

7.2 Sensitivity Analysis

In the event of an economic downturn, the business may have a decline in its revenues. Wine products, by most standards, are considered luxury products. As such, the business may see sluggish sales growth as the U.S. and global economies are currently reeling from a number of serious economic issues. However, the Company generates substantial gross margins from its sales, and this, coupled with the fact that the business is targeting higher-income individuals, will ensure that the business remains financially stable during the course of its operations.

7.3 Source of Funds

Financing

Equity contributions

Investor(s)	$ 5,000,000.00
Total equity financing	**$5,000,000.00**
Banks and lenders	
Total debt financing	**$ 0.00**
Total financing	**$5,000,000.00**

7.4 General Assumptions

General assumptions

Year	1	2	3
Short term interest rate	9.5%	9.5%	9.5%
Long term interest rate	10.0%	10.0%	10.0%
Federal tax rate	33.0%	33.0%	33.0%
State tax rate	5.0%	5.0%	5.0%
Personnel taxes	15.0%	15.0%	15.0%

7.5 Profit and Loss Statements

Proforma profit and loss (yearly)

Year	1	2	3
Sales	**$4,586,400**	**$5,503,680**	**$6,439,306**
Cost of goods sold	$1,719,900	$2,063,880	$2,414,740
Gross margin	62.50%	62.50%	62.50%
Operating income	**$2,866,500**	**$3,439,800**	**$4,024,566**
Expenses			
Payroll	$1,010,000	$1,040,300	$1,071,509
General and administrative	$ 145,200	$ 151,008	$ 157,048
Marketing expenses	$ 229,320	$ 275,184	$ 321,965
Professional fees and licensure	$ 25,000	$ 25,750	$ 26,523
Insurance costs	$ 50,000	$ 52,500	$ 55,125
Facility maintenance costs	$ 108,900	$ 119,790	$ 131,769
Utility expenses	$ 42,500	$ 44,625	$ 46,856
Miscellaneous costs	$ 55,037	$ 66,044	$ 77,272
Payroll taxes	$ 151,500	$ 156,045	$ 160,726
Total operating costs	**$1,817,457**	**$1,931,246**	**$2,048,793**
EBITDA	**$1,049,043**	**$1,508,554**	**$1,975,773**
Federal income tax	$ 346,184	$ 497,823	$ 652,005
State income tax	$ 52,452	$ 75,428	$ 98,789
Interest expense	$ 0	$ 0	$ 0
Depreciation expenses	$ 267,679	$ 267,679	$ 267,679
Net profit	**$ 382,728**	**$ 667,625**	**$ 957,300**
Profit margin	**8.34%**	**12.13%**	**14.87%**

Sales, operating costs, and profit forecast

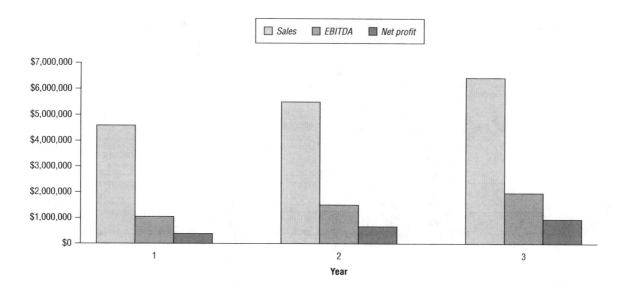

7.6 Cash Flow Analysis

Proforma cash flow analysis—yearly

Year	1	2	3
Cash from operations	$ 650,407	$ 935,303	$ 1,224,979
Cash from receivables	$ 0	$ 0	$ 0
Operating cash inflow	**$ 650,407**	**$ 935,303**	**$1,224,979**
Other cash inflows			
Equity investment	$ 5,000,000	$ 0	$ 0
Increased borrowings	$ 0	$ 0	$ 0
Sales of business assets	$ 0	$ 0	$ 0
A/P increases	$ 37,902	$ 43,587	$ 50,125
Total other cash inflows	**$5,037,902**	**$ 43,587**	**$ 50,125**
Total cash inflow	**$5,688,309**	**$ 978,891**	**$1,275,104**
Cash outflows			
Repayment of principal	$ 0	$ 0	$ 0
A/P decreases	$ 24,897	$ 29,876	$ 35,852
A/R increases	$ 0	$ 0	$ 0
Asset purchases	$ 3,650,000	$ 233,826	$ 306,245
Dividends	$ 455,285	$ 654,712	$ 857,485
Total cash outflows	**$4,130,182**	**$ 918,415**	**$1,199,582**
Net cash flow	**$1,558,127**	**$ 60,476**	**$ 75,523**
Cash balance	**$1,558,127**	**$1,618,603**	**$1,694,126**

Proforma cash flow (yearly)

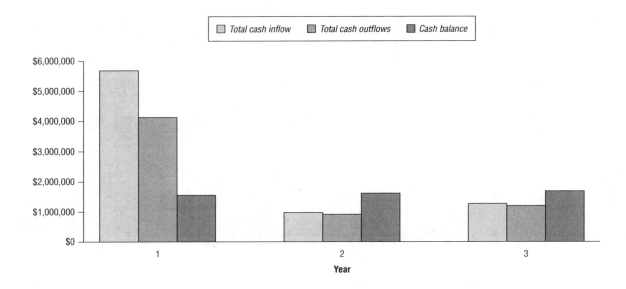

7.7 Balance Sheet

Proforma balance sheet—yearly

Year	1	2	3
Assets			
Cash	$1,558,127	$1,618,603	$1,694,126
Amortized development/expansion costs	$ 600,000	$ 623,383	$ 654,007
Property	$1,722,500	$1,825,850	$1,935,401
FF&E	$1,250,000	$1,343,530	$1,466,028
Wine inventories	$ 175,000	$ 291,913	$ 445,035
Accumulated depreciation	($ 267,679)	($ 535,357)	($ 803,036)
Total assets	**$5,037,948**	**$5,167,922**	**$5,391,562**
Liabilities and equity			
Accounts payable	$ 13,005	$ 26,716	$ 40,990
Long term liabilities	$ 0	$ 0	$ 0
Other liabilities	$ 0	$ 0	$ 0
Total liabilities	**$ 13,005**	**$ 26,716**	**$ 40,990**
Net worth	**$5,024,943**	**$5,141,206**	**$5,350,572**
Total liabilities and equity	**$5,037,948**	**$5,167,922**	**$5,391,562**

Proforma balance sheet

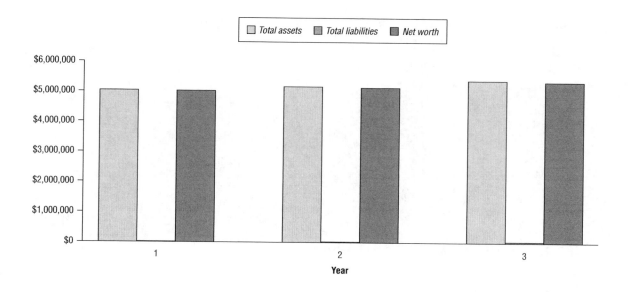

7.8 Breakeven Analysis

Monthly break even analysis

Year	1	2	3
Monthly revenue	$ 242,328	$ 257,499	$ 273,172
Yearly revenue	$2,907,931	$3,089,994	$3,278,069

Break even analysis

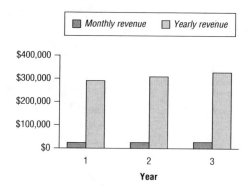

7.9 Business Ratios

Business ratios—yearly

Year	1	2	3
Sales			
Sales growth	0.00%	20.00%	17.00%
Gross margin	62.50%	62.50%	62.50%
Financials			
Profit margin	8.34%	12.13%	14.87%
Assets to liabilities	387.39	193.44	131.53
Equity to liabilities	386.39	192.44	130.53
Assets to equity	1.00	1.01	1.01
Liquidity			
Acid test	119.81	60.59	41.33
Cash to assets	0.31	0.31	0.31

7.10 Three Year Profit and Loss Statement

Profit and loss statement (first year)

Months	1	2	3	4	5	6	7
Sales	**$380,000**	**$380,400**	**$380,800**	**$381,200**	**$381,600**	**$382,000**	**$382,400**
Cost of goods sold	$142,500	$142,650	$142,800	$142,950	$143,100	$143,250	$143,400
Gross margin	62.5%	62.5%	62.5%	62.5%	62.5%	62.5%	62.5%
Operating income	**$237,500**	**$237,750**	**$238,000**	**$238,250**	**$238,500**	**$238,750**	**$239,000**
Expenses							
Payroll	$ 84,167	$ 84,167	$ 84,167	$ 84,167	$ 84,167	$ 84,167	$ 84,167
General and administrative	$ 12,100	$ 12,100	$ 12,100	$ 12,100	$ 12,100	$ 12,100	$ 12,100
Marketing expenses	$ 19,110	$ 19,110	$ 19,110	$ 19,110	$ 19,110	$ 19,110	$ 19,110
Professional fees and licensure	$ 2,083	$ 2,083	$ 2,083	$ 2,083	$ 2,083	$ 2,083	$ 2,083
Insurance costs	$ 4,167	$ 4,167	$ 4,167	$ 4,167	$ 4,167	$ 4,167	$ 4,167
Facility maintenance costs	$ 9,075	$ 9,075	$ 9,075	$ 9,075	$ 9,075	$ 9,075	$ 9,075
Utility expenses	$ 3,542	$ 3,542	$ 3,542	$ 3,542	$ 3,542	$ 3,542	$ 3,542
Miscellaneous costs	$ 4,586	$ 4,586	$ 4,586	$ 4,586	$ 4,586	$ 4,586	$ 4,586
Payroll taxes	$ 12,625	$ 12,625	$ 12,625	$ 12,625	$ 12,625	$ 12,625	$ 12,625
Total operating costs	**$151,455**	**$151,455**	**$151,455**	**$151,455**	**$151,455**	**$151,455**	**$151,455**
EBITDA	**$ 86,045**	**$ 86,295**	**$ 86,545**	**$ 86,795**	**$ 87,045**	**$ 87,295**	**$ 87,545**
Federal income tax	$ 28,683	$ 28,713	$ 28,743	$ 28,773	$ 28,803	$ 28,834	$ 28,864
State income tax	$ 4,346	$ 4,350	$ 4,355	$ 4,360	$ 4,364	$ 4,369	$ 4,373
Interest expense	$ 0	$ 0	$ 0	$ 0	$ 0	$ 0	$ 0
Depreciation expense	$ 22,307	$ 22,307	$ 22,307	$ 22,307	$ 22,307	$ 22,307	$ 22,307
Net profit	**$ 30,710**	**$ 30,925**	**$ 31,141**	**$ 31,356**	**$ 31,571**	**$ 31,786**	**$ 32,002**

Profit and loss statement (first year cont.)

Month	8	9	10	11	12	1
Sales	$382,800	$383,200	$383,600	$384,000	$384,400	$4,586,400
Cost of goods sold	$143,550	$143,700	$143,850	$144,000	$144,150	$1,719,900
Gross margin	62.5%	62.5%	62.5%	62.5%	62.5%	62.5%
Operating income	$239,250	$239,500	$239,750	$240,000	$240,250	$2,866,500
Expenses						
Payroll	$ 84,167	$ 84,167	$ 84,167	$ 84,167	$ 84,167	$1,010,000
General and administrative	$ 12,100	$ 12,100	$ 12,100	$ 12,100	$ 12,100	$ 145,200
Marketing expenses	$ 19,110	$ 19,110	$ 19,110	$ 19,110	$ 19,110	$ 229,320
Professional fees and licensure	$ 2,083	$ 2,083	$ 2,083	$ 2,083	$ 2,083	$ 25,000
Insurance costs	$ 4,167	$ 4,167	$ 4,167	$ 4,167	$ 4,167	$ 50,000
Facility maintenance costs	$ 9,075	$ 9,075	$ 9,075	$ 9,075	$ 9,075	$ 108,900
Utility expenses	$ 3,542	$ 3,542	$ 3,542	$ 3,542	$ 3,542	$ 42,500
Miscellaneous costs	$ 4,586	$ 4,586	$ 4,586	$ 4,586	$ 4,586	$ 55,037
Payroll taxes	$ 12,625	$ 12,625	$ 12,625	$ 12,625	$ 12,625	$ 151,500
Total operating costs	$151,455	$151,455	$151,455	$151,455	$151,455	$1,817,457
EBITDA	$ 87,795	$ 88,045	$ 88,295	$ 88,545	$ 88,795	$1,049,043
Federal income tax	$ 28,894	$ 28,924	$ 28,954	$ 28,985	$ 29,015	$ 346,184
State income tax	$ 4,378	$ 4,382	$ 4,387	$ 4,392	$ 4,396	$ 52,452
Interest expense	$ 0	$ 0	$ 0	$ 0	$ 0	$ 0
Depreciation expense	$ 22,307	$ 22,307	$ 22,307	$ 22,307	$ 22,307	$ 267,679
Net profit	$ 32,217	$ 32,432	$ 32,647	$ 32,863	$ 33,078	$ 382,728

Profit and loss statement (second year)

Quarter	Q1	2 Q2	Q3	Q4	2
Sales	$1,100,736	$1,375,920	$1,485,994	$1,541,030	$5,503,680
Cost of goods sold	$ 412,776	$ 515,970	$ 557,248	$ 577,886	$2,063,880
Gross margin	62.5%	62.5%	62.5%	62.5%	62.5%
Operating income	$ 687,960	$ 859,950	$ 928,746	$ 963,144	$3,439,800
Expenses					
Payroll	$ 208,060	$ 260,075	$ 280,881	$ 291,284	$1,040,300
General and administrative	$ 30,202	$ 37,752	$ 40,772	$ 42,282	$ 151,008
Marketing expenses	$ 55,037	$ 68,796	$ 74,300	$ 77,052	$ 275,184
Professional fees and licensure	$ 5,150	$ 6,438	$ 6,953	$ 7,210	$ 25,750
Insurance costs	$ 10,500	$ 13,125	$ 14,175	$ 14,700	$ 52,500
Facility maintenance costs	$ 23,958	$ 29,948	$ 32,343	$ 33,541	$ 119,790
Utility expenses	$ 8,925	$ 11,156	$ 12,049	$ 12,495	$ 44,625
Miscellaneous costs	$ 13,209	$ 16,511	$ 17,832	$ 18,492	$ 66,044
Payroll taxes	$ 31,209	$ 39,011	$ 42,132	$ 43,693	$ 156,045
Total operating costs	$ 386,249	$ 482,812	$ 521,436	$ 540,749	$1,931,246
EBITDA	$ 301,711	$ 377,138	$ 407,310	$ 422,395	$1,508,554
Federal income tax	$ 99,565	$ 124,456	$ 134,412	$ 139,390	$ 497,823
State income tax	$ 15,086	$ 18,857	$ 20,365	$ 21,120	$ 75,428
Interest expense	$ 0	$ 0	$ 0	$ 0	$ 0
Depreciation expense	$ 66,920	$ 66,920	$ 66,920	$ 66,920	$ 267,679
Net profit	$ 120,141	$ 166,906	$ 185,612	$ 194,965	$ 667,625

Profit and loss statement (third year)

Quarter	Q1	3 Q2	Q3	Q4	3
Sales	**$1,287,861**	**$1,609,826**	**$1,738,613**	**$1,803,006**	**$6,439,306**
Cost of goods sold	$ 482,948	$ 603,685	$ 651,980	$ 676,127	$2,414,740
Gross margin	62.5%	62.5%	62.5%	62.5%	62.5%
Operating income	**$ 804,913**	**$1,006,142**	**$1,086,633**	**$1,126,878**	**$4,024,566**
Expenses					
Payroll	$ 214,302	$ 267,877	$ 289,307	$ 300,023	$1,071,509
General and administrative	$ 31,410	$ 39,262	$ 42,403	$ 43,974	$ 157,048
Marketing expenses	$ 64,393	$ 80,491	$ 86,931	$ 90,150	$ 321,965
Professional fees and licensure	$ 5,305	$ 6,631	$ 7,161	$ 7,426	$ 26,523
Insurance costs	$ 11,025	$ 13,781	$ 14,884	$ 15,435	$ 55,125
Facility maintenance costs	$ 26,354	$ 32,942	$ 35,578	$ 36,895	$ 131,769
Utility expenses	$ 9,371	$ 11,714	$ 12,651	$ 13,120	$ 46,856
Miscellaneous costs	$ 15,454	$ 19,318	$ 20,863	$ 21,636	$ 77,272
Payroll taxes	$ 32,145	$ 40,182	$ 43,396	$ 45,003	$ 160,726
Total operating costs	**$ 409,759**	**$ 512,198**	**$ 553,174**	**$ 573,662**	**$2,048,793**
EBITDA	**$ 395,155**	**$ 493,943**	**$ 533,459**	**$ 553,216**	**$1,975,773**
Federal income tax	$ 130,401	$ 163,001	$ 176,041	$ 182,561	$ 652,005
State income tax	$ 19,758	$ 24,697	$ 26,673	$ 27,661	$ 98,789
Interest expense	$ 0	$ 0	$ 0	$ 0	$ 0
Depreciation expense	$ 66,920	$ 66,920	$ 66,920	$ 66,920	$ 267,679
Net profit	**$ 178,076**	**$ 239,325**	**$ 263,825**	**$ 276,074**	**$ 957,300**

7.11 Three Year Cash Flow Analysis

Cash flow analysis (first year)

Month	1	2	3	4	5	6	7
Cash from operations	$ 53,017	$ 53,232	$ 53,447	$ 53,662	$ 53,878	$ 54,093	$ 54,308
Cash from receivables	$ 0	$ 0	$ 0	$ 0	$ 0	$ 0	$ 0
Operating cash inflow	**$ 53,017**	**$ 53,232**	**$ 53,447**	**$ 53,662**	**$ 53,878**	**$ 54,093**	**$ 54,308**
Other cash inflows							
Equity investment	$5,000,000	$ 0	$ 0	$ 0	$ 0	$ 0	$ 0
Increased borrowings	$ 0	$ 0	$ 0	$ 0	$ 0	$ 0	$ 0
Sales of business assets	$ 0	$ 0	$ 0	$ 0	$ 0	$ 0	$ 0
A/P increases	$ 3,159	$ 3,159	$ 3,159	$ 3,159	$ 3,159	$ 3,159	$ 3,159
Total other cash inflows	**$5,003,159**	**$ 3,159**	**$ 3,159**	**$ 3,159**	**$ 3,159**	**$ 3,159**	**$ 3,159**
Total cash inflow	**$5,056,175**	**$ 56,391**	**$ 56,606**	**$ 56,821**	**$ 57,036**	**$ 57,251**	**$ 57,467**
Cash outflows							
Repayment of principal	$ 0	$ 0	$ 0	$ 0	$ 0	$ 0	$ 0
A/P decreases	$ 2,075	$ 2,075	$ 2,075	$ 2,075	$ 2,075	$ 2,075	$ 2,075
A/R increases	$ 0	$ 0	$ 0	$ 0	$ 0	$ 0	$ 0
Asset purchases	$3,650,000	$ 0	$ 0	$ 0	$ 0	$ 0	$ 0
Dividends	$ 0	$ 0	$ 0	$ 0	$ 0	$ 0	$ 0
Total cash outflows	**$3,652,075**	**$ 2,075**	**$ 2,075**	**$ 2,075**	**$ 2,075**	**$ 2,075**	**$ 2,075**
Net cash flow	**$1,404,101**	**$ 54,316**	**$ 54,531**	**$ 54,746**	**$ 54,961**	**$ 55,177**	**$ 55,392**
Cash balance	**$1,404,101**	**$1,458,416**	**$1,512,947**	**$1,567,694**	**$1,622,655**	**$1,677,832**	**$1,733,224**

Cash flow analysis (first year cont.)

Month	8	9	10	11	12	1
Cash from operations	$ 54,523	$ 54,739	$ 54,954	$ 55,169	$ 55,384	$ 650,407
Cash from receivables	$ 0	$ 0	$ 0	$ 0	$ 0	$ 0
Operating cash inflow	**$ 54,523**	**$ 54,739**	**$ 54,954**	**$ 55,169**	**$ 55,384**	**$ 650,407**
Other cash inflows						
Equity investment	$ 0	$ 0	$ 0	$ 0	$ 0	$ 5,000,000
Increased borrowings	$ 0	$ 0	$ 0	$ 0	$ 0	$ 0
Sales of business assets	$ 0	$ 0	$ 0	$ 0	$ 0	$ 0
A/P increases	$ 3,159	$ 3,159	$ 3,159	$ 3,159	$ 3,159	$ 37,902
Total other cash inflows	**$ 3,159**	**$ 3,159**	**$ 3,159**	**$ 3,159**	**$ 3,159**	**$5,037,902**
Total cash inflow	**$ 57,682**	**$ 57,897**	**$ 58,112**	**$ 58,328**	**$ 58,543**	**$5,688,309**
Cash outflows						
Repayment of principal	$ 0	$ 0	$ 0	$ 0	$ 0	$ 0
A/P decreases	$ 2,075	$ 2,075	$ 2,075	$ 2,075	$ 2,075	$ 24,897
A/R increases	$ 0	$ 0	$ 0	$ 0	$ 0	$ 0
Asset purchases	$ 0	$ 0	$ 0	$ 0	$ 0	$3,650,000
Dividends	$ 0	$ 0	$ 0	$ 0	$ 455,285	$ 455,285
Total cash outflows	**$ 2,075**	**$ 2,075**	**$ 2,075**	**$ 2,075**	**$ 457,360**	**$4,130,182**
Net cash flow	**$ 55,607**	**$ 55,822**	**$ 56,038**	**$ 56,253**	**−$ 398,817**	**$1,558,127**
Cash balance	**$1,788,831**	**$1,844,653**	**$1,900,691**	**$1,956,944**	**$1,558,127**	**$1,558,127**

Cash flow analysis (second year)

Quarter	Q1	2 Q2	Q3	Q4	2
Cash from operations	$ 187,061	$ 233,826	$ 252,532	$ 261,885	$ 935,303
Cash from receivables	$ 0	$ 0	$ 0	$ 0	$ 0
Operating cash inflow	**$ 187,061**	**$ 233,826**	**$ 252,532**	**$ 261,885**	**$ 935,303**
Other cash inflows					
Equity investment	$ 0	$ 0	$ 0	$ 0	$ 0
Increased borrowings	$ 0	$ 0	$ 0	$ 0	$ 0
Sales of business assets	$ 0	$ 0	$ 0	$ 0	$ 0
A/P increases	$ 8,717	$ 10,897	$ 11,769	$ 12,204	$ 43,587
Total other cash inflows	**$ 8,717**	**$ 10,897**	**$ 11,769**	**$ 12,204**	**$ 43,587**
Total cash inflow	**$ 195,778**	**$ 244,723**	**$ 264,300**	**$ 274,089**	**$ 978,891**
Cash outflows					
Repayment of principal	$ 0	$ 0	$ 0	$ 0	$ 0
A/P decreases	$ 5,975	$ 7,469	$ 8,067	$ 8,365	$ 29,876
A/R increases	$ 0	$ 0	$ 0	$ 0	$ 0
Asset purchases	$ 46,765	$ 58,456	$ 63,133	$ 65,471	$ 233,826
Dividends	$ 130,942	$ 163,678	$ 176,772	$ 183,319	$ 654,712
Total cash outflows	**$ 183,683**	**$ 229,604**	**$ 247,972**	**$ 257,156**	**$ 918,415**
Net cash flow	**$ 12,095**	**$ 15,119**	**$ 16,329**	**$ 16,933**	**$ 60,476**
Cash balance	**$1,570,222**	**$1,585,341**	**$1,601,670**	**$1,618,603**	**$1,618,603**

Cash flow analysis (third year)

Quarter	Q1	3 Q2	Q3	Q4	3
Cash from operations	$ 244,996	$ 306,245	$ 330,744	$ 342,994	$ 1,224,979
Cash from receivables	$ 0	$ 0	$ 0	$ 0	$ 0
Operating cash inflow	**$ 244,996**	**$ 306,245**	**$ 330,744**	**$ 342,994**	**$ 1,224,979**
Other cash inflows					
Equity investment	$ 0	$ 0	$ 0	$ 0	$ 0
Increased borrowings	$ 0	$ 0	$ 0	$ 0	$ 0
Sales of business assets	$ 0	$ 0	$ 0	$ 0	$ 0
A/P increases	$ 10,025	$ 12,531	$ 13,534	$ 14,035	$ 50,125
Total other cash inflows	**$ 10,025**	**$ 12,531**	**$ 13,534**	**$ 14,035**	**$ 50,125**
Total cash inflow	**$ 255,021**	**$ 318,776**	**$ 344,278**	**$ 357,029**	**$ 1,275,104**
Cash outflows					
Repayment of principal	$ 0	$ 0	$ 0	$ 0	$ 0
A/P decreases	$ 7,170	$ 8,963	$ 9,680	$ 10,038	$ 35,852
A/R increases	$ 0	$ 0	$ 0	$ 0	$ 0
Asset purchases	$ 61,249	$ 76,561	$ 82,686	$ 85,749	$ 306,245
Dividends	$ 171,497	$ 214,371	$ 231,521	$ 240,096	$ 857,485
Total cash outflows	**$ 239,916**	**$ 299,895**	**$ 323,887**	**$ 335,883**	**$ 1,199,582**
Net cash flow	**$ 15,105**	**$ 18,881**	**$ 20,391**	**$ 21,146**	**$ 75,523**
Cash balance	**$1,633,708**	**$1,652,588**	**$1,672,979**	**$1,694,126**	**$1,694,126**

BUSINESS PLAN TEMPLATE

USING THIS TEMPLATE

A business plan carefully spells out a company's projected course of action over a period of time, usually the first two to three years after the start-up. In addition, banks, lenders, and other investors examine the information and financial documentation before deciding whether or not to finance a new business venture. Therefore, a business plan is an essential tool in obtaining financing and should describe the business itself in detail as well as all important factors influencing the company, including the market, industry, competition, operations and management policies, problem solving strategies, financial resources and needs, and other vital information. The plan enables the business owner to anticipate costs, plan for difficulties, and take advantage of opportunities, as well as design and implement strategies that keep the company running as smoothly as possible.

This template has been provided as a model to help you construct your own business plan. Please keep in mind that there is no single acceptable format for a business plan, and that this template is in no way comprehensive, but serves as an example.

The business plans provided in this section are fictional and have been used by small business agencies as models for clients to use in compiling their own business plans.

GENERIC BUSINESS PLAN

Main headings included below are topics that should be covered in a comprehensive business plan. They include:

Business Summary

Purpose
Provides a brief overview of your business, succinctly highlighting the main ideas of your plan.

Includes

- Name and Type of Business
- Description of Product/Service
- Business History and Development
- Location
- Market

- Competition
- Management
- Financial Information
- Business Strengths and Weaknesses
- Business Growth

Table of Contents

Purpose
Organized in an Outline Format, the Table of Contents illustrates the selection and arrangement of information contained in your plan.

Includes

- Topic Headings and Subheadings
- Page Number References

Business History and Industry Outlook

Purpose

Examines the conception and subsequent development of your business within an industry specific context.

Includes

- Start-up Information
- Owner/Key Personnel Experience
- Location
- Development Problems and Solutions
- Investment/Funding Information
- Future Plans and Goals
- Market Trends and Statistics
- Major Competitors
- Product/Service Advantages
- National, Regional, and Local Economic Impact

Product/Service

Purpose

Introduces, defines, and details the product and/or service that inspired the information of your business.

Includes

- Unique Features
- Niche Served
- Market Comparison
- Stage of Product/Service Development
- Production
- Facilities, Equipment, and Labor
- Financial Requirements
- Product/Service Life Cycle
- Future Growth

Market Examination

Purpose

Assessment of product/service applications in relation to consumer buying cycles.

Includes

- Target Market
- Consumer Buying Habits
- Product/Service Applications
- Consumer Reactions
- Market Factors and Trends
- Penetration of the Market
- Market Share
- Research and Studies
- Cost
- Sales Volume and Goals

Competition

Purpose

Analysis of Competitors in the Marketplace.

Includes

- Competitor Information
- Product/Service Comparison
- Market Niche
- Product/Service Strengths and Weaknesses
- Future Product/Service Development

Marketing

Purpose

Identifies promotion and sales strategies for your product/service.

Includes

- Product/Service Sales Appeal
- Special and Unique Features
- Identification of Customers
- Sales and Marketing Staff
- Sales Cycles
- Type of Advertising/ Promotion
- Pricing
- Competition
- Customer Services

Operations

Purpose

Traces product/service development from production/inception to the market environment.

Includes

- Cost Effective Production Methods
- Facility
- Location
- Equipment
- Labor
- Future Expansion

Administration and Management

Purpose

Offers a statement of your management philosophy with an in-depth focus on processes and procedures.

Includes

- Management Philosophy
- Structure of Organization
- Reporting System
- Methods of Communication
- Employee Skills and Training
- Employee Needs and Compensation
- Work Environment
- Management Policies and Procedures
- Roles and Responsibilities

Key Personnel

Purpose

Describes the unique backgrounds of principle employees involved in business.

Includes

- Owner(s)/Employee Education and Experience
- Positions and Roles
- Benefits and Salary
- Duties and Responsibilities
- Objectives and Goals

Potential Problems and Solutions

Purpose

Discussion of problem solving strategies that change issues into opportunities.

Includes

- Risks
- Litigation
- Future Competition
- Economic Impact
- Problem Solving Skills

Financial Information

Purpose

Secures needed funding and assistance through worksheets and projections detailing financial plans, methods of repayment, and future growth opportunities.

Includes

- Financial Statements
- Bank Loans
- Methods of Repayment
- Tax Returns
- Start-up Costs
- Projected Income (3 years)
- Projected Cash Flow (3 Years)
- Projected Balance Statements (3 years)

Appendices

Purpose

Supporting documents used to enhance your business proposal.

Includes

- Photographs of product, equipment, facilities, etc.
- Copyright/Trademark Documents
- Legal Agreements
- Marketing Materials
- Research and or Studies
- Operation Schedules
- Organizational Charts
- Job Descriptions
- Resumes
- Additional Financial Documentation

Fictional Food Distributor

Commercial Foods, Inc.

3003 Avondale Ave.
Knoxville, TN 37920

This plan demonstrates how a partnership can have a positive impact on a new business. It demonstrates how two individuals can carve a niche in the specialty foods market by offering gourmet foods to upscale restaurants and fine hotels. This plan is fictional and has not been used to gain funding from a bank or other lending institution.

STATEMENT OF PURPOSE

Commercial Foods, Inc. seeks a loan of $75,000 to establish a new business. This sum, together with $5,000 equity investment by the principals, will be used as follows:

- Merchandise inventory $25,000
- Office fixture/equipment $12,000
- Warehouse equipment $14,000
- One delivery truck $10,000
- Working capital $39,000
- Total $100,000

DESCRIPTION OF THE BUSINESS

Commercial Foods, Inc. will be a distributor of specialty food service products to hotels and upscale restaurants in the geographical area of a 50 mile radius of Knoxville. Richard Roberts will direct the sales effort and John Williams will manage the warehouse operation and the office. One delivery truck will be used initially with a second truck added in the third year. We expect to begin operation of the business within 30 days after securing the requested financing.

MANAGEMENT

A. Richard Roberts is a native of Memphis, Tennessee. He is a graduate of Memphis State University with a Bachelor's degree from the School of Business. After graduation, he worked for a major manufacturer of specialty food service products as a detail sales person for five years, and, for the past three years, he has served as a product sales manager for this firm.

B. John Williams is a native of Nashville, Tennessee. He holds a B.S. Degree in Food Technology from the University of Tennessee. His career includes five years as a product development chemist in gourmet food products and five years as operations manager for a food service distributor.

Both men are healthy and energetic. Their backgrounds complement each other, which will ensure the success of Commercial Foods, Inc. They will set policies together and personnel decisions will be made jointly. Initial salaries for the owners will be $1,000 per month for the first few years. The spouses of both principals are successful in the business world and earn enough to support the families.

They have engaged the services of Foster Jones, CPA, and William Hale, Attorney, to assist them in an advisory capacity.

PERSONNEL

The firm will employ one delivery truck driver at a wage of $8.00 per hour. One office worker will be employed at $7.50 per hour. One part-time employee will be used in the office at $5.00 per hour. The driver will load and unload his own trucks. Mr. Williams will assist in the warehouse operation as needed to assist one stock person at $7.00 per hour. An additional delivery truck and driver will be added the third year.

LOCATION

The firm will lease a 20,000 square foot building at 3003 Avondale Ave., in Knoxville, which contains warehouse and office areas equipped with two-door truck docks. The annual rental is $9,000. The building was previously used as a food service warehouse and very little modification to the building will be required.

PRODUCTS AND SERVICES

The firm will offer specialty food service products such as soup bases, dessert mixes, sauce bases, pastry mixes, spices, and flavors, normally used by upscale restaurants and nice hotels. We are going after a niche in the market with high quality gourmet products. There is much less competition in this market than in standard run of the mill food service products. Through their work experiences, the principals have contacts with supply sources and with local chefs.

THE MARKET

We know from our market survey that there are over 200 hotels and upscale restaurants in the area we plan to serve. Customers will be attracted by a direct sales approach. We will offer samples of our products and product application data on use of our products in the finished prepared foods. We will cultivate the chefs in these establishments. The technical background of John Williams will be especially useful here.

COMPETITION

We find that we will be only distributor in the area offering a full line of gourmet food service products. Other foodservice distributors offer only a few such items in conjunction with their standard product line. Our survey shows that many of the chefs are ordering products from Atlanta and Memphis because of a lack of adequate local supply.

SUMMARY

Commercial Foods, Inc. will be established as a foodservice distributor of specialty food in Knoxville. The principals, with excellent experience in the industry, are seeking a $75,000 loan to establish the business. The principals are investing $25,000 as equity capital.

The business will be set up as an S Corporation with each principal owning 50% of the common stock in the corporation.

FICTIONAL HARDWARE STORE
OSHKOSH HARDWARE, INC.

123 Main St.
Oshkosh, WI 54901

The following plan outlines how a small hardware store can survive competition from large discount chains by offering products and providing expert advice in the use of any product it sells. This plan is fictional and has not been used to gain funding from a bank or other lending institution.

EXECUTIVE SUMMARY

Oshkosh Hardware, Inc. is a new corporation that is going to establish a retail hardware store in a strip mall in Oshkosh, Wisconsin. The store will sell hardware of all kinds, quality tools, paint, and housewares. The business will make revenue and a profit by servicing its customers not only with needed hardware but also with expert advice in the use of any product it sells.

Oshkosh Hardware, Inc. will be operated by its sole shareholder, James Smith. The company will have a total of four employees. It will sell its products in the local market. Customers will buy our products because we will provide free advice on the use of all of our products and will also furnish a full refund warranty.

Oshkosh Hardware, Inc. will sell its products in the Oshkosh store staffed by three sales representatives. No additional employees will be needed to achieve its short and long range goals. The primary short range goal is to open the store by October 1, 1994. In order to achieve this goal a lease must be signed by July 1, 1994 and the complete inventory ordered by August 1, 1994.

Mr. James Smith will invest $30,000 in the business. In addition, the company will have to borrow $150,000 during the first year to cover the investment in inventory, accounts receivable, and furniture and equipment. The company will be profitable after six months of operation and should be able to start repayment of the loan in the second year.

THE BUSINESS

The business will sell hardware of all kinds, quality tools, paint, and housewares. We will purchase our products from three large wholesale buying groups.

In general our customers are homeowners who do their own repair and maintenance, hobbyists, and housewives. Our business is unique in that we will have a complete line of all hardware items and will be able to get special orders by overnight delivery. The business makes revenue and profits by servicing our customers not only with needed hardware but also with expert advice in the use of any product we sell. Our major costs for bringing our products to market are cost of merchandise of 36%, salaries of $45,000, and occupancy costs of $60,000.

201

Oshkosh Hardware, Inc.'s retail outlet will be located at 1524 Frontage Road, which is in a newly developed retail center of Oshkosh. Our location helps facilitate accessibility from all parts of town and reduces our delivery costs. The store will occupy 7500 square feet of space. The major equipment involved in our business is counters and shelving, a computer, a paint mixing machine, and a truck.

THE MARKET

Oshkosh Hardware, Inc. will operate in the local market. There are 15,000 potential customers in this market area. We have three competitors who control approximately 98% of the market at present. We feel we can capture 25% of the market within the next four years. Our major reason for believing this is that our staff is technically competent to advise our customers in the correct use of all products we sell.

After a careful market analysis, we have determined that approximately 60% of our customers are men and 40% are women. The percentage of customers that fall into the following age categories are:

Under 16: 0%
17-21: 5%
22-30: 30%
31-40: 30%
41-50: 20%
51-60: 10%
61-70: 5%
Over 70: 0%

The reasons our customers prefer our products is our complete knowledge of their use and our full refund warranty.

We get our information about what products our customers want by talking to existing customers. There seems to be an increasing demand for our product. The demand for our product is increasing in size based on the change in population characteristics.

SALES

At Oshkosh Hardware, Inc. we will employ three sales people and will not need any additional personnel to achieve our sales goals. These salespeople will need several years experience in home repair and power tool usage. We expect to attract 30% of our customers from newspaper ads, 5% of our customers from local directories, 5% of our customers from the yellow pages, 10% of our customers from family and friends, and 50% of our customers from current customers. The most cost effect source will be current customers. In general our industry is growing.

MANAGEMENT

We would evaluate the quality of our management staff as being excellent. Our manager is experienced and very motivated to achieve the various sales and quality assurance objectives we have set. We will use a management information system that produces key inventory, quality assurance, and sales data on a weekly basis. All data is compared to previously established goals for that week, and deviations are the primary focus of the management staff.

GOALS IMPLEMENTATION

The short term goals of our business are:

1. Open the store by October 1, 1994
2. Reach our breakeven point in two months
3. Have sales of $100,000 in the first six months

In order to achieve our first short term goal we must:

1. Sign the lease by July 1, 1994
2. Order a complete inventory by August 1, 1994

In order to achieve our second short term goal we must:

1. Advertise extensively in Sept. and Oct.
2. Keep expenses to a minimum

In order to achieve our third short term goal we must:

1. Promote power tool sales for the Christmas season
2. Keep good customer traffic in Jan. and Feb.

The long term goals for our business are:

1. Obtain sales volume of $600,000 in three years
2. Become the largest hardware dealer in the city
3. Open a second store in Fond du Lac

The most important thing we must do in order to achieve the long term goals for our business is to develop a highly profitable business with excellent cash flow.

FINANCE

Oshkosh Hardware, Inc. Faces some potential threats or risks to our business. They are discount house competition. We believe we can avoid or compensate for this by providing quality products complimented by quality advice on the use of every product we sell. The financial projections we have prepared are located at the end of this document.

JOB DESCRIPTION-GENERAL MANAGER

The General Manager of the business of the corporation will be the president of the corporation. He will be responsible for the complete operation of the retail hardware store which is owned by the corporation. A detailed description of his duties and responsibilities is as follows.

Sales

Train and supervise the three sales people. Develop programs to motivate and compensate these employees. Coordinate advertising and sales promotion effects to achieve sales totals as outlined in budget. Oversee purchasing function and inventory control procedures to insure adequate merchandise at all times at a reasonable cost.

Finance

Prepare monthly and annual budgets. Secure adequate line of credit from local banks. Supervise office personnel to insure timely preparation of records, statements, all government reports, control of receivables and payables, and monthly financial statements.

Administration

Perform duties as required in the areas of personnel, building leasing and maintenance, licenses and permits, and public relations.

Organizations, Agencies, & Consultants

A listing of Associations and Consultants of interest to entrepreneurs, followed by the ten Small Business Administration Regional Offices, Small Business Development Centers, Service Corps of Retired Executives offices, and Venture Capital and Finance Companies.

Associations

This section contains a listing of associations and other agencies of interest to the small business owner. Entries are listed alphabetically by organization name.

American Business Women's Association
9100 Ward Pkwy.
PO Box 8728
Kansas City, MO 64114-0728
(800)228-0007
E-mail: abwa@abwa.org
Website: http://www.abwa.org
Jeanne Banks, National President

American Franchisee Association
53 W Jackson Blvd., Ste. 1157
Chicago, IL 60604
(312)431-0545
E-mail: info@franchisee.org
Website: http://www.franchisee.org
Susan P. Kezios, President

American Independent Business Alliance
222 S Black Ave.
Bozeman, MT 59715
(406)582-1255
E-mail: info@amiba.net
Website: http://www.amiba.net
Jennifer Rockne, Director

American Small Businesses Association
206 E College St., Ste. 201
Grapevine, TX 76051
800-942-2722
E-mail: info@asbaonline.org
Website: http://www.asbaonline.org/

American Women's Economic Development Corporation
216 East 45th St., 10th Floor
New York, NY 10017
(917)368-6100
Fax: (212)986-7114
E-mail: info@awed.org
Website: http://www.awed.org
Roseanne Antonucci, Exec. Dir.

Association for Enterprise Opportunity
1601 N Kent St., Ste. 1101
Arlington, VA 22209
(703)841-7760
Fax: (703)841-7748
E-mail: aeo@assoceo.org
Website: http://www.microenter
priseworks.org
Bill Edwards, Exec.Dir.

Association of Small Business Development Centers
c/o Don Wilson
8990 Burke Lake Rd.
Burke, VA 22015
(703)764-9850
Fax: (703)764-1234
E-mail: info@asbdc-us.org
Website: http://www.asbdc-us.org
Don Wilson, Pres./CEO

BEST Employers Association
2505 McCabe Way
Irvine, CA 92614
(949)253-4080
800-433-0088
Fax: (714)553-0883
E-mail: info@bestlife.com
Website: http://www.bestlife.com
Donald R. Lawrenz, CEO

Center for Family Business
PO Box 24219
Cleveland, OH 44124
(440)460-5409
E-mail: grummi@aol.com
Dr. Leon A. Danco, Chm.

Coalition for Government Procurement
1990 M St. NW, Ste. 400
Washington, DC 20036
(202)331-0975
E-mail: info@thecgp.org
Website: http://www.coalgovpro.org
Paul Caggiano, Pres.

Employers of America
PO Box 1874
Mason City, IA 50402-1874
(641)424-3187
800-728-3187
Fax: (641)424-1673
E-mail: employer@employerhelp.org
Website: http://www.employerhelp.org
Jim Collison, Pres.

Family Firm Institute
200 Lincoln St., Ste. 201
Boston, MA 02111
(617)482-3045
Fax: (617)482-3049
E-mail: ffi@ffi.org
Website: http://www.ffi.org
Judy L. Green, Ph.D., Exec.Dir.

Independent Visually Impaired Enterprisers
500 S 3rd St., Apt. H
Burbank, CA 91502
(818)238-9321
E-mail: abazyn@bazyn
communications.com
http://www.acb.org/affiliates
Adris Bazyn, Pres.

International Association for Business Organizations
3 Woodthorn Ct., Ste. 12
Owings Mills, MD 21117
(410)581-1373
E-mail: nahbb@msn.com
Rudolph Lewis, Exec. Officer

International Council for Small Business
The George Washington University
School of Business and Public
Management
2115 G St. NW, Ste. 403
Washington, DC 20052
(202)994-0704
Fax: (202)994-4930
E-mail: icsb@gwu.edu
Website: http://www.icsb.org
Susan G. Duffy. Admin.

International Small Business Consortium
3309 Windjammer St.
Norman, OK 73072
E-mail: sb@isbc.com
Website: http://www.isbc.com

Kauffman Center for Entrepreneurial Leadership
4801 Rockhill Rd.
Kansas City, MO 64110-2046
(816)932-1000
E-mail: info@kauffman.org
Website: http://www.entreworld.org

National Alliance for Fair Competition
3 Bethesda Metro Center, Ste. 1100
Bethesda, MD 20814
(410)235-7116
Fax: (410)235-7116
E-mail: ampesq@aol.com
Tony Ponticelli, Exec.Dir.

National Association for the Self-Employed
PO Box 612067
DFW Airport
Dallas, TX 75261-2067
(800)232-6273
E-mail: mpetron@nase.org
Website: http://www.nase.org
Robert Hughes, Pres.

National Association of Business Leaders
4132 Shoreline Dr., Ste. J & H
Earth City, MO 63045
Fax: (314)298-9110
E-mail: nabl@nabl.com
Website: http://www.nabl.com/
Gene Blumenthal, Contact

National Association of Private Enterprise
PO Box 15550
Long Beach, CA 90815
888-224-0953
Fax: (714)844-4942
Website: http://www.napeonline.net
Laura Squiers, Exec.Dir.

National Association of Small Business Investment Companies
666 11th St. NW, Ste. 750
Washington, DC 20001
(202)628-5055
Fax: (202)628-5080
E-mail: nasbic@nasbic.org
Website: http://www.nasbic.org
Lee W. Mercer, Pres.

National Business Association
PO Box 700728
5151 Beltline Rd., Ste. 1150
Dallas, TX 75370
(972)458-0900
800-456-0440
Fax: (972)960-9149
E-mail: info@nationalbusiness.org
Website: http://www.national
business.org
Raj Nisankarao, Pres.

National Business Owners Association
PO Box 111
Stuart, VA 24171
(276)251-7500
(866)251-7505
Fax: (276)251-2217
E-mail: membershipservices@nboa.org
Website: http://www.rvmdb.com.nboa
Paul LaBarr, Pres.

National Center for Fair Competition
PO Box 220
Annandale, VA 22003
(703)280-4622
Fax: (703)280-0942
E-mail: kentonp1@aol.com
Kenton Pattie, Pres.

National Family Business Council
1640 W. Kennedy Rd.
Lake Forest, IL 60045
(847)295-1040
Fax: (847)295-1898
E-mail: lmsnfbc@email.msn.com
Jogn E. Messervey, Pres.

National Federation of Independent Business
53 Century Blvd., Ste. 250
Nashville, TN 37214
(615)872-5800
800-NFIBNOW
Fax: (615)872-5353
Website: http://www.nfib.org
Jack Faris, Pres. and CEO

National Small Business Association
1156 15th St. NW, Ste. 1100
Washington, DC 20005

(202)293-8830
800-345-6728
Fax: (202)872-8543
E-mail: press@nsba.biz
Website: http://www.nsba.biz
Rob Yunich, Dir. of Communications

PUSH Commercial Division
930 E 50th St.
Chicago, IL 60615-2702
(773)373-3366
Fax: (773)373-3571
E-mail: info@rainbowpush.org
Website: http://www.rainbowpush.org
Rev. Willie T. Barrow, Co-Chm.

Research Institute for Small and Emerging Business
722 12th St. NW
Washington, DC 20005
(202)628-8382
Fax: (202)628-8392
E-mail: info@riseb.org
Website: http://www.riseb.org
Allan Neece, Jr., Chm.

Sales Professionals USA
PO Box 149
Arvada, CO 80001
(303)534-4937
888-736-7767
E-mail: salespro@salesprofessionals-usa
.com
Website: http://www.salesprofessionals-
usa.com
Sharon Herbert, Natl. Pres.

Score Association - Service Corps of Retired Executives
409 3rd St. SW, 6th Fl.
Washington, DC 20024
(202)205-6762
800-634-0245
Fax: (202)205-7636
E-mail: media@score.org
Website: http://www.score.org
W. Kenneth Yancey, Jr., CEO

Small Business and Entrepreneurship Council
1920 L St. NW, Ste. 200
Washington, DC 20036
(202)785-0238
Fax: (202)822-8118
E-mail: membership@sbec.org
Website: http://www.sbecouncil.org
Karen Kerrigan, Pres./CEO

Small Business in Telecommunications
1331 H St. NW, Ste. 500
Washington, DC 20005

(202)347-4511
Fax: (202)347-8607
E-mail: sbt@sbthome.org
Website: http://www.sbthome.org
Lonnie Danchik, Chm.

**Small Business Legislative
Council**
1010 Massachusetts Ave. NW, Ste. 540
Washington, DC 20005
(202)639-8500
Fax: (202)296-5333
E-mail: email@sblc.org
Website: http://www.sblc.org
John Satagaj, Pres.

Small Business Service Bureau
554 Main St.
PO Box 15014
Worcester, MA 01615-0014
(508)756-3513
800-343-0939
Fax: (508)770-0528
E-mail: membership@sbsb.com
Website: http://www.sbsb.com
Francis R. Carroll, Pres.

**Small Publishers Association of North
America**
1618 W Colorado Ave.
Colorado Springs, CO 80904
(719)475-1726
Fax: (719)471-2182
E-mail: span@spannet.org
Website: http://www.spannet.org
Scott Flora, Exec. Dir.

SOHO America
PO Box 941
Hurst, TX 76053-0941
800-495-SOHO
E-mail: soho@1sas.com
Website: http://www.soho.org

**Structured Employment Economic
Development Corporation**
915 Broadway, 17th Fl.
New York, NY 10010
(212)473-0255
Fax: (212)473-0357
E-mail: info@seedco.org
Website: http://www.seedco.org
William Grinker, CEO

Support Services Alliance
107 Prospect St.
Schoharie, NY 12157
800-836-4772
E-mail: info@ssamembers.com
Website: http://www.ssainfo.com
Steve COle, Pres.

**United States Association for Small
Business and Entrepreneurship**
975 University Ave., No. 3260
Madison, WI 53706
(608)262-9982
Fax: (608)263-0818
E-mail: jgillman@wisc.edu
Website: http://www.ususbe.org
Joan Gillman, Exec. Dir.

Consultants

*This section contains a listing of consul-
tants specializing in small business development. It is arranged alphabetically by
country, then by state or province, then by
city, then by firm name.*

Canada

Alberta

Tenato
1229A 9th Ave. SE
Calgary, AB, Canada T2G 0S9
(403)242-1127
Fax: (403)261-5693
E-mail: jdrew@tenato.com
Website: http://www.tenato.com

Varsity Consulting Group
School of Business
University of Alberta
Edmonton, AB, Canada T6G 2R6
(780)492-2994
Fax: (780)492-5400

British Columbia

Andrew R. De Boda Consulting
1523 Milford Ave.
Coquitlam, BC, Canada V3J 2V9
(604)936-4527
Fax: (604)936-4527
E-mail: deboda@intergate.bc.ca

Reality Marketing Associates
3049 Sienna Ct.
Coquitlam, BC, Canada V3E 3N7
(604)944-8603
Fax: (604)944-4708
E-mail: info@realityassociates.com
Website: http://www.realityassociates.com

Pinpoint Tactics Business Consulting
5525 West Blvd., Ste. 330
Vancouver, BC, Canada V6M 3W6
(604)263-4698
E-mail: info@pinpointtactics.com
Website: http://www.pinpointtactics.com

Ketch Consulting Inc.
6890 Winnifred Pl.
Victoria, BC, Canada V8M 1N1
(250)661-1208
E-mail: info@ketch.ca
Website: http://www.ketch.ca

Mahigan Consulting Services
334 Skawshen Rd.
West Vancouver, BC, Canada V7P 3T1
(604)210-3833
Fax: (778)285-2736
E-mail: info@mahiganconsulting.com
Website: http://www.mahiganconsulting
.com

Nova Scotia

The Marketing Clinic
1384 Bedford Hwy.
Bedford, NS, Canada B4A 1E2
(902)835-4122
Fax: (902)832-9389
E-mail: office@themarketingclinic.ca
Website: http://www.themarketing
clinic.ca

Ontario

The Cynton Co.
17 Massey St.
Brampton, ON, Canada L6S 2V6
(905)792-7769
Fax: (905)792-8116
E-mail: cynton@home.com
Website: http://www.cynton.com

CRO Engineering Ltd.
1895 William Hodgins Ln.
Carp, ON, Canada K0A 1L0
(613)839-1108
Fax: (613)839-1406
E-mail: J.Grefford@ieee.ca

Business Plan World
PO Box 1322, Sta. B
Mississauga, ON, Canada L4Y 4B6
(709)643-8544
E-mail: theboss@businessplanworld.com
Website: http://www.businessplanworld
.com

JPL Consulting
236 Millard Ave.
Newmarket, ON, Canada L3Y 1Z2
(416)606-9124
E-mail: sales@jplbiz.ca
Website: http://www.jplbiz.ca

Black Eagle Consulting 2000 Inc.
451 Barclay Cres.
Oakville, ON, Canada L6J 6H8

(905)842-3010
Fax: (905)842-9586
E-mail: info@blackeagle.ca
Website: http://www.blackeagle.ca

Care Concepts & Communications
21 Spruce Hill Rd.
Toronto, ON, Canada M4E 3G2
(416)420-8840
E-mail: info@cccbizconsultants.com
Website: http://www.cccbizconsultants
.com

FHG International Inc.
14 Glengrove Ave. W
Toronto, ON, Canada M4R 1N4
(416)402-8000
E-mail: info@fhgi.com
Website: http://www.fhgi.com

Harrison Pricing Strategy Group Inc.
1235 Bay St., Ste. 400
Toronto, ON, Canada M5R 3K4
(416)218-1103
Fax: (416) 827-8595

Ken Wyman & Associates Inc.
64 Lamb Ave.
Toronto, ON, Canada V
(416)362-2926
Fax: (416)362-3039
E-mail: kenwyman@compuserve.com

Quebec

PGP Consulting
17 Linton
Dollard-des-Ormeaux, QC, Canada H9B
1P2
(514)796-7613
Fax: (866)750-0947
E-mail: pierre@pgpconsulting.com
Website: http://www.pgpconsulting.com

Komand Consulting
1250 Rene Levesque Blvd.,W
22nd Fl., Ste. 2200
Montreal, QC, Canada H3B 4W8
(514)934-9281
Fax: (514)934-0770
E-mail: info@komand.ca
Website: http://www.komand.ca

Saskatchewan

Banda Marketing Group
410 - 22nd St. E, Ste. 810
Saskatoon, SK, Canada S7K 5T6
(306) 343-6100
Fax: (306) 652-1340
E-mail: admin@bandagroup.com
Website: http://www.bandagroup.com

Oracle Planning
106 28th St. W
Saskatoon, SK, Canada, S7L 0K2
(306) 717-5001
Fax: (650)618-2742

United states

Alabama

Business Planning Inc.
2090 Columbiana Rd., Ste. 2950
Vestavia Hills, AL 35216
(205)824-8969
Fax: (205)824-8939
E-mail:
kmiller@businessplanninginc.com
Website: http://www.businessplanning
inc.com

Tradebank of Eastern Alabama
400 S St. E
Talladega, AL 35160
(256)761-9051
Fax: (256)761-9227

Alaska

Alaska Business Development Center
840 K St., Ste. 202
Anchorage, AK 99501
(907)562-0335
Free: 800-478-3474
Fax: (907)562-6988
E-mail: info@abdc.org
Website: http://www.abdc.org

Arizona

Carefree Direct Marketing Corp.
8001 E Serene St.
PO Box 3737
Carefree, AZ 85377-3737
(480)488-4227
Fax: (480)488-2841

Management 2000
39342 S Winding Trl.
Oro Valley, AZ 85737
(520)818-9988
Fax: (520)818-3277
E-mail: m2000@mgmt2000.com
Website: http://www.mgmt2000.com

CMAS
5125 N 16th St.
Phoenix, AZ 85016
(602)395-1001
Fax: (602)604-8180

Moneysoft Inc.
1 E Camelback Rd. #550
Phoenix, AZ 85012

Free: 800-966-7797
E-mail: mbray@moneysoft.com
Website: http://www.moneysoft.com

Harvey C. Skoog
7151 E Addis Ave.
Prescott Valley, AZ 86314
(928)772-1448

The De Angelis Group Inc.
9815 E Bell Rd., Ste. 120
Scottsdale, AZ 85260
(480)609-4868
Fax: (480)452-0401
E-mail: info@thedeangelisgroup.com
Website: http://www.thedeangelisgroup
.com

Incendo Marketing L.L.C.
7687 E Thunderhawk Rd., Ste. 100
Scottsdale, AZ 85255
(480)513-4208
Fax: (509)561-9011

Sauerbrun Technology Group Ltd.
7979 E Princess Dr., Ste. 5
Scottsdale, AZ 85255-5878
(602)502-4950
Fax: (602)502-4292
E-mail: info@sauerbrun.com
Website: http://www.sauerbrun.com

Van Cleve Associates
6932 E 2nd St.
Tucson, AZ 85710
(520)296-2587
Fax: (520)296-3358

Variantia
6161 N Canon del Pajaro
Tucson, AZ 85750
(520)577-7680

Louws Management Corp.
PO Box 130
Vail, AZ 85641
(520)664-1881
Fax: (928)222-0086
E-mail: info@louwstraining.com
Website: http://www.louwsmanagement
.com

California

Thomas E. Church & Associates Inc.
PO Box 2439
Aptos, CA 95001
(831) 662-7950
Fax:(831) 684-0173
E-mail: thomase2@trueyellow.net
Website: http://www.thomas_church.
ypgs.net

AB Manley Partners Worldwide L.L.C.
1428 S Marengo Ave.
Alhambra, CA 91803-3096
(626) 457-8841

Lindquist Consultants-Venture Planning
225 Arlington Ave.
Berkeley, CA 94707
(510)524-6685
Fax: (510)527-6604

One Page Business Plan Co.
1798 Fifth St.
Berkeley, CA 94710
(510)705-8400
Fax: (510)705-8403
E-mail: info@onepagebusinessplan.com
Website: http://
www.onepagebusinessplan.com

WordCraft Creative Services
2687 Shasta Rd.
Berkeley, CA 94708
(510) 848-5177
Fax:(510) 868-1006
E-mail: info@wordcraftcreative.com
Website: http://www.wordcraftcreative
.com

Growth Partners
1566 La Pradera Dr., Ste. 5
Campbell, CA 95008
(408) 871-7925
Fax: (408) 871-7924
E-mail: mark@growth-partners.com
Website: http://www.growth-partners.com

The Success Resource
25773 Flanders Pl.
Carmel, CA 93923
(831) 236-0732

W and J PARTNERSHIP
PO Box 2499
18876 Edwin Markham Dr.
Castro Valley, CA 94546
(510)583-7751
Fax: (510)583-7645
E-mail: wamorgan@wjpartnership.com
Website: http://www.wjpartnership.com

JB Associates
21118 Gardena Dr.
Cupertino, CA 95014
(408)257-0214
Fax: (408)257-0216
E-mail: semarang@sirius.com

House Agricultural Consultants
1105 Kennedy Pl., Ste. 1
Davis, CA 95616

(916)753-3361
Fax: (916)753-0464
E-mail: infoag@houseag.com
Website: http://www.houseag.com/

3C Systems Co.
16161 Ventura Blvd., Ste. 815
Encino, CA 91436
(818)907-1302
Fax: (818)907-1357
E-mail: mark@3CSysCo.com
Website: http://www.3CSysCo.com

Technical Management Consultants
3624 Westfall Dr.
Encino, CA 91436-4154
(818)784-0626
Fax: (818)501-5575
E-mail: tmcrs@aol.com

Rainwater-Gish & Associates
317 3rd St., Ste. 3
Eureka, CA 95501
(707)443-0030
Fax: (707)443-5683

MedMarket Diligence L.L.C.
51 Fairfield
Foothill Ranch, CA 92610-1856
(949) 859-3401
Fax: (949) 837-4558
E-mail: info@mediligence.com
Website: http://www.mediligence.com

Global Tradelinks
451 Pebble Beach Pl.
Fullerton, CA 92835
(714)441-2280
Fax: (714)441-2281
E-mail: info@globaltradelinks.com
Website: http://www.globaltradelinks.com

Larson Associates
1440 Harbor Blvd., Ste. 800
Fullerton, CA 92835
(714)529-4121
Fax: (714)572-3606
E-mail: ray@consultlarson.com
Website: http://www.consultlarson.com

Strategic Business Group
800 Cienaga Dr.
Fullerton, CA 92835-1248
(714)449-1040
Fax: (714)525-1631

Burnes Consulting
20537 Wolf Creek Rd.
Grass Valley, CA 95949
(530)346-8188
Free: 800-949-9021
Fax: (530)346-7704

E-mail: kent@burnesconsulting.com
Website: http://www.burnesconsulting
.com

International Health Resources
PO Box 2738
Grass Valley, CA 95945
Website: http://
www.futureofhealthcare.com

Pioneer Business Consultants
9042 Garfield Ave., Ste. 211
Huntington Beach, CA 92646
(714)964-7600

Fluor Daniel Inc.
3353 Michelson Dr.
Irvine, CA 92612-0650
(949)975-2000
Fax: (949)975-5271
E-mail: sales.consulting@fluordaniel.com
Website: http://www.fluor.com

MCS Associates
18881 Von Karman, Ste. 1175
Irvine, CA 92612
(949)263-8700
Fax: (949)263-0770
E-mail: info@mcsassociates.com
Website: http://www.mcsassociates.com

Savvy Communications
9730 Soda Bay Rd., Ste. 5035
Kelseyville, CA 95451-9576
(707) 277-8078
Fax:(707) 277-8079

Sky Blue Consulting Inc.
4165 Executive Dr.
Lafayette, CA 94549
(925) 283-8272

Comprehensive Business Services
3201 Lucas Cir.
Lafayette, CA 94549
(925)283-8272
Fax: (925)283-8272

The Ribble Group
27601 Forbes Rd., Ste. 52
Laguna Niguel, CA 92677
(714)582-1085
Fax: (714)582-6420
E-mail: ribble@deltanet.com

Norris Bernstein, CMC
9309 Marina Pacifica Dr. N
Long Beach, CA 90803
(562)493-5458
Fax: (562)493-5459
E-mail: norris@ctecomputer.com
Website: http://foodconsultants.com/
bernstein/

Horizon Consulting Services
1315 Garthwick Dr.
Los Altos, CA 94024
(415)967-0906
Fax: (650)967-0906

Blue Garnet Associates L.L.C.
8055 W Manchester Ave., Ste. 430
Los Angeles, CA 90293
(310) 439-1930
Fax: (310) 388-1657
E-mail: hello@bluegarnet.net
Website: http://www.bluegarnet.net

CAST Management Consultants Inc.
700 S Flower St., Ste. 1900
Los Angeles, CA 90017
(213) 614-8066
Fax: (213) 614-0760
E-mail: info@castconsultants.com
Website: http://www.castconsultants.com

Rubenstein/Justman Management Consultants
11620 Wilshire Blvd., Ste. 750
Los Angeles, CA 90025
(310)445-5300
Fax: (310)496-1450
E-mail: info@rjmc.net
Website: http://www.rjmc.net

F.J. Schroeder & Associates
1926 Westholme Ave.
Los Angeles, CA 90025
(310)470-2655
Fax: (310)470-6378
E-mail: fjsacons@aol.com
Website: http://www.mcninet.com/
GlobalLook/Fjschroe.html

Western Management Associates
5777 W Century Blvd., Ste. 1220
Los Angeles, CA 90045
(310)645-1091
Free: (888)788-6534
Fax: (310)645-1092
E-mail: gene@cfoforrent.com
Website: http://www.cfoforrent.com

Inspiration Quest Inc.
PO Box 90
Mendocino, CA 95460
(415) 235-6002
E-mail: info@inspirationquest.com
Website: http://www.inspirationquest.com

Heron Advisory Group
9 Heron Dr.
Mill Valley, CA 94941
(415) 380-8611
Fax: (415) 381-9044
E-mail: janetmca@pacbell.net
Website: http://www.hagroup.biz

Emacula Consulting Group
131 Draeger Dr., Ste. A
Moraga, CA 94556
(925) 388-6083
Fax: (267) 589-3151
E-mail: drochlin@emacula.com
Website: http://www.emacula.com

BizplanSource
1048 Irvine Ave., Ste. 621
Newport Beach, CA 92660
Free: 888-253-0974
Fax: 800-859-8254
E-mail: info@bizplansource.com
Website: http://www.bizplansource.com
Adam Greengrass, President

The Market Connection
20051 SW Birch St., Ste 310
Newport Beach, CA 92660
(949)851-6313
Fax: (949)833-0283

Intelequest Corp.
722 Gailen Ave.
Palo Alto, CA 94303
(415)968-3443
Fax: (415)493-6954
E-mail: frits@iqix.com

Beblie, Brandt & Jacobs Inc.
19 Brista del Lago
Rancho Santa Margarita, CA 92618
(949)589-5120
Fax: (949)203-6225
E-mail: darcy@bbjinc.com

California Business Incubation Network
225 Broadway, Ste. 2250
San Diego, CA 92101
(619)237-0559
Fax: (619)237-0521

The Drake Group
824 Santa Clara Pl.
San Diego, CA 92109-7224
X(858) 488-3911
Fax: (810) 454-4593
E-mail: cdrake@drakegroup.com
Website: http://www.drakegroup.com

G.R. Gordetsky Consultants Inc.
11414 Windy Summit Pl.
San Diego, CA 92127
(858)487-4939
E-mail: gordet@pacbell.net

Noorany Marketing Resources
3830 Valley Centre Dr., Ste. 705
San Diego, CA 92130
(858) 792-9559

Fax: (858) 259-2320
E-mail: heidi@noorany.com
Website: http://www.noorany.com

Freeman, Sullivan & Co.
1101 Montgomery St., 15th Fl.
San Francisco, CA 94104
Website: http://www.fscgroup.com

PKF Consulting Corp.
50 California St., 19th Fl.
San Francisco, CA 94111
(415)788-3102
Fax: (415)433-7844
E-mail: callahan@pkfc.com
Website: http://www.pkfc.com

Welling & Woodard Inc.
1067 Broadway
San Francisco, CA 94133
(415)776-4500
Fax: (415)776-5067

Highland Associates
16174 Highland Dr.
San Jose, CA 95127
(408)272-7008
Fax: (408)272-4040

Leckrone Law Corp.
4010 Moorpark Ave., Ste. 215
San Jose, CA 95117-1843
(408) 243-9898
Fax: (408) 296-6637

ORDIS Inc.
6815 Trinidad Dr.
San Jose, CA 95120-2056
(408)268-3321
Free: 800-446-7347
Fax: (408)268-3582
E-mail: ordis@ordis.com
Website: http://www.ordis.com

Bay Area Tax Consultants and Bayhill Financial Consultants
1840 Gateway Dr.
San Mateo, CA 94404
(650)378-1373
Fax: (650)585-5444
E-mail: admin@baytax.com
Website: http://www.baytax.com/

Helfert Associates
111 St. Matthews, Ste. 307
San Mateo, CA 94401
(650)377-0540
Fax: (650)377-0472

Mykytyn Consulting Group Inc.
185 N Redwood Dr., Ste. 200
San Rafael, CA 94903
(415)491-1770

Fax: (415)491-1251
E-mail: info@mcgi.com

Omega Management Systems Inc.
3 Mount Darwin Ct.
San Rafael, CA 94903-1109
(415)499-1300
Fax: (415)492-9490
E-mail: information@omegamgt.com

Manex Consulting
2010 Crow Canyon Pl., Ste. 320
San Ramon, CA 94583
(925) 807-5100
Website: http://www.manexconsulting.com

Brincko Associates Inc.
530 Wilshire Blvd., Ste. 201
Santa Monica, CA 90401
(310)553-4523
Fax: (310)553-6782

E Myth
131B Stony Cir., Ste. 2000
Santa Rosa, CA 95401
(541)552-4600
Free: 800-300-3531
E-mail: info@emyth.com
Website: http://www.emyth.com

Figueroa Farms L.L.C.
PO Box 206
Santa Ynez, CA 93460
(805) 686-4890
Fax: (805) 686-2887
E-mail: info@figueroafarms.com
Website: http://www.FigueroaFarms.com

Reilly, Connors & Ray
1743 Canyon Rd.
Spring Valley, CA 91977
(619)698-4808
Fax: (619)460-3892
E-mail: davidray@adnc.com

RJR Associates
1639 Lewiston Dr.
Sunnyvale, CA 94087
(408)737-7720
E-mail: bobroy@rjrassoc.com
Website: http://www.rjrassoc.com

Schwafel Associates
333 Cobalt Way, Ste. 107
Sunnyvale, CA 94085
(408)720-0649
Fax: (408)720-1796
E-mail: schwafel@ricochet.net
Website: http://www.patca.org

The International Coverting Institute
5200 Badger Rd
Terrebonne, CA 97760

(503) 548-1447
Fax: (503) 548-1618

GlobalReady
1521 Kirk Ave.
Thousand Oaks, CA 91360
(805) 427-4131
E-mail: info@globalready.com
Website: http://www.globalready.com

Staubs Business Services
23320 S Vermont Ave.
Torrance, CA 90502-2940
(310)830-9128
Fax: (310)830-9128
E-mail: Harry_L_Staubs@Lamg.com

Enterprise Management Corp.
17461 Irvine Blvd., Ste. M
Tustin, CA 92780
(714) 505-1925
Fax: (714) 505-9691
E-mail: cfotogo@companycfo.com
Website: http://www.companycfo.com

Out of Your Mind...and Into the Marketplace
13381 White Sands Dr.
Tustin, CA 92780-4565
(714)544-0248
Free: 800-419-1513
Fax: (714)730-1414
Website: http://www.business-plan.com

Ingman Company Inc.
7949 Woodley Ave., Ste. 120
Van Nuys, CA 91406-1232
(805)650-9353
Fax: (805)984-2979

Innovative Technology Associates
3639 E Harbor Blvd., Ste. 203E
Ventura, CA 93001
(805)650-9353

Grid Technology Associates
20404 Tufts Cir.
Walnut, CA 91789
(909)444-0922
Fax: (909)444-0922

Bell Springs Publishing
PO Box 1240
Willits, CA 95490
(707)459-6372
E-mail: bellsprings@sabernet
Website: http://www.bellsprings.com

Hutchinson Consulting and Appraisal
23245 Sylvan St., Ste. 103
Woodland Hills, CA 91367
(818)888-8175
Free: 800-977-7548

Fax: (818)888-8220
E-mail: r.f.hutchinson-cpa@worldnet.att.net

Colorado

Sam Boyer & Associates
4255 S Buckley Rd., No. 136
Aurora, CO 80013
(303)766-1557
Free: 800-785-0485
Fax: (303)766-8740
E-mail: samboyer@samboyer.com
Website: http://www.samboyer.com/

Associated Enterprises Ltd.
183 Pauls Ln.
Bailey, CO 80421

Comer & Associates LLC
5255 Holmes Pl.
Boulder, CO 80303
(303) 786-7986
Fax: (303)895-2347
E-mail: jerry@comerassociates.com
Website: http://www.comerassociates.com

Ameriwest Business Consultants Inc.
3725 E. Wade Ln.
Colorado Springs, CO 80917
(719)380-7096
Fax: (719)380-7096
E-mail: email@abchelp.com
Website: http://www.abchelp.com

GVNW Consulting Inc.
2270 La Montana Way
Colorado Springs, CO 80936
(719)594-5800
Fax: (719)594-5803
Website: http://www.gvnw.com

M-Squared Inc.
755 San Gabriel Pl.
Colorado Springs, CO 80906
(719)576-2554
Fax: (719)576-2554

Foxhall Consulting Services
2532 Dahlia St.
Denver, CO 80207
(303)355-7995
Fax: (303)377-0716
E-mail: michael@foxhallconsulting.com
Website: http://www.foxhallconsulting.com

KLA Associates
2352 Humboldt St.
Denver, CO 80205-5332
(303)830-8042

Wilson Hughes Consulting LLC
2100 Humboldt St., Ste. 302
Denver, CO 80205
Website: http://www.wilsonhughes
consultingllc.com

Co-Active Communications Corp.
400 Inverness Pkwy., Ste. 200
Englewood, CO 80112-6415
(303)771-6181
Fax: (303)771-0080

Thornton Financial FNIC
1024 Centre Ave., Bldg. E
Fort Collins, CO 80526-1849
(970)221-2089
Fax: (970)484-5206

Extelligent Inc.
8400 E Crescent Pky., Ste. 600
Greenwood Village, CO 80111
(720)201-5672
E-mail: info@extelligent.com
Website: http://www.extelligent.com

Western Capital Holdings Inc.
10050 E Applwood Dr.
Parker, CO 80138
(303)841-1022
Fax: (303)770-1945

Connecticut

Christiansen Consulting
56 Scarborough St.
Hartford, CT 06105
(860)586-8265
Fax: (860)233-3420
Website: http://www.Christiansen
Consulting.com

Follow-up News
185 Pine St., Ste. 818
Manchester, CT 06040
(860)647-7542
Free: 800-708-0696
Fax: (860)646-6544
E-mail: Followupnews@aol.com

Musevue360
555 Millbrook Rd.
Middletown, CT 06457
(860)463-7722
Fax: (860)346-3013
E-mail: jennifer.eifrig@musevue360
.com
Website: http://www.musevue360.com

Alltis Corp.
747 Farmington Ave., Ste. 6
New Britain, CT 06053
(860)224-1300
Fax: (860)224-1700

E-mail: info@alltis.com
Website: http://www.alltis.com

Kalba International Inc.
116 McKinley Ave.
New Haven, CT 06515
(203)397-2199
Fax: (781)240-2657
E-mail: kalba@comcast.net
Website: http://www.kalbainternational
.com

Lovins & Associates Consulting
357 Whitney Ave.
New Haven, CT 06511
(203)787-3367
Fax: (203)624-7599
E-mail: Alovinsphd@aol.com
Website: http://www.lovinsgroup.com

JC Ventures Inc.
4 Arnold St.
Old Greenwich, CT 06870-1203
(203)698-1990
Free: 800-698-1997
Fax: (203)698-2638

Charles L. Hornung Associates
52 Ned's Mountain Rd.
Ridgefield, CT 06877
(203)431-0297

Greenwich Associates
6 High Ridge Park
Stamford, CT 06905
(203)629-1200
Fax: (203)629-1229
E-mail: lisa@greenwich.com
Website: http://www.greenwich.com

Management Practice Inc.
216 W Hill Rd.
Stamford, CT 06902
(203)973-0535
Fax: (203)978-9034
E-mail: mpayne@mpiweb.com
Website: http://www.mpiweb.com

RealBusinessPlans.com
156 Westport Rd.
Wilton, CT 06897
(914)837-2886
E-mail: ct@realbusinessplans.com
Website: http://www.RealBusinessPlans
.com

Wellspring Consulting LLC
198 Amity Rd., 2nd Fl.
Woodbridge, CT 06525
(203)387-7192
Fax: (203)387-1345
E-mail: info@wellspringconsulting.net

Website: http://www.wellspring
consulting.net

Delaware

Focus Marketing
61-7 Habor Dr.
Claymont, DE 19703
(302)793-3064

Daedalus Ventures Ltd.
PO Box 1474
Hockessin, DE 19707
(302)239-6758
Fax: (302)239-9991
E-mail: daedalus@mail.del.net

The Formula Group
PO Box 866
Hockessin, DE 19707
(302)456-0952
Fax: (302)456-1354
E-mail: formula@netaxs.com

Selden Enterprises Inc.
2502 Silverside Rd., Ste. 1
Wilmington, DE 19810-3740
(302)529-7113
Fax: (302)529-7442
E-mail: selden2@bellatlantic.net
Website: http://www.seldenenterprises
.com

District of Columbia

Bruce W. McGee and Associates
7826 Eastern Ave. NW, Ste. 30
Washington, DC 20012
(202)726-7272
Fax: (202)726-2946

McManis Associates Inc.
1900 K St. NW, Ste. 700
Washington, DC 20006
(202)466-7680
Fax: (202)872-1898
Website: http://www.mcmanis-mmi.com

Smith, Dawson & Andrews Inc.
1000 Connecticut Ave., Ste. 302
Washington, DC 20036
(202)835-0740
Fax: (202)775-8526
E-mail: webmaster@sda-inc.com
Website: http://www.sda-inc.com

Florida

BackBone, Inc.
20404 Hacienda Court
Boca Raton, FL 33498
(561)470-0965

Fax: 516-908-4038
E-mail: BPlans@backboneinc.com
Website: http://www.backboneinc.com
Charles Epstein, President

Whalen & Associates Inc.
4255 Northwest 26 Ct.
Boca Raton, FL 33434
(561)241-5950
Fax: (561)241-7414
E-mail: drwhalen@ix.netcom.com

E.N. Rysso & Associates
180 Bermuda Petrel Ct.
Daytona Beach, FL 32119
(386)760-3028
E-mail: erysso@aol.com

Virtual Technocrats LLC
560 Lavers Circle, #146
Delray Beach, FL 33444
(561)265-3509
E-mail: josh@virtualtechnocrats.com;
info@virtualtechnocrats.com
Website: http://www.virtualtechnocrats
.com
Josh Eikov, Managing Director

Eric Sands Consulting Services
6193 Rock Island Rd., Ste. 412
Fort Lauderdale, FL 33319
(954)721-4767
Fax: (954)720-2815
E-mail: easands@aol.com
Website: http://www.ericsandsconsultig
.com

Professional Planning Associates, Inc.
1975 E. Sunrise Blvd. Suite 607
Fort Lauderdale, FL 33304
(954)764-5204
Fax: 954-463-4172
E-mail: Mgoldstein@proplana.com
Website: http://proplana.com
Michael Goldstein, President

Host Media Corp.
3948 S 3rd St., Ste. 191
Jacksonville Beach, FL 32250
(904)285-3239
Fax: (904)285-5618
E-mail: msconsulting@compuserve.com
Website: http://www.mediaservicesgroup
.com

William V. Hall
1925 Brickell, Ste. D-701
Miami, FL 33129
(305)856-9622
Fax: (305)856-4113
E-mail: williamvhall@compuserve.com

F.A. McGee Inc.
800 Claughton Island Dr., Ste. 401
Miami, FL 33131
(305)377-9123

Taxplan Inc.
Mirasol International Ctr.
2699 Collins Ave.
Miami Beach, FL 33140
(305)538-3303

T.C. Brown & Associates
8415 Excalibur Cir., Apt. B1
Naples, FL 34108
(941)594-1949
Fax: (941)594-0611
E-mail: tcater@naples.net.com

RLA International Consulting
713 Lagoon Dr.
North Palm Beach, FL 33408
(407)626-4258
Fax: (407)626-5772

Comprehensive Franchising Inc.
2465 Ridgecrest Ave.
Orange Park, FL 32065
(904)272-6567
Free: 800-321-6567
Fax: (904)272-6750
E-mail: theimp@cris.com
Website: http://www.franchise411.com

Hunter G. Jackson Jr. - Consulting Environmental Physicist
PO Box 618272
Orlando, FL 32861-8272
(407)295-4188
E-mail: hunterjackson@juno.com

F. Newton Parks
210 El Brillo Way
Palm Beach, FL 33480
(561)833-1727
Fax: (561)833-4541

Avery Business Development Services
2506 St. Michel Ct.
Ponte Vedra Beach, FL 32082
(904)285-6033
Fax: (904)285-6033

Strategic Business Planning Co.
PO Box 821006
South Florida, FL 33082-1006
(954)704-9100
Fax: (954)438-7333
E-mail: info@bizplan.com
Website: http://www.bizplan.com

Dufresne Consulting Group Inc.
10014 N Dale Mabry, Ste. 101
Tampa, FL 33618-4426

(813)264-4775
Fax: (813)264-9300
Website: http://www.dcgconsult.com

Agrippa Enterprises Inc.
PO Box 175
Venice, FL 34284-0175
(941)355-7876
E-mail: webservices@agrippa.com
Website: http://www.agrippa.com

Center for Simplified Strategic Planning Inc.
PO Box 3324
Vero Beach, FL 32964-3324
(561)231-3636
Fax: (561)231-1099
Website: http://www.cssp.com

Georgia

Marketing Spectrum Inc.
115 Perimeter Pl., Ste. 440
Atlanta, GA 30346
(770)395-7244
Fax: (770)393-4071

Business Ventures Corp.
1650 Oakbrook Dr., Ste. 405
Norcross, GA 30093
(770)729-8000
Fax: (770)729-8028

Informed Decisions Inc.
100 Falling Cheek
Sautee Nacoochee, GA 30571
(706)878-1905
Fax: (706)878-1802
E-mail: skylake@compuserve.com

Tom C. Davis & Associates, P.C.
3189 Perimeter Rd.
Valdosta, GA 31602
(912)247-9801
Fax: (912)244-7704
E-mail: mail@tcdcpa.com
Website: http://www.tcdcpa.com/

Illinois

TWD and Associates
431 S Patton
Arlington Heights, IL 60005
(847)398-6410
Fax: (847)255-5095
E-mail: tdoo@aol.com

Management Planning Associates Inc.
2275 Half Day Rd., Ste. 350
Bannockburn, IL 60015-1277
(847)945-2421
Fax: (847)945-2425

Phil Faris Associates
86 Old Mill Ct.
Barrington, IL 60010
(847)382-4888
Fax: (847)382-4890
E-mail: pfaris@meginsnet.net

Seven Continents Technology
787 Stonebridge
Buffalo Grove, IL 60089
(708)577-9653
Fax: (708)870-1220

Grubb & Blue Inc.
2404 Windsor Pl.
Champaign, IL 61820
(217)366-0052
Fax: (217)356-0117

ACE Accounting Service Inc.
3128 N Bernard St.
Chicago, IL 60618
(773)463-7854
Fax: (773)463-7854

AON Consulting Worldwide
200 E Randolph St., 10th Fl.
Chicago, IL 60601
(312)381-4800
Free: 800-438-6487
Fax: (312)381-0240
Website: http://www.aon.com

FMS Consultants
5801 N Sheridan Rd., Ste. 3D
Chicago, IL 60660
(773)561-7362
Fax: (773)561-6274

Grant Thornton
800 1 Prudential Plz.
130 E Randolph St.
Chicago, IL 60601
(312)856-0001
Fax: (312)861-1340
E-mail: gtinfo@gt.com
Website: http://www.grantthornton.com

Kingsbury International Ltd.
5341 N Glenwood Ave.
Chicago, IL 60640
(773)271-3030
Fax: (773)728-7080
E-mail: jetlag@mcs.com
Website: http://www.kingbiz.com

MacDougall & Blake Inc.
1414 N Wells St., Ste. 311
Chicago, IL 60610-1306
(312)587-3330
Fax: (312)587-3699
E-mail: jblake@compuserve.com

James C. Osburn Ltd.
6445 N. Western Ave., Ste. 304
Chicago, IL 60645
(773)262-4428
Fax: (773)262-6755
E-mail: osburnltd@aol.com

Tarifero & Tazewell Inc.
211 S Clark
Chicago, IL 60690
(312)665-9714
Fax: (312)665-9716

Human Energy Design Systems
620 Roosevelt Dr.
Edwardsville, IL 62025
(618)692-0258
Fax: (618)692-0819

China Business Consultants Group
931 Dakota Cir.
Naperville, IL 60563
(630)778-7992
Fax: (630)778-7915
E-mail: cbcq@aol.com

Center for Workforce Effectiveness
500 Skokie Blvd., Ste. 222
Northbrook, IL 60062
(847)559-8777
Fax: (847)559-8778
E-mail: office@cwelink.com
Website: http://www.cwelink.com

Smith Associates
1320 White Mountain Dr.
Northbrook, IL 60062
(847)480-7200
Fax: (847)480-9828

Francorp Inc.
20200 Governors Dr.
Olympia Fields, IL 60461
(708)481-2900
Free: 800-372-6244
Fax: (708)481-5885
E-mail: francorp@aol.com
Website: http://www.francorpinc.com

Camber Business Strategy Consultants
1010 S Plum Tree Ct
Palatine, IL 60078-0986
(847)202-0101
Fax: (847)705-7510
E-mail: camber@ameritech.net

Partec Enterprise Group
5202 Keith Dr.
Richton Park, IL 60471
(708)503-4047
Fax: (708)503-9468

Rockford Consulting Group Ltd.
Century Plz., Ste. 206
7210 E State St.
Rockford, IL 61108
(815)229-2900
Free: 800-667-7495
Fax: (815)229-2612
E-mail: rligus@RockfordConsulting.com
Website: http://www.Rockford
Consulting.com

RSM McGladrey Inc.
1699 E Woodfield Rd., Ste. 300
Schaumburg, IL 60173-4969
(847)413-6900
Fax: (847)517-7067
Website: http://www.rsmmcgladrey.com

A.D. Star Consulting
320 Euclid
Winnetka, IL 60093
(847)446-7827
Fax: (847)446-7827
E-mail: startwo@worldnet.att.net

Indiana

Modular Consultants Inc.
3109 Crabtree Ln.
Elkhart, IN 46514
(219)264-5761
Fax: (219)264-5761
E-mail: sasabo5313@aol.com

Midwest Marketing Research
PO Box 1077
Goshen, IN 46527
(219)533-0548
Fax: (219)533-0540
E-mail: 103365.654@compuserve

Ketchum Consulting Group
8021 Knue Rd., Ste. 112
Indianapolis, IN 46250
(317)845-5411
Fax: (317)842-9941

MDI Management Consulting
1519 Park Dr.
Munster, IN 46321
(219)838-7909
Fax: (219)838-7909

Iowa

McCord Consulting Group Inc.
4533 Pine View Dr. NE
PO Box 11024
Cedar Rapids, IA 52410
(319)378-0077
Fax: (319)378-1577
E-mail: smmccord@hom.com
Website: http://www.mccordgroup.com

Management Solutions L.C.
3815 Lincoln Pl. Dr.
Des Moines, IA 50312
(515)277-6408
Fax: (515)277-3506
E-mail: wasunimers@uswest.net

Grandview Marketing
15 Red Bridge Dr.
Sioux City, IA 51104
(712)239-3122
Fax: (712)258-7578
E-mail: eandrews@pionet.net

Kansas

Assessments in Action
513A N Mur-Len
Olathe, KS 66062
(913)764-6270
Free: (888)548-1504
Fax: (913)764-6495
E-mail: lowdene@qni.com
Website: http://www.assessments-in-action.com

Maine

Pan Atlantic SMS Group Inc.
6 City Ctr., Ste. 200
Portland, ME 04101
(207)871-8622
Fax: (207)772-4842
E-mail: pmurphy@panatlanticsmsgroup.com
Website: http://www.panatlanticsms group.com

Maryland

Clemons & Associates Inc.
5024-R Campbell Blvd.
Baltimore, MD 21236
(410)931-8100
Fax: (410)931-8111
E-mail: info@clemonsmgmt.com
Website: http://www.clemonsmgmt.com

Employee Benefits Group Inc.
4405 E West Hwy., Ste. 202
Bethesda, MD 20814
(301) 718-4637
Fax: (301) 907-0176
E-mail: info@ebg.com
Website: http://www.ebg.com

Burdeshaw Associates Ltd.
4701 Sangamore Rd.
Bethesda, MD 20816-2508
(301)229-5800

Fax: (301)229-5045
E-mail: jstacy@burdeshaw.com
Website: http://www.burdeshaw.com

Michael E. Cohen
5225 Pooks Hill Rd., Ste. 1119 S
Bethesda, MD 20814
(301)530-5738
Fax: (301)530-2988
E-mail: mecohen@crosslink.net

World Development Group Inc.
5800 Madaket Rd., Ste. 100
Bethesda, MD 20816
(301) 320-0971
Fax: (301) 320-0978
E-mail: wdg@worlddg.com
Website: http://www.worlddg.com

Creative Edge Consulting
6047 Wild Ginger Ct.
Columbia, MD 21044
(443) 545-5863
Website: http://www.creativeedge consulting.org

Paul Yelder Consulting
9581 Standon Pl.
Columbia, MD 21045
(410) 740-8417
E-mail: consulting@yelder.com
Website: http://www.yelder.com

Hammer Marketing Resources
19118 Silver Maple Ct.
Hagerstown, MD 21742
(301) 733-8891
Fax: (305) 675-3277

Strategies
8 Park Center Ct., Ste. 200
Owings Mills, MD 21117
(410)363-6669
Fax: (410)363-1231
E-mail: info@strategiescorp.net
Website: http://www.strategiescorp.net

Managance Consulting and Coaching
1708 Chester Mill Rd.
Silver Spring, MD 20906
(301) 260-9503
E-mail: info@managance.com
Website: http://www.managance.com

Andrew Sussman & Associates
13731 Kretsinger
Smithsburg, MD 21783
(301)824-2943
Fax: (301)824-2943

Massachusetts

Geibel Marketing and Public Relations
PO Box 611
Belmont, MA 02478-0005
(617)484-8285
Fax: (617)489-3567
E-mail: jgeibel@geibelpr.com
Website: http://www.geibelpr.com

Bain & Co.
2 Copley Pl.
Boston, MA 02116
(617)572-2000
Fax: (617)572-2427
E-mail: corporate.inquiries@bain.com
Website: http://www.bain.com

Mehr & Co.
62 Kinnaird St.
Cambridge, MA 02139
(617)876-3311
Fax: (617)876-3023
E-mail: mehrco@aol.com

Monitor Company Inc.
2 Canal Park
Cambridge, MA 02141
(617)252-2000
Fax: (617)252-2100
Website: http://www.monitor.com

Information & Research Associates
PO Box 3121
Framingham, MA 01701
(508)788-0784

Walden Consultants Ltd.
252 Pond St.
Hopkinton, MA 01748
(508)435-4882
Fax: (508)435-3971
Website: http://www.waldenconsultants .com

Jeffrey D. Marshall
102 Mitchell Rd.
Ipswich, MA 01938-1219
(508)356-1113
Fax: (508)356-2989

Consulting Resources Corp.
6 Northbrook Park
Lexington, MA 02420
(781)863-1222
Fax: (781)863-1441
E-mail: res@consultingresources.net
Website: http://www.consultingresources .net

Planning Technologies Group L.L.C.
92 Hayden Ave.
Lexington, MA 02421

(781)778-4678
Fax: (781)861-1099
E-mail: ptg@plantech.com
Website: http://www.plantech.com

Kalba International Inc.
23 Sandy Pond Rd.
Lincoln, MA 01773
(781)259-9589
Fax: (781)259-1460
E-mail: info@kalbainternational.com
Website: http://www.kalbainternational
.com

VMB Associates Inc.
115 Ashland St.
Melrose, MA 02176
(781)665-0623
Fax: (425)732-7142
E-mail: vmbinc@aol.com

The Company Doctor
14 Pudding Stone Ln.
Mendon, MA 01756
(508)478-1747
Fax: (508)478-0520

Data and Strategies Group Inc.
190 N Main St.
Natick, MA 01760
(508)653-9990
Fax: (508)653-7799
E-mail: dsginc@dsggroup.com
Website: http://www.dsggroup.com

The Enterprise Group
73 Parker Rd.
Needham, MA 02494
(617)444-6631
Fax: (617)433-9991
E-mail: lsacco@world.std.com
Website: http://www.enterprise-
group.com

PSMJ Resources Inc.
10 Midland Ave.
Newton, MA 02458
(617)965-0055
Free: 800-537-7765
Fax: (617)965-5152
E-mail: psmj@tiac.net
Website: http://www.psmj.com

Scheur Management Group Inc.
255 Washington St., Ste. 100
Newton, MA 02458-1611
(617)969-7500
Fax: (617)969-7508
E-mail: smgnow@scheur.com
Website: http://www.scheur.com

I.E.E.E., Boston Section
240 Bear Hill Rd., 202B
Waltham, MA 02451-1017
(781)890-5294
Fax: (781)890-5290

Business Planning and Consulting Services
20 Beechwood Ter.
Wellesley, MA 02482
(617)237-9151
Fax: (617)237-9151

Michigan

BBC Entrepreneurial Training & Consulting LLC
803 N Main St.
Ann Arbor, MI 48104
(734)930-9741
Fax: (734)930-6629
E-mail: info@bioconsultants.com
Website: http://www.bioconsultants.com

Center for Simplified Strategic Planning Inc.
2219 Packard Rd., Ste. 13
Ann Arbor, MI 48104
(734)995-3465
E-mail: tidd@cssp.com
Website: http://www.cssp.com

Walter Frederick Consulting
1719 South Blvd.
Ann Arbor, MI 48104
(313)662-4336
Fax: (313)769-7505

Aimattech Consulting LLC
568 Woodway Ct., Ste. 1
Bloomfield Hills, MI 48302
(248) 540-3758
Fax: (248) 540-3011
E-mail: dpwconsult@aol.com
Website: http://www.aimattech.com

QualSAT International Inc.
30777 NW Highway., Ste. 101
Farmington Hills, MI 48334
866-899-0020
Fax: (248)932-3801
E-mail: info@qualsat.com
Website: http://www.qualsat.com

Fox Enterprises
6220 W Freeland Rd.
Freeland, MI 48623
(989)695-9170
Fax: (989)695-9174

T. L. Cramer Associates LLC
1788 Broadstone Rd.
Grosse Pointe Woods, MI 48236

(313)332-0182
E-mail: info@tlcramerassociates.com
Website: http://www.tlcramerassociates
.com

G.G.W. and Associates
1213 Hampton
Jackson, MI 49203
(517)782-2255
Fax: (517)782-2255

BHM Associates Inc.
2817 Canterbury Dr.
Midland, MI 48642
(989) 631-7109
E-mail: smiller@bhmassociates.net
Website: http://www.bhmassociates.net

MarketingHelp Inc.
6647 Riverwoods Ct. NE
Rockford, MI 49341
(616) 866-1198
Website: http://www.mktghelp.com

Rehmann, Robson PC
5800 Gratiot
Saginaw, MI 48605
(989)799-9580
Fax: (989)799-0227
E-mail: info@rehmann.com
Website: http://www.rehmann.com

Private Ventures Inc.
16000 W 9 Mile Rd., Ste. 504
Southfield, MI 48075
(248)569-1977
Free: 800-448-7614
Fax: (248)569-1838
E-mail: pventuresi@aol.com

JGK Associates
14464 Kerner Dr.
Sterling Heights, MI 48313
(810)247-9055
Fax: (248)822-4977
E-mail: kozlowski@home.com

Cool & Associates Inc.
921 Village Green Ln., Ste. 1068
Waterford, MI 48328
(248)683-1130
E-mail: jcool@cool-associates.com
Website: http://www.cool-associates.com

Griffioen Consulting Group Inc.
6689 Orchard Lake Rd., Ste. 295
West Bloomfield, MI 48322
(888)262-5850
Fax: (248)855-4084
Website: http://www.griffioenconsulting
.com

Minnesota

Health Fitness Corp.
31700 W 82nd St., Ste. 200
Minneapolis, MN 55431
(952)831-6830
E-mail: info@hfit.com
Website: http://www.hfit.com

Consatech Inc.
PO Box 1047
Burnsville, MN 55337
(612)953-1088
Fax: (612)435-2966

Kaes Analytics Inc.
14960 Ironwood Ct.
Eden Prairie, MN 55346
(952)942-2912

DRI Consulting
2 Otter Ln.
Saint Paul, MN 55127
(651)415-1400
Fax: (651)415-9968
E-mail: dric@dric.com
Website: http://www.dric.com

Markin Consulting
12072 87th Pl. N
Maple Grove, MN 55369
(763)493-3568
Fax: (763)322-5013
E-mail: markin@markinconsulting.com
Website: http://
www.markinconsulting.com

**Minnesota Cooperation Office for
Small Business & Job Creation Inc.**
5001 W 80th St., Ste. 825
Minneapolis, MN 55437
(612)830-1230
Fax: (612)830-1232
E-mail: mncoop@msn.com
Website: http://www.mnco.org

Power Systems Research
1365 Corporate Center Curve, 2nd Fl.
St. Paul, MN 55121
(612)905-8400
Free: (888)625-8612
Fax: (612)454-0760
E-mail: Barb@Powersys.com
Website: http://www.powersys.com

Missouri

**Business Planning and Development
Corp.**
4030 Charlotte St.
Kansas City, MO 64110
(816)753-0495

E-mail: humph@bpdev.demon.co.uk
Website: http://www.bpdev.demon.co.uk

CFO Service
10336 Donoho
St. Louis, MO 63131
(314)750-2940
E-mail: jskae@cfoservice.com
Website: http://www.cfoservice.com

Nebraska

**International Management Consulting
Group Inc.**
1309 Harlan Dr., Ste. 205
Bellevue, NE 68005
(402)291-4545
Free: 800-665-IMCG
Fax: (402)291-4343
E-mail: imcg@neonramp.com
Website: http://www.mgtconsulting.com

**Heartland Management Consulting
Group**
1904 Barrington Pky.
Papillion, NE 68046
(402)339-2387
Fax: (402)339-1319

Nevada

The DuBois Group
865 Tahoe Blvd., Ste. 108
Incline Village, NV 89451
(775)832-0550
Free: 800-375-2935
Fax: (775)832-0556
E-mail: DuBoisGrp@aol.com

New Hampshire

Wolff Consultants
10 Buck Rd.
Hanover, NH 03755
(603)643-6015

BPT Consulting Associates Ltd.
12 Parmenter Rd., Ste. B-6
Londonderry, NH 03053
(603)437-8484
Free: (888)278-0030
Fax: (603)434-5388
E-mail: bptcons@tiac.net
Website: http://www.bptconsulting.com

New Jersey

Bedminster Group Inc.
1170 Rte. 22 E
Bridgewater, NJ 08807
(908)500-4155
Fax: (908)766-0780

E-mail: info@bedminstergroup.com
Website: http://www.bedminstergroup
.com
Fax: (202)806-1777
Terry Strong, Acting Regional Dir.

Delta Planning Inc.
PO Box 425
Denville, NJ 07834
(913)625-1742
Free: 800-672-0762
Fax: (973)625-3531
E-mail: DeltaP@worldnet.att.net
Website: http://deltaplanning.com

Kumar Associates Inc.
1004 Cumbermeade Rd.
Fort Lee, NJ 07024
(201)224-9480
Fax: (201)585-2343
E-mail: mail@kumarassociates.com
Website: http://kumarassociates.com

John Hall & Company Inc.
PO Box 187
Glen Ridge, NJ 07028
(973)680-4449
Fax: (973)680-4581
E-mail: jhcompany@aol.com

Market Focus
PO Box 402
Maplewood, NJ 07040
(973)378-2470
Fax: (973)378-2470
E-mail: mcss66@marketfocus.com

Vanguard Communications Corp.
100 American Rd.
Morris Plains, NJ 07950
(973)605-8000
Fax: (973)605-8329
Website: http://www.vanguard.net/

ConMar International Ltd.
1901 US Hwy. 130
North Brunswick, NJ 08902
(732)940-8347
Fax: (732)274-1199

KLW New Products
156 Cedar Dr.
Old Tappan, NJ 07675
(201)358-1300
Fax: (201)664-2594
E-mail: lrlarsen@usa.net
Website: http://www.klwnewproducts
.com

PA Consulting Group
315A Enterprise Dr.
Plainsboro, NJ 08536

(609)936-8300
Fax: (609)936-8811
E-mail: info@paconsulting.com
Website: http://www.pa-consulting.com

Aurora Marketing Management Inc.

66 Witherspoon St., Ste. 600
Princeton, NJ 08542
(908)904-1125
Fax: (908)359-1108
E-mail: aurora2@voicenet.com
Website: http://www.auroramarketing.net

Smart Business Supersite

88 Orchard Rd., CN-5219
Princeton, NJ 08543
(908)321-1924
Fax: (908)321-5156
E-mail: irv@smartbiz.com
Website: http://www.smartbiz.com

Tracelin Associates

1171 Main St., Ste. 6K
Rahway, NJ 07065
(732)381-3288

Schkeeper Inc.

130-6 Bodman Pl.
Red Bank, NJ 07701
(732)219-1965
Fax: (732)530-3703

Henry Branch Associates

2502 Harmon Cove Twr.
Secaucus, NJ 07094
(201)866-2008
Fax: (201)601-0101
E-mail: hbranch161@home.com

Robert Gibbons & Company Inc.

46 Knoll Rd.
Tenafly, NJ 07670-1050
(201)871-3933
Fax: (201)871-2173
E-mail: crisisbob@aol.com

PMC Management Consultants Inc.

6 Thistle Ln.
Three Bridges, NJ 08887-0332
(908)788-1014
Free: 800-PMC-0250
Fax: (908)806-7287
E-mail: int@pmc-management.com
Website: http://www.pmc-management.com

R.W. Bankart & Associates

20 Valley Ave., Ste. D-2
Westwood, NJ 07675-3607
(201)664-7672

New Mexico

Vondle & Associates Inc.

4926 Calle de Tierra, NE
Albuquerque, NM 87111
(505)292-8961
Fax: (505)296-2790
E-mail: vondle@aol.com

InfoNewMexico

2207 Black Hills Rd., NE
Rio Rancho, NM 87124
(505)891-2462
Fax: (505)896-8971

New York

Powers Research and Training Institute

PO Box 78
Bayville, NY 11709
(516)628-2250
Fax: (516)628-2252
E-mail: powercocch@compuserve.com
Website: http://www.nancypowers.com

Consortium House

296 Wittenberg Rd.
Bearsville, NY 12409
(845)679-8867
Fax: (845)679-9248
E-mail: eugenegs@aol.com
Website: http://www.chpub.com

Progressive Finance Corp.

3549 Tiemann Ave.
Bronx, NY 10469
(718)405-9029
Free: 800-225-8381
Fax: (718)405-1170

Wave Hill Associates Inc.

2621 Palisade Ave., Ste. 15-C
Bronx, NY 10463
(718)549-7368
Fax: (718)601-9670
E-mail: pepper@compuserve.com

Management Insight

96 Arlington Rd.
Buffalo, NY 14221
(716)631-3319
Fax: (716)631-0203
E-mail: michalski@foodserviceinsight.com
Website: http://www.foodserviceinsight.com

Samani International Enterprises, Marions Panyaught Consultancy

2028 Parsons
Flushing, NY 11357-3436

(917)287-8087
Fax: 800-873-8939
E-mail: vjp2@biostrategist.com
Website: http://www.biostrategist.com

Marketing Resources Group

71-58 Austin St.
Forest Hills, NY 11375
(718)261-8882

Mangabay Business Plans & Development

125-10 Queens Blvd., Ste. 2202
Kew Gardens, NY 11415
(905)527-1947
Fax: 509-472-1935
E-mail: mangabay@mangabay.com
Website: http://www.mangabay.com
Lee Toh, Managing Partner

ComputerEase Co.

1301 Monmouth Ave.
Lakewood, NY 08701
(212)406-9464
Fax: (914)277-5317
E-mail: crawfordc@juno.com

Boice Dunham Group

30 W 13th St.
New York, NY 10011
(212)924-2200
Fax: (212)924-1108

Elizabeth Capen

27 E 95th St.
New York, NY 10128
(212)427-7654
Fax: (212)876-3190

Haver Analytics

60 E 42nd St., Ste. 2424
New York, NY 10017
(212)986-9300
Fax: (212)986-5857
E-mail: data@haver.com
Website: http://www.haver.com

The Jordan, Edmiston Group Inc.

150 E 52nd Ave., 18th Fl.
New York, NY 10022
(212)754-0710
Fax: (212)754-0337

KPMG International

345 Park Ave.
New York, NY 10154-0102
(212)758-9700
Fax: (212)758-9819
Website: http://www.kpmg.com

Mahoney Cohen Consulting Corp.
111 W 40th St., 12th Fl.
New York, NY 10018
(212)490-8000
Fax: (212)790-5913

Management Practice Inc.
342 Madison Ave.
New York, NY 10173-1230
(212)867-7948
Fax: (212)972-5188
Website: http://www.mpiweb.com

Moseley Associates Inc.
342 Madison Ave., Ste. 1414
New York, NY 10016
(212)213-6673
Fax: (212)687-1520

Practice Development Counsel
60 Sutton Pl. S
New York, NY 10022
(212)593-1549
Fax: (212)980-7940
E-mail: pwhaserot@pdcounsel.com
Website: http://www.pdcounsel.com

Unique Value International Inc.
575 Madison Ave., 10th Fl.
New York, NY 10022-1304
(212)605-0590
Fax: (212)605-0589

The Van Tulleken Co.
126 E 56th St.
New York, NY 10022
(212)355-1390
Fax: (212)755-3061
E-mail: newyork@vantulleken.com

Vencon Management Inc.
301 W 53rd St.
New York, NY 10019
(212)581-8787
Fax: (212)397-4126
Website: http://www.venconinc.com

Werner International Inc.
55 E 52nd, 29th Fl.
New York, NY 10055
(212)909-1260
Fax: (212)909-1273
E-mail: richard.downing@rgh.com
Website: http://www.wernertex.com

Zimmerman Business Consulting Inc.
44 E 92nd St., Ste. 5-B
New York, NY 10128
(212)860-3107
Fax: (212)860-7730
E-mail: ljzzbci@aol.com
Website: http://www.zbcinc.com

Overton Financial
7 Allen Rd.
Peekskill, NY 10566
(914)737-4649
Fax: (914)737-4696

Stromberg Consulting
2500 Westchester Ave.
Purchase, NY 10577
(914)251-1515
Fax: (914)251-1562
E-mail: strategy@stromberg_
consulting.com
Website: http://www.stromberg_
consulting.com

Innovation Management Consulting Inc.
209 Dewitt Rd.
Syracuse, NY 13214-2006
(315)425-5144
Fax: (315)445-8989
E-mail: missonneb@axess.net

M. Clifford Agress
891 Fulton St.
Valley Stream, NY 11580
(516)825-8955
Fax: (516)825-8955

Destiny Kinal Marketing Consultancy
105 Chemung St.
Waverly, NY 14892
(607)565-8317
Fax: (607)565-4083

Valutis Consulting Inc.
5350 Main St., Ste. 7
Williamsville, NY 14221-5338
(716)634-2553
Fax: (716)634-2554
E-mail: valutis@localnet.com
Website: http://www.valutisconsulting
.com

North Carolina

Best Practices L.L.C.
6320 Quadrangle Dr., Ste. 200
Chapel Hill, NC 27514
(919)403-0251
Fax: (919)403-0144
E-mail: best@best:in/class
Website: http://www.best-in-class.com

Norelli & Co.
Bank of America Corporate Ctr.
100 N Tyron St., Ste. 5160
Charlotte, NC 28202-4000
(704)376-5484
Fax: (704)376-5485
E-mail: consult@norelli.com
Website: http://www.norelli.com

North Dakota

Center for Innovation
4300 Dartmouth Dr.
PO Box 8372
Grand Forks, ND 58202
(701)777-3132
Fax: (701)777-2339
E-mail: bruce@innovators.net
Website: http://www.innovators.net

Ohio

Transportation Technology Services
208 Harmon Rd.
Aurora, OH 44202
(330)562-3596

Empro Systems Inc.
4777 Red Bank Expy., Ste. 1
Cincinnati, OH 45227-1542
(513)271-2042
Fax: (513)271-2042

Alliance Management International Ltd.
1440 Windrow Ln.
Cleveland, OH 44147-3200
(440)838-1922
Fax: (440)838-0979
E-mail: bgruss@amiltd.com
Website: http://www.amiltd.com

Bozell Kamstra Public Relations
1301 E 9th St., Ste. 3400
Cleveland, OH 44114
(216)623-1511
Fax: (216)623-1501
E-mail: jfeniger@cleveland.bozellkamstra
.com
Website: http://www.bozellkamstra.com

Cory Dillon Associates
111 Schreyer Pl. E
Columbus, OH 43214
(614)262-8211
Fax: (614)262-3806

Holcomb Gallagher Adams
300 Marconi, Ste. 303
Columbus, OH 43215
(614)221-3343
Fax: (614)221-3367
E-mail: riadams@acme.freenet.oh.us

Young & Associates
PO Box 711
Kent, OH 44240
(330)678-0524
Free: 800-525-9775
Fax: (330)678-6219
E-mail: online@younginc.com
Website: http://www.younginc.com

Robert A. Westman & Associates
8981 Inversary Dr. SE
Warren, OH 44484-2551
(330)856-4149
Fax: (330)856-2564

Oklahoma

Innovative Partners L.L.C.
4900 Richmond Sq., Ste. 100
Oklahoma City, OK 73118
(405)840-0033
Fax: (405)843-8359
E-mail: ipartners@juno.com

Oregon

INTERCON - The International Converting Institute
5200 Badger Rd.
Crooked River Ranch, OR 97760
(541)548-1447
Fax: (541)548-1618
E-mail: johnbowler@crookedriverranch
.com

Talbott ARM
HC 60, Box 5620
Lakeview, OR 97630
(541)635-8587
Fax: (503)947-3482

Management Technology Associates Ltd.
2768 SW Sherwood Dr, Ste. 105
Portland, OR 97201-2251
(503)224-5220
Fax: (503)224-5334
E-mail: lcuster@mta-ltd.com
Website: http://www.mgmt-tech.com

Pennsylvania

Healthscope Inc.
400 Lancaster Ave.
Devon, PA 19333
(610)687-6199
Fax: (610)687-6376
E-mail: health@voicenet.com
Website: http://www.healthscope.net/

Elayne Howard & Associates Inc.
3501 Masons Mill Rd., Ste. 501
Huntingdon Valley, PA 19006-3509
(215)657-9550

GRA Inc.
115 West Ave., Ste. 201
Jenkintown, PA 19046
(215)884-7500
Fax: (215)884-1385
E-mail: gramail@gra-inc.com
Website: http://www.gra-inc.com

Mifflin County Industrial Development Corp.
Mifflin County Industrial Plz.
6395 SR 103 N
Bldg. 50
Lewistown, PA 17044
(717)242-0393
Fax: (717)242-1842
E-mail: mcide@acsworld.net

Autech Products
1289 Revere Rd.
Morrisville, PA 19067
(215)493-3759
Fax: (215)493-9791
E-mail: autech4@yahoo.com

Advantage Associates
434 Avon Dr.
Pittsburgh, PA 15228
(412)343-1558
Fax: (412)362-1684
E-mail: ecocba1@aol.com

Regis J. Sheehan & Associates
Pittsburgh, PA 15220
(412)279-1207

James W. Davidson Company Inc.
23 Forest View Rd.
Wallingford, PA 19086
(610)566-1462

Puerto Rico

Diego Chevere & Co.
Metro Parque 7, Ste. 204
Metro Office
Caparra Heights, PR 00920
(787)774-9595
Fax: (787)774-9566
E-mail: dcco@coqui.net

Manuel L. Porrata and Associates
898 Munoz Rivera Ave., Ste. 201
San Juan, PR 00927
(787)765-2140
Fax: (787)754-3285
E-mail: m_porrata@manuelporrata.com
Website: http://manualporrata.com

South Carolina

Aquafood Business Associates
PO Box 13267
Charleston, SC 29422
(843)795-9506
Fax: (843)795-9477
E-mail: rraba@aol.com

Profit Associates Inc.
PO Box 38026
Charleston, SC 29414

(803)763-5718
Fax: (803)763-5719
E-mail: bobrog@awod.com
Website: http://www.awod.com/gallery/
business/proasc

Strategic Innovations International
12 Executive Ct.
Lake Wylie, SC 29710
(803)831-1225
Fax: (803)831-1177
E-mail: stratinnov@aol.com
Website: http://www.strategicinnovations
.com

Minus Stage
Box 4436
Rock Hill, SC 29731
(803)328-0705
Fax: (803)329-9948

Tennessee

Daniel Petchers & Associates
8820 Fernwood CV
Germantown, TN 38138
(901)755-9896

Business Choices
1114 Forest Harbor, Ste. 300
Hendersonville, TN 37075-9646
(615)822-8692
Free: 800-737-8382
Fax: (615)822-8692
E-mail: bz-ch@juno.com

RCFA Healthcare Management Services L.L.C.
9648 Kingston Pke., Ste. 8
Knoxville, TN 37922
(865)531-0176
Free: 800-635-4040
Fax: (865)531-0722
E-mail: info@rcfa.com
Website: http://www.rcfa.com

Growth Consultants of America
3917 Trimble Rd.
Nashville, TN 37215
(615)383-0550
Fax: (615)269-8940
E-mail: 70244.451@compuserve.com

Texas

Integrated Cost Management Systems Inc.
6001 W I-20, Ste. 209
Arlington, TX 76094-0206
(817)475-2945
E-mail: abm@icms.net
Website: http://www.icms.net

Business Resource Software Inc.
1779 Wells Branch Pky.
Austin, TX 78728
Free: 800-423-1228
Fax: (512)251-4401
E-mail: info@brs-inc.com
Website: http://www.brs-inc.com

Erisa Adminstrative Services Inc.
12325 Hymeadow Dr., Bldg. 4
Austin, TX 78750-1847
(512)250-9020
Fax: (512)250-9487
Website: http://www.cserisa.com

R. Miller Hicks & Co.
1011 W 11th St.
Austin, TX 78703
(512)477-7000
Fax: (512)477-9697
E-mail: millerhicks@rmhicks.com
Website: http://www.rmhicks.com

Pragmatic Tactics Inc.
3303 Westchester Ave.
College Station, TX 77845
(409)696-5294
Free: 800-570-5294
Fax: (409)696-4994
E-mail: ptactics@aol.com
Website: http://www.ptatics.com

Zaetric Business Solutions LLC
27350 Blueberry Hill, Ste. 14
Conroe, TX 77385
(713)621-4885
Fax: (713)824-1654
E-mail: inquiries@zaetric.com
Website: http://www.zaetric.com

Perot Systems
12404 Park Central Dr.
Dallas, TX 75251
(972)340-5000
Free: 800-688-4333
Fax: (972)455-4100
E-mail: corp.comm@ps.net
Website: http://www.perotsystems.com

ReGENERATION Partners
3811 Turtle Creek Blvd., Ste. 300
Dallas, TX 75219
(214)559-3999
Free: 800-406-1112
E-mail: info@regeneration-partner.com
Website: http://www.regeneration-partners.com

High Technology Associates
5739 Longmont Ln.
Houston, TX 77057
(713)963-9300

Fax: (713)963-8341
E-mail: baker@hta-usa.com
Website: http://www.high-technology-associates.com

SynerImages LLC
1 Riverway, Ste. 1700
Houston, TX 77056
(713)840-6442
Fax: (713)963-8341
Website: http://www.synerimages.com

PROTEC
4607 Linden Pl.
Pearland, TX 77584
(281)997-9872
Fax: (281)997-9895
E-mail: p.oman@ix.netcom.com

Bastian Public Relations
614 San Dizier
San Antonio, TX 78232
(210)404-1839
E-mail: lisa@bastianpr.com
Website: http://www.bastianpr.com
Lisa Bastian CBC

Business Strategy Development Consultants
PO Box 690365
San Antonio, TX 78269
(210)696-8000
Free: 800-927-BSDC
Fax: (210)696-8000

Utah

Vector Resources
7651 S Main St., Ste. 106
Midvale, UT 84047-7158
(801) 352-8500
Fax: (801) 352-8506
E-mail: info@vectorresources.com
Website: http://www.vectorresources.com

StreetMaker Inc.
524 West 440 South
Orem, UT 84058-6115
(801)607-2246
Fax: (800)561-4928
E-mail: contact@streetmaker.com
Website: http://www.streetmaker.com

Biomedical Management Resources
PO Box 521125
Salt Lake City, UT 84152-1125
(801)272-4668
Fax: (801)277-3290
E-mail: SeniorManagement@BiomedicalManagement.com
Website: http://www.biomedicalmanagement.com

Marriott Consulting Inc.
6945 S Knudsen Ridge Cir.
Salt Lake City, UT 84121
(801)944-5000
Fax: (801)947-9022
E-mail: info@marriottconsulting.com
Website: http://www.marriottconsulting.com

Virginia

Crown Consulting Inc.
1400 Key Blvd., Ste. 1100
Arlington, VA 22209
(703)650-0663
Fax: (703)243-1280
E-mail: info@crownci.com
Website: http://www.crownci.com

Dare Mighty Things
901 N Glebe Rd., Ste. 1005
Arlington, VA 22203
(703)752-4331
Fax: (703)752-4332
E-mail: info@daremightythings.com
Website: http://www.daremightythings.com

Elliott B. Jaffa
2530-B S Walter Reed Dr.
Arlington, VA 22206
(703)931-0040

Koach Enterprises - USA
5529 N 18th St.
Arlington, VA 22205
(703)241-8361
Fax: (703)241-8623

AMX International Inc.
9016 Triple Ridge Rd.
Fairfax Station, VA 22039-3003
(703)864-7046
Fax: (703)690-9994
E-mail: info@amxi.com
Website: http://www.amxi.com

Joel Greenstein & Associates
6212 Nethercombe Ct.
McLean, VA 22101
(703) 893-1888

John C. Randall and Associates Inc.
10197 Georgetown Rd.
Mechanicsville, VA 23116
(804)746-4450

Charles Scott Pugh (Investor)
4101 Pittaway Dr.
Richmond, VA 23235-1022
(804)560-0979
Fax: (804)560-4670

Robert Martens & Co.
2226 Floyd Ave.
Richmond, VA 23220
(804) 342-8850
Fax: (804)342-8860
E-mail: rm@robertmartens.com
Website: http://www.robertmartens.com

William W. Garry Inc.
PO Box 61662
Virginia Beach, VA 23466
(757) 467-7874
E-mail: drbillgarry@freeyellow.com

Regis J. Sheehan & Associates
500 Belmont Bay Dr.
Woodbridge, VA 22191-5445
(703)491-7377

Washington

Burlington Consultants
10900 NE 8th St., Ste. 900
Bellevue, WA 98004
(425)688-3060
Fax: (425)454-4383
E-mail:
partners@burlingtonconsultants.com
Website: http://www.burlington
consultants.com

Perry L. Smith Consulting
800 Bellevue Way NE, Ste. 400
Bellevue, WA 98004-4208
(425)462-2072
Fax: (425)462-5638

St. Charles Consulting Group
1420 NW Gilman Blvd.
Issaquah, WA 98027
(425)557-8708
Fax: (425)557-8731
E-mail: info@stcharlesconsulting.com
Website: http://www.stcharlesconsulting
.com

Independent Automotive Training Services
PO Box 334
Kirkland, WA 98083
(425)822-5715
E-mail: ltunney@autosvccon.com
Website: http://www.autosvccon.com

Kahle Associate Inc.
6203 204th Dr. NE
Redmond, WA 98053
(425)836-8763
Fax: (425)868-3770
E-mail: randykahle@kahleassociates.com
Website: http://www.kahleassociates.com

Dan Collin
3419 Wallingord Ave N, No. 2
Seattle, WA 98103
(206)634-9469
E-mail: dc@dancollin.com
Website: http://members.home.net/
dcollin/

ECG Management Consultants Inc.
1111 3rd Ave., Ste. 2700
Seattle, WA 98101-3201
(206)689-2200
Fax: (206)689-2209
E-mail: ecg@ecgmc.com
Website: http://www.ecgmc.com

Northwest Trade Adjustment Assistance Center
900 4th Ave., Ste. 2430
Seattle, WA 98164-1001
(206)622-2730
Free: 800-667-8087
Fax: (206)622-1105
E-mail: matchingfunds@nwtaac.org
Website: http://www.taacenters.org

Business Planning Consultants
S 3510 Ridgeview Dr.
Spokane, WA 99206
(509)928-0332
Fax: (509)921-0842
E-mail: bpci@nextdim.com

West Virginia

**Stanley & Associates Inc./
BusinessandMarketingPlans.com**
1687 Robert C. Byrd Dr.
Beckley, WV 25801
(304)252-0324
Free: 888-752-6720
Fax: (304)252-0470
E-mail: cclay@charterinternet.com
Website: http://www.Businessand
MarketingPlans.com
Christopher Clay

Wisconsin

White & Associates Inc.
5349 Somerset Ln. S
Greenfield, WI 53221
(414)281-7373
Fax: (414)281-7006
E-mail: wnaconsult@aol.com

Small business administration regional offices

This section contains a listing of Small Business Administration offices arranged numerically by region. Service areas are provided. Contact the appropriate office for a referral to the nearest field office, or visit the Small Business Administration online at www.sba.gov.

Region 1

U.S. Small Business Administration
Region I Office
10 Causeway St., Ste. 812
Boston, MA 02222-1093
Phone: (617)565-8415
Fax: (617)565-8420
Serves Connecticut, Maine, Massachusetts, New Hampshire, Rhode Island, and Vermont.

Region 2

U.S. Small Business Administration
Region II Office
26 Federal Plaza, Ste. 3108
New York, NY 10278
Phone: (212)264-1450
Fax: (212)264-0038
Serves New Jersey, New York, Puerto Rico, and the Virgin Islands.

Region 3

U.S. Small Business Administration
Region III Office
1150 First Avenue Suite 1001
King of Prussia, PA 19406
(610)382-3092
Serves Delaware, the District of Columbia, Maryland, Pennsylvania, Virginia, and West Virginia.

Region 4

U.S. Small Business Administration
Region IV Office
233 Peachtree St. NE
Harris Tower 1800
Atlanta, GA 30303
Phone: (404)331-4999
Fax: (404)331-2354
Serves Alabama, Florida, Georgia, Kentucky, Mississippi, North Carolina, South Carolina, and Tennessee.

Region 5

U.S. Small Business Administration
Region V Office
500 W. Madison St.
Citicorp Center, Ste. 1150
Chicago, IL 60661
Phone: (312)353-0357

Fax: (312)353-3426
Serves Illinois, Indiana, Michigan, Minnesota, Ohio, and Wisconsin.

Region 6

U.S. Small Business Administration
Region VI Office
4300 Amon Carter Blvd., Ste. 108
Fort Worth, TX 76155
Phone: (817)684-5581
Fax: (817)684-5588
Serves Arkansas, Louisiana, New Mexico, Oklahoma, and Texas.

Region 7

U.S. Small Business Administration
Region VII Office
1000 Walnut Suite 530
Kansas City, MO 64106
Phone: (816)426-4840
Fax: (816)426-4848
Serves Iowa, Kansas, Missouri, and Nebraska.

Region 8

U.S. Small Business Administration
Region VIII Office
721 19th St., Ste. 400
Denver, CO 80202
Phone: (303)844-0500
Fax: (303)844-0506
Serves Colorado, Montana, North Dakota, South Dakota, Utah, and Wyoming.

Region 9

U.S. Small Business Administration
Region IX Office
330 N Brand Blvd., Ste. 1200
Glendale, CA 91203
Phone: (818)552-3437
Fax: (818)552-0344
Serves American Samoa, Arizona, California, Guam, Hawaii, Nevada, and the Trust Territory of the Pacific Islands.

Region 10

U.S. Small Business Administration
Region X Office
2401 Fourth Ave., Ste. 400
Seattle, WA 98121
Phone: (206)553-5676
Fax: (206)553-4155
Serves Alaska, Idaho, Oregon, and Washington.

Small business development centers

This section contains a listing of all Small Business Development Centers, organized alphabetically by state/U.S. territory, then by city, then by agency name.

Alabama

Alabama SBDC

UNIVERSITY OF ALABAMA
2800 Milan Court Suite 124
Birmingham, AL 35211-6908
Phone: 205-943-6750
Fax: 205-943-6752
E-Mail: wcampbell@provost.uab.edu
Website: http://www.asbdc.org
Mr. William Campbell Jr, State Director

Alaska

Alaska SBDC

UNIVERSITY OF ALASKA - ANCHORAGE
430 West Seventh Avenue, Suite 110
Anchorage, AK 99501
Phone: 907-274 -7232
Fax: 907-272-0565
E-Mail: Isaac.Vanderburg@aksbdc.org
Website: http://www.aksbdc.org
Isaac Vanderburg, State Director

American Samoa

American Samoa SBDC

AMERICAN SAMOA COMMUNITY COLLEGE
P.O. Box 2609
Pago Pago, American Samoa 96799
Phone: 011-684-699-4830
Fax: 011-684-699-6132
E-Mail: hthweatt.sbdc@hotmail.com
Website: www.as-sbdc.org
Mr. Herbert Thweatt, Director

Arizona

Arizona SBDC

MARICOPA COUNTY COMMUNITY COLLEGE
2411 West 14th Street, Suite 114
Tempe, AZ 85281
Phone: 480-731-8720
Fax: 480-731-8729
E-Mail: janice.washington@domail.maricopa.edu
Website: http://www.azsbdc.net
Janice Washington, State Director

Arkansas

Arkansas SBDC

UNIVERSITY OF ARKANSAS
2801 South University Avenue
Little Rock, AR 72204
Phone: 501-683-7700
Fax: 501-683-7720
E-Mail: jmroderick@ualr.edu
Website: http://asbtdc.org
Ms. Janet M. Roderick, State Director

California

California - Northern California Regional SBDC

Northern California SBDC

HUMBOLDT STATE UNIVERSITY
1 Harpst Street 2006A, 209 Siemens Hall
Arcata, CA, 95521
Phone: 707-826-3920
Fax: 707-826-3912
E-Mail: Kristin.Johnson@humboldt.edu
Website: https://www.norcalsbdc.org
Kristin Johnson, Regional Director

California - Northern California SBDC

CALIFORNIA STATE UNIVERSITY - CHICO
35 Main St., Rm 203rr
Chico, CA 95929-0765
Phone: 530-898-5443
Fax: 530-898-4734
E-Mail: dripke@csuchico.edu
Website: https://www.necsbdc.org
Mr. Dan Ripke, Interim Regional Director

California - San Diego and Imperial SBDC

SOUTHWESTERN COMMUNITY COLLEGE
880 National City Boulevard, Suite 103
National City, CA 91950
Phone: 619-216-6721
Fax: 619-216-6692
E-Mail: awilson@swccd.edu
Website: http://www.SBDCRegional Network.org
Aleta Wilson, Regional Director

California - UC Merced SBDC

UC Merced Lead Center

UNIVERSITY OF CALIFORNIA - MERCED
550 East Shaw, Suite 105A
Fresno, CA 93710

Organizations, Agencies, & Consultants

Phone: 559-241-6590
Fax: 559-241-7422
E-Mail: dhowerton@ucmerced.edu
Website: http://sbdc.ucmerced.edu
Diane Howerton, State Director

California - Orange County/Inland Empire SBDC

Tri-County Lead SBDC

CALIFORNIA STATE UNIVERSITY - FULLERTON
800 North State College Boulevard, SGMH 5313
Fullerton, CA 92834
Phone: 714-278-5168
Fax: 714-278-7101
E-Mail: kmpayne@fullerton.edu
Website: http://www.leadsbdc.org
Katrina Payne Smith, Lead Center Director

California - Los Angeles Region SBDC

LONG BEACH CITY COLLEGE
4900 E. Conant Street, Building 2
Long Beach, CA 90808
Phone: 562-938-5006
Fax: 562-938-5030
E-Mail: jtorres@lbcc.edu
Website: http://www.smallbizla.org
Jesse Torres, Lead Center Director

Colorado

Colorado SBDC

COLORADO SBDC
1625 Broadway, Suite 2700
Denver, CO 80202
Phone: 303-892-3864
Fax: 303-892-3848
E-Mail: Kelly.Manning@state.co.us
Website: http://www.www.coloradosbdc .org
Ms. Kelly Manning, State Director

Connecticut

Connecticut SBDC

UNIVERSITY OF CONNECTICUT
2100 Hillside Road, Unit 1044
Storrs, CT 06269
Phone: 855-428-7232
E-Mail: ecarter@uconn.edu
Website: www.ctsbdc.com
Emily Carter, State Director

Delaware

Delaware SBDC

DELAWARE TECHNOLOGY PARK
1 Innovation Way, Suite 301
Newark, DE 19711
Phone: 302-831-4283
Fax: 302-831-1423
E-Mail: jmbowman@udel.edu
Website: http://www.delawaresbdc.org
Mike Bowman, State Director

District of Columbia

District of Columbia SBDC

HOWARD UNIVERSITY
2600 6th Street, NW Room 128
Washington, DC 20059
Phone: 202-806-1550
Fax: 202-806-1777
E-Mail: darrell.brown@howard.edu
Website: http://www.dcsbdc.com/
Darrell Brown, Executive Director

Florida

Florida SBDC

UNIVERSITY OF WEST FLORIDA
11000 University Parkway, Building 38
Pensacola, FL 32514
Phone: 850-473-7800
Fax: 850-473-7813
E-Mail: mmyhre@uwf.edu
Website: http://www.floridasbdc.com
Michael Myhre, State Director

Georgia

Georgia SBDC

UNIVERSITY OF GEORGIA
1180 East Broad Street
Athens, GA 30602
Phone: 706-542-6762
Fax: 706-542-7935
E-mail: aadams@georgiasbdc.org
Website: http://www.georgiasbdc.org
Mr. Allan Adams, State Director

Guam

Guam Small Business Development Center

UNIVERSITY OF GUAM
Pacific Islands SBDC
P.O. Box 5014 - U.O.G. Station
Mangilao, GU 96923
Phone: 671-735-2590
Fax: 671-734-2002
E-mail: casey@pacificsbdc.com

Website: http://www.uog.edu/sbdc
Mr. Casey Jeszenka, Director

Hawaii

Hawaii SBDC

UNIVERSITY OF HAWAII - HILO
200 W. Kawili Street, Suite 107
Hilo, HI 96720
Phone: 808-974-7515
Fax: 808-974-7683
E-Mail: cathy.wiltse@hisbdc.org
Website: http://www.hisbdc.org
Cathy Wiltse, State Director

Idaho

Idaho SBDC

BOISE STATE UNIVERSITY
1910 University Drive
Boise, ID 83725
Phone: 208-426-3838
Fax: 208-426-3877
E-mail: ksewell@boisestate.edu
Website: http://www.idahosbdc.org
Katie Sewell, State Director

Illinois

Illinois SBDC

DEPARTMENT OF COMMERCE AND ECONOMIC OPPORTUNITY
500 E. Monroe
Springfield, IL 62701
Phone: 217-524-5700
Fax: 217-524-0171
E-mail: mark.petrilli@illinois.gov
Website: http://www.ilsbdc.biz
Mr. Mark Petrilli, State Director

Indiana

Indiana SBDC

INDIANA ECONOMIC DEVELOPMENT CORPORATION
One North Capitol, Suite 700
Indianapolis, IN 46204
Phone: 317-232-8805
Fax: 317-232-8872
E-mail: JSchpok@iedc.in.gov
Website: http://www.isbdc.org
Jacob Schpok, State Director

Iowa

Iowa SBDC

IOWA STATE UNIVERSITY
2321 North Loop Drive, Suite 202
Ames, IA 50010

Phone: 515-294-2030
Fax: 515-294-6522
E-mail: lshimkat@iastate.edu
Website: http://www.iowasbdc.org
Lisa Shimkat, State Director

Kansas

Kansas SBDC

FORT HAYS STATE UNIVERSITY

214 SW Sixth Street, Suite 301
Topeka, KS 66603
Phone: 785-296-6514
Fax: 785-291-3261
E-mail: panichello@ksbdc.net
Website: http://www.fhsu.edu/ksbdc
Greg Panichello, State Director

Kentucky

Kentucky SBDC

UNIVERSITY OF KENTUCKY

One Quality Street
Lexington, KY 40507
Phone: 859-257-7668
Fax: 859-323-1907
E-mail: lrnaug0@uky.edu
Website: http://www.ksbdc.org
Becky Naugle, State Director

Louisiana

Louisiana SBDC

UNIVERSITY OF LOUISIANA - MONROE

College of Business Administration
700 University Avenue
Monroe, LA 71209
Phone: 318-342-5507
Fax: 318-342-5510
E-mail: rkessler@lsbdc.org
Website: http://www.lsbdc.org
Rande Kessler, State Director

Maine

Maine SBDC

UNIVERSITY OF SOUTHERN MAINE

96 Falmouth Street P.O. Box 9300
Portland, ME 04104
Phone: 207-780-4420
Fax: 207-780-4810
E-mail: mark.delisle@maine.edu
Website: http://www.mainesbdc.org
Mark Delisle, State Director

Maryland

Maryland SBDC

UNIVERSITY OF MARYLAND

7100 Baltimore Avenue, Suite 401
College Park, MD 20742
Phone: 301-403-8300
Fax: 301-403-8303
E-mail: rsprow@mdsbdc.umd.edu
Website: http://www.mdsbdc.umd.edu
Renee Sprow, State Director

Massachusetts

Massachusetts SBDC

UNIVERSITY OF MASSACHUSETTS

23 Tillson Farm Road
Amherst, MA 01003
Phone: 413-545-6301
Fax: 413-545-1273
E-mail: gparkin@msbdc.umass.edu
Website: http://www.www.msbdc.org
Georgianna Parkin, State Director

Michigan

Michigan SBTDC

GRAND VALLEY STATE UNIVERSITY

510 West Fulton Avenue
Grand Rapids, MI 49504
Phone: 616-331-7480
Fax: 616-331-7485
E-mail: boesen@gvsu.edu
Website: http://www.misbtdc.org
Nancy Boese, State Director

Minnesota

Minnesota SBDC

MINNESOTA SMALL BUSINESS DEVELOPMENT CENTER

1st National Bank Building
332 Minnesota Street, Suite E200
St. Paul, MN 55101-1349
Phone: 651-259-7420
Fax: 651-296-5287
E-mail: Bruce.Strong@state.mn.us
Website: http://www.mnsbdc.com
Bruce H. Strong, State Director

Mississippi

Mississippi SBDC

UNIVERSITY OF MISSISSIPPI

122 Jeanette Phillips Drive
P.O. Box 1848
University, MS 38677
Phone: 662-915-5001

Fax: 662-915-5650
E-mail: wgurley@olemiss.edu
Website: http://www.mssbdc.org
Doug Gurley, Jr., State Director

Missouri

Missouri SBDC

UNIVERSITY OF MISSOURI

410 South 6th Street, ?200 Engineering
North
Columbia, MO 65211
Phone: 573-882-9206
Fax: 573-884-4297
E-mail: bouchardc@missouri.edu
Website: http://www.missouribusiness
.net
Chris Bouchard, State Director

Montana

Montana SBDC

DEPARTMENT OF COMMERCE

301 S. Park Avenue, Room 114
Helena, MT 59601
Phone: 406-841-2746
Fax: 406-841-2728
E-mail: adesch@mt.gov
Website: http://www.sbdc.mt.gov
Ms. Ann Desch, State Director

Nebraska

Nebraska SBDC

UNIVERSITY OF NEBRASKA - OMAHA

200 Mammel Hall, 67th & Pine Streets
Omaha, NE 68182
Phone: 402-554-2521
Fax: 402-554-3473
E-mail: rbernier@unomaha.edu
Website: http://nbdc.unomaha.edu
Robert Bernier, State Director

Nevada

Nevada SBDC

UNIVERSITY OF NEVADA - RENO

Reno College of Business, Room 411
Reno, NV 89557-0100
Phone: 775-784-1717
Fax: 775-784-4337
E-mail: males@unr.edu
Website: http://www.nsbdc.org
Sam Males, State Director

ORGANIZATIONS, AGENCIES, & CONSULTANTS

New Hampshire

New Hampshire SBDC

UNIVERSITY OF NEW HAMPSHIRE
10 Garrison Avenue
Durham, NH 03824-3593
Phone: 603-862-2200
Fax: 603-862-4876
E-mail: Mary.Collins@unh.edu
Website: http://www.nhsbdc.org
Mary Collins, State Director

New Jersey

New Jersey SBDC

RUTGERS UNIVERSITY
1 Washington Park, 3rd Floor
Newark, NJ 07102
Phone: 973-353-1927
Fax: 973-353-1110
E-mail: bhopper@njsbdc.com
Website: http://www.njsbdc.com
Brenda Hopper, State Director

New Mexico

New Mexico SBDC

SANTA FE COMMUNITY COLLEGE
6401 Richards Avenue
Santa Fe, NM 87508
Phone: 505-428-1362
Fax: 505-428-1469
E-mail: russell.wyrick@sfcc.edu
Website: http://www.nmsbdc.org
Russell Wyrick, State Director

New York

New York SBDC

STATE UNIVERSITY OF NEW YORK
22 Corporate Woods, 3rd Floor
Albany, NY 12246
Phone: 518-443-5398
Fax: 518-443-5275
E-mail: j.king@nyssbdc.org
Website: http://www.nyssbdc.org
Jim King, State Director

North Carolina

North Carolina SBDTC

UNIVERSITY OF NORTH CAROLINA
5 West Hargett Street, Suite 600
Raleigh, NC 27601
Phone: 919-715-7272
Fax: 919-715-7777
E-mail: sdaugherty@sbtdc.org
Website: http://www.sbtdc.org
Scott Daugherty, State Director

North Dakota

North Dakota SBDC

UNIVERSITY OF NORTH DAKOTA
1200 Memorial Highway, PO Box 5509
Bismarck, ND 58506
Phone: 701-328-5375
Fax: 701-250-4304
E-mail: dkmartin@ndsbdc.org
Website: http://www.ndsbdc.org
David Martin, State Director

Ohio

Ohio SBDC

OHIO DEPARTMENT OF DEVELOPMENT
77 South High Street, 28th Floor
Columbus, OH 43216
Phone: 614-466-2711
Fax: 614-466-1789
E-mail: ezra.escudero@development.ohio.gov
Website: http://www.ohiosbdc.org
Ezra Escudero, State Director

Oklahoma

Oklahoma SBDC

SOUTHEAST OKLAHOMA STATE UNIVERSITY
1405 N. 4th Avenue, PMB 2584
Durant, OK 74701
Phone: 580-745-2955
Fax: 580-745-7471
E-mail: wcarter@se.edu
Website: http://www.osbdc.org
Grady Pennington, State Director

Oregon

Oregon SBDC

LANE COMMUNITY COLLEGE
1445 Willamette Street, Suite 5
Eugene, OR 97401
Phone: 541-463-5250
Fax: 541-345-6006
E-mail: gregorym@lanecc.edu
Website: http://www.bizcenter.org
Mark Gregory, State Director

Pennsylvania

Pennsylvania SBDC

UNIVERSITY OF PENNSYLVANIA

The Wharton School
3819-33 Chestnut Street, Suite 325
Philadelphia, PA 19104
Phone: 215-898-1219
Fax: 215-573-2135
E-mail: cconroy@wharton.upenn.edu
Website: http://pasbdc.org
Christian Conroy, State Director

Puerto Rico

Puerto Rico SBDC

INTER-AMERICAN UNIVERSITY OF PUERTO RICO
416 Ponce de Leon Avenue, Union Plaza, Tenth Floor
Hato Rey, PR 00918
Phone: 787-763-6811
Fax: 787-763-6875
E-mail: cmarti@prsbdc.org
Website: http://www.prsbdc.org
Carmen Marti, Executive Director

Rhode Island

Rhode Island SBDC

UNIVERSITY OF RHODE ISLAND
75 Lower College Road, 2nd Floor
Kingston, RI 02881
Phone: 401-874-4576
E-mail: gsonnenfeld@uri.edu
Website: http://www.risbdc.org
Gerald Sonnenfeld, State Director

South Carolina

South Carolina SBDC

UNIVERSITY OF SOUTH CAROLINA

Moore School of Business
1014 Greene Street
Columbia, SC 29208
Phone: 803-777-0749
Fax: 803-777-6876
E-mail: michele.abraham@moore.sc.edu
Website: http://www.scsbdc.com
Michele Abraham, State Director

South Dakota

South Dakota SBDC

UNIVERSITY OF SOUTH DAKOTA
414 East Clark Street, Patterson Hall
Vermillion, SD 57069
Phone: 605-677-5103
Fax: 605-677-5427
E-mail: jeff.eckhoff@usd.edu
Website: http://www.usd.edu/sbdc
Jeff Eckhoff, State Director

Tennessee

Tennessee SBDC

MIDDLE TENNESSEE STATE UNIVERSITY
3050 Medical Center Parkway, Ste. 200
Nashville, TN 37129
Phone: 615-849-9999
Fax: 615-893-7089
E-mail: pgeho@tsbdc.org
Website: http://www.tsbdc.org
Patrick Geho, State Director

Texas

Texas-North SBDC

DALLAS COUNTY COMMUNITY COLLEGE
1402 Corinth Street
Dallas, TX 75215
Phone: 214-860-5832
Fax: 214-860-5813
E-mail: m.langford@dcccd.edu
Website: http://www.ntsbdc.org
Mark Langford, Region Director

Texas Gulf Coast SBDC

UNIVERSITY OF HOUSTON
2302 Fannin, Suite 200
Houston, TX 77002
Phone: 713-752-8444
Fax: 713-756-1500
E-mail: fyoung@uh.edu
Website: http://sbdcnetwork.uh.edu
Mike Young, Executive Director

Texas-NW SBDC

TEXAS TECH UNIVERSITY
2579 South Loop 289, Suite 114
Lubbock, TX 79423
Phone: 806-745-3973
Fax: 806-745-6207
E-mail: c.bean@nwtsbdc.org
Website: http://www.nwtsbdc.org
Craig Bean, Executive Director

Texas-South-West Texas Border Region SBDC

UNIVERSITY OF TEXAS - SAN ANTONIO
501 West Durango Boulevard
San Antonio, TX 78207-4415
Phone: 210-458-2480
Fax: 210-458-2425
E-mail: albert.salgado@utsa.edu
Website: https://www.txsbdc.org
Alberto Salgado, Region Director

Utah

Utah SBDC

SALT LAKE COMMUNITY COLLEGE
9750 South 300 West
Salt Lake City, UT 84070
Phone: 801-957-5384
Fax: 801-985-5300
E-mail: Sherm.Wilkinson@slcc.edu
Website: http://www.utahsbdc.org
Sherm Wilkinson, State Director

Vermont

Vermont SBDC

VERMONT TECHNICAL COLLEGE
PO Box 188, 1 Main Street
Randolph Center, VT 05061-0188
Phone: 802-728-9101
Fax: 802-728-3026
E-mail: lrossi@vtsbdc.org
Website: http://www.vtsbdc.org
Linda Rossi, State Director

Virgin Islands

Virgin Islands SBDC

UNIVERSITY OF THE VIRGIN ISLANDS
8000 Nisky Center, Suite 720
St. Thomas, VI 00802
Phone: 340-776-3206
Fax: 340-775-3756
E-mail: ldottin@uvi.edu
Website: http://www.sbdcvi.org
Leonor Dottin, State Director

Virginia

Virginia SBDC

GEORGE MASON UNIVERSITY
4031 University Drive, Suite100
Fairfax, VA 22030
Phone: 703-277-7727
Fax: 703-352-8518
E-mail: jkeenan@gmu.edu
Website: http://www.virginiasbdc.org
Jody Keenan, Director

Washington

Washington SBDC

WASHINGTON STATE UNIVERSITY
1235 N. Post Street, Suite 201
Spokane, WA 99201
Phone: 509-358-7765
Fax: 509-358-7764

E-mail: duane.fladland@wsbdc.org
Website: http://www.wsbdc.org
Duane Fladland, State Director

West Virginia

West Virginia SBDC

WEST VIRGINIA DEVELOPMENT OFFICE
Capital Complex, Building 6, Room 652
1900 Kanawha Boulevard
Charleston, WV 25305
Phone: 304-957-2087
Fax: 304-558-0127
E-mail: Kristina.J.Oliver@wv.gov
Website: http://www.wvsbdc.org
Mr. Conley Salyor, State Director

Wisconsin

Wisconsin SBDC

UNIVERSITY OF WISCONSIN
432 North Lake Street, Room 423
Madison, WI 53706
Phone: 608-263-7794
Fax: 608-263-7830
E-mail: bon.wikenheiser@uwex.edu
Website: http://www.uwex.edu/sbdc
Bon Wikenheiser, State Director

Wyoming

Wyoming SBDC

UNIVERSITY OF WYOMING
1000 E. University Ave., Dept. 3922
Laramie, WY 82071-3922
Phone: 307-766-3405
Fax: 307-766-3406
E-mail: jkline@uwyo.edu
Website: http://www.wyomingentrepreneur.biz
Jill Kline, Acting State Director

Service corps of retired executives (score) offices

This section contains a listing of all SCORE offices organized alphabetically by state/U.S. territory, then by city, then by agency name.

Alabama

SCORE Office (Northeast Alabama)
1400 Commerce Blvd., Northeast
Anniston, AL 36207
(256)241-6111

SCORE Office (North Alabama)
1731 1st Ave. North, Ste. 200
Birmingham, AL 35203
(205)264-8425
Fax: (205)934-0538

SCORE Office (Baldwin County)
327 Fairhope Avenue
Fairhope, AL 36532
(251)928-6387

SCORE Office (Mobile)
451 Government Street
Mobile, AL 36652
(251)431-8614
Fax: (251)431-8646

SCORE Office (Alabama Capitol City)
600 S. Court St.
Montgomery, AL 36104
(334)240-6868
Fax: (334)240-6869

SCORE Office (Tuscaloosa)
2200 University Blvd.
Tuscaloosa, AL 35402
(205)758-7588

Alaska

SCORE Office (Anchorage)
420 L St., Ste. 300
Anchorage, AK 99501
(907)271-4022
Fax: (907)271-4545

Arizona

SCORE Office (Greater Phoenix)
2828 N. Central Ave., Ste. 800
Phoenix, AZ 85004
(602)745-7250
Fax: (602)745-7210
E-mail: e-mail@SCORE-phoenix.org
Website: http://www.greaterphoenix
.score.org/

SCORE Office (Northern Arizona)
1228 Willow Creek Rd., Ste. 2
Prescott, AZ 86301
(928)778-7438
Fax: (928)778-0812
Website: http://
www.northernarizona.score.org/

SCORE Office (Southern Arizona)
1400 W Speedway Blvd.
Tucson, AZ 85745
(520)505-3636
Fax: (520)670-5011
Website: http://www.southernarizona
.score.org/

Arkansas

SCORE Office (South Central)
201 N. Jackson Ave.
El Dorado, AR 71730-5803
(870)863-6113
Fax: (870)863-6115

SCORE Office (Northwest Arkansas)
614 E. Emma St., Room M412
Springdale, AR 72764
(479)725-1809
Website: http://www.northwestarkansas
.score.org

SCORE Office (Little Rock)
2120 Riverfront Dr., Ste. 250
Little Rock, AR 72202-1747
(501)324-7379
Fax: (501)324-5199
Website: http://www.littlerock.score
.org

SCORE Office (Southeast Arkansas)
P.O. Box 5069
Pine Bluff, AR 71611-5069
(870)535-0110
Fax: (870)535-1643

California

SCORE Office (Bakersfield)
P.O. Box 2426
Bakersfield, CA 93303
(661)861-9249
Fax: (661)395-4134
Website: http://www.bakersfield.score.org

SCORE Office (Santa Cruz County)
716 G Capitola Ave.
Capitola, CA 95010
(831)621-3735
Fax: (831)475-6530
Website: http://santacruzcounty.score.org

SCORE Office (Greater Chico Area)
1324 Mangrove St., Ste. 114
Chico, CA 95926
(530)342-8932
Fax: (530)342-8932
Website: http://www.greaterchicoarea.
score.org

SCORE Office (El Centro)
1850 W. Main St, Ste. C
El Centro, CA 92243
(760)337-2692
Website: http://www.sandiego.score.org/

SCORE Office (Central Valley)
801 R St., Ste. 201
Fresno, CA 93721
(559)487-5605

Fax: (559)487-5636
Website: http://www.centralvalley.
score.org

SCORE Office (Los Angeles)
330 N. Brand Blvd., Ste. 190
Glendale, CA 91203-2304
(818)552-3206
Fax: (818)552-3323
Website: http://www.greaterlosangeles.
score.org

SCORE Office (Modesto Merced)
1880 W. Wardrobe Ave.
Merced, CA 95340
(209)725-2033
Fax: (209)577-2673
Website: http://www.modestomerced.
score.org

SCORE Office (Monterey Bay)
Monterey Chamber of Commerce
30 Ragsdale Dr.
Monterey, CA 93940
(831)648-5360
Website: http://www.montereybay.score
.org

SCORE Office (East Bay)
492 9th St., Ste. 350
Oakland, CA 94607
(510)273-6611
Fax: (510)273-6015
E-mail: webmaster@eastbayscore.org
Website: http://www.eastbay.score.org/

SCORE Office (Ventura County)
400 E. Esplanade Dr., Ste. 301
Oxnard, CA 93036
(805)204-6022
Fax: (805)650-1414
Website: http://www.ventura.score.org

SCORE Office (Coachella)
43100 Cook St., Ste. 104
Palm Desert, CA 92211
(760)773-6507
Fax: (760)773-6514
Website: http://
www.coachellavalley.score.org

SCORE Office (Antelope Valley)
1212 E. Avenue, S Ste. A3
Palmdale, CA 93550
(661)947-7679
Website: http://www.antelopevalley.score
.org/

SCORE Office (Inland Empire)
11801 Pierce St., 2nd Fl.
Riverside, CA 92505
(951)-652-4390

Fax: (951)929-8543
Website: http://www.inlandempire.score
.org/

SCORE Office (Sacramento)
4990 Stockton Blvd.
Sacramento, CA 95820
(916)635-9085
Fax: (916)635-9089
Website: http://www.sacramento.score
.org

SCORE Office (San Diego)
550 West C. St., Ste. 550
San Diego, CA 92101-3540
(619)557-7272
Website: http://www.sandiego.score.org/

SCORE Office (San Francisco)
455 Market St., 6th Fl.
San Francisco, CA 94105
(415)744-6827
Fax: (415)744-6750
E-mail: sfscore@sfscore.
Website: http://www.sanfrancisco.score
.org/

SCORE Office (Silicon Valley)
234 E. Gish Rd., Ste. 100
San Jose, CA 95112
(408)453-6237
Fax: (408)494-0214
E-mail: info@svscore.org
Website: http://www.siliconvalley.score
.org/

SCORE Office (San Luis Obispo)
711 Tank Farm Rd., Ste. 210
San Luis Obispo, CA 93401
(805)547-0779
Website: http://www.sanluisobispo.score
.org

SCORE Office (Orange County)
200 W. Santa Anna Blvd., Ste. 700
Santa Ana, CA 92701
(714)550-7369
Fax: (714)550-0191
Website: http://www.orangecounty.score
.org

SCORE Office (Santa Barbara)
924 Anacapa St.
Santa Barbara, CA 93101
(805)563-0084
Website: http://www.santabarbara.score
.org/

SCORE Office (North Coast)
777 Sonoma Ave., Rm. 115E
Santa Rosa, CA 95404
(707)571-8342

Fax: (707)541-0331
Website: http://www.northcoast.score
.org

SCORE Office (Tuolumne County)
222 S. Shepherd St.
Sonora, CA 95370
(209)532-4316
Fax: (209)588-0673
Website: http://www.tuolumnecounty.
score.org/

Colorado

SCORE Office (Colorado Springs)
3595 E. Fountain Blvd., Ste. E-1
Colorado Springs, CO 80910
(719)636-3074
Fax: (719)635-1571
Website: http://www.coloradosprings.
score.org/

SCORE Office (Denver)
US Custom's House, 4th Fl.
721 19th St.
Denver, CO 80202
(303)844-3985
Fax: (303)844-6490
Website: http://www.denver.score.org/

SCORE Office (Tri-River)
1102 Grand Ave.
Glenwood Springs, CO 81601
(970)945-6589

SCORE Office (Grand Junction)
2591 B & 3/4 Rd.
Grand Junction, CO 81503
(970)243-5242

SCORE Office (Gunnison)
608 N. 11th
Gunnison, CO 81230
(303)641-4422

SCORE Office (Montrose)
1214 Peppertree Dr.
Montrose, CO 81401
(970)249-6080

SCORE Office (Pagosa Springs)
PO Box 4381
Pagosa Springs, CO 81157
(970)731-4890

SCORE Office (Rifle)
0854 W. Battlement Pky., Apt. C106
Parachute, CO 81635
(970)285-9390

SCORE Office (Pueblo)
302 N. Santa Fe
Pueblo, CO 81003

(719)542-1704
Fax: (719)542-1624
Website: http://www.pueblo.score.org

SCORE Office (Ridgway)
143 Poplar Pl.
Ridgway, CO 81432

SCORE Office (Silverton)
PO Box 480
Silverton, CO 81433
(303)387-5430

SCORE Office (Minturn)
PO Box 2066
Vail, CO 81658
(970)476-1224

Connecticut

SCORE Office (Greater Bridgeport)
230 Park Ave.
Bridgeport, CT 06604
(203)450-9484
Fax: (203)576-4388

SCORE Office (Western Connecticut)
155 Deer Hill Ave.
Danbury, CT 06010
(203)794-1404
Website: http://www.westernconnecticut
.score.org

SCORE Office (Greater Hartford County)
330 Main St., 2nd Fl.
Hartford, CT 06106
(860)240-4700
Fax: (860)240-4659
Website: http://www.greaterhartford
.score.org

SCORE Office (Manchester)
20 Hartford Rd.
Manchester, CT 06040
(203)646-2223
Fax: (203)646-5871

SCORE Office (New Britain)
185 Main St., Ste. 431
New Britain, CT 06051
(203)827-4492
Fax: (203)827-4480

SCORE Office (New Haven)
60 Sargent Dr.
New Haven, CT 06511
(203)865-7645
Website: http://www.newhaven.score.org

SCORE Office (Fairfield County)
111 East Ave.
Norwalk, CT 06851

(203)847-7348
Fax: (203)849-9308
Website: http://www.fairfieldcounty
.score.org

**SCORE Office (Southeastern
Connecticut)**
665 Boston Post Rd.
Old Saybrook, CT 06475
(860)388-9508
Website: http://www.southeastern
connecticut.score.org

SCORE Office (Northwest Connecticut)
333 Kennedy Dr.
Torrington, CT 06790
(560)482-6586
Website: http://www.northwest
connecticut.score.org

Delaware

SCORE Office (Dover)
Treadway Towers
PO Box 576
Dover, DE 19903
(302)678-0892
Fax: (302)678-0189

SCORE Office (Lewes)
PO Box 1
Lewes, DE 19958
(302)645-8073
Fax: (302)645-8412

SCORE Office (Milford)
204 NE Front St.
Milford, DE 19963
(302)422-3301

SCORE Office (Wilmington)
824 Market St., Ste. 610
Wilmington, DE 19801
(302)573-6652
Fax: (302)573-6092
Website: http://www.scoredelaware.com

District of Columbia

**SCORE Office (George Mason
University)**
409 3rd St. SW, 4th Fl.
Washington, DC 20024
800-634-0245

SCORE Office (Washington DC)
1110 Vermont Ave. NW, 9th Fl.
Washington, DC 20043
(202)606-4000
Fax: (202)606-4225
E-mail: dcscore@hotmail.com
Website: http://www.scoredc.org/

Florida

**SCORE Office (Desota County
Chamber of Commerce)**
16 South Velucia Ave.
Arcadia, FL 34266
(941)494-4033

SCORE Office (Suncoast/Pinellas)
Airport Business Ctr.
4707 - 140th Ave. N, No. 311
Clearwater, FL 33755
(813)532-6800
Fax: (813)532-6800

SCORE Office (DeLand)
336 N. Woodland Blvd.
DeLand, FL 32720
(904)734-4331
Fax: (904)734-4333

SCORE Office (South Palm Beach)
1050 S. Federal Hwy., Ste. 132
Delray Beach, FL 33483
(561)278-7752
Fax: (561)278-0288

SCORE Office (Ft. Lauderdale)
Federal Bldg., Ste. 123
299 E. Broward Blvd.
Ft. Lauderdale, FL 33301
(954)356-7263
Fax: (954)356-7145

SCORE Office (Southwest Florida)
The Renaissance
8695 College Pky., Ste. 345 & 346
Ft. Myers, FL 33919
(941)489-2935
Fax: (941)489-1170

SCORE Office (Treasure Coast)
Professional Center, Ste. 2
3220 S. US, No. 1
Ft. Pierce, FL 34982
(561)489-0548

SCORE Office (Gainesville)
101 SE 2nd Pl., Ste. 104
Gainesville, FL 32601
(904)375-8278

SCORE Office (Hialeah Dade Chamber)
59 W. 5th St.
Hialeah, FL 33010
(305)887-1515
Fax: (305)887-2453

SCORE Office (Daytona Beach)
921 Nova Rd., Ste. A
Holly Hills, FL 32117
(904)255-6889
Fax: (904)255-0229
E-mail: score87@dbeach.com

SCORE Office (South Broward)
3475 Sheridian St., Ste. 203
Hollywood, FL 33021
(305)966-8415

SCORE Office (Citrus County)
5 Poplar Ct.
Homosassa, FL 34446
(352)382-1037

SCORE Office (Jacksonville)
7825 Baymeadows Way, Ste. 100-B
Jacksonville, FL 32256
(904)443-1911
Fax: (904)443-1980
E-mail: scorejax@juno.com
Website: http://www.scorejax.org/

SCORE Office (Jacksonville Satellite)
3 Independent Dr.
Jacksonville, FL 32256
(904)366-6600
Fax: (904)632-0617

SCORE Office (Central Florida)
5410 S. Florida Ave., No. 3
Lakeland, FL 33801
(941)687-5783
Fax: (941)687-6225

SCORE Office (Lakeland)
100 Lake Morton Dr.
Lakeland, FL 33801
(941)686-2168

SCORE Office (St. Petersburg)
800 W. Bay Dr., Ste. 505
Largo, FL 33712
(813)585-4571

SCORE Office (Leesburg)
9501 US Hwy. 441
Leesburg, FL 34788-8751
(352)365-3556
Fax: (352)365-3501

SCORE Office (Cocoa)
1600 Farno Rd., Unit 205
Melbourne, FL 32935
(407)254-2288

SCORE Office (Melbourne)
Melbourne Professional Complex
1600 Sarno, Ste. 205
Melbourne, FL 32935
(407)254-2288
Fax: (407)245-2288

SCORE Office (Merritt Island)
1600 Sarno Rd., Ste. 205
Melbourne, FL 32935
(407)254-2288
Fax: (407)254-2288

SCORE Office (Space Coast)
Melbourn Professional Complex
1600 Sarno, Ste. 205
Melbourne, FL 32935
(407)254-2288
Fax: (407)254-2288

SCORE Office (Dade)
49 NW 5th St.
Miami, FL 33128
(305)371-6889
Fax: (305)374-1882
E-mail: score@netrox.net
Website: http://www.netrox.net/~score/

SCORE Office (Naples of Collier)
International College
2654 Tamiami Trl. E
Naples, FL 34112
(941)417-1280
Fax: (941)417-1281
E-mail: score@naples.net
Website: http://www.naples.net/clubs/
score/index.htm

SCORE Office (Pasco County)
6014 US Hwy. 19, Ste. 302
New Port Richey, FL 34652
(813)842-4638

SCORE Office (Southeast Volusia)
115 Canal St.
New Smyrna Beach, FL 32168
(904)428-2449
Fax: (904)423-3512

SCORE Office (Ocala)
110 E. Silver Springs Blvd.
Ocala, FL 34470
(352)629-5959

Clay County SCORE Office
Clay County Chamber of Commerce
1734 Kingsdey Ave.
PO Box 1441
Orange Park, FL 32073
(904)264-2651
Fax: (904)269-0363

SCORE Office (Orlando)
80 N. Hughey Ave.
Rm. 445 Federal Bldg.
Orlando, FL 32801
(407)648-6476
Fax: (407)648-6425

SCORE Office (Emerald Coast)
19 W. Garden St., No. 325
Pensacola, FL 32501
(904)444-2060
Fax: (904)444-2070

SCORE Office (Charlotte County)
201 W. Marion Ave., Ste. 211
Punta Gorda, FL 33950
(941)575-1818
E-mail: score@gls3c.com
Website: http://www.charlotte-
florida.com/business/scorepg01.htm

SCORE Office (St. Augustine)
1 Riberia St.
St. Augustine, FL 32084
(904)829-5681
Fax: (904)829-6477

SCORE Office (Bradenton)
2801 Fruitville, Ste. 280
Sarasota, FL 34237
(813)955-1029

SCORE Office (Manasota)
2801 Fruitville Rd., Ste. 280
Sarasota, FL 34237
(941)955-1029
Fax: (941)955-5581
E-mail: score116@gte.net
Website: http://www.score-suncoast.org/

SCORE Office (Tallahassee)
200 W. Park Ave.
Tallahassee, FL 32302
(850)487-2665

SCORE Office (Hillsborough)
4732 Dale Mabry Hwy. N, Ste. 400
Tampa, FL 33614-6509
(813)870-0125

SCORE Office (Lake Sumter)
122 E. Main St.
Tavares, FL 32778-3810
(352)365-3556

SCORE Office (Titusville)
2000 S. Washington Ave.
Titusville, FL 32780
(407)267-3036
Fax: (407)264-0127

SCORE Office (Venice)
257 N. Tamiami Trl.
Venice, FL 34285
(941)488-2236
Fax: (941)484-5903

SCORE Office (Palm Beach)
500 Australian Ave. S, Ste. 100
West Palm Beach, FL 33401
(561)833-1672
Fax: (561)833-1712

SCORE Office (Wildwood)
103 N. Webster St.
Wildwood, FL 34785

Georgia

SCORE Office (Atlanta)
Harris Tower, Suite 1900
233 Peachtree Rd., NE
Atlanta, GA 30309
(404)347-2442
Fax: (404)347-1227

SCORE Office (Augusta)
3126 Oxford Rd.
Augusta, GA 30909
(706)869-9100

SCORE Office (Columbus)
School Bldg.
PO Box 40
Columbus, GA 31901
(706)327-3654

SCORE Office (Dalton-Whitfield)
305 S. Thorton Ave.
Dalton, GA 30720
(706)279-3383

SCORE Office (Gainesville)
PO Box 374
Gainesville, GA 30503
(770)532-6206
Fax: (770)535-8419

SCORE Office (Macon)
711 Grand Bldg.
Macon, GA 31201
(912)751-6160

SCORE Office (Brunswick)
4 Glen Ave.
St. Simons Island, GA 31520
(912)265-0620
Fax: (912)265-0629

SCORE Office (Savannah)
111 E. Liberty St., Ste. 103
Savannah, GA 31401
(912)652-4335
Fax: (912)652-4184
E-mail: info@scoresav.org
Website: http://www.coastalempire.com/
score/index.htm

Guam

SCORE Office (Guam)
Pacific News Bldg., Rm. 103
238 Archbishop Flores St.
Agana, GU 96910-5100
(671)472-7308

Hawaii

SCORE Office (Hawaii, Inc.)
1111 Bishop St., Ste. 204
PO Box 50207

Honolulu, HI 96813
(808)522-8132
Fax: (808)522-8135
E-mail: hnlscore@juno.com

SCORE Office (Kahului)
250 Alamaha, Unit N16A
Kahului, HI 96732
(808)871-7711

SCORE Office (Maui, Inc.)
590 E. Lipoa Pkwy., Ste. 227
Kihei, HI 96753
(808)875-2380

Idaho

SCORE Office (Treasure Valley)
1020 Main St., No. 290
Boise, ID 83702
(208)334-1696
Fax: (208)334-9353

SCORE Office (Eastern Idaho)
2300 N. Yellowstone, Ste. 119
Idaho Falls, ID 83401
(208)523-1022
Fax: (208)528-7127

Illinois

SCORE Office (Fox Valley)
40 W. Downer Pl.
PO Box 277
Aurora, IL 60506
(630)897-9214
Fax: (630)897-7002

SCORE Office (Greater Belvidere)
419 S. State St.
Belvidere, IL 61008
(815)544-4357
Fax: (815)547-7654

SCORE Office (Bensenville)
1050 Busse Hwy. Suite 100
Bensenville, IL 60106
(708)350-2944
Fax: (708)350-2979

SCORE Office (Central Illinois)
402 N. Hershey Rd.
Bloomington, IL 61704
(309)644-0549
Fax: (309)663-8270
E-mail: webmaster@central-illinois-score.org
Website: http://www.central-illinois-score.org/

SCORE Office (Southern Illinois)
150 E. Pleasant Hill Rd.
Box 1

Carbondale, IL 62901
(618)453-6654
Fax: (618)453-5040

SCORE Office (Chicago)
Northwest Atrium Ctr.
500 W. Madison St., No. 1250
Chicago, IL 60661
(312)353-7724
Fax: (312)886-5688
Website: http://www.mcs.net/~bic/

SCORE Office (Chicago–Oliver Harvey College)
Pullman Bldg.
1000 E. 11th St., 7th Fl.
Chicago, IL 60628
Fax: (312)468-8086

SCORE Office (Danville)
28 W. N. Street
Danville, IL 61832
(217)442-7232
Fax: (217)442-6228

SCORE Office (Decatur)
Milliken University
1184 W. Main St.
Decatur, IL 62522
(217)424-6297
Fax: (217)424-3993
E-mail: charding@mail.millikin.edu
Website: http://www.millikin.edu/academics/Tabor/score.html

SCORE Office (Downers Grove)
925 Curtis
Downers Grove, IL 60515
(708)968-4050
Fax: (708)968-8368

SCORE Office (Elgin)
24 E. Chicago, 3rd Fl.
PO Box 648
Elgin, IL 60120
(847)741-5660
Fax: (847)741-5677

SCORE Office (Freeport Area)
26 S. Galena Ave.
Freeport, IL 61032
(815)233-1350
Fax: (815)235-4038

SCORE Office (Galesburg)
292 E. Simmons St.
PO Box 749
Galesburg, IL 61401
(309)343-1194
Fax: (309)343-1195

SCORE Office (Glen Ellyn)
500 Pennsylvania
Glen Ellyn, IL 60137
(708)469-0907
Fax: (708)469-0426

SCORE Office (Greater Alton)
Alden Hall
5800 Godfrey Rd.
Godfrey, IL 62035-2466
(618)467-2280
Fax: (618)466-8289
Website: http://www.altonweb.com/score/

SCORE Office (Grayslake)
19351 W. Washington St.
Grayslake, IL 60030
(708)223-3633
Fax: (708)223-9371

SCORE Office (Harrisburg)
303 S. Commercial
Harrisburg, IL 62946-1528
(618)252-8528
Fax: (618)252-0210

SCORE Office (Joliet)
100 N. Chicago
Joliet, IL 60432
(815)727-5371
Fax: (815)727-5374

SCORE Office (Kankakee)
101 S. Schuyler Ave.
Kankakee, IL 60901
(815)933-0376
Fax: (815)933-0380

SCORE Office (Macomb)
216 Seal Hall, Rm. 214
Macomb, IL 61455
(309)298-1128
Fax: (309)298-2520

SCORE Office (Matteson)
210 Lincoln Mall
Matteson, IL 60443
(708)709-3750
Fax: (708)503-9322

SCORE Office (Mattoon)
1701 Wabash Ave.
Mattoon, IL 61938
(217)235-5661
Fax: (217)234-6544

SCORE Office (Quad Cities)
622 19th St.
Moline, IL 61265
(309)797-0082
Fax: (309)757-5435
E-mail: score@qconline.com

Website: http://www.qconline.com/
business/score/

SCORE Office (Naperville)
131 W. Jefferson Ave.
Naperville, IL 60540
(708)355-4141
Fax: (708)355-8355

SCORE Office (Northbrook)
2002 Walters Ave.
Northbrook, IL 60062
(847)498-5555
Fax: (847)498-5510

SCORE Office (Palos Hills)
10900 S. 88th Ave.
Palos Hills, IL 60465
(847)974-5468
Fax: (847)974-0078

SCORE Office (Peoria)
124 SW Adams, Ste. 300
Peoria, IL 61602
(309)676-0755
Fax: (309)676-7534

SCORE Office (Prospect Heights)
1375 Wolf Rd.
Prospect Heights, IL 60070
(847)537-8660
Fax: (847)537-7138

SCORE Office (Quincy Tri-State)
300 Civic Center Plz., Ste. 245
Quincy, IL 62301
(217)222-8093
Fax: (217)222-3033

SCORE Office (River Grove)
2000 5th Ave.
River Grove, IL 60171
(708)456-0300
Fax: (708)583-3121

SCORE Office (Northern Illinois)
515 N. Court St.
Rockford, IL 61103
(815)962-0122
Fax: (815)962-0122

SCORE Office (St. Charles)
103 N. 1st Ave.
St. Charles, IL 60174-1982
(847)584-8384
Fax: (847)584-6065

SCORE Office (Springfield)
511 W. Capitol Ave., Ste. 302
Springfield, IL 62704
(217)492-4416
Fax: (217)492-4867

SCORE Office (Sycamore)
112 Somunak St.
Sycamore, IL 60178
(815)895-3456
Fax: (815)895-0125

SCORE Office (University)
Hwy. 50 & Stuenkel Rd. Ste. C3305
University Park, IL 60466
(708)534-5000
Fax: (708)534-8457

Indiana

SCORE Office (Anderson)
205 W. 11th St.
Anderson, IN 46015
(317)642-0264

SCORE Office (Bloomington)
Star Center
216 W. Allen
Bloomington, IN 47403
(812)335-7334
E-mail: wtfische@indiana.edu
Website: http://www.brainfreezemedia
.com/score527/

SCORE Office (South East Indiana)
500 Franklin St.
Box 29
Columbus, IN 47201
(812)379-4457

SCORE Office (Corydon)
310 N. Elm St.
Corydon, IN 47112
(812)738-2137
Fax: (812)738-6438

SCORE Office (Crown Point)
Old Courthouse Sq. Ste. 206
PO Box 43
Crown Point, IN 46307
(219)663-1800

SCORE Office (Elkhart)
418 S. Main St.
Elkhart, IN 46515
(219)293-1531
Fax: (219)294-1859

SCORE Office (Evansville)
1100 W. Lloyd Expy., Ste. 105
Evansville, IN 47708
(812)426-6144

SCORE Office (Fort Wayne)
1300 S. Harrison St.
Ft. Wayne, IN 46802
(219)422-2601
Fax: (219)422-2601

SCORE Office (Gary)
973 W. 6th Ave., Rm. 326
Gary, IN 46402
(219)882-3918

SCORE Office (Hammond)
7034 Indianapolis Blvd.
Hammond, IN 46324
(219)931-1000
Fax: (219)845-9548

SCORE Office (Indianapolis)
429 N. Pennsylvania St., Ste. 100
Indianapolis, IN 46204-1873
(317)226-7264
Fax: (317)226-7259
E-mail: inscore@indy.net
Website: http://www.score-
indianapolis.org/

SCORE Office (Jasper)
PO Box 307
Jasper, IN 47547-0307
(812)482-6866

**SCORE Office (Kokomo/Howard
Counties)**
106 N. Washington St.
Kokomo, IN 46901
(765)457-5301
Fax: (765)452-4564

SCORE Office (Logansport)
300 E. Broadway, Ste. 103
Logansport, IN 46947
(219)753-6388

SCORE Office (Madison)
301 E. Main St.
Madison, IN 47250
(812)265-3135
Fax: (812)265-2923

SCORE Office (Marengo)
Rt. 1 Box 224D
Marengo, IN 47140
Fax: (812)365-2793

**SCORE Office (Marion/Grant
Counties)**
215 S. Adams
Marion, IN 46952
(765)664-5107

SCORE Office (Merrillville)
255 W. 80th Pl.
Merrillville, IN 46410
(219)769-8180
Fax: (219)736-6223

SCORE Office (Michigan City)
200 E. Michigan Blvd.
Michigan City, IN 46360

(219)874-6221
Fax: (219)873-1204

SCORE Office (South Central Indiana)
4100 Charleston Rd.
New Albany, IN 47150-9538
(812)945-0066

SCORE Office (Rensselaer)
104 W. Washington
Rensselaer, IN 47978

SCORE Office (Salem)
210 N. Main St.
Salem, IN 47167
(812)883-4303
Fax: (812)883-1467

SCORE Office (South Bend)
300 N. Michigan St.
South Bend, IN 46601
(219)282-4350
E-mail: chair@southbend-score.org
Website: http://www.southbend-score.org/

SCORE Office (Valparaiso)
150 Lincolnway
Valparaiso, IN 46383
(219)462-1105
Fax: (219)469-5710

SCORE Office (Vincennes)
27 N. 3rd
PO Box 553
Vincennes, IN 47591
(812)882-6440
Fax: (812)882-6441

SCORE Office (Wabash)
PO Box 371
Wabash, IN 46992
(219)563-1168
Fax: (219)563-6920

Iowa

SCORE Office (Burlington)
Federal Bldg.
300 N. Main St.
Burlington, IA 52601
(319)752-2967

SCORE Office (Cedar Rapids)
2750 1st Ave. NE, Ste 350
Cedar Rapids, IA 52401-1806
(319)362-6405
Fax: (319)362-7861
E:mail: score@scorecr.org
Website: http://www.scorecr.org

SCORE Office (Illowa)
333 4th Ave. S
Clinton, IA 52732
(319)242-5702

SCORE Office (Council Bluffs)
7 N. 6th St.
Council Bluffs, IA 51502
(712)325-1000

SCORE Office (Northeast Iowa)
3404 285th St.
Cresco, IA 52136
(319)547-3377

SCORE Office (Des Moines)
Federal Bldg., Rm. 749
210 Walnut St.
Des Moines, IA 50309-2186
(515)284-4760

SCORE Office (Ft. Dodge)
Federal Bldg., Rm. 436
205 S. 8th St.
Ft. Dodge, IA 50501
(515)955-2622

SCORE Office (Independence)
110 1st. St. east
Independence, IA 50644
(319)334-7178
Fax: (319)334-7179

SCORE Office (Iowa City)
210 Federal Bldg.
PO Box 1853
Iowa City, IA 52240-1853
(319)338-1662

SCORE Office (Keokuk)
401 Main St.
Pierce Bldg., No. 1
Keokuk, IA 52632
(319)524-5055

SCORE Office (Central Iowa)
Fisher Community College
709 S. Center
Marshalltown, IA 50158
(515)753-6645

SCORE Office (River City)
15 West State St.
Mason City, IA 50401
(515)423-5724

SCORE Office (South Central)
SBDC, Indian Hills Community College
525 Grandview Ave.
Ottumwa, IA 52501
(515)683-5127
Fax: (515)683-5263

SCORE Office (Dubuque)
10250 Sundown Rd.
Peosta, IA 52068
(319)556-5110

SCORE Office (Southwest Iowa)
614 W. Sheridan
Shenandoah, IA 51601
(712)246-3260

SCORE Office (Sioux City)
Federal Bldg.
320 6th St.
Sioux City, IA 51101
(712)277-2324
Fax: (712)277-2325

SCORE Office (Iowa Lakes)
122 W. 5th St.
Spencer, IA 51301
(712)262-3059

SCORE Office (Vista)
119 W. 6th St.
Storm Lake, IA 50588
(712)732-3780

SCORE Office (Waterloo)
215 E. 4th
Waterloo, IA 50703
(319)233-8431

Kansas

SCORE Office (Southwest Kansas)
501 W. Spruce
Dodge City, KS 67801
(316)227-3119

SCORE Office (Emporia)
811 Homewood
Emporia, KS 66801
(316)342-1600

SCORE Office (Golden Belt)
1307 Williams
Great Bend, KS 67530
(316)792-2401

SCORE Office (Hays)
PO Box 400
Hays, KS 67601
(913)625-6595

SCORE Office (Hutchinson)
1 E. 9th St.
Hutchinson, KS 67501
(316)665-8468
Fax: (316)665-7619

SCORE Office (Southeast Kansas)
404 Westminster Pl.
PO Box 886
Independence, KS 67301
(316)331-4741

SCORE Office (McPherson)
306 N. Main
PO Box 616

McPherson, KS 67460
(316)241-3303

SCORE Office (Salina)
120 Ash St.
Salina, KS 67401
(785)243-4290
Fax: (785)243-1833

SCORE Office (Topeka)
1700 College
Topeka, KS 66621
(785)231-1010

SCORE Office (Wichita)
100 E. English, Ste. 510
Wichita, KS 67202
(316)269-6273
Fax: (316)269-6499

SCORE Office (Ark Valley)
205 E. 9th St.
Winfield, KS 67156
(316)221-1617

Kentucky

SCORE Office (Ashland)
PO Box 830
Ashland, KY 41105
(606)329-8011
Fax: (606)325-4607

SCORE Office (Bowling Green)
812 State St.
PO Box 51
Bowling Green, KY 42101
(502)781-3200
Fax: (502)843-0458

SCORE Office (Tri-Lakes)
508 Barbee Way
Danville, KY 40422-1548
(606)231-9902

SCORE Office (Glasgow)
301 W. Main St.
Glasgow, KY 42141
(502)651-3161
Fax: (502)651-3122

SCORE Office (Hazard)
B & I Technical Center
100 Airport Gardens Rd.
Hazard, KY 41701
(606)439-5856
Fax: (606)439-1808

SCORE Office (Lexington)
410 W. Vine St., Ste. 290, Civic C
Lexington, KY 40507
(606)231-9902
Fax: (606)253-3190
E-mail: scorelex@uky.campus.mci.net

SCORE Office (Louisville)
188 Federal Office Bldg.
600 Dr. Martin L. King Jr. Pl.
Louisville, KY 40202
(502)582-5976

SCORE Office (Madisonville)
257 N. Main
Madisonville, KY 42431
(502)825-1399
Fax: (502)825-1396

SCORE Office (Paducah)
Federal Office Bldg.
501 Broadway, Rm. B-36
Paducah, KY 42001
(502)442-5685

Louisiana

SCORE Office (Central Louisiana)
802 3rd St.
Alexandria, LA 71309
(318)442-6671

SCORE Office (Baton Rouge)
564 Laurel St.
PO Box 3217
Baton Rouge, LA 70801
(504)381-7130
Fax: (504)336-4306

SCORE Office (North Shore)
2 W. Thomas
Hammond, LA 70401
(504)345-4457
Fax: (504)345-4749

SCORE Office (Lafayette)
804 St. Mary Blvd.
Lafayette, LA 70505-1307
(318)233-2705
Fax: (318)234-8671
E-mail: score302@aol.com

SCORE Office (Lake Charles)
120 W. Pujo St.
Lake Charles, LA 70601
(318)433-3632

SCORE Office (New Orleans)
365 Canal St., Ste. 3100
New Orleans, LA 70130
(504)589-2356
Fax: (504)589-2339

SCORE Office (Shreveport)
400 Edwards St.
Shreveport, LA 71101
(318)677-2536
Fax: (318)677-2541

Maine

SCORE Office (Augusta)
40 Western Ave.
Augusta, ME 04330
(207)622-8509

SCORE Office (Bangor)
Peabody Hall, Rm. 229
One College Cir.
Bangor, ME 04401
(207)941-9707

SCORE Office (Central & Northern Arroostock)
111 High St.
Caribou, ME 04736
(207)492-8010
Fax: (207)492-8010

SCORE Office (Penquis)
South St.
Dover Foxcroft, ME 04426
(207)564-7021

SCORE Office (Maine Coastal)
Mill Mall
Box 1105
Ellsworth, ME 04605-1105
(207)667-5800
E-mail: score@arcadia.net

SCORE Office (Lewiston-Auburn)
BIC of Maine-Bates Mill Complex
35 Canal St.
Lewiston, ME 04240-7764
(207)782-3708
Fax: (207)783-7745

SCORE Office (Portland)
66 Pearl St., Rm. 210
Portland, ME 04101
(207)772-1147
Fax: (207)772-5581
E-mail: Score53@score.maine.org
Website: http://www.score.maine.org/
chapter53/

SCORE Office (Western Mountains)
255 River St.
PO Box 252
Rumford, ME 04257-0252
(207)369-9976

SCORE Office (Oxford Hills)
166 Main St.
South Paris, ME 04281
(207)743-0499

Maryland

SCORE Office (Southern Maryland)
2525 Riva Rd., Ste. 110
Annapolis, MD 21401

(410)266-9553
Fax: (410)573-0981
E-mail: score390@aol.com
Website: http://members.aol.com/
score390/index.htm

SCORE Office (Baltimore)
The City Crescent Bldg., 6th Fl.
10 S. Howard St.
Baltimore, MD 21201
(410)962-2233
Fax: (410)962-1805

SCORE Office (Bel Air)
108 S. Bond St.
Bel Air, MD 21014
(410)838-2020
Fax: (410)893-4715

SCORE Office (Bethesda)
7910 Woodmont Ave., Ste. 1204
Bethesda, MD 20814
(301)652-4900
Fax: (301)657-1973

SCORE Office (Bowie)
6670 Race Track Rd.
Bowie, MD 20715
(301)262-0920
Fax: (301)262-0921

SCORE Office (Dorchester County)
203 Sunburst Hwy.
Cambridge, MD 21613
(410)228-3575

SCORE Office (Upper Shore)
210 Marlboro Ave.
Easton, MD 21601
(410)822-4606
Fax: (410)822-7922

SCORE Office (Frederick County)
43A S. Market St.
Frederick, MD 21701
(301)662-8723
Fax: (301)846-4427

SCORE Office (Gaithersburg)
9 Park Ave.
Gaithersburg, MD 20877
(301)840-1400
Fax: (301)963-3918

SCORE Office (Glen Burnie)
103 Crain Hwy. SE
Glen Burnie, MD 21061
(410)766-8282
Fax: (410)766-9722

SCORE Office (Hagerstown)
111 W. Washington St.
Hagerstown, MD 21740

(301)739-2015
Fax: (301)739-1278

SCORE Office (Laurel)
7901 Sandy Spring Rd. Ste. 501
Laurel, MD 20707
(301)725-4000
Fax: (301)725-0776

SCORE Office (Salisbury)
300 E. Main St.
Salisbury, MD 21801
(410)749-0185
Fax: (410)860-9925

Massachusetts

SCORE Office (NE Massachusetts)
100 Cummings Ctr., Ste. 101 K
Beverly, MA 01923
(978)922-9441
Website: http://www1.shore.net/~score/

SCORE Office (Boston)
10 Causeway St., Rm. 265
Boston, MA 02222-1093
(617)565-5591
Fax: (617)565-5598
E-mail: boston-score-
20@worldnet.att.net
Website: http://www.scoreboston.org/

SCORE office (Bristol/Plymouth County)
53 N. 6th St., Federal Bldg.
Bristol, MA 02740
(508)994-5093

SCORE Office (SE Massachusetts)
60 School St.
Brockton, MA 02401
(508)587-2673
Fax: (508)587-1340
Website: http://www.metrosouth
chamber.com/score.html

SCORE Office (North Adams)
820 N. State Rd.
Cheshire, MA 01225
(413)743-5100

SCORE Office (Clinton Satellite)
1 Green St.
Clinton, MA 01510
Fax: (508)368-7689

SCORE Office (Greenfield)
PO Box 898
Greenfield, MA 01302
(413)773-5463
Fax: (413)773-7008

SCORE Office (Haverhill)
87 Winter St.
Haverhill, MA 01830
(508)373-5663
Fax: (508)373-8060

SCORE Office (Hudson Satellite)
PO Box 578
Hudson, MA 01749
(508)568-0360
Fax: (508)568-0360

SCORE Office (Cape Cod)
Independence Pk., Ste. 5B
270 Communications Way
Hyannis, MA 02601
(508)775-4884
Fax: (508)790-2540

SCORE Office (Lawrence)
264 Essex St.
Lawrence, MA 01840
(508)686-0900
Fax: (508)794-9953

SCORE Office (Leominster Satellite)
110 Erdman Way
Leominster, MA 01453
(508)840-4300
Fax: (508)840-4896

SCORE Office (Bristol/Plymouth Counties)
53 N. 6th St., Federal Bldg.
New Bedford, MA 02740
(508)994-5093

SCORE Office (Newburyport)
29 State St.
Newburyport, MA 01950
(617)462-6680

SCORE Office (Pittsfield)
66 West St.
Pittsfield, MA 01201
(413)499-2485

SCORE Office (Haverhill-Salem)
32 Derby Sq.
Salem, MA 01970
(508)745-0330
Fax: (508)745-3855

SCORE Office (Springfield)
1350 Main St.
Federal Bldg.
Springfield, MA 01103
(413)785-0314

SCORE Office (Carver)
12 Taunton Green, Ste. 201
Taunton, MA 02780
(508)824-4068
Fax: (508)824-4069

SCORE Office (Worcester)
33 Waldo St.
Worcester, MA 01608
(508)753-2929
Fax: (508)754-8560

Michigan

SCORE Office (Allegan)
PO Box 338
Allegan, MI 49010
(616)673-2479

SCORE Office (Ann Arbor)
425 S. Main St., Ste. 103
Ann Arbor, MI 48104
(313)665-4433

SCORE Office (Battle Creek)
34 W. Jackson Ste. 4A
Battle Creek, MI 49017-3505
(616)962-4076
Fax: (616)962-6309

SCORE Office (Cadillac)
222 Lake St.
Cadillac, MI 49601
(616)775-9776
Fax: (616)768-4255

SCORE Office (Detroit)
477 Michigan Ave., Rm. 515
Detroit, MI 48226
(313)226-7947
Fax: (313)226-3448

SCORE Office (Flint)
708 Root Rd., Rm. 308
Flint, MI 48503
(810)233-6846

SCORE Office (Grand Rapids)
111 Pearl St. NW
Grand Rapids, MI 49503-2831
(616)771-0305
Fax: (616)771-0328
E-mail: scoreone@iserv.net
Website: http://www.iserv.net/
~scoreone/

SCORE Office (Holland)
480 State St.
Holland, MI 49423
(616)396-9472

SCORE Office (Jackson)
209 East Washington
PO Box 80
Jackson, MI 49204
(517)782-8221
Fax: (517)782-0061

SCORE Office (Kalamazoo)
345 W. Michigan Ave.
Kalamazoo, MI 49007
(616)381-5382
Fax: (616)384-0096
E-mail: score@nucleus.net

SCORE Office (Lansing)
117 E. Allegan
PO Box 14030
Lansing, MI 48901
(517)487-6340
Fax: (517)484-6910

SCORE Office (Livonia)
15401 Farmington Rd.
Livonia, MI 48154
(313)427-2122
Fax: (313)427-6055

SCORE Office (Madison Heights)
26345 John R
Madison Heights, MI 48071
(810)542-5010
Fax: (810)542-6821

SCORE Office (Monroe)
111 E. 1st
Monroe, MI 48161
(313)242-3366
Fax: (313)242-7253

SCORE Office (Mt. Clemens)
58 S/B Gratiot
Mt. Clemens, MI 48043
(810)463-1528
Fax: (810)463-6541

SCORE Office (Muskegon)
PO Box 1087
230 Terrace Plz.
Muskegon, MI 49443
(616)722-3751
Fax: (616)728-7251

SCORE Office (Petoskey)
401 E. Mitchell St.
Petoskey, MI 49770
(616)347-4150

SCORE Office (Pontiac)
Executive Office Bldg.
1200 N. Telegraph Rd.
Pontiac, MI 48341
(810)975-9555

SCORE Office (Pontiac)
PO Box 430025
Pontiac, MI 48343
(810)335-9600

SCORE Office (Port Huron)
920 Pinegrove Ave.
Port Huron, MI 48060
(810)985-7101

SCORE Office (Rochester)
71 Walnut Ste. 110
Rochester, MI 48307
(810)651-6700
Fax: (810)651-5270

SCORE Office (Saginaw)
901 S. Washington Ave.
Saginaw, MI 48601
(517)752-7161
Fax: (517)752-9055

SCORE Office (Upper Peninsula)
2581 I-75 Business Spur
Sault Ste. Marie, MI 49783
(906)632-3301

SCORE Office (Southfield)
21000 W. 10 Mile Rd.
Southfield, MI 48075
(810)204-3050
Fax: (810)204-3099

SCORE Office (Traverse City)
202 E. Grandview Pkwy.
PO Box 387
Traverse City, MI 49685
(616)947-5075
Fax: (616)946-2565

SCORE Office (Warren)
30500 Van Dyke, Ste. 118
Warren, MI 48093
(810)751-3939

Minnesota

SCORE Office (Aitkin)
Aitkin, MN 56431
(218)741-3906

SCORE Office (Albert Lea)
202 N. Broadway Ave.
Albert Lea, MN 56007
(507)373-7487

SCORE Office (Austin)
PO Box 864
Austin, MN 55912
(507)437-4561
Fax: (507)437-4869

SCORE Office (South Metro)
Ames Business Ctr.
2500 W. County Rd., No. 42
Burnsville, MN 55337
(612)898-5645
Fax: (612)435-6972

E-mail: southmetro@scoreminn.org
Website: http://www.scoreminn.org/
southmetro/

SCORE Office (Duluth)
1717 Minnesota Ave.
Duluth, MN 55802
(218)727-8286
Fax: (218)727-3113
E-mail: duluth@scoreminn.org
Website: http://www.scoreminn.org

SCORE Office (Fairmont)
PO Box 826
Fairmont, MN 56031
(507)235-5547
Fax: (507)235-8411

SCORE Office (Southwest Minnesota)
112 Riverfront St.
Box 999
Mankato, MN 56001
(507)345-4519
Fax: (507)345-4451
Website: http://www.scoreminn.org/

SCORE Office (Minneapolis)
North Plaza Bldg., Ste. 51
5217 Wayzata Blvd.
Minneapolis, MN 55416
(612)591-0539
Fax: (612)544-0436
Website: http://www.scoreminn.org/

SCORE Office (Owatonna)
PO Box 331
Owatonna, MN 55060
(507)451-7970
Fax: (507)451-7972

SCORE Office (Red Wing)
2000 W. Main St., Ste. 324
Red Wing, MN 55066
(612)388-4079

SCORE Office (Southeastern Minnesota)
220 S. Broadway, Ste. 100
Rochester, MN 55901
(507)288-1122
Fax: (507)282-8960
Website: http://www.scoreminn.org/

SCORE Office (Brainerd)
St. Cloud, MN 56301

SCORE Office (Central Area)
1527 Northway Dr.
St. Cloud, MN 56301
(320)240-1332
Fax: (320)255-9050
Website: http://www.scoreminn.org/

SCORE Office (St. Paul)
350 St. Peter St., No. 295
Lowry Professional Bldg.
St. Paul, MN 55102
(651)223-5010
Fax: (651)223-5048
Website: http://www.scoreminn.org/

SCORE Office (Winona)
Box 870
Winona, MN 55987
(507)452-2272
Fax: (507)454-8814

SCORE Office (Worthington)
1121 3rd Ave.
Worthington, MN 56187
(507)372-2919
Fax: (507)372-2827

Mississippi

SCORE Office (Delta)
915 Washington Ave.
PO Box 933
Greenville, MS 38701
(601)378-3141

SCORE Office (Gulfcoast)
1 Government Plaza
2909 13th St., Ste. 203
Gulfport, MS 39501
(228)863-0054

SCORE Office (Jackson)
1st Jackson Center, Ste. 400
101 W. Capitol St.
Jackson, MS 39201
(601)965-5533

SCORE Office (Meridian)
5220 16th Ave.
Meridian, MS 39305
(601)482-4412

Missouri

SCORE Office (Lake of the Ozark)
University Extension
113 Kansas St.
PO Box 1405
Camdenton, MO 65020
(573)346-2644
Fax: (573)346-2694
E-mail: score@cdoc.net
Website: http://sites.cdoc.net/score/

Chamber of Commerce (Cape Girardeau)
PO Box 98
Cape Girardeau, MO 63702-0098
(314)335-3312

SCORE Office (Mid-Missouri)
1705 Halstead Ct.
Columbia, MO 65203
(573)874-1132

SCORE Office (Ozark-Gateway)
1486 Glassy Rd.
Cuba, MO 65453-1640
(573)885-4954

SCORE Office (Kansas City)
323 W. 8th St., Ste. 104
Kansas City, MO 64105
(816)374-6675
Fax: (816)374-6692
E-mail: SCOREBIC@AOL.COM
Website: http://www.crn.org/score/

SCORE Office (Sedalia)
Lucas Place
323 W. 8th St., Ste.104
Kansas City, MO 64105
(816)374-6675

SCORE office (Tri-Lakes)
PO Box 1148
Kimberling, MO 65686
(417)739-3041

SCORE Office (Tri-Lakes)
HCRI Box 85
Lampe, MO 65681
(417)858-6798

SCORE Office (Mexico)
111 N. Washington St.
Mexico, MO 65265
(314)581-2765

SCORE Office (Southeast Missouri)
Rte. 1, Box 280
Neelyville, MO 63954
(573)989-3577

SCORE office (Poplar Bluff Area)
806 Emma St.
Poplar Bluff, MO 63901
(573)686-8892

SCORE Office (St. Joseph)
3003 Frederick Ave.
St. Joseph, MO 64506
(816)232-4461

SCORE Office (St. Louis)
815 Olive St., Rm. 242
St. Louis, MO 63101-1569
(314)539-6970
Fax: (314)539-3785
E-mail: info@stlscore.org
Website: http://www.stlscore.org/

SCORE Office (Lewis & Clark)
425 Spencer Rd.
St. Peters, MO 63376
(314)928-2900
Fax: (314)928-2900
E-mail: score01@mail.win.org

SCORE Office (Springfield)
620 S. Glenstone, Ste. 110
Springfield, MO 65802-3200
(417)864-7670
Fax: (417)864-4108

SCORE office (Southeast Kansas)
1206 W. First St.
Webb City, MO 64870
(417)673-3984

Montana

SCORE Office (Billings)
815 S. 27th St.
Billings, MT 59101
(406)245-4111

SCORE Office (Bozeman)
1205 E. Main St.
Bozeman, MT 59715
(406)586-5421

SCORE Office (Butte)
1000 George St.
Butte, MT 59701
(406)723-3177

SCORE Office (Great Falls)
710 First Ave. N
Great Falls, MT 59401
(406)761-4434
E-mail: scoregtf@in.tch.com

SCORE Office (Havre, Montana)
518 First St.
Havre, MT 59501
(406)265-4383

SCORE Office (Helena)
Federal Bldg.
301 S. Park
Helena, MT 59626-0054
(406)441-1081

SCORE Office (Kalispell)
2 Main St.
Kalispell, MT 59901
(406)756-5271
Fax: (406)752-6665

SCORE Office (Missoula)
723 Ronan
Missoula, MT 59806
(406)327-8806

E-mail: score@safeshop.com
Website: http://missoula.bigsky.net/
score/

Nebraska

SCORE Office (Columbus)
Columbus, NE 68601
(402)564-2769

SCORE Office (Fremont)
92 W. 5th St.
Fremont, NE 68025
(402)721-2641

SCORE Office (Hastings)
Hastings, NE 68901
(402)463-3447

SCORE Office (Lincoln)
8800 O St.
Lincoln, NE 68520
(402)437-2409

SCORE Office (Panhandle)
150549 CR 30
Minatare, NE 69356
(308)632-2133
Website: http://www.tandt.com/SCORE

SCORE Office (Norfolk)
3209 S. 48th Ave.
Norfolk, NE 68106
(402)564-2769

SCORE Office (North Platte)
3301 W. 2nd St.
North Platte, NE 69101
(308)532-4466

SCORE Office (Omaha)
11145 Mill Valley Rd.
Omaha, NE 68154
(402)221-3606
Fax: (402)221-3680
E-mail: infoctr@ne.uswest.net
Website: http://www.tandt.com/score/

Nevada

SCORE Office (Incline Village)
969 Tahoe Blvd.
Incline Village, NV 89451
(702)831-7327
Fax: (702)832-1605

SCORE Office (Carson City)
301 E. Stewart
PO Box 7527
Las Vegas, NV 89125
(702)388-6104

SCORE Office (Las Vegas)
300 Las Vegas Blvd. S, Ste. 1100
Las Vegas, NV 89101
(702)388-6104

SCORE Office (Northern Nevada)
SBDC, College of Business
Administration
Univ. of Nevada
Reno, NV 89557-0100
(702)784-4436
Fax: (702)784-4337

New Hampshire

SCORE Office (North Country)
PO Box 34
Berlin, NH 03570
(603)752-1090

SCORE Office (Concord)
143 N. Main St., Rm. 202A
PO Box 1258
Concord, NH 03301
(603)225-1400
Fax: (603)225-1409

SCORE Office (Dover)
299 Central Ave.
Dover, NH 03820
(603)742-2218
Fax: (603)749-6317

SCORE Office (Monadnock)
34 Mechanic St.
Keene, NH 03431-3421
(603)352-0320

SCORE Office (Lakes Region)
67 Water St., Ste. 105
Laconia, NH 03246
(603)524-9168

SCORE Office (Upper Valley)
Citizens Bank Bldg., Rm. 310
20 W. Park St.
Lebanon, NH 03766
(603)448-3491
Fax: (603)448-1908
E-mail: billt@valley.net
Website: http://www.valley.net/~score/

SCORE Office (Merrimack Valley)
275 Chestnut St., Rm. 618
Manchester, NH 03103
(603)666-7561
Fax: (603)666-7925

SCORE Office (Mt. Washington Valley)
PO Box 1066
North Conway, NH 03818
(603)383-0800

SCORE Office (Seacoast)
195 Commerce Way, Unit-A
Portsmouth, NH 03801-3251
(603)433-0575

New Jersey

SCORE Office (Somerset)
Paritan Valley Community College, Rte. 28
Branchburg, NJ 08807
(908)218-8874
E-mail: nj-score@grizbiz.com.
Website: http://www.nj-score.org/

SCORE Office (Chester)
5 Old Mill Rd.
Chester, NJ 07930
(908)879-7080

SCORE Office (Greater Princeton)
4 A George Washington Dr.
Cranbury, NJ 08512
(609)520-1776

SCORE Office (Freehold)
36 W. Main St.
Freehold, NJ 07728
(908)462-3030
Fax: (908)462-2123

SCORE Office (North West)
Picantinny Innovation Ctr.
3159 Schrader Rd.
Hamburg, NJ 07419
(973)209-8525
Fax: (973)209-7252
E-mail: nj-score@grizbiz.com
Website: http://www.nj-score.org/

SCORE Office (Monmouth)
765 Newman Springs Rd.
Lincroft, NJ 07738
(908)224-2573
E-mail: nj-score@grizbiz.com
Website: http://www.nj-score.org/

SCORE Office (Manalapan)
125 Symmes Dr.
Manalapan, NJ 07726
(908)431-7220

SCORE Office (Jersey City)
2 Gateway Ctr., 4th Fl.
Newark, NJ 07102
(973)645-3982
Fax: (973)645-2375

SCORE Office (Newark)
2 Gateway Center, 15th Fl.
Newark, NJ 07102-5553
(973)645-3982
Fax: (973)645-2375
E-mail: nj-score@grizbiz.com
Website: http://www.nj-score.org

SCORE Office (Bergen County)
327 E. Ridgewood Ave.
Paramus, NJ 07652
(201)599-6090
E-mail: nj-score@grizbiz.com
Website: http://www.nj-score.org/

SCORE Office (Pennsauken)
4900 Rte. 70
Pennsauken, NJ 08109
(609)486-3421

SCORE Office (Southern New Jersey)
4900 Rte. 70
Pennsauken, NJ 08109
(609)486-3421
E-mail: nj-score@grizbiz.com
Website: http://www.nj-score.org/

SCORE Office (Greater Princeton)
216 Rockingham Row
Princeton Forrestal Village
Princeton, NJ 08540
(609)520-1776
Fax: (609)520-9107
E-mail: nj-score@grizbiz.com
Website: http://www.nj-score.org/

SCORE Office (Shrewsbury)
Hwy. 35
Shrewsbury, NJ 07702
(908)842-5995
Fax: (908)219-6140

SCORE Office (Ocean County)
33 Washington St.
Toms River, NJ 08754
(732)505-6033
E-mail: nj-score@grizbiz.com
Website: http://www.nj-score.org/

SCORE Office (Wall)
2700 Allaire Rd.
Wall, NJ 07719
(908)449-8877

SCORE Office (Wayne)
2055 Hamburg Tpke.
Wayne, NJ 07470
(201)831-7788
Fax: (201)831-9112

New Mexico

SCORE Office (Albuquerque)
525 Buena Vista, SE
Albuquerque, NM 87106
(505)272-7999
Fax: (505)272-7963

SCORE Office (Las Cruces)
Loretto Towne Center
505 S. Main St., Ste. 125

Las Cruces, NM 88001
(505)523-5627
Fax: (505)524-2101
E-mail: score.397@zianet.com

SCORE Office (Roswell)
Federal Bldg., Rm. 237
Roswell, NM 88201
(505)625-2112
Fax: (505)623-2545

SCORE Office (Santa Fe)
Montoya Federal Bldg.
120 Federal Place, Rm. 307
Santa Fe, NM 87501
(505)988-6302
Fax: (505)988-6300

New York

SCORE Office (Northeast)
1 Computer Dr. S
Albany, NY 12205
(518)446-1118
Fax: (518)446-1228

SCORE Office (Auburn)
30 South St.
PO Box 675
Auburn, NY 13021
(315)252-7291

SCORE Office (South Tier Binghamton)
Metro Center, 2nd Fl.
49 Court St.
PO Box 995
Binghamton, NY 13902
(607)772-8860

SCORE Office (Queens County City)
12055 Queens Blvd., Rm. 333
Borough Hall, NY 11424
(718)263-8961

SCORE Office (Buffalo)
Federal Bldg., Rm. 1311
111 W. Huron St.
Buffalo, NY 14202
(716)551-4301
Website: http://www2.pcom.net/score/
buf45.html

SCORE Office (Canandaigua)
Chamber of Commerce Bldg.
113 S. Main St.
Canandaigua, NY 14424
(716)394-4400
Fax: (716)394-4546

SCORE Office (Chemung)
333 E. Water St., 4th Fl.
Elmira, NY 14901
(607)734-3358

SCORE Office (Geneva)
Chamber of Commerce Bldg.
PO Box 587
Geneva, NY 14456
(315)789-1776
Fax: (315)789-3993

SCORE Office (Glens Falls)
84 Broad St.
Glens Falls, NY 12801
(518)798-8463
Fax: (518)745-1433

SCORE Office (Orange County)
40 Matthews St.
Goshen, NY 10924
(914)294-8080
Fax: (914)294-6121

SCORE Office (Huntington Area)
151 W. Carver St.
Huntington, NY 11743
(516)423-6100

SCORE Office (Tompkins County)
904 E. Shore Dr.
Ithaca, NY 14850
(607)273-7080

SCORE Office (Long Island City)
120-55 Queens Blvd.
Jamaica, NY 11424
(718)263-8961
Fax: (718)263-9032

SCORE Office (Chatauqua)
101 W. 5th St.
Jamestown, NY 14701
(716)484-1103

SCORE Office (Westchester)
2 Caradon Ln.
Katonah, NY 10536
(914)948-3907
Fax: (914)948-4645
E-mail: score@w-w-w.com
Website: http://w-w-w.com/score/

SCORE Office (Queens County)
Queens Borough Hall
120-55 Queens Blvd. Rm. 333
Kew Gardens, NY 11424
(718)263-8961
Fax: (718)263-9032

SCORE Office (Brookhaven)
3233 Rte. 112
Medford, NY 11763
(516)451-6563
Fax: (516)451-6925

SCORE Office (Melville)
35 Pinelawn Rd., Rm. 207-W

Melville, NY 11747
(516)454-0771

SCORE Office (Nassau County)
400 County Seat Dr., No. 140
Mineola, NY 11501
(516)571-3303
E-mail: Counse1998@aol.com
Website: http://members.aol.com/
Counse1998/Default.htm

SCORE Office (Mt. Vernon)
4 N. 7th Ave.
Mt. Vernon, NY 10550
(914)667-7500

SCORE Office (New York)
26 Federal Plz., Rm. 3100
New York, NY 10278
(212)264-4507
Fax: (212)264-4963
E-mail: score1000@erols.com
Website: http://users.erols.com/
score-nyc/

SCORE Office (Newburgh)
47 Grand St.
Newburgh, NY 12550
(914)562-5100

SCORE Office (Owego)
188 Front St.
Owego, NY 13827
(607)687-2020

SCORE Office (Peekskill)
1 S. Division St.
Peekskill, NY 10566
(914)737-3600
Fax: (914)737-0541

SCORE Office (Penn Yan)
2375 Rte. 14A
Penn Yan, NY 14527
(315)536-3111

SCORE Office (Dutchess)
110 Main St.
Poughkeepsie, NY 12601
(914)454-1700

SCORE Office (Rochester)
601 Keating Federal Bldg., Rm. 410
100 State St.
Rochester, NY 14614
(716)263-6473
Fax: (716)263-3146
Website: http://www.ggw.org/score/

SCORE Office (Saranac Lake)
30 Main St.
Saranac Lake, NY 12983
(315)448-0415

SCORE Office (Suffolk)
286 Main St.
Setauket, NY 11733
(516)751-3886

SCORE Office (Staten Island)
130 Bay St.
Staten Island, NY 10301
(718)727-1221

SCORE Office (Ulster)
Clinton Bldg., Rm. 107
Stone Ridge, NY 12484
(914)687-5035
Fax: (914)687-5015
Website: http://www.scoreulster.org/

SCORE Office (Syracuse)
401 S. Salina, 5th Fl.
Syracuse, NY 13202
(315)471-9393

SCORE Office (Utica)
SUNY Institute of Technology, Route 12
Utica, NY 13504-3050
(315)792-7553

SCORE Office (Watertown)
518 Davidson St.
Watertown, NY 13601
(315)788-1200
Fax: (315)788-8251

North Carolina

SCORE office (Asheboro)
317 E. Dixie Dr.
Asheboro, NC 27203
(336)626-2626
Fax: (336)626-7077

SCORE Office (Asheville)
Federal Bldg., Rm. 259
151 Patton
Asheville, NC 28801-5770
(828)271-4786
Fax: (828)271-4009

SCORE Office (Chapel Hill)
104 S. Estes Dr.
PO Box 2897
Chapel Hill, NC 27514
(919)967-7075

SCORE Office (Coastal Plains)
PO Box 2897
Chapel Hill, NC 27515
(919)967-7075
Fax: (919)968-6874

SCORE Office (Charlotte)
200 N. College St., Ste. A-2015
Charlotte, NC 28202

(704)344-6576
Fax: (704)344-6769
E-mail: CharlotteSCORE47@AOL.com
Website: http://www.charweb.org/
business/score/

SCORE Office (Durham)
411 W. Chapel Hill St.
Durham, NC 27707
(919)541-2171

SCORE Office (Gastonia)
PO Box 2168
Gastonia, NC 28053
(704)864-2621
Fax: (704)854-8723

SCORE Office (Greensboro)
400 W. Market St., Ste. 103
Greensboro, NC 27401-2241
(910)333-5399

SCORE Office (Henderson)
PO Box 917
Henderson, NC 27536
(919)492-2061
Fax: (919)430-0460

SCORE Office (Hendersonville)
Federal Bldg., Rm. 108
W. 4th Ave. & Church St.
Hendersonville, NC 28792
(828)693-8702
E-mail: score@circle.net
Website: http://www.wncguide.com/
score/Welcome.html

SCORE Office (Unifour)
PO Box 1828
Hickory, NC 28603
(704)328-6111

SCORE Office (High Point)
1101 N. Main St.
High Point, NC 27262
(336)882-8625
Fax: (336)889-9499

SCORE Office (Outer Banks)
Collington Rd. and Mustain
Kill Devil Hills, NC 27948
(252)441-8144

SCORE Office (Down East)
312 S. Front St., Ste. 6
New Bern, NC 28560
(252)633-6688
Fax: (252)633-9608

SCORE Office (Kinston)
PO Box 95
New Bern, NC 28561
(919)633-6688

SCORE Office (Raleigh)
Century Post Office Bldg., Ste. 306
300 Federal St. Mall
Raleigh, NC 27601
(919)856-4739
E-mail: jendres@ibm.net
Website: http://www.intrex.net/score96/
score96.htm

SCORE Office (Sanford)
1801 Nash St.
Sanford, NC 27330
(919)774-6442
Fax: (919)776-8739

SCORE Office (Sandhills Area)
1480 Hwy. 15-501
PO Box 458
Southern Pines, NC 28387
(910)692-3926

SCORE Office (Wilmington)
Corps of Engineers Bldg.
96 Darlington Ave., Ste. 207
Wilmington, NC 28403
(910)815-4576
Fax: (910)815-4658

North Dakota

SCORE Office (Bismarck-Mandan)
700 E. Main Ave., 2nd Fl.
PO Box 5509
Bismarck, ND 58506-5509
(701)250-4303

SCORE Office (Fargo)
657 2nd Ave., Rm. 225
Fargo, ND 58108-3083
(701)239-5677

SCORE Office (Upper Red River)
4275 Technology Dr., Rm. 156
Grand Forks, ND 58202-8372
(701)777-3051

SCORE Office (Minot)
100 1st St. SW
Minot, ND 58701-3846
(701)852-6883
Fax: (701)852-6905

Ohio

SCORE Office (Akron)
1 Cascade Plz., 7th Fl.
Akron, OH 44308
(330)379-3163
Fax: (330)379-3164

SCORE Office (Ashland)
Gill Center
47 W. Main St.

Ashland, OH 44805
(419)281-4584

SCORE Office (Canton)
116 Cleveland Ave. NW, Ste. 601
Canton, OH 44702-1720
(330)453-6047

SCORE Office (Chillicothe)
165 S. Paint St.
Chillicothe, OH 45601
(614)772-4530

SCORE Office (Cincinnati)
Ameritrust Bldg., Rm. 850
525 Vine St.
Cincinnati, OH 45202
(513)684-2812
Fax: (513)684-3251
Website: http://www.score.chapter34
.org/

SCORE Office (Cleveland)
Eaton Center, Ste. 620
1100 Superior Ave.
Cleveland, OH 44114-2507
(216)522-4194
Fax: (216)522-4844

SCORE Office (Columbus)
2 Nationwide Plz., Ste. 1400
Columbus, OH 43215-2542
(614)469-2357
Fax: (614)469-2391
E-mail: info@scorecolumbus.org
Website: http://www.scorecolumbus
.org/

SCORE Office (Dayton)
Dayton Federal Bldg., Rm. 505
200 W. Second St.
Dayton, OH 45402-1430
(513)225-2887
Fax: (513)225-7667

SCORE Office (Defiance)
615 W. 3rd St.
PO Box 130
Defiance, OH 43512
(419)782-7946

SCORE Office (Findlay)
123 E. Main Cross St.
PO Box 923
Findlay, OH 45840
(419)422-3314

SCORE Office (Lima)
147 N. Main St.
Lima, OH 45801
(419)222-6045
Fax: (419)229-0266

SCORE Office (Mansfield)
55 N. Mulberry St.
Mansfield, OH 44902
(419)522-3211

SCORE Office (Marietta)
Thomas Hall
Marietta, OH 45750
(614)373-0268

SCORE Office (Medina)
County Administrative Bldg.
144 N. Broadway
Medina, OH 44256
(216)764-8650

SCORE Office (Licking County)
50 W. Locust St.
Newark, OH 43055
(614)345-7458

SCORE Office (Salem)
2491 State Rte. 45 S
Salem, OH 44460
(216)332-0361

SCORE Office (Tiffin)
62 S. Washington St.
Tiffin, OH 44883
(419)447-4141
Fax: (419)447-5141

SCORE Office (Toledo)
608 Madison Ave, Ste. 910
Toledo, OH 43624
(419)259-7598
Fax: (419)259-6460

SCORE Office (Heart of Ohio)
377 W. Liberty St.
Wooster, OH 44691
(330)262-5735
Fax: (330)262-5745

SCORE Office (Youngstown)
306 Williamson Hall
Youngstown, OH 44555
(330)746-2687

Oklahoma

SCORE Office (Anadarko)
PO Box 366
Anadarko, OK 73005
(405)247-6651

SCORE Office (Ardmore)
410 W. Main
Ardmore, OK 73401
(580)226-2620

SCORE Office (Northeast Oklahoma)
210 S. Main
Grove, OK 74344

(918)787-2796
Fax: (918)787-2796
E-mail: Score595@greencis.net

SCORE Office (Lawton)
4500 W. Lee Blvd., Bldg. 100, Ste. 107
Lawton, OK 73505
(580)353-8727
Fax: (580)250-5677

SCORE Office (Oklahoma City)
210 Park Ave., No. 1300
Oklahoma City, OK 73102
(405)231-5163
Fax: (405)231-4876
E-mail: score212@usa.net

SCORE Office (Stillwater)
439 S. Main
Stillwater, OK 74074
(405)372-5573
Fax: (405)372-4316

SCORE Office (Tulsa)
616 S. Boston, Ste. 406
Tulsa, OK 74119
(918)581-7462
Fax: (918)581-6908
Website: http://www.ionet.net/~tulscore/

Oregon

SCORE Office (Bend)
63085 N. Hwy. 97
Bend, OR 97701
(541)923-2849
Fax: (541)330-6900

SCORE Office (Willamette)
1401 Willamette St.
PO Box 1107
Eugene, OR 97401-4003
(541)465-6600
Fax: (541)484-4942

SCORE Office (Florence)
3149 Oak St.
Florence, OR 97439
(503)997-8444
Fax: (503)997-8448

SCORE Office (Southern Oregon)
33 N. Central Ave., Ste. 216
Medford, OR 97501
(541)776-4220
E-mail: pgr134f@prodigy.com

SCORE Office (Portland)
1515 SW 5th Ave., Ste. 1050
Portland, OR 97201
(503)326-3441
Fax: (503)326-2808
E-mail: gr134@prodigy.com

SCORE Office (Salem)
416 State St. (corner of Liberty)
Salem, OR 97301
(503)370-2896

Pennsylvania

SCORE Office (Altoona-Blair)
1212 12th Ave.
Altoona, PA 16601-3493
(814)943-8151

SCORE Office (Lehigh Valley)
Rauch Bldg. 37
Lehigh University
621 Taylor St.
Bethlehem, PA 18015
(610)758-4496
Fax: (610)758-5205

SCORE Office (Butler County)
100 N. Main St.
PO Box 1082
Butler, PA 16003
(412)283-2222
Fax: (412)283-0224

SCORE Office (Harrisburg)
4211 Trindle Rd.
Camp Hill, PA 17011
(717)761-4304
Fax: (717)761-4315

SCORE Office (Cumberland Valley)
75 S. 2nd St.
Chambersburg, PA 17201
(717)264-2935

SCORE Office (Monroe County-Stroudsburg)
556 Main St.
East Stroudsburg, PA 18301
(717)421-4433

SCORE Office (Erie)
120 W. 9th St.
Erie, PA 16501
(814)871-5650
Fax: (814)871-7530

SCORE Office (Bucks County)
409 Hood Blvd.
Fairless Hills, PA 19030
(215)943-8850
Fax: (215)943-7404

SCORE Office (Hanover)
146 Broadway
Hanover, PA 17331
(717)637-6130
Fax: (717)637-9127

SCORE Office (Harrisburg)
100 Chestnut, Ste. 309
Harrisburg, PA 17101
(717)782-3874

SCORE Office (East Montgomery County)
Baederwood Shopping Center
1653 The Fairways, Ste. 204
Jenkintown, PA 19046
(215)885-3027

SCORE Office (Kittanning)
2 Butler Rd.
Kittanning, PA 16201
(412)543-1305
Fax: (412)543-6206

SCORE Office (Lancaster)
118 W. Chestnut St.
Lancaster, PA 17603
(717)397-3092

SCORE Office (Westmoreland County)
300 Fraser Purchase Rd.
Latrobe, PA 15650-2690
(412)539-7505
Fax: (412)539-1850

SCORE Office (Lebanon)
252 N. 8th St.
PO Box 899
Lebanon, PA 17042-0899
(717)273-3727
Fax: (717)273-7940

SCORE Office (Lewistown)
3 W. Monument Sq., Ste. 204
Lewistown, PA 17044
(717)248-6713
Fax: (717)248-6714

SCORE Office (Delaware County)
602 E. Baltimore Pike
Media, PA 19063
(610)565-3677
Fax: (610)565-1606

SCORE Office (Milton Area)
112 S. Front St.
Milton, PA 17847
(717)742-7341
Fax: (717)792-2008

SCORE Office (Mon-Valley)
435 Donner Ave.
Monessen, PA 15062
(412)684-4277
Fax: (412)684-7688

SCORE Office (Monroeville)
William Penn Plaza
2790 Mosside Blvd., Ste. 295

Monroeville, PA 15146
(412)856-0622
Fax: (412)856-1030

SCORE Office (Airport Area)
986 Brodhead Rd.
Moon Township, PA 15108-2398
(412)264-6270
Fax: (412)264-1575

SCORE Office (Northeast)
8601 E. Roosevelt Blvd.
Philadelphia, PA 19152
(215)332-3400
Fax: (215)332-6050

SCORE Office (Philadelphia)
1315 Walnut St., Ste. 500
Philadelphia, PA 19107
(215)790-5050
Fax: (215)790-5057
E-mail: score46@bellatlantic.net
Website: http://www.pgweb.net/score46/

SCORE Office (Pittsburgh)
1000 Liberty Ave., Rm. 1122
Pittsburgh, PA 15222
(412)395-6560
Fax: (412)395-6562

SCORE Office (Tri-County)
801 N. Charlotte St.
Pottstown, PA 19464
(610)327-2673

SCORE Office (Reading)
601 Penn St.
Reading, PA 19601
(610)376-3497

SCORE Office (Scranton)
Oppenheim Bldg.
116 N. Washington Ave., Ste. 650
Scranton, PA 18503
(717)347-4611
Fax: (717)347-4611

SCORE Office (Central Pennsylvania)
200 Innovation Blvd., Ste. 242-B
State College, PA 16803
(814)234-9415
Fax: (814)238-9686
Website: http://countrystore.org/business/score.htm

SCORE Office (Monroe-Stroudsburg)
556 Main St.
Stroudsburg, PA 18360
(717)421-4433

SCORE Office (Uniontown)
Federal Bldg.
Pittsburg St.

PO Box 2065 DTS
Uniontown, PA 15401
(412)437-4222
E-mail: uniontownscore@lcsys.net

SCORE Office (Warren County)
315 2nd Ave.
Warren, PA 16365
(814)723-9017

SCORE Office (Waynesboro)
323 E. Main St.
Waynesboro, PA 17268
(717)762-7123
Fax: (717)962-7124

SCORE Office (Chester County)
Government Service Center, Ste. 281
601 Westtown Rd.
West Chester, PA 19382-4538
(610)344-6910
Fax: (610)344-6919
E-mail: score@locke.ccil.org

SCORE Office (Wilkes-Barre)
7 N. Wilkes-Barre Blvd.
Wilkes Barre, PA 18702-5241
(717)826-6502
Fax: (717)826-6287

SCORE Office (North Central Pennsylvania)
240 W. 3rd St., Rm. 227
PO Box 725
Williamsport, PA 17703
(717)322-3720
Fax: (717)322-1607
E-mail: score234@mail.csrlink.net
Website: http://www.lycoming.org/score/

SCORE Office (York)
Cyber Center
2101 Pennsylvania Ave.
York, PA 17404
(717)845-8830
Fax: (717)854-9333

Puerto Rico

SCORE Office (Puerto Rico & Virgin Islands)
PO Box 12383-96
San Juan, PR 00914-0383
(787)726-8040
Fax: (787)726-8135

Rhode Island

SCORE Office (Barrington)
281 County Rd.
Barrington, RI 02806
(401)247-1920
Fax: (401)247-3763

SCORE Office (Woonsocket)
640 Washington Hwy.
Lincoln, RI 02865
(401)334-1000
Fax: (401)334-1009

SCORE Office (Wickford)
8045 Post Rd.
North Kingstown, RI 02852
(401)295-5566
Fax: (401)295-8987

SCORE Office (J.G.E. Knight)
380 Westminster St.
Providence, RI 02903
(401)528-4571
Fax: (401)528-4539
Website: http://www.riscore.org

SCORE Office (Warwick)
3288 Post Rd.
Warwick, RI 02886
(401)732-1100
Fax: (401)732-1101

SCORE Office (Westerly)
74 Post Rd.
Westerly, RI 02891
(401)596-7761
800-732-7636
Fax: (401)596-2190

South Carolina

SCORE Office (Aiken)
PO Box 892
Aiken, SC 29802
(803)641-1111
800-542-4536
Fax: (803)641-4174

SCORE Office (Anderson)
Anderson Mall
3130 N. Main St.
Anderson, SC 29621
(864)224-0453

SCORE Office (Coastal)
284 King St.
Charleston, SC 29401
(803)727-4778
Fax: (803)853-2529

SCORE Office (Midlands)
Strom Thurmond Bldg., Rm. 358
1835 Assembly St., Rm 358
Columbia, SC 29201
(803)765-5131
Fax: (803)765-5962
Website: http://www.scoremidlands
.org/

SCORE Office (Piedmont)
Federal Bldg., Rm. B-02
300 E. Washington St.
Greenville, SC 29601
(864)271-3638

SCORE Office (Greenwood)
PO Drawer 1467
Greenwood, SC 29648
(864)223-8357

SCORE Office (Hilton Head Island)
52 Savannah Trail
Hilton Head, SC 29926
(803)785-7107
Fax: (803)785-7110

SCORE Office (Grand Strand)
937 Broadway
Myrtle Beach, SC 29577
(803)918-1079
Fax: (803)918-1083
E-mail: score381@aol.com

SCORE Office (Spartanburg)
PO Box 1636
Spartanburg, SC 29304
(864)594-5000
Fax: (864)594-5055

South Dakota

SCORE Office (West River)
Rushmore Plz. Civic Ctr.
444 Mount Rushmore Rd., No. 209
Rapid City, SD 57701
(605)394-5311
E-mail: score@gwtc.net

SCORE Office (Sioux Falls)
First Financial Center
110 S. Phillips Ave., Ste. 200
Sioux Falls, SD 57104-6727
(605)330-4231
Fax: (605)330-4231

Tennessee

SCORE Office (Chattanooga)
Federal Bldg., Rm. 26
900 Georgia Ave.
Chattanooga, TN 37402
(423)752-5190
Fax: (423)752-5335

SCORE Office (Cleveland)
PO Box 2275
Cleveland, TN 37320
(423)472-6587
Fax: (423)472-2019

SCORE Office (Upper Cumberland Center)
1225 S. Willow Ave.
Cookeville, TN 38501
(615)432-4111
Fax: (615)432-6010

SCORE Office (Unicoi County)
PO Box 713
Erwin, TN 37650
(423)743-3000
Fax: (423)743-0942

SCORE Office (Greeneville)
115 Academy St.
Greeneville, TN 37743
(423)638-4111
Fax: (423)638-5345

SCORE Office (Jackson)
194 Auditorium St.
Jackson, TN 38301
(901)423-2200

SCORE Office (Northeast Tennessee)
1st Tennessee Bank Bldg.
2710 S. Roan St., Ste. 584
Johnson City, TN 37601
(423)929-7686
Fax: (423)461-8052

SCORE Office (Kingsport)
151 E. Main St.
Kingsport, TN 37662
(423)392-8805

SCORE Office (Greater Knoxville)
Farragot Bldg., Ste. 224
530 S. Gay St.
Knoxville, TN 37902
(423)545-4203
E-mail: scoreknox@ntown.com
Website: http://www.scoreknox.org/

SCORE Office (Maryville)
201 S. Washington St.
Maryville, TN 37804-5728
(423)983-2241
800-525-6834
Fax: (423)984-1386

SCORE Office (Memphis)
Federal Bldg., Ste. 390
167 N. Main St.
Memphis, TN 38103
(901)544-3588

SCORE Office (Nashville)
50 Vantage Way, Ste. 201
Nashville, TN 37228-1500
(615)736-7621

Texas

SCORE Office (Abilene)
2106 Federal Post Office and Court Bldg.
Abilene, TX 79601
(915)677-1857

SCORE Office (Austin)
2501 S. Congress
Austin, TX 78701
(512)442-7235
Fax: (512)442-7528

SCORE Office (Golden Triangle)
450 Boyd St.
Beaumont, TX 77704
(409)838-6581
Fax: (409)833-6718

SCORE Office (Brownsville)
3505 Boca Chica Blvd., Ste. 305
Brownsville, TX 78521
(210)541-4508

SCORE Office (Brazos Valley)
3000 Briarcrest, Ste. 302
Bryan, TX 77802
(409)776-8876
E-mail: 102633.2612@compuserve.com

SCORE Office (Cleburne)
Watergarden Pl., 9th Fl., Ste. 400
Cleburne, TX 76031
(817)871-6002

SCORE Office (Corpus Christi)
651 Upper North Broadway, Ste. 654
Corpus Christi, TX 78477
(512)888-4322
Fax: (512)888-3418

SCORE Office (Dallas)
6260 E. Mockingbird
Dallas, TX 75214-2619
(214)828-2471
Fax: (214)821-8033

SCORE Office (El Paso)
10 Civic Center Plaza
El Paso, TX 79901
(915)534-0541
Fax: (915)534-0513

SCORE Office (Bedford)
100 E. 15th St., Ste. 400
Ft. Worth, TX 76102
(817)871-6002

SCORE Office (Ft. Worth)
100 E. 15th St., No. 24
Ft. Worth, TX 76102
(817)871-6002
Fax: (817)871-6031
E-mail: fwbac@onramp.net

SCORE Office (Garland)
2734 W. Kingsley Rd.
Garland, TX 75041
(214)271-9224

SCORE Office (Granbury Chamber of Commerce)
416 S. Morgan
Granbury, TX 76048
(817)573-1622
Fax: (817)573-0805

SCORE Office (Lower Rio Grande Valley)
222 E. Van Buren, Ste. 500
Harlingen, TX 78550
(956)427-8533
Fax: (956)427-8537

SCORE Office (Houston)
9301 Southwest Fwy., Ste. 550
Houston, TX 77074
(713)773-6565
Fax: (713)773-6550

SCORE Office (Irving)
3333 N. MacArthur Blvd., Ste. 100
Irving, TX 75062
(214)252-8484
Fax: (214)252-6710

SCORE Office (Lubbock)
1205 Texas Ave., Rm. 411D
Lubbock, TX 79401
(806)472-7462
Fax: (806)472-7487

SCORE Office (Midland)
Post Office Annex
200 E. Wall St., Rm. P121
Midland, TX 79701
(915)687-2649

SCORE Office (Orange)
1012 Green Ave.
Orange, TX 77630-5620
(409)883-3536
800-528-4906
Fax: (409)886-3247

SCORE Office (Plano)
1200 E. 15th St.
PO Drawer 940287
Plano, TX 75094-0287
(214)424-7547
Fax: (214)422-5182

SCORE Office (Port Arthur)
4749 Twin City Hwy., Ste. 300
Port Arthur, TX 77642
(409)963-1107
Fax: (409)963-3322

SCORE Office (Richardson)
411 Belle Grove
Richardson, TX 75080
(214)234-4141
800-777-8001
Fax: (214)680-9103

SCORE Office (San Antonio)
Federal Bldg., Rm. A527
727 E. Durango
San Antonio, TX 78206
(210)472-5931
Fax: (210)472-5935

SCORE Office (Texarkana State College)
819 State Line Ave.
Texarkana, TX 75501
(903)792-7191
Fax: (903)793-4304

SCORE Office (East Texas)
RTDC
1530 SSW Loop 323, Ste. 100
Tyler, TX 75701
(903)510-2975
Fax: (903)510-2978

SCORE Office (Waco)
401 Franklin Ave.
Waco, TX 76701
(817)754-8898
Fax: (817)756-0776
Website: http://www.brc-waco.com/

SCORE Office (Wichita Falls)
Hamilton Bldg.
900 8th St.
Wichita Falls, TX 76307
(940)723-2741
Fax: (940)723-8773

Utah

SCORE Office (Northern Utah)
160 N. Main
Logan, UT 84321
(435)746-2269

SCORE Office (Ogden)
1701 E. Windsor Dr.
Ogden, UT 84604
(801)629-8613
E-mail: score158@netscape.net

SCORE Office (Central Utah)
1071 E. Windsor Dr.
Provo, UT 84604
(801)373-8660

SCORE Office (Southern Utah)
225 South 700 East
St. George, UT 84770
(435)652-7751

SCORE Office (Salt Lake)
310 S Main St.
Salt Lake City, UT 84101
(801)746-2269
Fax: (801)746-2273

Vermont

SCORE Office (Champlain Valley)
Winston Prouty Federal Bldg.
11 Lincoln St., Rm. 106
Essex Junction, VT 05452
(802)951-6762

SCORE Office (Montpelier)
87 State St., Rm. 205
PO Box 605
Montpelier, VT 05601
(802)828-4422
Fax: (802)828-4485

SCORE Office (Marble Valley)
256 N. Main St.
Rutland, VT 05701-2413
(802)773-9147

SCORE Office (Northeast Kingdom)
20 Main St.
PO Box 904
St. Johnsbury, VT 05819
(802)748-5101

Virgin Islands

SCORE Office (St. Croix)
United Plaza Shopping Center
PO Box 4010, Christiansted
St. Croix, VI 00822
(809)778-5380

SCORE Office (St. Thomas-St. John)
Federal Bldg., Rm. 21
Veterans Dr.
St. Thomas, VI 00801
(809)774-8530

Virginia

SCORE Office (Arlington)
2009 N. 14th St., Ste. 111
Arlington, VA 22201
(703)525-2400

SCORE Office (Blacksburg)
141 Jackson St.
Blacksburg, VA 24060
(540)552-4061

SCORE Office (Bristol)
20 Volunteer Pkwy.
Bristol, VA 24203
(540)989-4850

SCORE Office (Central Virginia)
1001 E. Market St., Ste. 101
Charlottesville, VA 22902
(804)295-6712
Fax: (804)295-7066

SCORE Office (Alleghany Satellite)
241 W. Main St.
Covington, VA 24426
(540)962-2178
Fax: (540)962-2179

SCORE Office (Central Fairfax)
3975 University Dr., Ste. 350
Fairfax, VA 22030
(703)591-2450

SCORE Office (Falls Church)
PO Box 491
Falls Church, VA 22040
(703)532-1050
Fax: (703)237-7904

SCORE Office (Glenns)
Glenns Campus
Box 287
Glenns, VA 23149
(804)693-9650

SCORE Office (Peninsula)
6 Manhattan Sq.
PO Box 7269
Hampton, VA 23666
(757)766-2000
Fax: (757)865-0339
E-mail: score100@seva.net

SCORE Office (Tri-Cities)
108 N. Main St.
Hopewell, VA 23860
(804)458-5536

SCORE Office (Lynchburg)
Federal Bldg.
1100 Main St.
Lynchburg, VA 24504-1714
(804)846-3235

SCORE Office (Greater Prince William)
8963 Center St
Manassas, VA 20110
(703)368-4813
Fax: (703)368-4733

SCORE Office (Martinsvile)
115 Broad St.
Martinsville, VA 24112-0709
(540)632-6401
Fax: (540)632-5059

SCORE Office (Hampton Roads)
Federal Bldg., Rm. 737
200 Grandby St.

Norfolk, VA 23510
(757)441-3733
Fax: (757)441-3733
E-mail: scorehr60@juno.com

SCORE Office (Norfolk)
Federal Bldg., Rm. 737
200 Granby St.
Norfolk, VA 23510
(757)441-3733
Fax: (757)441-3733

SCORE Office (Virginia Beach)
Chamber of Commerce
200 Grandby St., Rm 737
Norfolk, VA 23510
(804)441-3733

SCORE Office (Radford)
1126 Norwood St.
Radford, VA 24141
(540)639-2202

SCORE Office (Richmond)
Federal Bldg.
400 N. 8th St., Ste. 1150
PO Box 10126
Richmond, VA 23240-0126
(804)771-2400
Fax: (804)771-8018
E-mail: scorechapter12@yahoo.com
Website: http://www.cvco.org/score/

SCORE Office (Roanoke)
Federal Bldg., Rm. 716
250 Franklin Rd.
Roanoke, VA 24011
(540)857-2834
Fax: (540)857-2043
E-mail: scorerva@juno.com
Website: http://hometown.aol.com/
scorerv/Index.html

SCORE Office (Fairfax)
8391 Old Courthouse Rd., Ste. 300
Vienna, VA 22182
(703)749-0400

SCORE Office (Greater Vienna)
513 Maple Ave. West
Vienna, VA 22180
(703)281-1333
Fax: (703)242-1482

SCORE Office (Shenandoah Valley)
301 W. Main St.
Waynesboro, VA 22980
(540)949-8203
Fax: (540)949-7740
E-mail: score427@intelos.net

SCORE Office (Williamsburg)
201 Penniman Rd.
Williamsburg, VA 23185
(757)229-6511
E-mail: wacc@williamsburgcc.com

SCORE Office (Northern Virginia)
1360 S. Pleasant Valley Rd.
Winchester, VA 22601
(540)662-4118

Washington

SCORE Office (Gray's Harbor)
506 Duffy St.
Aberdeen, WA 98520
(360)532-1924
Fax: (360)533-7945

SCORE Office (Bellingham)
101 E. Holly St.
Bellingham, WA 98225
(360)676-3307

SCORE Office (Everett)
2702 Hoyt Ave.
Everett, WA 98201-3556
(206)259-8000

SCORE Office (Gig Harbor)
3125 Judson St.
Gig Harbor, WA 98335
(206)851-6865

SCORE Office (Kennewick)
PO Box 6986
Kennewick, WA 99336
(509)736-0510

SCORE Office (Puyallup)
322 2nd St. SW
PO Box 1298
Puyallup, WA 98371
(206)845-6755
Fax: (206)848-6164

SCORE Office (Seattle)
1200 6th Ave., Ste. 1700
Seattle, WA 98101
(206)553-7320
Fax: (206)553-7044
E-mail: score55@aol.com
Website: http://www.scn.org/civic/score-online/index55.html

SCORE Office (Spokane)
801 W. Riverside Ave., No. 240
Spokane, WA 99201
(509)353-2820
Fax: (509)353-2600
E-mail: score@dmi.net
Website: http://www.dmi.net/score/

SCORE Office (Clover Park)
PO Box 1933
Tacoma, WA 98401-1933
(206)627-2175

SCORE Office (Tacoma)
1101 Pacific Ave.
Tacoma, WA 98402
(253)274-1288
Fax: (253)274-1289

SCORE Office (Fort Vancouver)
1701 Broadway, S-1
Vancouver, WA 98663
(360)699-1079

SCORE Office (Walla Walla)
500 Tausick Way
Walla Walla, WA 99362
(509)527-4681

SCORE Office (Mid-Columbia)
1113 S. 14th Ave.
Yakima, WA 98907
(509)574-4944
Fax: (509)574-2943
Website: http://www.ellensburg.com/~score/

West Virginia

SCORE Office (Charleston)
1116 Smith St.
Charleston, WV 25301
(304)347-5463
E-mail: score256@juno.com

SCORE Office (Virginia Street)
1116 Smith St., Ste. 302
Charleston, WV 25301
(304)347-5463

SCORE Office (Marion County)
PO Box 208
Fairmont, WV 26555-0208
(304)363-0486

SCORE Office (Upper Monongahela Valley)
1000 Technology Dr., Ste. 1111
Fairmont, WV 26555
(304)363-0486
E-mail: score537@hotmail.com

SCORE Office (Huntington)
1101 6th Ave., Ste. 220
Huntington, WV 25701-2309
(304)523-4092

SCORE Office (Wheeling)
1310 Market St.
Wheeling, WV 26003
(304)233-2575
Fax: (304)233-1320

Wisconsin

SCORE Office (Fox Cities)
227 S. Walnut St.
Appleton, WI 54913
(920)734-7101
Fax: (920)734-7161

SCORE Office (Beloit)
136 W. Grand Ave., Ste. 100
PO Box 717
Beloit, WI 53511
(608)365-8835
Fax: (608)365-9170

SCORE Office (Eau Claire)
Federal Bldg., Rm. B11
510 S. Barstow St.
Eau Claire, WI 54701
(715)834-1573
E-mail: score@ecol.net
Website: http://www.ecol.net/~score/

SCORE Office (Fond du Lac)
207 N. Main St.
Fond du Lac, WI 54935
(414)921-9500
Fax: (414)921-9559

SCORE Office (Green Bay)
835 Potts Ave.
Green Bay, WI 54304
(414)496-8930
Fax: (414)496-6009

SCORE Office (Janesville)
20 S. Main St., Ste. 11
PO Box 8008
Janesville, WI 53547
(608)757-3160
Fax: (608)757-3170

SCORE Office (La Crosse)
712 Main St.
La Crosse, WI 54602-0219
(608)784-4880

SCORE Office (Madison)
505 S. Rosa Rd.
Madison, WI 53719
(608)441-2820

SCORE Office (Manitowoc)
1515 Memorial Dr.
PO Box 903
Manitowoc, WI 54221-0903
(414)684-5575
Fax: (414)684-1915

SCORE Office (Milwaukee)
310 W. Wisconsin Ave., Ste. 425
Milwaukee, WI 53203
(414)297-3942
Fax: (414)297-1377

SCORE Office (Central Wisconsin)
1224 Lindbergh Ave.
Stevens Point, WI 54481
(715)344-7729

SCORE Office (Superior)
Superior Business Center Inc.
1423 N. 8th St.
Superior, WI 54880
(715)394-7388
Fax: (715)393-7414

SCORE Office (Waukesha)
223 Wisconsin Ave.
Waukesha, WI 53186-4926
(414)542-4249

SCORE Office (Wausau)
300 3rd St., Ste. 200
Wausau, WI 54402-6190
(715)845-6231

SCORE Office (Wisconsin Rapids)
2240 Kingston Rd.
Wisconsin Rapids, WI 54494
(715)423-1830

Wyoming

SCORE Office (Casper)
Federal Bldg., No. 2215
100 East B St.
Casper, WY 82602
(307)261-6529
Fax: (307)261-6530

Venture capital & financing companies

This section contains a listing of financing and loan companies in the United States and Canada. These listing are arranged alphabetically by country, then by state or province, then by city, then by organization name.

Canada

Alberta

Launchworks Inc.
1902J 11th St., S.E.
Calgary, AB, Canada T2G 3G2
(403)269-1119
Fax: (403)269-1141
Website: http://www.launchworks.com

Native Venture Capital Company, Inc.
21 Artist View Point, Box 7
Site 25, RR 12
Calgary, AB, Canada T3E 6W3
(903)208-5380

Miralta Capital Inc.
4445 Calgary Trail South
888 Terrace Plaza Alberta
Edmonton, AB, Canada T6H 5R7
(780)438-3535
Fax: (780)438-3129

Vencap Equities Alberta Ltd.
10180-101st St., Ste. 1980
Edmonton, AB, Canada T5J 3S4
(403)420-1171
Fax: (403)429-2541

British Columbia

Discovery Capital
5th Fl., 1199 West Hastings
Vancouver, BC, Canada V6E 3T5
(604)683-3000
Fax: (604)662-3457
E-mail: info@discoverycapital.com
Website: http://www.discoverycapital.com

Greenstone Venture Partners
1177 West Hastings St.
Ste. 400
Vancouver, BC, Canada V6E 2K3
(604)717-1977
Fax: (604)717-1976
Website: http://www.greenstonevc.com

Growthworks Capital
2600-1055 West Georgia St.
Box 11170 Royal Centre
Vancouver, BC, Canada V6E 3R5
(604)895-7259
Fax: (604)669-7605
Website: http://www.wofund.com

MDS Discovery Venture Management, Inc.
555 W. Eighth Ave., Ste. 305
Vancouver, BC, Canada V5Z 1C6
(604)872-8464
Fax: (604)872-2977
E-mail: info@mds-ventures.com

Ventures West Management Inc.
1285 W. Pender St., Ste. 280
Vancouver, BC, Canada V6E 4B1
(604)688-9495
Fax: (604)687-2145
Website: http://www.ventureswest.com

Nova Scotia

ACF Equity Atlantic Inc.
Purdy's Wharf Tower II
Ste. 2106
Halifax, NS, Canada B3J 3R7
(902)421-1965
Fax: (902)421-1808

Montgomerie, Huck & Co.
146 Bluenose Dr.
PO Box 538
Lunenburg, NS, Canada B0J 2C0
(902)634-7125
Fax: (902)634-7130

Ontario

IPS Industrial Promotion Services Ltd.
60 Columbia Way, Ste. 720
Markham, ON, Canada L3R 0C9
(905)475-9400
Fax: (905)475-5003

Betwin Investments Inc.
Box 23110
Sault Ste. Marie, ON, Canada P6A 6W6
(705)253-0744
Fax: (705)253-0744

Bailey & Company, Inc.
594 Spadina Ave.
Toronto, ON, Canada M5S 2H4
(416)921-6930
Fax: (416)925-4670

BCE Capital
200 Bay St.
South Tower, Ste. 3120
Toronto, ON, Canada M5J 2J2
(416)815-0078
Fax: (416)941-1073
Website: http://www.bcecapital.com

Castlehill Ventures
55 University Ave., Ste. 500
Toronto, ON, Canada M5J 2H7
(416)862-8574
Fax: (416)862-8875

CCFL Mezzanine Partners of Canada
70 University Ave.
Ste. 1450
Toronto, ON, Canada M5J 2M4
(416)977-1450
Fax: (416)977-6764
E-mail: info@ccfl.com
Website: http://www.ccfl.com

Celtic House International
100 Simcoe St., Ste. 100
Toronto, ON, Canada M5H 3G2
(416)542-2436
Fax: (416)542-2435
Website: http://www.celtic-house.com

Clairvest Group Inc.
22 St. Clair Ave. East
Ste. 1700
Toronto, ON, Canada M4T 2S3
(416)925-9270
Fax: (416)925-5753

Crosbie & Co., Inc.
One First Canadian Place
9th Fl.
PO Box 116
Toronto, ON, Canada M5X 1A4
(416)362-7726
Fax: (416)362-3447
E-mail: info@crosbieco.com
Website: http://www.crosbieco.com

Drug Royalty Corp.
Eight King St. East
Ste. 202
Toronto, ON, Canada M5C 1B5
(416)863-1865
Fax: (416)863-5161

Grieve, Horner, Brown & Asculai
8 King St. E, Ste. 1704
Toronto, ON, Canada M5C 1B5
(416)362-7668
Fax: (416)362-7660

Jefferson Partners
77 King St. West
Ste. 4010
PO Box 136
Toronto, ON, Canada M5K 1H1
(416)367-1533
Fax: (416)367-5827
Website: http://www.jefferson.com

J.L. Albright Venture Partners
Canada Trust Tower, 161 Bay St.
Ste. 4440
PO Box 215
Toronto, ON, Canada M5J 2S1
(416)367-2440
Fax: (416)367-4604
Website: http://www.jlaventures.com

McLean Watson Capital Inc.
One First Canadian Place
Ste. 1410
PO Box 129
Toronto, ON, Canada M5X 1A4
(416)363-2000
Fax: (416)363-2010
Website: http://www.mcleanwatson.com

Middlefield Capital Fund
One First Canadian Place
85th Fl.
PO Box 192
Toronto, ON, Canada M5X 1A6
(416)362-0714
Fax: (416)362-7925
Website: http://www.middlefield.com

Mosaic Venture Partners
24 Duncan St.
Ste. 300

Toronto, ON, Canada M5V 3M6
(416)597-8889
Fax: (416)597-2345

Onex Corp.
161 Bay St.
PO Box 700
Toronto, ON, Canada M5J 2S1
(416)362-7711
Fax: (416)362-5765

Penfund Partners Inc.
145 King St. West
Ste. 1920
Toronto, ON, Canada M5H 1J8
(416)865-0300
Fax: (416)364-6912
Website: http://www.penfund.com

Primaxis Technology Ventures Inc.
1 Richmond St. West, 8th Fl.
Toronto, ON, Canada M5H 3W4
(416)313-5210
Fax: (416)313-5218
Website: http://www.primaxis.com

Priveq Capital Funds
240 Duncan Mill Rd., Ste. 602
Toronto, ON, Canada M3B 3P1
(416)447-3330
Fax: (416)447-3331
E-mail: priveq@sympatico.ca

Roynat Ventures
40 King St. West, 26th Fl.
Toronto, ON, Canada M5H 1H1
(416)933-2667
Fax: (416)933-2783
Website: http://www.roynatcapital.com

Tera Capital Corp.
366 Adelaide St. East, Ste. 337
Toronto, ON, Canada M5A 3X9
(416)368-1024
Fax: (416)368-1427

Working Ventures Canadian Fund Inc.
250 Bloor St. East, Ste. 1600
Toronto, ON, Canada M4W 1E6
(416)934-7718
Fax: (416)929-0901
Website: http://www.working ventures.ca

Quebec

Altamira Capital Corp.
202 University
Niveau de Maisoneuve, Bur. 201
Montreal, QC, Canada H3A 2A5

(514)499-1656
Fax: (514)499-9570

Federal Business Development Bank
Venture Capital Division
Five Place Ville Marie, Ste. 600
Montreal, QC, Canada H3B 5E7
(514)283-1896
Fax: (514)283-5455

Hydro-Quebec Capitech Inc.
75 Boul, Rene Levesque Quest
Montreal, QC, Canada H2Z 1A4
(514)289-4783
Fax: (514)289-5420
Website: http://www.hqcapitech.com

Investissement Desjardins
2 complexe Desjardins
C.P. 760
Montreal, QC, Canada H5B 1B8
(514)281-7131
Fax: (514)281-7808
Website: http://www.desjardins.com/id

Marleau Lemire Inc.
One Place Ville-Marie, Ste. 3601
Montreal, QC, Canada H3B 3P2
(514)877-3800
Fax: (514)875-6415

Speirs Consultants Inc.
365 Stanstead
Montreal, QC, Canada H3R 1X5
(514)342-3858
Fax: (514)342-1977

Tecnocap Inc.
4028 Marlowe
Montreal, QC, Canada H4A 3M2
(514)483-6009
Fax: (514)483-6045
Website: http://www.technocap.com

Telsoft Ventures
1000, Rue de la Gauchetiere
Quest, 25eme Etage
Montreal, QC, Canada H3B 4W5
(514)397-8450
Fax: (514)397-8451

Saskatchewan

Saskatchewan Government Growth Fund
1801 Hamilton St., Ste. 1210
Canada Trust Tower
Regina, SK, Canada S4P 4B4
(306)787-2994
Fax: (306)787-2086

United states

Alabama

FHL Capital Corp.
600 20th Street North
Suite 350
Birmingham, AL 35203
(205)328-3098
Fax: (205)323-0001

Harbert Management Corp.
One Riverchase Pkwy. South
Birmingham, AL 35244
(205)987-5500
Fax: (205)987-5707
Website: http://www.harbert.net

Jefferson Capital Fund
PO Box 13129
Birmingham, AL 35213
(205)324-7709

Private Capital Corp.
100 Brookwood Pl., 4th Fl.
Birmingham, AL 35209
(205)879-2722
Fax: (205)879-5121

21st Century Health Ventures
One Health South Pkwy.
Birmingham, AL 35243
(256)268-6250
Fax: (256)970-8928

FJC Growth Capital Corp.
200 W. Side Sq., Ste. 340
Huntsville, AL 35801
(256)922-2918
Fax: (256)922-2909

Hickory Venture Capital Corp.
301 Washington St. NW
Suite 301
Huntsville, AL 35801
(256)539-1931
Fax: (256)539-5130
E-mail: hvcc@hvcc.com
Website: http://www.hvcc.com

Southeastern Technology Fund
7910 South Memorial Pkwy., Ste. F
Huntsville, AL 35802
(256)883-8711
Fax: (256)883-8558

Cordova Ventures
4121 Carmichael Rd., Ste. 301
Montgomery, AL 36106
(334)271-6011
Fax: (334)260-0120
Website: http://www.cordovaventures.com

Small Business Clinic of Alabama/AG Bartholomew & Associates
PO Box 231074
Montgomery, AL 36123-1074
(334)284-3640

Arizona

Miller Capital Corp.
4909 E. McDowell Rd.
Phoenix, AZ 85008
(602)225-0504
Fax: (602)225-9024
Website: http://www.themillergroup.com

The Columbine Venture Funds
9449 North 90th St., Ste. 200
Scottsdale, AZ 85258
(602)661-9222
Fax: (602)661-6262

Koch Ventures
17767 N. Perimeter Dr., Ste. 101
Scottsdale, AZ 85255
(480)419-3600
Fax: (480)419-3606
Website: http://www.kochventures.com

McKee & Co.
7702 E. Doubletree Ranch Rd.
Suite 230
Scottsdale, AZ 85258
(480)368-0333
Fax: (480)607-7446

Merita Capital Ltd.
7350 E. Stetson Dr., Ste. 108-A
Scottsdale, AZ 85251
(480)947-8700
Fax: (480)947-8766

Valley Ventures / Arizona Growth Partners L.P.
6720 N. Scottsdale Rd., Ste. 208
Scottsdale, AZ 85253
(480)661-6600
Fax: (480)661-6262

Estreetcapital.com
660 South Mill Ave., Ste. 315
Tempe, AZ 85281
(480)968-8400
Fax: (480)968-8480
Website: http://www.estreetcapital.com

Coronado Venture Fund
PO Box 65420
Tucson, AZ 85728-5420
(520)577-3764
Fax: (520)299-8491

Arkansas

Arkansas Capital Corp.
225 South Pulaski St.
Little Rock, AR 72201
(501)374-9247
Fax: (501)374-9425
Website: http://www.arcapital.com

California

Sundance Venture Partners, L.P.
100 Clocktower Place, Ste. 130
Carmel, CA 93923
(831)625-6500
Fax: (831)625-6590

Westar Capital (Costa Mesa)
949 South Coast Dr., Ste. 650
Costa Mesa, CA 92626
(714)481-5160
Fax: (714)481-5166
E-mail: mailbox@westarcapital.com
Website: http://www.westarcapital.com

Alpine Technology Ventures
20300 Stevens Creek Boulevard, Ste. 495
Cupertino, CA 95014
(408)725-1810
Fax: (408)725-1207
Website: http://www.alpineventures.com

Bay Partners
10600 N. De Anza Blvd.
Cupertino, CA 95014-2031
(408)725-2444
Fax: (408)446-4502
Website: http://www.baypartners.com

Novus Ventures
20111 Stevens Creek Blvd., Ste. 130
Cupertino, CA 95014
(408)252-3900
Fax: (408)252-1713
Website: http://www.novusventures.com

Triune Capital
19925 Stevens Creek Blvd., Ste. 200
Cupertino, CA 95014
(310)284-6800
Fax: (310)284-3290

Acorn Ventures
268 Bush St., Ste. 2829
Daly City, CA 94014
(650)994-7801
Fax: (650)994-3305
Website: http://www.acornventures.com

Digital Media Campus
2221 Park Place
El Segundo, CA 90245
(310)426-8000

Fax: (310)426-8010
E-mail: info@thecampus.com
Website: http://www.digitalmediacampus
.com

**BankAmerica Ventures / BA Venture
Partners**
950 Tower Ln., Ste. 700
Foster City, CA 94404
(650)378-6000
Fax: (650)378-6040
Website: http://www.baventurepartners
.com

Starting Point Partners
666 Portofino Lane
Foster City, CA 94404
(650)722-1035
Website: http://
www.startingpointpartners.com

Opportunity Capital Partners
2201 Walnut Ave., Ste. 210
Fremont, CA 94538
(510)795-7000
Fax: (510)494-5439
Website: http://www.ocpcapital.com

Imperial Ventures Inc.
9920 S. La Cienega Boulevar, 14th Fl.
Inglewood, CA 90301
(310)417-5409
Fax: (310)338-6115

Ventana Global (Irvine)
18881 Von Karman Ave., Ste. 1150
Irvine, CA 92612
(949)476-2204
Fax: (949)752-0223
Website: http://www.ventanaglobal.com

Integrated Consortium Inc.
50 Ridgecrest Rd.
Kentfield, CA 94904
(415)925-0386
Fax: (415)461-2726

Enterprise Partners
979 Ivanhoe Ave., Ste. 550
La Jolla, CA 92037
(858)454-8833
Fax: (858)454-2489
Website: http://www.epvc.com

Domain Associates
28202 Cabot Rd., Ste. 200
Laguna Niguel, CA 92677
(949)347-2446
Fax: (949)347-9720
Website: http://www.domainvc.com

**Cascade Communications
Ventures**
60 E. Sir Francis Drake Blvd., Ste. 300
Larkspur, CA 94939
(415)925-6500
Fax: (415)925-6501

Allegis Capital
One First St., Ste. Two
Los Altos, CA 94022
(650)917-5900
Fax: (650)917-5901
Website: http://www.allegiscapital.com

Aspen Ventures
1000 Fremont Ave., Ste. 200
Los Altos, CA 94024
(650)917-5670
Fax: (650)917-5677
Website: http://www.aspenventures.com

AVI Capital L.P.
1 First St., Ste. 2
Los Altos, CA 94022
(650)949-9862
Fax: (650)949-8510
Website: http://www.avicapital.com

Bastion Capital Corp.
1999 Avenue of the Stars, Ste. 2960
Los Angeles, CA 90067
(310)788-5700
Fax: (310)277-7582
E-mail: ga@bastioncapital.com
Website: http://www.bastion
capital.com

Davis Group
PO Box 69953
Los Angeles, CA 90069-0953
(310)659-6327
Fax: (310)659-6337

Developers Equity Corp.
1880 Century Park East, Ste. 211
Los Angeles, CA 90067
(213)277-0300

Far East Capital Corp.
350 S. Grand Ave., Ste. 4100
Los Angeles, CA 90071
(213)687-1361
Fax: (213)617-7939
E-mail: free@fareastnationalbank.com

Kline Hawkes & Co.
11726 San Vicente Blvd., Ste. 300
Los Angeles, CA 90049
(310)442-4700
Fax: (310)442-4707
Website: http://www.klinehawkes.com

Lawrence Financial Group
701 Teakwood
PO Box 491773
Los Angeles, CA 90049
(310)471-4060
Fax: (310)472-3155

Riordan Lewis & Haden
300 S. Grand Ave., 29th Fl.
Los Angeles, CA 90071
(213)229-8500
Fax: (213)229-8597

Union Venture Corp.
445 S. Figueroa St., 9th Fl.
Los Angeles, CA 90071
(213)236-4092
Fax: (213)236-6329

Wedbush Capital Partners
1000 Wilshire Blvd.
Los Angeles, CA 90017
(213)688-4545
Fax: (213)688-6642
Website: http://www.wedbush.com

Advent International Corp.
2180 Sand Hill Rd., Ste. 420
Menlo Park, CA 94025
(650)233-7500
Fax: (650)233-7515
Website: http://www.adventinternational
.com

Altos Ventures
2882 Sand Hill Rd., Ste. 100
Menlo Park, CA 94025
(650)234-9771
Fax: (650)233-9821
Website: http://www.altosvc.com

Applied Technology
1010 El Camino Real, Ste. 300
Menlo Park, CA 94025
(415)326-8622
Fax: (415)326-8163

APV Technology Partners
535 Middlefield, Ste. 150
Menlo Park, CA 94025
(650)327-7871
Fax: (650)327-7631
Website: http://www.apvtp.com

August Capital Management
2480 Sand Hill Rd., Ste. 101
Menlo Park, CA 94025
(650)234-9900
Fax: (650)234-9910
Website: http://www.augustcap.com

Baccharis Capital Inc.
2420 Sand Hill Rd., Ste. 100
Menlo Park, CA 94025
(650)324-6844
Fax: (650)854-3025

Benchmark Capital
2480 Sand Hill Rd., Ste. 200
Menlo Park, CA 94025
(650)854-8180
Fax: (650)854-8183
E-mail: info@benchmark.com
Website: http://www.benchmark.com

Bessemer Venture Partners (Menlo Park)
535 Middlefield Rd., Ste. 245
Menlo Park, CA 94025
(650)853-7000
Fax: (650)853-7001
Website: http://www.bvp.com

The Cambria Group
1600 El Camino Real Rd., Ste. 155
Menlo Park, CA 94025
(650)329-8600
Fax: (650)329-8601
Website: http://www.cambriagroup.com

Canaan Partners
2884 Sand Hill Rd., Ste. 115
Menlo Park, CA 94025
(650)854-8092
Fax: (650)854-8127
Website: http://www.canaan.com

Capstone Ventures
3000 Sand Hill Rd., Bldg. One, Ste. 290
Menlo Park, CA 94025
(650)854-2523
Fax: (650)854-9010
Website: http://www.capstonevc.com

Comdisco Venture Group (Silicon Valley)
3000 Sand Hill Rd., Bldg. 1, Ste. 155
Menlo Park, CA 94025
(650)854-9484
Fax: (650)854-4026

Commtech International
535 Middlefield Rd., Ste. 200
Menlo Park, CA 94025
(650)328-0190
Fax: (650)328-6442

Compass Technology Partners
1550 El Camino Real, Ste. 275
Menlo Park, CA 94025-4111
(650)322-7595
Fax: (650)322-0588

Website: http://www.compasstech
partners.com

Convergence Partners
3000 Sand Hill Rd., Ste. 235
Menlo Park, CA 94025
(650)854-3010
Fax: (650)854-3015
Website: http://www.convergence
partners.com

The Dakota Group
PO Box 1025
Menlo Park, CA 94025
(650)853-0600
Fax: (650)851-4899
E-mail: info@dakota.com

Delphi Ventures
3000 Sand Hill Rd.
Bldg. One, Ste. 135
Menlo Park, CA 94025
(650)854-9650
Fax: (650)854-2961
Website: http://www.delphiventures.com

El Dorado Ventures
2884 Sand Hill Rd., Ste. 121
Menlo Park, CA 94025
(650)854-1200
Fax: (650)854-1202
Website: http://www.eldoradoventures
.com

Glynn Ventures
3000 Sand Hill Rd., Bldg. 4, Ste. 235
Menlo Park, CA 94025
(650)854-2215

Indosuez Ventures
2180 Sand Hill Rd., Ste. 450
Menlo Park, CA 94025
(650)854-0587
Fax: (650)323-5561
Website: http://
www.indosuezventures.com

Institutional Venture Partners
3000 Sand Hill Rd., Bldg. 2, Ste. 290
Menlo Park, CA 94025
(650)854-0132
Fax: (650)854-5762
Website: http://www.ivp.com

Interwest Partners (Menlo Park)
3000 Sand Hill Rd., Bldg. 3, Ste. 255
Menlo Park, CA 94025-7112
(650)854-8585
Fax: (650)854-4706
Website: http://www.interwest.com

Kleiner Perkins Caufield & Byers (Menlo Park)
2750 Sand Hill Rd.
Menlo Park, CA 94025
(650)233-2750
Fax: (650)233-0300
Website: http://www.kpcb.com

Magic Venture Capital LLC
1010 El Camino Real, Ste. 300
Menlo Park, CA 94025
(650)325-4149

Matrix Partners
2500 Sand Hill Rd., Ste. 113
Menlo Park, CA 94025
(650)854-3131
Fax: (650)854-3296
Website: http://www.matrixpartners.com

Mayfield Fund
2800 Sand Hill Rd.
Menlo Park, CA 94025
(650)854-5560
Fax: (650)854-5712
Website: http://www.mayfield.com

McCown De Leeuw and Co. (Menlo Park)
3000 Sand Hill Rd., Bldg. 3, Ste. 290
Menlo Park, CA 94025-7111
(650)854-6000
Fax: (650)854-0853
Website: http://www.mdcpartners.com

Menlo Ventures
3000 Sand Hill Rd., Bldg. 4, Ste. 100
Menlo Park, CA 94025
(650)854-8540
Fax: (650)854-7059
Website: http://www.menloventures.com

Merrill Pickard Anderson & Eyre
2480 Sand Hill Rd., Ste. 200
Menlo Park, CA 94025
(650)854-8600
Fax: (650)854-0345

New Enterprise Associates (Menlo Park)
2490 Sand Hill Rd.
Menlo Park, CA 94025
(650)854-9499
Fax: (650)854-9397
Website: http://www.nea.com

Onset Ventures
2400 Sand Hill Rd., Ste. 150
Menlo Park, CA 94025
(650)529-0700
Fax: (650)529-0777
Website: http://www.onset.com

Paragon Venture Partners
3000 Sand Hill Rd., Bldg. 1, Ste. 275
Menlo Park, CA 94025
(650)854-8000
Fax: (650)854-7260

**Pathfinder Venture Capital Funds
(Menlo Park)**
3000 Sand Hill Rd., Bldg. 3, Ste. 255
Menlo Park, CA 94025
(650)854-0650
Fax: (650)854-4706

Rocket Ventures
3000 Sandhill Rd., Bldg. 1, Ste. 170
Menlo Park, CA 94025
(650)561-9100
Fax: (650)561-9183
Website: http://www.rocketventures.com

Sequoia Capital
3000 Sand Hill Rd., Bldg. 4, Ste. 280
Menlo Park, CA 94025
(650)854-3927
Fax: (650)854-2977
E-mail: sequoia@sequioacap.com
Website: http://www.sequoiacap.com

Sierra Ventures
3000 Sand Hill Rd., Bldg. 4, Ste. 210
Menlo Park, CA 94025
(650)854-1000
Fax: (650)854-5593
Website: http://www.sierraventures.com

Sigma Partners
2884 Sand Hill Rd., Ste. 121
Menlo Park, CA 94025-7022
(650)853-1700
Fax: (650)853-1717
E-mail: info@sigmapartners.com
Website: http://www.sigmapartners.com

Sprout Group (Menlo Park)
3000 Sand Hill Rd.
Bldg. 3, Ste. 170
Menlo Park, CA 94025
(650)234-2700
Fax: (650)234-2779
Website: http://www.sproutgroup.com

TA Associates (Menlo Park)
70 Willow Rd., Ste. 100
Menlo Park, CA 94025
(650)328-1210
Fax: (650)326-4933
Website: http://www.ta.com

Thompson Clive & Partners Ltd.
3000 Sand Hill Rd., Bldg. 1, Ste. 185
Menlo Park, CA 94025-7102
(650)854-0314

Fax: (650)854-0670
E-mail: mail@tcvc.com
Website: http://www.tcvc.com

Trinity Ventures Ltd.
3000 Sand Hill Rd., Bldg. 1, Ste. 240
Menlo Park, CA 94025
(650)854-9500
Fax: (650)854-9501
Website: http://www.trinityventures.com

U.S. Venture Partners
2180 Sand Hill Rd., Ste. 300
Menlo Park, CA 94025
(650)854-9080
Fax: (650)854-3018
Website: http://www.usvp.com

USVP-Schlein Marketing Fund
2180 Sand Hill Rd., Ste. 300
Menlo Park, CA 94025
(415)854-9080
Fax: (415)854-3018
Website: http://www.usvp.com

Venrock Associates
2494 Sand Hill Rd., Ste. 200
Menlo Park, CA 94025
(650)561-9580
Fax: (650)561-9180
Website: http://www.venrock.com

Brad Peery Capital Inc.
145 Chapel Pkwy.
Mill Valley, CA 94941
(415)389-0625
Fax: (415)389-1336

Dot Edu Ventures
650 Castro St., Ste. 270
Mountain View, CA 94041
(650)575-5638
Fax: (650)325-5247
Website: http://www.doteduventures.com

Forrest, Binkley & Brown
840 Newport Ctr. Dr., Ste. 480
Newport Beach, CA 92660
(949)729-3222
Fax: (949)729-3226
Website: http://www.fbbvc.com

Marwit Capital LLC
180 Newport Center Dr., Ste. 200
Newport Beach, CA 92660
(949)640-6234
Fax: (949)720-8077
Website: http://www.marwit.com

**Kaiser Permanente / National Venture
Development**
1800 Harrison St., 22nd Fl.
Oakland, CA 94612

(510)267-4010
Fax: (510)267-4036
Website: http://www.kpventures.com

Nu Capital Access Group, Ltd.
7677 Oakport St., Ste. 105
Oakland, CA 94621
(510)635-7345
Fax: (510)635-7068

Inman and Bowman
4 Orinda Way, Bldg. D, Ste. 150
Orinda, CA 94563
(510)253-1611
Fax: (510)253-9037

Accel Partners (San Francisco)
428 University Ave.
Palo Alto, CA 94301
(650)614-4800
Fax: (650)614-4880
Website: http://www.accel.com

Advanced Technology Ventures
485 Ramona St., Ste. 200
Palo Alto, CA 94301
(650)321-8601
Fax: (650)321-0934
Website: http://www.atvcapital.com

Anila Fund
400 Channing Ave.
Palo Alto, CA 94301
(650)833-5790
Fax: (650)833-0590
Website: http://www.anila.com

**Asset Management Company Venture
Capital**
2275 E. Bayshore, Ste. 150
Palo Alto, CA 94303
(650)494-7400
Fax: (650)856-1826
E-mail: postmaster@assetman.com
Website: http://www.assetman.com

**BancBoston Capital / BancBoston
Ventures**
435 Tasso St., Ste. 250
Palo Alto, CA 94305
(650)470-4100
Fax: (650)853-1425
Website: http://www.bancbostoncapital
.com

Charter Ventures
525 University Ave., Ste. 1400
Palo Alto, CA 94301
(650)325-6953
Fax: (650)325-4762
Website: http://www.charterventures.com

Communications Ventures
505 Hamilton Avenue, Ste. 305
Palo Alto, CA 94301
(650)325-9600
Fax: (650)325-9608
Website: http://www.comven.com

HMS Group
2468 Embarcadero Way
Palo Alto, CA 94303-3313
(650)856-9862
Fax: (650)856-9864

Jafco America Ventures, Inc.
505 Hamilton Ste. 310
Palto Alto, CA 94301
(650)463-8800
Fax: (650)463-8801
Website: http://www.jafco.com

New Vista Capital
540 Cowper St., Ste. 200
Palo Alto, CA 94301
(650)329-9333
Fax: (650)328-9434
E-mail: fgreene@nvcap.com
Website: http://www.nvcap.com

Norwest Equity Partners (Palo Alto)
245 Lytton Ave., Ste. 250
Palo Alto, CA 94301-1426
(650)321-8000
Fax: (650)321-8010
Website: http://www.norwestvp.com

Oak Investment Partners
525 University Ave., Ste. 1300
Palo Alto, CA 94301
(650)614-3700
Fax: (650)328-6345
Website: http://www.oakinv.com

Patricof & Co. Ventures, Inc. (Palo Alto)
2100 Geng Rd., Ste. 150
Palo Alto, CA 94303
(650)494-9944
Fax: (650)494-6751
Website: http://www.patricof.com

RWI Group
835 Page Mill Rd.
Palo Alto, CA 94304
(650)251-1800
Fax: (650)213-8660
Website: http://www.rwigroup.com

Summit Partners (Palo Alto)
499 Hamilton Ave., Ste. 200
Palo Alto, CA 94301
(650)321-1166
Fax: (650)321-1188
Website: http://www.summitpartners.com

Sutter Hill Ventures
755 Page Mill Rd., Ste. A-200
Palo Alto, CA 94304
(650)493-5600
Fax: (650)858-1854
E-mail: shv@shv.com

Vanguard Venture Partners
525 University Ave., Ste. 600
Palo Alto, CA 94301
(650)321-2900
Fax: (650)321-2902
Website: http://www.vanguardventures
.com

Venture Growth Associates
2479 East Bayshore St., Ste. 710
Palo Alto, CA 94303
(650)855-9100
Fax: (650)855-9104

Worldview Technology Partners
435 Tasso St., Ste. 120
Palo Alto, CA 94301
(650)322-3800
Fax: (650)322-3880
Website: http://www.worldview.com

Draper, Fisher, Jurvetson / Draper Associates
400 Seaport Ct., Ste.250
Redwood City, CA 94063
(415)599-9000
Fax: (415)599-9726
Website: http://www.dfj.com

Gabriel Venture Partners
350 Marine Pkwy., Ste. 200
Redwood Shores, CA 94065
(650)551-5000
Fax: (650)551-5001
Website: http://www.gabrielvp.com

Hallador Venture Partners, L.L.C.
740 University Ave., Ste. 110
Sacramento, CA 95825-6710
(916)920-0191
Fax: (916)920-5188
E-mail: chris@hallador.com

Emerald Venture Group
12396 World Trade Dr., Ste. 116
San Diego, CA 92128
(858)451-1001
Fax: (858)451-1003
Website: http://www.emeraldventure
.com

Forward Ventures
9255 Towne Centre Dr.
San Diego, CA 92121
(858)677-6077

Fax: (858)452-8799
E-mail: info@forwardventure.com
Website: http://www.forwardventure.com

Idanta Partners Ltd.
4660 La Jolla Village Dr., Ste. 850
San Diego, CA 92122
(619)452-9690
Fax: (619)452-2013
Website: http://www.idanta.com

Kingsbury Associates
3655 Nobel Dr., Ste. 490
San Diego, CA 92122
(858)677-0600
Fax: (858)677-0800

Kyocera International Inc.
Corporate Development
8611 Balboa Ave.
San Diego, CA 92123
(858)576-2600
Fax: (858)492-1456

Sorrento Associates, Inc.
4370 LaJolla Village Dr., Ste. 1040
San Diego, CA 92122
(619)452-3100
Fax: (619)452-7607
Website: http://www.sorrentoventures
.com

Western States Investment Group
9191 Towne Ctr. Dr., Ste. 310
San Diego, CA 92122
(619)678-0800
Fax: (619)678-0900

Aberdare Ventures
One Embarcadero Center, Ste. 4000
San Francisco, CA 94111
(415)392-7442
Fax: (415)392-4264
Website: http://www.aberdare.com

Acacia Venture Partners
101 California St., Ste. 3160
San Francisco, CA 94111
(415)433-4200
Fax: (415)433-4250
Website: http://www.acaciavp.com

Access Venture Partners
319 Laidley St.
San Francisco, CA 94131
(415)586-0132
Fax: (415)392-6310
Website: http://www.accessventure
partners.com

Alta Partners
One Embarcadero Center, Ste. 4050
San Francisco, CA 94111

(415)362-4022
Fax: (415)362-6178
E-mail: alta@altapartners.com
Website: http://www.altapartners.com

Bangert Dawes Reade Davis & Thom
220 Montgomery St., Ste. 424
San Francisco, CA 94104
(415)954-9900
Fax: (415)954-9901
E-mail: bdrdt@pacbell.net

Berkeley International Capital Corp.
650 California St., Ste. 2800
San Francisco, CA 94108-2609
(415)249-0450
Fax: (415)392-3929
Website: http://www.berkeleyvc.com

Blueprint Ventures LLC
456 Montgomery St., 22nd Fl.
San Francisco, CA 94104
(415)901-4000
Fax: (415)901-4035
Website: http://www.blueprintventures
.com

Blumberg Capital Ventures
580 Howard St., Ste. 401
San Francisco, CA 94105
(415)905-5007
Fax: (415)357-5027
Website: http://www.blumberg-
capital.com

Burr, Egan, Deleage, and Co. (San Francisco)
1 Embarcadero Center, Ste. 4050
San Francisco, CA 94111
(415)362-4022
Fax: (415)362-6178

Burrill & Company
120 Montgomery St., Ste. 1370
San Francisco, CA 94104
(415)743-3160
Fax: (415)743-3161
Website: http://www.burrillandco.com

CMEA Ventures
235 Montgomery St., Ste. 920
San Francisco, CA 94401
(415)352-1520
Fax: (415)352-1524
Website: http://www.cmeaventures.com

Crocker Capital
1 Post St., Ste. 2500
San Francisco, CA 94101
(415)956-5250
Fax: (415)959-5710

Dominion Ventures, Inc.
44 Montgomery St., Ste. 4200
San Francisco, CA 94104
(415)362-4890
Fax: (415)394-9245

Dorset Capital
Pier 1
Bay 2
San Francisco, CA 94111
(415)398-7101
Fax: (415)398-7141
Website: http://www.dorsetcapital.com

Gatx Capital
Four Embarcadero Center, Ste. 2200
San Francisco, CA 94904
(415)955-3200
Fax: (415)955-3449

IMinds
135 Main St., Ste. 1350
San Francisco, CA 94105
(415)547-0000
Fax: (415)227-0300
Website: http://www.iminds.com

LF International Inc.
360 Post St., Ste. 705
San Francisco, CA 94108
(415)399-0110
Fax: (415)399-9222
Website: http://www.lfvc.com

Newbury Ventures
535 Pacific Ave., 2nd Fl.
San Francisco, CA 94133
(415)296-7408
Fax: (415)296-7416
Website: http://www.newburyven.com

Quest Ventures (San Francisco)
333 Bush St., Ste. 1750
San Francisco, CA 94104
(415)782-1414
Fax: (415)782-1415

Robertson-Stephens Co.
555 California St., Ste. 2600
San Francisco, CA 94104
(415)781-9700
Fax: (415)781-2556
Website: http://www.omegaadventures
.com

Rosewood Capital, L.P.
One Maritime Plaza, Ste. 1330
San Francisco, CA 94111-3503
(415)362-5526
Fax: (415)362-1192
Website: http://www.rosewoodvc.com

Ticonderoga Capital Inc.
555 California St., No. 4950
San Francisco, CA 94104
(415)296-7900
Fax: (415)296-8956

21st Century Internet Venture Partners
Two South Park
2nd Floor
San Francisco, CA 94107
(415)512-1221
Fax: (415)512-2650
Website: http://www.21vc.com

VK Ventures
600 California St., Ste.1700
San Francisco, CA 94111
(415)391-5600
Fax: (415)397-2744

Walden Group of Venture Capital Funds
750 Battery St., Seventh Floor
San Francisco, CA 94111
(415)391-7225
Fax: (415)391-7262

Acer Technology Ventures
2641 Orchard Pkwy.
San Jose, CA 95134
(408)433-4945
Fax: (408)433-5230

Authosis
226 Airport Pkwy., Ste. 405
San Jose, CA 95110
(650)814-3603
Website: http://www.authosis.com

Western Technology Investment
2010 N. First St., Ste. 310
San Jose, CA 95131
(408)436-8577
Fax: (408)436-8625
E-mail: mktg@westerntech.com

Drysdale Enterprises
177 Bovet Rd., Ste. 600
San Mateo, CA 94402
(650)341-6336
Fax: (650)341-1329
E-mail: drysdale@aol.com

Greylock
2929 Campus Dr., Ste. 400
San Mateo, CA 94401
(650)493-5525
Fax: (650)493-5575
Website: http://www.greylock.com

Technology Funding
2000 Alameda de las Pulgas, Ste. 250
San Mateo, CA 94403

(415)345-2200
Fax: (415)345-1797

2M Invest Inc.
1875 S. Grant St.
Suite 750
San Mateo, CA 94402
(650)655-3765
Fax: (650)372-9107
E-mail: 2minfo@2minvest.com
Website: http://www.2minvest.com

Phoenix Growth Capital Corp.
2401 Kerner Blvd.
San Rafael, CA 94901
(415)485-4569
Fax: (415)485-4663

NextGen Partners LLC
1705 East Valley Rd.
Santa Barbara, CA 93108
(805)969-8540
Fax: (805)969-8542
Website: http://www.nextgenpartners.com

Denali Venture Capital
1925 Woodland Ave.
Santa Clara, CA 95050
(408)690-4838
Fax: (408)247-6979
E-mail: wael@denaliventurecapital.com
Website: http://www.denaliventure
capital.com

Dotcom Ventures LP
3945 Freedom Circle, Ste. 740
Santa Clara, CA 95045
(408)919-9855
Fax: (408)919-9857
Website: http://www.dotcomventuresatl
.com

Silicon Valley Bank
3003 Tasman
Santa Clara, CA 95054
(408)654-7400
Fax: (408)727-8728

Al Shugart International
920 41st Ave.
Santa Cruz, CA 95062
(831)479-7852
Fax: (831)479-7852
Website: http://www.alshugart.com

Leonard Mautner Associates
1434 Sixth St.
Santa Monica, CA 90401
(213)393-9788
Fax: (310)459-9918

Palomar Ventures
100 Wilshire Blvd., Ste. 450

Santa Monica, CA 90401
(310)260-6050
Fax: (310)656-4150
Website: http://www.palomarventures.com

Medicus Venture Partners
12930 Saratoga Ave., Ste. D8
Saratoga, CA 95070
(408)447-8600
Fax: (408)447-8599
Website: http://www.medicusvc.com

Redleaf Venture Management
14395 Saratoga Ave., Ste. 130
Saratoga, CA 95070
(408)868-0800
Fax: (408)868-0810
E-mail: nancy@redleaf.com
Website: http://www.redleaf.com

Artemis Ventures
207 Second St., Ste. E
3rd Fl.
Sausalito, CA 94965
(415)289-2500
Fax: (415)289-1789
Website: http://www.artemisventures.com

Deucalion Venture Partners
19501 Brooklime
Sonoma, CA 95476
(707)938-4974
Fax: (707)938-8921

Windward Ventures
PO Box 7688
Thousand Oaks, CA 91359-7688
(805)497-3332
Fax: (805)497-9331

National Investment Management, Inc.
2601 Airport Dr., Ste.210
Torrance, CA 90505
(310)784-7600
Fax: (310)784-7605

Southern California Ventures
406 Amapola Ave. Ste. 125
Torrance, CA 90501
(310)787-4381
Fax: (310)787-4382

Sandton Financial Group
21550 Oxnard St., Ste. 300
Woodland Hills, CA 91367
(818)702-9283

Woodside Fund
850 Woodside Dr.
Woodside, CA 94062
(650)368-5545
Fax: (650)368-2416
Website: http://www.woodsidefund.com

Colorado

Colorado Venture Management
Ste. 300
Boulder, CO 80301
(303)440-4055
Fax: (303)440-4636

Dean & Associates
4362 Apple Way
Boulder, CO 80301
Fax: (303)473-9900

Roser Ventures LLC
1105 Spruce St.
Boulder, CO 80302
(303)443-6436
Fax: (303)443-1885
Website: http://www.roserventures.com

Sequel Venture Partners
4430 Arapahoe Ave., Ste. 220
Boulder, CO 80303
(303)546-0400
Fax: (303)546-9728
E-mail: tom@sequelvc.com
Website: http://www.sequelvc.com

New Venture Resources
445C E. Cheyenne Mtn. Blvd.
Colorado Springs, CO 80906-4570
(719)598-9272
Fax: (719)598-9272

The Centennial Funds
1428 15th St.
Denver, CO 80202-1318
(303)405-7500
Fax: (303)405-7575
Website: http://www.centennial.com

Rocky Mountain Capital Partners
1125 17th St., Ste. 2260
Denver, CO 80202
(303)291-5200
Fax: (303)291-5327

Sandlot Capital LLC
600 South Cherry St., Ste. 525
Denver, CO 80246
(303)893-3400
Fax: (303)893-3403
Website: http://www.sandlotcapital.com

Wolf Ventures
50 South Steele St., Ste. 777
Denver, CO 80209
(303)321-4800
Fax: (303)321-4848
E-mail: businessplan@wolfventures.com
Website: http://www.wolfventures.com

The Columbine Venture Funds
5460 S. Quebec St., Ste. 270
Englewood, CO 80111
(303)694-3222
Fax: (303)694-9007

Investment Securities of Colorado, Inc.
4605 Denice Dr.
Englewood, CO 80111
(303)796-9192

Kinship Partners
6300 S. Syracuse Way, Ste. 484
Englewood, CO 80111
(303)694-0268
Fax: (303)694-1707
E-mail: block@vailsys.com

Boranco Management, L.L.C.
1528 Hillside Dr.
Fort Collins, CO 80524-1969
(970)221-2297
Fax: (970)221-4787

Aweida Ventures
890 West Cherry St., Ste. 220
Louisville, CO 80027
(303)664-9520
Fax: (303)664-9530
Website: http://www.aweida.com

Access Venture Partners
8787 Turnpike Dr., Ste. 260
Westminster, CO 80030
(303)426-8899
Fax: (303)426-8828

Medmax Ventures LP
1 Northwestern Dr., Ste. 203
Bloomfield, CT 06002
(860)286-2960
Fax: (860)286-9960

James B. Kobak & Co.
Four Mansfield Place
Darien, CT 06820
(203)656-3471
Fax: (203)655-2905

Orien Ventures
1 Post Rd.
Fairfield, CT 06430
(203)259-9933
Fax: (203)259-5288

ABP Acquisition Corporation
115 Maple Ave.
Greenwich, CT 06830
(203)625-8287
Fax: (203)447-6187

Catterton Partners
9 Greenwich Office Park
Greenwich, CT 06830
(203)629-4901
Fax: (203)629-4903
Website: http://www.cpequity.com

Consumer Venture Partners
3 Pickwick Plz.
Greenwich, CT 06830
(203)629-8800
Fax: (203)629-2019

Insurance Venture Partners
31 Brookside Dr., Ste. 211
Greenwich, CT 06830
(203)861-0030
Fax: (203)861-2745

The NTC Group
Three Pickwick Plaza
Ste. 200
Greenwich, CT 06830
(203)862-2800
Fax: (203)622-6538

Regulus International Capital Co., Inc.
140 Greenwich Ave.
Greenwich, CT 06830
(203)625-9700
Fax: (203)625-9706

Axiom Venture Partners
City Place II
185 Asylum St., 17th Fl.
Hartford, CT 06103
(860)548-7799
Fax: (860)548-7797
Website: http://www.axiomventures.com

Conning Capital Partners
City Place II
185 Asylum St.
Hartford, CT 06103-4105
(860)520-1289
Fax: (860)520-1299
E-mail: pe@conning.com
Website: http://www.conning.com

First New England Capital L.P.
100 Pearl St.
Hartford, CT 06103
(860)293-3333
Fax: (860)293-3338
E-mail: info@firstnewengland
capital.com
Website: http://www.firstnewengland
capital.com

Northeast Ventures
One State St., Ste. 1720
Hartford, CT 06103

(860)547-1414
Fax: (860)246-8755

Windward Holdings
38 Sylvan Rd.
Madison, CT 06443
(203)245-6870
Fax: (203)245-6865

Advanced Materials Partners, Inc.
45 Pine St.
PO Box 1022
New Canaan, CT 06840
(203)966-6415
Fax: (203)966-8448
E-mail: wkb@amplink.com

RFE Investment Partners
36 Grove St.
New Canaan, CT 06840
(203)966-2800
Fax: (203)966-3109
Website: http://www.rfeip.com

Connecticut Innovations, Inc.
999 West St.
Rocky Hill, CT 06067
(860)563-5851
Fax: (860)563-4877
E-mail: pamela.hartley@ctinnovations.com
Website: http://www.ctinnovations.com

Canaan Partners
105 Rowayton Ave.
Rowayton, CT 06853
(203)855-0400
Fax: (203)854-9117
Website: http://www.canaan.com

Landmark Partners, Inc.
10 Mill Pond Ln.
Simsbury, CT 06070
(860)651-9760
Fax: (860)651-8890
Website: http://www.landmarkpartners
.com

Sweeney & Company
PO Box 567
Southport, CT 06490
(203)255-0220
Fax: (203)255-0220
E-mail: sweeney@connix.com

Baxter Associates, Inc.
PO Box 1333
Stamford, CT 06904
(203)323-3143
Fax: (203)348-0622

Beacon Partners Inc.
6 Landmark Sq., 4th Fl.
Stamford, CT 06901-2792

(203)359-5776
Fax: (203)359-5876

Collinson, Howe, and Lennox, LLC
1055 Washington Blvd., 5th Fl.
Stamford, CT 06901
(203)324-7700
Fax: (203)324-3636
E-mail: info@chlmedical.com
Website: http://www.chlmedical.com

Prime Capital Management Co.
550 West Ave.
Stamford, CT 06902
(203)964-0642
Fax: (203)964-0862

Saugatuck Capital Co.
1 Canterbury Green
Stamford, CT 06901
(203)348-6669
Fax: (203)324-6995
Website: http://www.saugatuckcapital.com

Soundview Financial Group Inc.
22 Gatehouse Rd.
Stamford, CT 06902
(203)462-7200
Fax: (203)462-7350
Website: http://www.sndv.com

TSG Ventures, L.L.C.
177 Broad St., 12th Fl.
Stamford, CT 06901
(203)406-1500
Fax: (203)406-1590

Whitney & Company
177 Broad St.
Stamford, CT 06901
(203)973-1400
Fax: (203)973-1422
Website: http://www.jhwhitney.com

Cullinane & Donnelly Venture Partners L.P.
970 Farmington Ave.
West Hartford, CT 06107
(860)521-7811

The Crestview Investment and Financial Group
431 Post Rd. E, Ste. 1
Westport, CT 06880-4403
(203)222-0333
Fax: (203)222-0000

Marketcorp Venture Associates, L.P. (MCV)
274 Riverside Ave.
Westport, CT 06880
(203)222-3030
Fax: (203)222-3033

Oak Investment Partners (Westport)
1 Gorham Island
Westport, CT 06880
(203)226-8346
Fax: (203)227-0372
Website: http://www.oakinv.com

Oxford Bioscience Partners
315 Post Rd. W
Westport, CT 06880-5200
(203)341-3300
Fax: (203)341-3309
Website: http://www.oxbio.com

Prince Ventures (Westport)
25 Ford Rd.
Westport, CT 06880
(203)227-8332
Fax: (203)226-5302

LTI Venture Leasing Corp.
221 Danbury Rd.
Wilton, CT 06897
(203)563-1100
Fax: (203)563-1111
Website: http://www.ltileasing.com

Delaware

Blue Rock Capital
5803 Kennett Pike, Ste. A
Wilmington, DE 19807
(302)426-0981
Fax: (302)426-0982
Website: http://www.bluerockcapital.com

District of Columbia

Allied Capital Corp.
1919 Pennsylvania Ave. NW
Washington, DC 20006-3434
(202)331-2444
Fax: (202)659-2053
Website: http://www.alliedcapital.com

Atlantic Coastal Ventures, L.P.
3101 South St. NW
Washington, DC 20007
(202)293-1166
Fax: (202)293-1181
Website: http://www.atlanticcv.com

Columbia Capital Group, Inc.
1660 L St. NW, Ste. 308
Washington, DC 20036
(202)775-8815
Fax: (202)223-0544

Core Capital Partners
901 15th St., NW
9th Fl.
Washington, DC 20005

(202)589-0090
Fax: (202)589-0091
Website: http://www.core-capital.com

Next Point Partners
701 Pennsylvania Ave. NW, Ste. 900
Washington, DC 20004
(202)661-8703
Fax: (202)434-7400
E-mail: mf@nextpoint.vc
Website: http://www.nextpointvc.com

Telecommunications Development Fund
2020 K. St. NW
Ste. 375
Washington, DC 20006
(202)293-8840
Fax: (202)293-8850
Website: http://www.tdfund.com

Wachtel & Co., Inc.
1101 4th St. NW
Washington, DC 20005-5680
(202)898-1144

Winslow Partners LLC
1300 Connecticut Ave. NW
Washington, DC 20036-1703
(202)530-5000
Fax: (202)530-5010
E-mail: winslow@winslowpartners.com

Women's Growth Capital Fund
1054 31st St., NW
Ste. 110
Washington, DC 20007
(202)342-1431
Fax: (202)341-1203
Website: http://www.wgcf.com

Sigma Capital Corp.
22668 Caravelle Circle
Boca Raton, FL 33433
(561)368-9783

North American Business Development Co., L.L.C.
111 East Las Olas Blvd.
Ft. Lauderdale, FL 33301
(305)463-0681
Fax: (305)527-0904
Website: http://www.northamericanfund.com

Chartwell Capital Management Co. Inc.
1 Independent Dr., Ste. 3120
Jacksonville, FL 32202
(904)355-3519
Fax: (904)353-5833
E-mail: info@chartwellcap.com

CEO Advisors
1061 Maitland Center Commons
Ste. 209
Maitland, FL 32751
(407)660-9327
Fax: (407)660-2109

Henry & Co.
8201 Peters Rd., Ste. 1000
Plantation, FL 33324
(954)797-7400

Avery Business Development Services
2506 St. Michel Ct.
Ponte Vedra, FL 32082
(904)285-6033

New South Ventures
5053 Ocean Blvd.
Sarasota, FL 34242
(941)358-6000
Fax: (941)358-6078
Website: http://www.newsouthventures
.com

Venture Capital Management Corp.
PO Box 2626
Satellite Beach, FL 32937
(407)777-1969

Florida Capital Venture Ltd.
325 Florida Bank Plaza
100 W. Kennedy Blvd.
Tampa, FL 33602
(813)229-2294
Fax: (813)229-2028

Quantum Capital Partners
339 South Plant Ave.
Tampa, FL 33606
(813)250-1999
Fax: (813)250-1998
Website: http://www.quantumcapital
partners.com

South Atlantic Venture Fund
614 W. Bay St.
Tampa, FL 33606-2704
(813)253-2500
Fax: (813)253-2360
E-mail: venture@southatlantic.com
Website: http://www.southatlantic.com

LM Capital Corp.
120 S. Olive, Ste. 400
West Palm Beach, FL 33401
(561)833-9700
Fax: (561)655-6587
Website: http://www.lmcapitalsecurities
.com

Georgia

Venture First Associates
4811 Thornwood Dr.
Acworth, GA 30102
(770)928-3733
Fax: (770)928-6455

Alliance Technology Ventures
8995 Westside Pkwy., Ste. 200
Alpharetta, GA 30004
(678)336-2000
Fax: (678)336-2001
E-mail: info@atv.com
Website: http://www.atv.com

Cordova Ventures
2500 North Winds Pkwy., Ste. 475
Alpharetta, GA 30004
(678)942-0300
Fax: (678)942-0301
Website: http://www.cordovaventures.com

Advanced Technology Development Fund
1000 Abernathy, Ste. 1420
Atlanta, GA 30328-5614
(404)668-2333
Fax: (404)668-2333

CGW Southeast Partners
12 Piedmont Center, Ste. 210
Atlanta, GA 30305
(404)816-3255
Fax: (404)816-3258
Website: http://www.cgwlp.com

Cyberstarts
1900 Emery St., NW
3rd Fl.
Atlanta, GA 30318
(404)267-5000
Fax: (404)267-5200
Website: http://www.cyberstarts.com

EGL Holdings, Inc.
10 Piedmont Center, Ste. 412
Atlanta, GA 30305
(404)949-8300
Fax: (404)949-8311

Equity South
1790 The Lenox Bldg.
3399 Peachtree Rd. NE
Atlanta, GA 30326
(404)237-6222
Fax: (404)261-1578

Five Paces
3400 Peachtree Rd., Ste. 200
Atlanta, GA 30326
(404)439-8300
Fax: (404)439-8301
Website: http://www.fivepaces.com

Frontline Capital, Inc.
3475 Lenox Rd., Ste. 400
Atlanta, GA 30326
(404)240-7280
Fax: (404)240-7281

Fuqua Ventures LLC
1201 W. Peachtree St. NW, Ste. 5000
Atlanta, GA 30309
(404)815-4500
Fax: (404)815-4528
Website: http://www.fuquaventures.com

Noro-Moseley Partners
4200 Northside Pkwy., Bldg. 9
Atlanta, GA 30327
(404)233-1966
Fax: (404)239-9280
Website: http://www.noro-moseley.com

Renaissance Capital Corp.
34 Peachtree St. NW, Ste. 2230
Atlanta, GA 30303
(404)658-9061
Fax: (404)658-9064

River Capital, Inc.
Two Midtown Plaza
1360 Peachtree St. NE, Ste. 1430
Atlanta, GA 30309
(404)873-2166
Fax: (404)873-2158

State Street Bank & Trust Co.
3414 Peachtree Rd. NE, Ste. 1010
Atlanta, GA 30326
(404)364-9500
Fax: (404)261-4469

UPS Strategic Enterprise Fund
55 Glenlake Pkwy. NE
Atlanta, GA 30328
(404)828-8814
Fax: (404)828-8088
E-mail: jcacyce@ups.com
Website: http://www.ups.com/sef/
sef_home

Wachovia
191 Peachtree St. NE, 26th Fl.
Atlanta, GA 30303
(404)332-1000
Fax: (404)332-1392
Website: http://www.wachovia.com/wca

Brainworks Ventures
4243 Dunwoody Club Dr.
Chamblee, GA 30341
(770)239-7447

First Growth Capital Inc.
Best Western Plaza, Ste. 105
PO Box 815

Forsyth, GA 31029
(912)781-7131

Financial Capital Resources, Inc.
21 Eastbrook Bend, Ste. 116
Peachtree City, GA 30269
(404)487-6650

Hawaii

HMS Hawaii Management Partners
Davies Pacific Center
841 Bishop St., Ste. 860
Honolulu, HI 96813
(808)545-3755
Fax: (808)531-2611

Idaho

Sun Valley Ventures
160 Second St.
Ketchum, ID 83340
(208)726-5005
Fax: (208)726-5094

Illinois

Open Prairie Ventures
115 N. Neil St., Ste. 209
Champaign, IL 61820
(217)351-7000
Fax: (217)351-7051
E-mail: inquire@openprairie.com
Website: http://www.openprairie.com

ABN AMRO Private Equity
208 S. La Salle St., 10th Fl.
Chicago, IL 60604
(312)855-7079
Fax: (312)553-6648
Website: http://www.abnequity.com

Alpha Capital Partners, Ltd.
122 S. Michigan Ave., Ste. 1700
Chicago, IL 60603
(312)322-9800
Fax: (312)322-9808
E-mail: acp@alphacapital.com

Ameritech Development Corp.
30 S. Wacker Dr., 37th Fl.
Chicago, IL 60606
(312)750-5083
Fax: (312)609-0244

Apex Investment Partners
225 W. Washington, Ste. 1450
Chicago, IL 60606
(312)857-2800
Fax: (312)857-1800
E-mail: apex@apexvc.com
Website: http://www.apexvc.com

Arch Venture Partners
8725 W. Higgins Rd., Ste. 290
Chicago, IL 60631
(773)380-6600
Fax: (773)380-6606
Website: http://www.archventure.com

The Bank Funds
208 South LaSalle St., Ste. 1680
Chicago, IL 60604
(312)855-6020
Fax: (312)855-8910

Batterson Venture Partners
303 W. Madison St., Ste. 1110
Chicago, IL 60606-3309
(312)269-0300
Fax: (312)269-0021
Website: http://www.battersonvp.com

William Blair Capital Partners, L.L.C.
222 W. Adams St., Ste. 1300
Chicago, IL 60606
(312)364-8250
Fax: (312)236-1042
E-mail: privateequity@wmblair.com
Website: http://www.wmblair.com

Bluestar Ventures
208 South LaSalle St., Ste. 1020
Chicago, IL 60604
(312)384-5000
Fax: (312)384-5005
Website: http://www.bluestarventures.com

The Capital Strategy Management Co.
233 S. Wacker Dr.
Box 06334
Chicago, IL 60606
(312)444-1170

DN Partners
77 West Wacker Dr., Ste. 4550
Chicago, IL 60601
(312)332-7960
Fax: (312)332-7979

Dresner Capital Inc.
29 South LaSalle St., Ste. 310
Chicago, IL 60603
(312)726-3600
Fax: (312)726-7448

Eblast Ventures LLC
11 South LaSalle St., 5th Fl.
Chicago, IL 60603
(312)372-2600
Fax: (312)372-5621
Website: http://www.eblastventures.com

Essex Woodlands Health Ventures, L.P.
190 S. LaSalle St., Ste. 2800
Chicago, IL 60603

(312)444-6040
Fax: (312)444-6034
Website: http://www.essexwoodlands.com

First Analysis Venture Capital
233 S. Wacker Dr., Ste. 9500
Chicago, IL 60606
(312)258-1400
Fax: (312)258-0334
Website: http://www.firstanalysis.com

Frontenac Co.
135 S. LaSalle St., Ste.3800
Chicago, IL 60603
(312)368-0044
Fax: (312)368-9520
Website: http://www.frontenac.com

GTCR Golder Rauner, LLC
6100 Sears Tower
Chicago, IL 60606
(312)382-2200
Fax: (312)382-2201
Website: http://www.gtcr.com

High Street Capital LLC
311 South Wacker Dr., Ste. 4550
Chicago, IL 60606
(312)697-4990
Fax: (312)697-4994
Website: http://www.highstr.com

IEG Venture Management, Inc.
70 West Madison
Chicago, IL 60602
(312)644-0890
Fax: (312)454-0369
Website: http://www.iegventure.com

JK&B Capital
180 North Stetson, Ste. 4500
Chicago, IL 60601
(312)946-1200
Fax: (312)946-1103
E-mail: gspencer@jkbcapital.com
Website: http://www.jkbcapital.com

Kettle Partners L.P.
350 W. Hubbard, Ste. 350
Chicago, IL 60610
(312)329-9300
Fax: (312)527-4519
Website: http://www.kettlevc.com

Lake Shore Capital Partners
20 N. Wacker Dr., Ste. 2807
Chicago, IL 60606
(312)803-3536
Fax: (312)803-3534

LaSalle Capital Group Inc.
70 W. Madison St., Ste. 5710
Chicago, IL 60602

(312)236-7041
Fax: (312)236-0720

Linc Capital, Inc.
303 E. Wacker Pkwy., Ste. 1000
Chicago, IL 60601
(312)946-2670
Fax: (312)938-4290
E-mail: bdemars@linccap.com

Madison Dearborn Partners, Inc.
3 First National Plz., Ste. 3800
Chicago, IL 60602
(312)895-1000
Fax: (312)895-1001
E-mail: invest@mdcp.com
Website: http://www.mdcp.com

Mesirow Private Equity Investments Inc.
350 N. Clark St.
Chicago, IL 60610
(312)595-6950
Fax: (312)595-6211
Website: http://www.meisrowfinancial.com

Mosaix Ventures LLC
1822 North Mohawk
Chicago, IL 60614
(312)274-0988
Fax: (312)274-0989
Website: http://www.mosaixventures.com

Nesbitt Burns
111 West Monroe St.
Chicago, IL 60603
(312)416-3855
Fax: (312)765-8000
Website: http://www.harrisbank.com

Polestar Capital, Inc.
180 N. Michigan Ave., Ste. 1905
Chicago, IL 60601
(312)984-9090
Fax: (312)984-9877
E-mail: wl@polestarvc.com
Website: http://www.polestarvc.com

Prince Ventures (Chicago)
10 S. Wacker Dr., Ste. 2575
Chicago, IL 60606-7407
(312)454-1408
Fax: (312)454-9125

Prism Capital
444 N. Michigan Ave.
Chicago, IL 60611
(312)464-7900
Fax: (312)464-7915
Website: http://www.prismfund.com

Third Coast Capital
900 N. Franklin St., Ste. 700
Chicago, IL 60610
(312)337-3303
Fax: (312)337-2567
E-mail: manic@earthlink.com
Website: http://www.thirdcoastcapital.com

Thoma Cressey Equity Partners
4460 Sears Tower, 92nd Fl.
233 S. Wacker Dr.
Chicago, IL 60606
(312)777-4444
Fax: (312)777-4445
Website: http://www.thomacressey.com

Tribune Ventures
435 N. Michigan Ave., Ste. 600
Chicago, IL 60611
(312)527-8797
Fax: (312)222-5993
Website: http://www.tribuneventures.com

Wind Point Partners (Chicago)
676 N. Michigan Ave., Ste. 330
Chicago, IL 60611
(312)649-4000
Website: http://www.wppartners.com

Marquette Venture Partners
520 Lake Cook Rd., Ste. 450
Deerfield, IL 60015
(847)940-1700
Fax: (847)940-1724
Website: http://www.marquetteventures.com

Duchossois Investments Limited, LLC
845 Larch Ave.
Elmhurst, IL 60126
(630)530-6105
Fax: (630)993-8644
Website: http://www.duchtec.com

Evanston Business Investment Corp.
1840 Oak Ave.
Evanston, IL 60201
(847)866-1840
Fax: (847)866-1808
E-mail: t-parkinson@nwu.com
Website: http://www.ebic.com

Inroads Capital Partners L.P.
1603 Orrington Ave., Ste. 2050
Evanston, IL 60201-3841
(847)864-2000
Fax: (847)864-9692

The Cerulean Fund/WGC Enterprises
1701 E. Lake Ave., Ste. 170
Glenview, IL 60025
(847)657-8002
Fax: (847)657-8168

Ventana Financial Resources, Inc.
249 Market Sq.
Lake Forest, IL 60045
(847)234-3434

Beecken, Petty & Co.
901 Warrenville Rd., Ste. 205
Lisle, IL 60532
(630)435-0300
Fax: (630)435-0370
E-mail: hep@bpcompany.com
Website: http://www.bpcompany.com

Allstate Private Equity
3075 Sanders Rd., Ste. G5D
Northbrook, IL 60062-7127
(847)402-8247
Fax: (847)402-0880

KB Partners
1101 Skokie Blvd., Ste. 260
Northbrook, IL 60062-2856
(847)714-0444
Fax: (847)714-0445
E-mail: keith@kbpartners.com
Website: http://www.kbpartners.com

Transcap Associates Inc.
900 Skokie Blvd., Ste. 210
Northbrook, IL 60062
(847)753-9600
Fax: (847)753-9090

Graystone Venture Partners, L.L.C. / Portage Venture Partners
One Northfield Plaza, Ste. 530
Northfield, IL 60093
(847)446-9460
Fax: (847)446-9470
Website: http://www.portageventures.com

Motorola Inc.
1303 E. Algonquin Rd.
Schaumburg, IL 60196-1065
(847)576-4929
Fax: (847)538-2250
Website: http://www.mot.com/mne

Indiana

Irwin Ventures LLC
500 Washington St.
Columbus, IN 47202
(812)373-1434
Fax: (812)376-1709
Website: http://www.irwinventures.com

Cambridge Venture Partners
4181 East 96th St., Ste. 200
Indianapolis, IN 46240
(317)814-6192
Fax: (317)944-9815

CID Equity Partners
One American Square, Ste. 2850
Box 82074
Indianapolis, IN 46282
(317)269-2350
Fax: (317)269-2355
Website: http://www.cidequity.com

Gazelle Techventures
6325 Digital Way, Ste. 460
Indianapolis, IN 46278
(317)275-6800
Fax: (317)275-1101
Website: http://www.gazellevc.com

Monument Advisors Inc.
Bank One Center/Circle
111 Monument Circle, Ste. 600
Indianapolis, IN 46204-5172
(317)656-5065
Fax: (317)656-5060
Website: http://www.monumentadv.com

MWV Capital Partners
201 N. Illinois St., Ste. 300
Indianapolis, IN 46204
(317)237-2323
Fax: (317)237-2325
Website: http://www.mwvcapital.com

First Source Capital Corp.
100 North Michigan St.
PO Box 1602
South Bend, IN 46601
(219)235-2180
Fax: (219)235-2227

Iowa

Allsop Venture Partners
118 Third Ave. SE, Ste. 837
Cedar Rapids, IA 52401
(319)368-6675
Fax: (319)363-9515

InvestAmerica Investment Advisors, Inc.
101 2nd St. SE, Ste. 800
Cedar Rapids, IA 52401
(319)363-8249
Fax: (319)363-9683

Pappajohn Capital Resources
2116 Financial Center
Des Moines, IA 50309
(515)244-5746
Fax: (515)244-2346
Website: http://www.pappajohn.com

Berthel Fisher & Company Planning Inc.
701 Tama St.
PO Box 609
Marion, IA 52302

(319)497-5700
Fax: (319)497-4244

Kansas

Enterprise Merchant Bank
7400 West 110th St., Ste. 560
Overland Park, KS 66210
(913)327-8500
Fax: (913)327-8505

Kansas Venture Capital, Inc. (Overland Park)
6700 Antioch Plz., Ste. 460
Overland Park, KS 66204
(913)262-7117
Fax: (913)262-3509
E-mail: jdalton@kvci.com

Child Health Investment Corp.
6803 W. 64th St., Ste. 208
Shawnee Mission, KS 66202
(913)262-1436
Fax: (913)262-1575
Website: http://www.chca.com

Kansas Technology Enterprise Corp.
214 SW 6th, 1st Fl.
Topeka, KS 66603-3719
(785)296-5272
Fax: (785)296-1160
E-mail: ktec@ktec.com
Website: http://www.ktec.com

Kentucky

Kentucky Highlands Investment Corp.
362 Old Whitley Rd.
London, KY 40741
(606)864-5175
Fax: (606)864-5194
Website: http://www.khic.org

Chrysalis Ventures, L.L.C.
1850 National City Tower
Louisville, KY 40202
(502)583-7644
Fax: (502)583-7648
E-mail: bobsany@chrysalisventures.com
Website: http://www.chrysalisventures.com

Humana Venture Capital
500 West Main St.
Louisville, KY 40202
(502)580-3922
Fax: (502)580-2051
E-mail: gemont@humana.com
George Emont, Director

Summit Capital Group, Inc.
6510 Glenridge Park Pl., Ste. 8
Louisville, KY 40222
(502)332-2700

Louisiana

Bank One Equity Investors, Inc.
451 Florida St.
Baton Rouge, LA 70801
(504)332-4421
Fax: (504)332-7377

Advantage Capital Partners
LLE Tower
909 Poydras St., Ste. 2230
New Orleans, LA 70112
(504)522-4850
Fax: (504)522-4950
Website: http://www.advantagecap.com

Maine

CEI Ventures / Coastal Ventures LP
2 Portland Fish Pier, Ste. 201
Portland, ME 04101
(207)772-5356
Fax: (207)772-5503
Website: http://www.ceiventures.com

Commwealth Bioventures, Inc.
4 Milk St.
Portland, ME 04101
(207)780-0904
Fax: (207)780-0913

Maryland

Annapolis Ventures LLC
151 West St., Ste. 302
Annapolis, MD 21401
(443)482-9555
Fax: (443)482-9565
Website: http://www.annapolisventures.com

Delmag Ventures
220 Wardour Dr.
Annapolis, MD 21401
(410)267-8196
Fax: (410)267-8017
Website: http://www.delmagventures.com

Abell Venture Fund
111 S. Calvert St., Ste. 2300
Baltimore, MD 21202
(410)547-1300
Fax: (410)539-6579
Website: http://www.abell.org

ABS Ventures (Baltimore)
1 South St., Ste. 2150
Baltimore, MD 21202
(410)895-3895
Fax: (410)895-3899
Website: http://www.absventures.com

Anthem Capital, L.P.
16 S. Calvert St., Ste. 800
Baltimore, MD 21202-1305
(410)625-1510
Fax: (410)625-1735
Website: http://www.anthemcapital.com

Catalyst Ventures
1119 St. Paul St.
Baltimore, MD 21202
(410)244-0123
Fax: (410)752-7721

Maryland Venture Capital Trust
217 E. Redwood St., Ste. 2200
Baltimore, MD 21202
(410)767-6361
Fax: (410)333-6931

New Enterprise Associates (Baltimore)
1119 St. Paul St.
Baltimore, MD 21202
(410)244-0115
Fax: (410)752-7721
Website: http://www.nea.com

T. Rowe Price Threshold Partnerships
100 E. Pratt St., 8th Fl.
Baltimore, MD 21202
(410)345-2000
Fax: (410)345-2800

Spring Capital Partners
16 W. Madison St.
Baltimore, MD 21201
(410)685-8000
Fax: (410)727-1436
E-mail: mailbox@springcap.com

Arete Corporation
3 Bethesda Metro Ctr., Ste. 770
Bethesda, MD 20814
(301)657-6268
Fax: (301)657-6254
Website: http://www.arete-microgen.com

Embryon Capital
7903 Sleaford Place
Bethesda, MD 20814
(301)656-6837
Fax: (301)656-8056

Potomac Ventures
7920 Norfolk Ave., Ste. 1100
Bethesda, MD 20814
(301)215-9240
Website: http://www.potomacventures
.com

Toucan Capital Corp.
3 Bethesda Metro Center, Ste. 700
Bethesda, MD 20814
(301)961-1970

Fax: (301)961-1969
Website: http://www.toucancapital.com

Kinetic Ventures LLC
2 Wisconsin Cir., Ste. 620
Chevy Chase, MD 20815
(301)652-8066
Fax: (301)652-8310
Website: http://www.kineticventures.com

Boulder Ventures Ltd.
4750 Owings Mills Blvd.
Owings Mills, MD 21117
(410)998-3114
Fax: (410)356-5492
Website: http://www.boulderventures.com

Grotech Capital Group
9690 Deereco Rd., Ste. 800
Timonium, MD 21093
(410)560-2000
Fax: (410)560-1910
Website: http://www.grotech.com

Massachusetts

Adams, Harkness & Hill, Inc.
60 State St.
Boston, MA 02109
(617)371-3900

Advent International
75 State St., 29th Fl.
Boston, MA 02109
(617)951-9400
Fax: (617)951-0566
Website: http://
www.adventinernational.com

American Research and Development
30 Federal St.
Boston, MA 02110-2508
(617)423-7500
Fax: (617)423-9655

Ascent Venture Partners
255 State St., 5th Fl.
Boston, MA 02109
(617)270-9400
Fax: (617)270-9401
E-mail: info@ascentvp.com
Website: http://www.ascentvp.com

Atlas Venture
222 Berkeley St.
Boston, MA 02116
(617)488-2200
Fax: (617)859-9292
Website: http://www.atlasventure.com

Axxon Capital
28 State St., 37th Fl.
Boston, MA 02109

(617)722-0980
Fax: (617)557-6014
Website: http://www.axxoncapital.com

BancBoston Capital/BancBoston Ventures
175 Federal St., 10th Fl.
Boston, MA 02110
(617)434-2509
Fax: (617)434-6175
Website: http://www.bancbostoncapital
.com

Boston Capital Ventures
Old City Hall
45 School St.
Boston, MA 02108
(617)227-6550
Fax: (617)227-3847
E-mail: info@bcv.com
Website: http://www.bcv.com

Boston Financial & Equity Corp.
20 Overland St.
PO Box 15071
Boston, MA 02215
(617)267-2900
Fax: (617)437-7601
E-mail: debbie@bfec.com

Boston Millennia Partners
30 Rowes Wharf
Boston, MA 02110
(617)428-5150
Fax: (617)428-5160
Website: http://www.millenniapartners.com

Bristol Investment Trust
842A Beacon St.
Boston, MA 02215-3199
(617)566-5212
Fax: (617)267-0932

Brook Venture Management LLC
50 Federal St., 5th Fl.
Boston, MA 02110
(617)451-8989
Fax: (617)451-2369
Website: http://www.brookventure.com

Burr, Egan, Deleage, and Co. (Boston)
200 Clarendon St., Ste. 3800
Boston, MA 02116
(617)262-7770
Fax: (617)262-9779

Cambridge/Samsung Partners
One Exeter Plaza
Ninth Fl.
Boston, MA 02116
(617)262-4440
Fax: (617)262-5562

Chestnut Street Partners, Inc.
75 State St., Ste. 2500
Boston, MA 02109
(617)345-7220
Fax: (617)345-7201
E-mail: chestnut@chestnutp.com

Claflin Capital Management, Inc.
10 Liberty Sq., Ste. 300
Boston, MA 02109
(617)426-6505
Fax: (617)482-0016
Website: http://www.claflincapital.com

Copley Venture Partners
99 Summer St., Ste. 1720
Boston, MA 02110
(617)737-1253
Fax: (617)439-0699

Corning Capital / Corning Technology Ventures
121 High Street, Ste. 400
Boston, MA 02110
(617)338-2656
Fax: (617)261-3864
Website: http://www.corningventures.com

Downer & Co.
211 Congress St.
Boston, MA 02110
(617)482-6200
Fax: (617)482-6201
E-mail: cdowner@downer.com
Website: http://www.downer.com

Fidelity Ventures
82 Devonshire St.
Boston, MA 02109
(617)563-6370
Fax: (617)476-9023
Website: http://www.fidelityventures.com

Greylock Management Corp. (Boston)
1 Federal St.
Boston, MA 02110-2065
(617)423-5525
Fax: (617)482-0059

Gryphon Ventures
222 Berkeley St., Ste.1600
Boston, MA 02116
(617)267-9191
Fax: (617)267-4293
E-mail: all@gryphoninc.com

Halpern, Denny & Co.
500 Boylston St.
Boston, MA 02116
(617)536-6602
Fax: (617)536-8535

Harbourvest Partners, LLC
1 Financial Center, 44th Fl.
Boston, MA 02111
(617)348-3707
Fax: (617)350-0305
Website: http://www.hvpllc.com

Highland Capital Partners
2 International Pl.
Boston, MA 02110
(617)981-1500
Fax: (617)531-1550
E-mail: info@hcp.com
Website: http://www.hcp.com

Lee Munder Venture Partners
John Hancock Tower T-53
200 Clarendon St.
Boston, MA 02103
(617)380-5600
Fax: (617)380-5601
Website: http://www.leemunder.com

M/C Venture Partners
75 State St., Ste. 2500
Boston, MA 02109
(617)345-7200
Fax: (617)345-7201
Website: http://
www.mcventurepartners.com

Massachusetts Capital Resources Co.
420 Boylston St.
Boston, MA 02116
(617)536-3900
Fax: (617)536-7930

Massachusetts Technology Development Corp. (MTDC)
148 State St.
Boston, MA 02109
(617)723-4920
Fax: (617)723-5983
E-mail: jhodgman@mtdc.com
Website: http://www.mtdc.com

New England Partners
One Boston Place, Ste. 2100
Boston, MA 02108
(617)624-8400
Fax: (617)624-8999
Website: http://www.nepartners.com

North Hill Ventures
Ten Post Office Square
11th Fl.
Boston, MA 02109
(617)788-2112
Fax: (617)788-2152
Website: http://www.northhillventures
.com

OneLiberty Ventures
150 Cambridge Park Dr.
Boston, MA 02140
(617)492-7280
Fax: (617)492-7290
Website: http://www.oneliberty.com

Schroder Ventures
Life Sciences
60 State St., Ste. 3650
Boston, MA 02109
(617)367-8100
Fax: (617)367-1590
Website: http://www.shroderventures
.com

Shawmut Capital Partners
75 Federal St., 18th Fl.
Boston, MA 02110
(617)368-4900
Fax: (617)368-4910
Website: http://www.shawmutcapital
.com

Solstice Capital LLC
15 Broad St., 3rd Fl.
Boston, MA 02109
(617)523-7733
Fax: (617)523-5827
E-mail: solticecapital@solcap.com

Spectrum Equity Investors
One International Pl., 29th Fl.
Boston, MA 02110
(617)464-4600
Fax: (617)464-4601
Website: http://www.spectrumequity.com

Spray Venture Partners
One Walnut St.
Boston, MA 02108
(617)305-4140
Fax: (617)305-4144
Website: http://www.sprayventure.com

The Still River Fund
100 Federal St., 29th Fl.
Boston, MA 02110
(617)348-2327
Fax: (617)348-2371
Website: http://www.stillriverfund.com

Summit Partners
600 Atlantic Ave., Ste. 2800
Boston, MA 02210-2227
(617)824-1000
Fax: (617)824-1159
Website: http://www.summitpartners.com

TA Associates, Inc. (Boston)
High Street Tower
125 High St., Ste. 2500

Boston, MA 02110
(617)574-6700
Fax: (617)574-6728
Website: http://www.ta.com

TVM Techno Venture Management
101 Arch St., Ste. 1950
Boston, MA 02110
(617)345-9320
Fax: (617)345-9377
E-mail: info@tvmvc.com
Website: http://www.tvmvc.com

UNC Ventures
64 Burough St.
Boston, MA 02130-4017
(617)482-7070
Fax: (617)522-2176

Venture Investment Management Company (VIMAC)
177 Milk St.
Boston, MA 02190-3410
(617)292-3300
Fax: (617)292-7979
E-mail: bzeisig@vimac.com
Website: http://www.vimac.com

MDT Advisers, Inc.
125 Cambridge Park Dr.
Cambridge, MA 02140-2314
(617)234-2200
Fax: (617)234-2210
Website: http://www.mdtai.com

TTC Ventures
One Main St., 6th Fl.
Cambridge, MA 02142
(617)528-3137
Fax: (617)577-1715
E-mail: info@ttcventures.com

Zero Stage Capital Co. Inc.
101 Main St., 17th Fl.
Cambridge, MA 02142
(617)876-5355
Fax: (617)876-1248
Website: http://www.zerostage.com

Atlantic Capital
164 Cushing Hwy.
Cohasset, MA 02025
(617)383-9449
Fax: (617)383-6040
E-mail: info@atlanticcap.com
Website: http://www.atlanticcap.com

Seacoast Capital Partners
55 Ferncroft Rd.
Danvers, MA 01923
(978)750-1300
Fax: (978)750-1301

E-mail: gdeli@seacoastcapital.com
Website: http://www.seacoastcapital.com

Sage Management Group
44 South Street
PO Box 2026
East Dennis, MA 02641
(508)385-7172
Fax: (508)385-7272
E-mail: sagemgt@capecod.net

Applied Technology
1 Cranberry Hill
Lexington, MA 02421-7397
(617)862-8622
Fax: (617)862-8367

Royalty Capital Management
5 Downing Rd.
Lexington, MA 02421-6918
(781)861-8490

Argo Global Capital
210 Broadway, Ste. 101
Lynnfield, MA 01940
(781)592-5250
Fax: (781)592-5230
Website: http://www.gsmcapital.com

Industry Ventures
6 Bayne Lane
Newburyport, MA 01950
(978)499-7606
Fax: (978)499-0686
Website: http://www.industryventures.com

Softbank Capital Partners
10 Langley Rd., Ste. 202
Newton Center, MA 02459
(617)928-9300
Fax: (617)928-9305
E-mail: clax@bvc.com

Advanced Technology Ventures (Boston)
281 Winter St., Ste. 350
Waltham, MA 02451
(781)290-0707
Fax: (781)684-0045
E-mail: info@atvcapital.com
Website: http://www.atvcapital.com

Castile Ventures
890 Winter St., Ste. 140
Waltham, MA 02451
(781)890-0060
Fax: (781)890-0065
Website: http://www.castileventures.com

Charles River Ventures
1000 Winter St., Ste. 3300
Waltham, MA 02451
(781)487-7060

Fax: (781)487-7065
Website: http://www.crv.com

Comdisco Venture Group (Waltham)
Totton Pond Office Center
400-1 Totten Pond Rd.
Waltham, MA 02451
(617)672-0250
Fax: (617)398-8099

Marconi Ventures
890 Winter St., Ste. 310
Waltham, MA 02451
(781)839-7177
Fax: (781)522-7477
Website: http://www.marconi.com

Matrix Partners
Bay Colony Corporate Center
1000 Winter St., Ste.4500
Waltham, MA 02451
(781)890-2244
Fax: (781)890-2288
Website: http://www.matrixpartners.com

North Bridge Venture Partners
950 Winter St. Ste. 4600
Waltham, MA 02451
(781)290-0004
Fax: (781)290-0999
E-mail: eta@nbvp.com

Polaris Venture Partners
Bay Colony Corporate Ctr.
1000 Winter St., Ste. 3500
Waltham, MA 02451
(781)290-0770
Fax: (781)290-0880
E-mail: partners@polarisventures.com
Website: http://www.polarisventures.com

Seaflower Ventures
Bay Colony Corporate Ctr.
1000 Winter St. Ste. 1000
Waltham, MA 02451
(781)466-9552
Fax: (781)466-9553
E-mail: moot@seaflower.com
Website: http://www.seaflower.com

Ampersand Ventures
55 William St., Ste. 240
Wellesley, MA 02481
(617)239-0700
Fax: (617)239-0824
E-mail: info@ampersandventures.com
Website: http://www.ampersandventures
.com

Battery Ventures (Boston)
20 William St., Ste. 200
Wellesley, MA 02481

(781)577-1000
Fax: (781)577-1001
Website: http://www.battery.com

Commonwealth Capital Ventures, L.P.
20 William St., Ste.225
Wellesley, MA 02481
(781)237-7373
Fax: (781)235-8627
Website: http://www.ccvlp.com

Fowler, Anthony & Company
20 Walnut St.
Wellesley, MA 02481
(781)237-4201
Fax: (781)237-7718

Gemini Investors
20 William St.
Wellesley, MA 02481
(781)237-7001
Fax: (781)237-7233

Grove Street Advisors Inc.
20 William St., Ste. 230
Wellesley, MA 02481
(781)263-6100
Fax: (781)263-6101
Website: http://www.grovestreetadvisors
.com

Mees Pierson Investeringsmaat B.V.
20 William St., Ste. 210
Wellesley, MA 02482
(781)239-7600
Fax: (781)239-0377

Norwest Equity Partners
40 William St., Ste. 305
Wellesley, MA 02481-3902
(781)237-5870
Fax: (781)237-6270
Website: http://www.norwestvp.com

Bessemer Venture Partners (Wellesley Hills)
83 Walnut St.
Wellesley Hills, MA 02481
(781)237-6050
Fax: (781)235-7576
E-mail: travis@bvpny.com
Website: http://www.bvp.com

Venture Capital Fund of New England
20 Walnut St., Ste. 120
Wellesley Hills, MA 02481-2175
(781)239-8262
Fax: (781)239-8263

Prism Venture Partners
100 Lowder Brook Dr., Ste. 2500
Westwood, MA 02090
(781)302-4000

Fax: (781)302-4040
E-mail: dwbaum@prismventure.com

Palmer Partners LP
200 Unicorn Park Dr.
Woburn, MA 01801
(781)933-5445
Fax: (781)933-0698

Michigan

Arbor Partners, L.L.C.
130 South First St.
Ann Arbor, MI 48104
(734)668-9000
Fax: (734)669-4195
Website: http://www.arborpartners.com

EDF Ventures
425 N. Main St.
Ann Arbor, MI 48104
(734)663-3213
Fax: (734)663-7358
E-mail: edf@edfvc.com
Website: http://www.edfvc.com

White Pines Management, L.L.C.
2401 Plymouth Rd., Ste. B
Ann Arbor, MI 48105
(734)747-9401
Fax: (734)747-9704
E-mail: ibund@whitepines.com
Website: http://www.whitepines.com

Wellmax, Inc.
3541 Bendway Blvd., Ste. 100
Bloomfield Hills, MI 48301
(248)646-3554
Fax: (248)646-6220

Venture Funding, Ltd.
Fisher Bldg.
3011 West Grand Blvd., Ste. 321
Detroit, MI 48202
(313)871-3606
Fax: (313)873-4935

Investcare Partners L.P. / GMA Capital LLC
32330 W. Twelve Mile Rd.
Farmington Hills, MI 48334
(248)489-9000
Fax: (248)489-8819
E-mail: gma@gmacapital.com
Website: http://www.gmacapital.com

Liberty Bidco Investment Corp.
30833 Northwestern Highway, Ste. 211
Farmington Hills, MI 48334
(248)626-6070
Fax: (248)626-6072

Seaflower Ventures
5170 Nicholson Rd.
PO Box 474
Fowlerville, MI 48836
(517)223-3335
Fax: (517)223-3337
E-mail: gibbons@seaflower.com
Website: http://www.seaflower.com

Ralph Wilson Equity Fund LLC
15400 E. Jefferson Ave.
Gross Pointe Park, MI 48230
(313)821-9122
Fax: (313)821-9101
Website: http://www.RalphWilsonEquity
Fund.com
J. Skip Simms, President

Minnesota

Development Corp. of Austin
1900 Eighth Ave., NW
Austin, MN 55912
(507)433-0346
Fax: (507)433-0361
E-mail: dca@smig.net
Website: http://www.spamtownusa.com

Northeast Ventures Corp.
802 Alworth Bldg.
Duluth, MN 55802
(218)722-9915
Fax: (218)722-9871

Medical Innovation Partners, Inc.
6450 City West Pkwy.
Eden Prairie, MN 55344-3245
(612)828-9616
Fax: (612)828-9596

St. Paul Venture Capital, Inc.
10400 Vicking Dr., Ste. 550
Eden Prairie, MN 55344
(612)995-7474
Fax: (612)995-7475
Website: http://www.stpaulvc.com

Cherry Tree Investments, Inc.
7601 France Ave. S, Ste. 150
Edina, MN 55435
(612)893-9012
Fax: (612)893-9036
Website: http://www.cherrytree.com

Shared Ventures, Inc.
6550 York Ave. S
Edina, MN 55435
(612)925-3411

Sherpa Partners LLC
5050 Lincoln Dr., Ste. 490
Edina, MN 55436
(952)942-1070

Fax: (952)942-1071
Website: http://www.sherpapartners.com

Affinity Capital Management
901 Marquette Ave., Ste. 1810
Minneapolis, MN 55402
(612)252-9900
Fax: (612)252-9911
Website: http://www.affinitycapital.com

Artesian Capital
1700 Foshay Tower
821 Marquette Ave.
Minneapolis, MN 55402
(612)334-5600
Fax: (612)334-5601
E-mail: artesian@artesian.com

Coral Ventures
60 S. 6th St., Ste. 3510
Minneapolis, MN 55402
(612)335-8666
Fax: (612)335-8668
Website: http://www.coralventures.com

Crescendo Venture Management, L.L.C.
800 LaSalle Ave., Ste. 2250
Minneapolis, MN 55402
(612)607-2800
Fax: (612)607-2801
Website: http://www.crescendoventures
.com

Gideon Hixon Venture
1900 Foshay Tower
821 Marquette Ave.
Minneapolis, MN 55402
(612)904-2314
Fax: (612)204-0913

Norwest Equity Partners
3600 IDS Center
80 S. 8th St.
Minneapolis, MN 55402
(612)215-1600
Fax: (612)215-1601
Website: http://www.norwestvp.com

Oak Investment Partners (Minneapolis)
4550 Norwest Center
90 S. 7th St.
Minneapolis, MN 55402
(612)339-9322
Fax: (612)337-8017
Website: http://www.oakinv.com

Pathfinder Venture Capital Funds (Minneapolis)
7300 Metro Blvd., Ste. 585
Minneapolis, MN 55439
(612)835-1121

Fax: (612)835-8389
E-mail: jahrens620@aol.com

U.S. Bancorp Piper Jaffray Ventures, Inc.
800 Nicollet Mall, Ste. 800
Minneapolis, MN 55402
(612)303-5686
Fax: (612)303-1350
Website: http://www.paperjaffrey
ventures.com

The Food Fund, Ltd. Partnership
5720 Smatana Dr., Ste. 300
Minnetonka, MN 55343
(612)939-3950
Fax: (612)939-8106

Mayo Medical Ventures
200 First St. SW
Rochester, MN 55905
(507)266-4586
Fax: (507)284-5410
Website: http://www.mayo.edu

Missouri

Bankers Capital Corp.
3100 Gillham Rd.
Kansas City, MO 64109
(816)531-1600
Fax: (816)531-1334

Capital for Business, Inc. (Kansas City)
1000 Walnut St., 18th Fl.
Kansas City, MO 64106
(816)234-2357
Fax: (816)234-2952
Website: http://www.capitalforbusiness
.com

De Vries & Co. Inc.
800 West 47th St.
Kansas City, MO 64112
(816)756-0055
Fax: (816)756-0061

InvestAmerica Venture Group Inc. (Kansas City)
Commerce Tower
911 Main St., Ste. 2424
Kansas City, MO 64105
(816)842-0114
Fax: (816)471-7339

Kansas City Equity Partners
233 W. 47th St.
Kansas City, MO 64112
(816)960-1771
Fax: (816)960-1777
Website: http://www.kcep.com

Bome Investors, Inc.
8000 Maryland Ave., Ste. 1190
St. Louis, MO 63105
(314)721-5707
Fax: (314)721-5135
Website: http://www.gatewayventures.com

Capital for Business, Inc. (St. Louis)
11 S. Meramac St., Ste. 1430
St. Louis, MO 63105
(314)746-7427
Fax: (314)746-8739
Website: http://www.capitalforbusiness
.com

Crown Capital Corp.
540 Maryville Centre Dr., Ste. 120
Saint Louis, MO 63141
(314)576-1201
Fax: (314)576-1525
Website: http://www.crown-cap.com

Gateway Associates L.P.
8000 Maryland Ave., Ste. 1190
St. Louis, MO 63105
(314)721-5707
Fax: (314)721-5135

Harbison Corp.
8112 Maryland Ave., Ste. 250
Saint Louis, MO 63105
(314)727-8200
Fax: (314)727-0249

Heartland Capital Fund, Ltd.
PO Box 642117
Omaha, NE 68154
(402)778-5124
Fax: (402)445-2370
Website: http://www.heartlandcapital
fund.com

Odin Capital Group
1625 Farnam St., Ste. 700
Omaha, NE 68102
(402)346-6200
Fax: (402)342-9311
Website: http://www.odincapital.com

Nevada

Edge Capital Investment Co. LLC
1350 E. Flamingo Rd., Ste. 3000
Las Vegas, NV 89119
(702)438-3343
E-mail: info@edgecapital.net
Website: http://www.edgecapital.net

The Benefit Capital Companies Inc.
PO Box 542
Logandale, NV 89021
(702)398-3222
Fax: (702)398-3700

Millennium Three Venture Group LLC
6880 South McCarran Blvd., Ste. A-11
Reno, NV 89509
(775)954-2020
Fax: (775)954-2023
Website: http://www.m3vg.com

New Jersey

Alan I. Goldman & Associates
497 Ridgewood Ave.
Glen Ridge, NJ 07028
(973)857-5680
Fax: (973)509-8856

CS Capital Partners LLC
328 Second St., Ste. 200
Lakewood, NJ 08701
(732)901-1111
Fax: (212)202-5071
Website: http://www.cs-capital.com

Edison Venture Fund
1009 Lenox Dr., Ste. 4
Lawrenceville, NJ 08648
(609)896-1900
Fax: (609)896-0066
E-mail: info@edisonventure.com
Website: http://www.edisonventure.com

Tappan Zee Capital Corp.
(New Jersey)
201 Lower Notch Rd.
PO Box 416
Little Falls, NJ 07424
(973)256-8280
Fax: (973)256-2841

The CIT Group/Venture Capital, Inc.
650 CIT Dr.
Livingston, NJ 07039
(973)740-5429
Fax: (973)740-5555
Website: http://www.cit.com

Capital Express, L.L.C.
1100 Valleybrook Ave.
Lyndhurst, NJ 07071
(201)438-8228
Fax: (201)438-5131
E-mail: niles@capitalexpress.com
Website: http://www.capitalexpress.com

Westford Technology Ventures, L.P.
17 Academy St.
Newark, NJ 07102
(973)624-2131
Fax: (973)624-2008

Accel Partners
1 Palmer Sq.
Princeton, NJ 08542
(609)683-4500

Fax: (609)683-4880
Website: http://www.accel.com

Cardinal Partners
221 Nassau St.
Princeton, NJ 08542
(609)924-6452
Fax: (609)683-0174
Website: http://www.cardinalhealth
partners.com

Domain Associates L.L.C.
One Palmer Sq., Ste. 515
Princeton, NJ 08542
(609)683-5656
Fax: (609)683-9789
Website: http://www.domainvc.com

Johnston Associates, Inc.
181 Cherry Valley Rd.
Princeton, NJ 08540
(609)924-3131
Fax: (609)683-7524
E-mail: jaincorp@aol.com

Kemper Ventures
Princeton Forrestal Village
155 Village Blvd.
Princeton, NJ 08540
(609)936-3035
Fax: (609)936-3051

Penny Lane Parnters
One Palmer Sq., Ste. 309
Princeton, NJ 08542
(609)497-4646
Fax: (609)497-0611

Early Stage Enterprises L.P.
995 Route 518
Skillman, NJ 08558
(609)921-8896
Fax: (609)921-8703
Website: http://www.esevc.com

MBW Management Inc.
1 Springfield Ave.
Summit, NJ 07901
(908)273-4060
Fax: (908)273-4430

BCI Advisors, Inc.
Glenpointe Center W.
Teaneck, NJ 07666
(201)836-3900
Fax: (201)836-6368
E-mail: info@bciadvisors.com
Website: http://www.bci partners.com

**Demuth, Folger & Wetherill / DFW
Capital Partners**
Glenpointe Center E., 5th Fl.
300 Frank W. Burr Blvd.

Teaneck, NJ 07666
(201)836-2233
Fax: (201)836-5666
Website: http://www.dfwcapital.com

First Princeton Capital Corp.
189 Berdan Ave., No. 131
Wayne, NJ 07470-3233
(973)278-3233
Fax: (973)278-4290
Website: http://www.lytellcatt.net

Edelson Technology Partners
300 Tice Blvd.
Woodcliff Lake, NJ 07675
(201)930-9898
Fax: (201)930-8899
Website: http://www.edelsontech.com

New Mexico

Bruce F. Glaspell & Associates
10400 Academy Rd. NE, Ste. 313
Albuquerque, NM 87111
(505)292-4505
Fax: (505)292-4258

High Desert Ventures, Inc.
6101 Imparata St. NE, Ste. 1721
Albuquerque, NM 87111
(505)797-3330
Fax: (505)338-5147

New Business Capital Fund, Ltd.
5805 Torreon NE
Albuquerque, NM 87109
(505)822-8445

SBC Ventures
10400 Academy Rd. NE, Ste. 313
Albuquerque, NM 87111
(505)292-4505
Fax: (505)292-4528

Technology Ventures Corp.
1155 University Blvd. SE
Albuquerque, NM 87106
(505)246-2882
Fax: (505)246-2891

New York

**New York State Science & Technology
Foundation**

**Small Business Technology
Investment Fund**
99 Washington Ave., Ste. 1731
Albany, NY 12210
(518)473-9741
Fax: (518)473-6876

Rand Capital Corp.
2200 Rand Bldg.
Buffalo, NY 14203
(716)853-0802
Fax: (716)854-8480
Website: http://www.randcapital.com

Seed Capital Partners
620 Main St.
Buffalo, NY 14202
(716)845-7520
Fax: (716)845-7539
Website: http://www.seedcp.com

Coleman Venture Group
5909 Northern Blvd.
PO Box 224
East Norwich, NY 11732
(516)626-3642
Fax: (516)626-9722

Vega Capital Corp.
45 Knollwood Rd.
Elmsford, NY 10523
(914)345-9500
Fax: (914)345-9505

Herbert Young Securities, Inc.
98 Cuttermill Rd.
Great Neck, NY 11021
(516)487-8300
Fax: (516)487-8319

Sterling/Carl Marks Capital, Inc.
175 Great Neck Rd., Ste. 408
Great Neck, NY 11021
(516)482-7374
Fax: (516)487-0781
E-mail: stercrlmar@aol.com
Website: http://
www.serlingcarlmarks.com

Impex Venture Management Co.
PO Box 1570
Green Island, NY 12183
(518)271-8008
Fax: (518)271-9101

Corporate Venture Partners L.P.
200 Sunset Park
Ithaca, NY 14850
(607)257-6323
Fax: (607)257-6128

Arthur P. Gould & Co.
One Wilshire Dr.
Lake Success, NY 11020
(516)773-3000
Fax: (516)773-3289

Dauphin Capital Partners
108 Forest Ave.
Locust Valley, NY 11560

(516)759-3339
Fax: (516)759-3322
Website: http://www.dauphincapital.com

550 Digital Media Ventures
555 Madison Ave., 10th Fl.
New York, NY 10022
Website: http://www.550dmv.com

Aberlyn Capital Management Co., Inc.
500 Fifth Ave.
New York, NY 10110
(212)391-7750
Fax: (212)391-7762

Adler & Company
342 Madison Ave., Ste. 807
New York, NY 10173
(212)599-2535
Fax: (212)599-2526

Alimansky Capital Group, Inc.
605 Madison Ave., Ste. 300
New York, NY 10022-1901
(212)832-7300
Fax: (212)832-7338

Allegra Partners
515 Madison Ave., 29th Fl.
New York, NY 10022
(212)826-9080
Fax: (212)759-2561

The Argentum Group
The Chyrsler Bldg.
405 Lexington Ave.
New York, NY 10174
(212)949-6262
Fax: (212)949-8294
Website: http://www.argentumgroup.com

Axavision Inc.
14 Wall St., 26th Fl.
New York, NY 10005
(212)619-4000
Fax: (212)619-7202

Bedford Capital Corp.
18 East 48th St., Ste. 1800
New York, NY 10017
(212)688-5700
Fax: (212)754-4699
E-mail: info@bedfordnyc.com
Website: http://www.bedfordnyc.com

Bloom & Co.
950 Third Ave.
New York, NY 10022
(212)838-1858
Fax: (212)838-1843

Bristol Capital Management
300 Park Ave., 17th Fl.
New York, NY 10022
(212)572-6306
Fax: (212)705-4292

**Citicorp Venture Capital Ltd.
(New York City)**
399 Park Ave., 14th Fl.
Zone 4
New York, NY 10043
(212)559-1127
Fax: (212)888-2940

CM Equity Partners
135 E. 57th St.
New York, NY 10022
(212)909-8428
Fax: (212)980-2630

Cohen & Co., L.L.C.
800 Third Ave.
New York, NY 10022
(212)317-2250
Fax: (212)317-2255
E-mail: nlcohen@aol.com

**Cornerstone Equity Investors,
L.L.C.**
717 5th Ave., Ste. 1100
New York, NY 10022
(212)753-0901
Fax: (212)826-6798
Website: http://www.cornerstone-
equity.com

CW Group, Inc.
1041 3rd Ave., 2nd fl.
New York, NY 10021
(212)308-5266
Fax: (212)644-0354
Website: http://www.cwventures.com

DH Blair Investment Banking Corp.
44 Wall St., 2nd Fl.
New York, NY 10005
(212)495-5000
Fax: (212)269-1438

Dresdner Kleinwort Capital
75 Wall St.
New York, NY 10005
(212)429-3131
Fax: (212)429-3139
Website: http://www.dresdnerkb.com

East River Ventures, L.P.
645 Madison Ave., 22nd Fl.
New York, NY 10022
(212)644-2322
Fax: (212)644-5498

Easton Hunt Capital Partners
641 Lexington Ave., 21st Fl.
New York, NY 10017
(212)702-0950
Fax: (212)702-0952
Website: http://www.eastoncapital.com

Elk Associates Funding Corp.
747 3rd Ave., Ste. 4C
New York, NY 10017
(212)355-2449
Fax: (212)759-3338

EOS Partners, L.P.
320 Park Ave., 22nd Fl.
New York, NY 10022
(212)832-5800
Fax: (212)832-5815
E-mail: mfirst@eospartners.com
Website: http://www.eospartners.com

Euclid Partners
45 Rockefeller Plaza, Ste. 3240
New York, NY 10111
(212)218-6880
Fax: (212)218-6877
E-mail: graham@euclidpartners.com
Website: http://www.euclidpartners.com

Evergreen Capital Partners, Inc.
150 East 58th St.
New York, NY 10155
(212)813-0758
Fax: (212)813-0754

Exeter Capital L.P.
10 E. 53rd St.
New York, NY 10022
(212)872-1172
Fax: (212)872-1198
E-mail: exeter@usa.net

Financial Technology Research Corp.
518 Broadway
Penthouse
New York, NY 10012
(212)625-9100
Fax: (212)431-0300
E-mail: fintek@financier.com

4C Ventures
237 Park Ave., Ste. 801
New York, NY 10017
(212)692-3680
Fax: (212)692-3685
Website: http://www.4cventures.com

Fusient Ventures
99 Park Ave., 20th Fl.
New York, NY 10016
(212)972-8999
Fax: (212)972-9876

E-mail: info@fusient.com
Website: http://www.fusient.com

Generation Capital Partners
551 Fifth Ave., Ste. 3100
New York, NY 10176
(212)450-8507
Fax: (212)450-8550
Website: http://www.genpartners.com

Golub Associates, Inc.
555 Madison Ave.
New York, NY 10022
(212)750-6060
Fax: (212)750-5505

Hambro America Biosciences Inc.
650 Madison Ave., 21st Floor
New York, NY 10022
(212)223-7400
Fax: (212)223-0305

Hanover Capital Corp.
505 Park Ave., 15th Fl.
New York, NY 10022
(212)755-1222
Fax: (212)935-1787

Harvest Partners, Inc.
280 Park Ave, 33rd Fl.
New York, NY 10017
(212)559-6300
Fax: (212)812-0100
Website: http://www.harvpart.com

Holding Capital Group, Inc.
10 E. 53rd St., 30th Fl.
New York, NY 10022
(212)486-6670
Fax: (212)486-0843

Hudson Venture Partners
660 Madison Ave., 14th Fl.
New York, NY 10021-8405
(212)644-9797
Fax: (212)644-7430
Website: http://www.hudsonptr.com

IBJS Capital Corp.
1 State St., 9th Fl.
New York, NY 10004
(212)858-2018
Fax: (212)858-2768

InterEquity Capital Partners, L.P.
220 5th Ave.
New York, NY 10001
(212)779-2022
Fax: (212)779-2103
Website: http://www.interequity-capital.com

The Jordan Edmiston Group Inc.
150 East 52nd St., 18th Fl.
New York, NY 10022
(212)754-0710
Fax: (212)754-0337

Josephberg, Grosz and Co., Inc.
633 3rd Ave., 13th Fl.
New York, NY 10017
(212)974-9926
Fax: (212)397-5832

J.P. Morgan Capital Corp.
60 Wall St.
New York, NY 10260-0060
(212)648-9000
Fax: (212)648-5002
Website: http://www.jpmorgan.com

The Lambda Funds
380 Lexington Ave., 54th Fl.
New York, NY 10168
(212)682-3454
Fax: (212)682-9231

Lepercq Capital Management Inc.
1675 Broadway
New York, NY 10019
(212)698-0795
Fax: (212)262-0155

Loeb Partners Corp.
61 Broadway, Ste. 2400
New York, NY 10006
(212)483-7000
Fax: (212)574-2001

Madison Investment Partners
660 Madison Ave.
New York, NY 10021
(212)223-2600
Fax: (212)223-8208

MC Capital Inc.
520 Madison Ave., 16th Fl.
New York, NY 10022
(212)644-0841
Fax: (212)644-2926

McCown, De Leeuw and Co. (New York)
65 E. 55th St., 36th Fl.
New York, NY 10022
(212)355-5500
Fax: (212)355-6283
Website: http://www.mdcpartners.com

Morgan Stanley Venture Partners
1221 Avenue of the Americas, 33rd Fl.
New York, NY 10020
(212)762-7900
Fax: (212)762-8424
E-mail: msventures@ms.com
Website: http://www.msvp.com

Nazem and Co.
645 Madison Ave., 12th Fl.
New York, NY 10022
(212)371-7900
Fax: (212)371-2150

Needham Capital Management, L.L.C.
445 Park Ave.
New York, NY 10022
(212)371-8300
Fax: (212)705-0299
Website: http://www.needhamco.com

Norwood Venture Corp.
1430 Broadway, Ste. 1607
New York, NY 10018
(212)869-5075
Fax: (212)869-5331
E-mail: nvc@mail.idt.net
Website: http://www.norven.com

Noveltek Venture Corp.
521 Fifth Ave., Ste. 1700
New York, NY 10175
(212)286-1963

Paribas Principal, Inc.
787 7th Ave.
New York, NY 10019
(212)841-2005
Fax: (212)841-3558

Patricof & Co. Ventures, Inc. (New York)
445 Park Ave.
New York, NY 10022
(212)753-6300
Fax: (212)319-6155
Website: http://www.patricof.com

The Platinum Group, Inc.
350 Fifth Ave, Ste. 7113
New York, NY 10118
(212)736-4300
Fax: (212)736-6086
Website: http://www.platinumgroup.com

Pomona Capital
780 Third Ave., 28th Fl.
New York, NY 10017
(212)593-3639
Fax: (212)593-3987
Website: http://www.pomonacapital.com

Prospect Street Ventures
10 East 40th St., 44th Fl.
New York, NY 10016
(212)448-0702
Fax: (212)448-9652
E-mail: wkohler@prospectstreet.com
Website: http://www.prospectstreet.com

Regent Capital Management
505 Park Ave., Ste. 1700
New York, NY 10022
(212)735-9900
Fax: (212)735-9908

Rothschild Ventures, Inc.
1251 Avenue of the Americas, 51st Fl.
New York, NY 10020
(212)403-3500
Fax: (212)403-3652
Website: http://www.nmrothschild.com

Sandler Capital Management
767 Fifth Ave., 45th Fl.
New York, NY 10153
(212)754-8100
Fax: (212)826-0280

Siguler Guff & Company
630 Fifth Ave., 16th Fl.
New York, NY 10111
(212)332-5100
Fax: (212)332-5120

Spencer Trask Ventures Inc.
535 Madison Ave.
New York, NY 10022
(212)355-5565
Fax: (212)751-3362
Website: http://www.spencertrask.com

Sprout Group (New York City)
277 Park Ave.
New York, NY 10172
(212)892-3600
Fax: (212)892-3444
E-mail: info@sproutgroup.com
Website: http://www.sproutgroup.com

US Trust Private Equity
114 W.47th St.
New York, NY 10036
(212)852-3949
Fax: (212)852-3759
Website: http://www.ustrust.com/privateequity

Vencon Management Inc.
301 West 53rd St., Ste. 10F
New York, NY 10019
(212)581-8787
Fax: (212)397-4126
Website: http://www.venconinc.com

Venrock Associates
30 Rockefeller Plaza, Ste. 5508
New York, NY 10112
(212)649-5600
Fax: (212)649-5788
Website: http://www.venrock.com

Venture Capital Fund of America, Inc.
509 Madison Ave., Ste. 812
New York, NY 10022
(212)838-5577
Fax: (212)838-7614
E-mail: mail@vcfa.com
Website: http://www.vcfa.com

Venture Opportunities Corp.
150 E. 58th St.
New York, NY 10155
(212)832-3737
Fax: (212)980-6603

Warburg Pincus Ventures, Inc.
466 Lexington Ave., 11th Fl.
New York, NY 10017
(212)878-9309
Fax: (212)878-9200
Website: http://www.warburgpincus.com

Wasserstein, Perella & Co. Inc.
31 W. 52nd St., 27th Fl.
New York, NY 10019
(212)702-5691
Fax: (212)969-7879

Welsh, Carson, Anderson, & Stowe
320 Park Ave., Ste. 2500
New York, NY 10022-6815
(212)893-9500
Fax: (212)893-9575

Whitney and Co. (New York)
630 Fifth Ave. Ste. 3225
New York, NY 10111
(212)332-2400
Fax: (212)332-2422
Website: http://www.jhwitney.com

Winthrop Ventures
74 Trinity Place, Ste. 600
New York, NY 10006
(212)422-0100

The Pittsford Group
8 Lodge Pole Rd.
Pittsford, NY 14534
(716)223-3523

Genesee Funding
70 Linden Oaks, 3rd Fl.
Rochester, NY 14625
(716)383-5550
Fax: (716)383-5305

Gabelli Multimedia Partners
One Corporate Center
Rye, NY 10580
(914)921-5395
Fax: (914)921-5031

Stamford Financial
108 Main St.
Stamford, NY 12167
(607)652-3311
Fax: (607)652-6301
Website: http://www.stamfordfinancial
.com

Northwood Ventures LLC
485 Underhill Blvd., Ste. 205
Syosset, NY 11791
(516)364-5544
Fax: (516)364-0879
E-mail: northwood@northwood.com
Website: http://www.northwoodventures
.com

Exponential Business Development Co.
216 Walton St.
Syracuse, NY 13202-1227
(315)474-4500
Fax: (315)474-4682
E-mail: dirksonn@aol.com
Website: http://www.exponential-ny.com

Onondaga Venture Capital Fund Inc.
714 State Tower Bldg.
Syracuse, NY 13202
(315)478-0157
Fax: (315)478-0158

Bessemer Venture Partners (Westbury)
1400 Old Country Rd., Ste. 109
Westbury, NY 11590
(516)997-2300
Fax: (516)997-2371
E-mail: bob@bvpny.com
Website: http://www.bvp.com

Ovation Capital Partners
120 Bloomingdale Rd., 4th Fl.
White Plains, NY 10605
(914)258-0011
Fax: (914)684-0848
Website: http://www.ovationcapital.com

North Carolina

Carolinas Capital Investment Corp.
1408 Biltmore Dr.
Charlotte, NC 28207
(704)375-3888
Fax: (704)375-6226

First Union Capital Partners
1st Union Center, 12th Fl.
301 S. College St.
Charlotte, NC 28288-0732
(704)383-0000
Fax: (704)374-6711
Website: http://www.fucp.com

Frontier Capital LLC
525 North Tryon St., Ste. 1700
Charlotte, NC 28202
(704)414-2880
Fax: (704)414-2881
Website: http://www.frontierfunds.com

Kitty Hawk Capital
2700 Coltsgate Rd., Ste. 202
Charlotte, NC 28211
(704)362-3909
Fax: (704)362-2774
Website: http://www.kittyhawkcapital.com

Piedmont Venture Partners
One Morrocroft Centre
6805 Morisson Blvd., Ste. 380
Charlotte, NC 28211
(704)731-5200
Fax: (704)365-9733
Website: http://www.piedmontvp.com

Ruddick Investment Co.
1800 Two First Union Center
Charlotte, NC 28282
(704)372-5404
Fax: (704)372-6409

The Shelton Companies Inc.
3600 One First Union Center
301 S. College St.
Charlotte, NC 28202
(704)348-2200
Fax: (704)348-2260

Wakefield Group
1110 E. Morehead St.
PO Box 36329
Charlotte, NC 28236
(704)372-0355
Fax: (704)372-8216
Website: http://
www.wakefieldgroup.com

Aurora Funds, Inc.
2525 Meridian Pkwy., Ste. 220
Durham, NC 27713
(919)484-0400
Fax: (919)484-0444
Website: http://www.aurora funds.com

Intersouth Partners
3211 Shannon Rd., Ste. 610
Durham, NC 27707
(919)493-6640
Fax: (919)493-6649
E-mail: info@intersouth.com
Website: http://www.intersouth.com

Geneva Merchant Banking Partners
PO Box 21962
Greensboro, NC 27420

(336)275-7002
Fax: (336)275-9155
Website: http://www.genevamerchant
bank.com

The North Carolina Enterprise Fund, L.P.
3600 Glenwood Ave., Ste. 107
Raleigh, NC 27612
(919)781-2691
Fax: (919)783-9195
Website: http://www.ncef.com

Ohio

Senmend Medical Ventures
4445 Lake Forest Dr., Ste. 600
Cincinnati, OH 45242
(513)563-3264
Fax: (513)563-3261

The Walnut Group
312 Walnut St., Ste. 1151
Cincinnati, OH 45202
(513)651-3300
Fax: (513)929-4441
Website: http://www.thewalnutgroup.com

Brantley Venture Partners
20600 Chagrin Blvd., Ste. 1150
Cleveland, OH 44122
(216)283-4800
Fax: (216)283-5324

Clarion Capital Corp.
1801 E. 9th St., Ste. 1120
Cleveland, OH 44114
(216)687-1096
Fax: (216)694-3545

Crystal Internet Venture Fund, L.P.
1120 Chester Ave., Ste. 418
Cleveland, OH 44114
(216)263-5515
Fax: (216)263-5518
E-mail: jf@crystalventure.com
Website: http://www.crystalventure.com

Key Equity Capital Corp.
127 Public Sq., 28th Fl.
Cleveland, OH 44114
(216)689-3000
Fax: (216)689-3204
Website: http://www.keybank.com

Morgenthaler Ventures
Terminal Tower
50 Public Square, Ste. 2700
Cleveland, OH 44113
(216)416-7500
Fax: (216)416-7501
Website: http://www.morgenthaler.com

National City Equity Partners Inc.
1965 E. 6th St.
Cleveland, OH 44114
(216)575-2491
Fax: (216)575-9965
E-mail: nccap@aol.com
Website: http://www.nccapital.com

Primus Venture Partners, Inc.
5900 LanderBrook Dr., Ste. 2000
Cleveland, OH 44124-4020
(440)684-7300
Fax: (440)684-7342
E-mail: info@primusventure.com
Website: http://www.primusventure.com

Banc One Capital Partners (Columbus)
150 East Gay St., 24th Fl.
Columbus, OH 43215
(614)217-1100
Fax: (614)217-1217

Battelle Venture Partners
505 King Ave.
Columbus, OH 43201
(614)424-7005
Fax: (614)424-4874

Ohio Partners
62 E. Board St., 3rd Fl.
Columbus, OH 43215
(614)621-1210
Fax: (614)621-1240

Capital Technology Group, L.L.C.
400 Metro Place North, Ste. 300
Dublin, OH 43017
(614)792-6066
Fax: (614)792-6036
E-mail: info@capitaltech.com
Website: http://www.capitaltech.com

Northwest Ohio Venture Fund
4159 Holland-Sylvania R., Ste. 202
Toledo, OH 43623
(419)824-8144
Fax: (419)882-2035
E-mail: bwalsh@novf.com

Oklahoma

Moore & Associates
1000 W. Wilshire Blvd., Ste. 370
Oklahoma City, OK 73116
(405)842-3660
Fax: (405)842-3763

Chisholm Private Capital Partners
100 West 5th St., Ste. 805
Tulsa, OK 74103
(918)584-0440
Fax: (918)584-0441
Website: http://www.chisholmvc.com

Davis, Tuttle Venture Partners (Tulsa)
320 S. Boston, Ste. 1000
Tulsa, OK 74103-3703
(918)584-7272
Fax: (918)582-3404
Website: http://www.davistuttle.com

RBC Ventures
2627 E. 21st St.
Tulsa, OK 74114
(918)744-5607
Fax: (918)743-8630

Oregon

Utah Ventures II LP
10700 SW Beaverton-Hillsdale Hwy., Ste. 548
Beaverton, OR 97005
(503)574-4125
E-mail: adishlip@uven.com
Website: http://www.uven.com

Orien Ventures
14523 SW Westlake Dr.
Lake Oswego, OR 97035
(503)699-1680
Fax: (503)699-1681

OVP Venture Partners (Lake Oswego)
340 Oswego Pointe Dr., Ste. 200
Lake Oswego, OR 97034
(503)697-8766
Fax: (503)697-8863
E-mail: info@ovp.com
Website: http://www.ovp.com

Oregon Resource and Technology Development Fund
4370 NE Halsey St., Ste. 233
Portland, OR 97213-1566
(503)282-4462
Fax: (503)282-2976

Shaw Venture Partners
400 SW 6th Ave., Ste. 1100
Portland, OR 97204-1636
(503)228-4884
Fax: (503)227-2471
Website: http://www.shawventures.com

Pennsylvania

Mid-Atlantic Venture Funds
125 Goodman Dr.
Bethlehem, PA 18015
(610)865-6550
Fax: (610)865-6427
Website: http://www.mavf.com

Newspring Ventures
100 W. Elm St., Ste. 101
Conshohocken, PA 19428

(610)567-2380
Fax: (610)567-2388
Website: http://www.newsprintventures.com

Patricof & Co. Ventures, Inc.
455 S. Gulph Rd., Ste. 410
King of Prussia, PA 19406
(610)265-0286
Fax: (610)265-4959
Website: http://www.patricof.com

Loyalhanna Venture Fund
527 Cedar Way, Ste. 104
Oakmont, PA 15139
(412)820-7035
Fax: (412)820-7036

Innovest Group Inc.
2000 Market St., Ste. 1400
Philadelphia, PA 19103
(215)564-3960
Fax: (215)569-3272

Keystone Venture Capital Management Co.
1601 Market St., Ste. 2500
Philadelphia, PA 19103
(215)241-1200
Fax: (215)241-1211
Website: http://www.keystonevc.com

Liberty Venture Partners
2005 Market St., Ste. 200
Philadelphia, PA 19103
(215)282-4484
Fax: (215)282-4485
E-mail: info@libertyvp.com
Website: http://www.libertyvp.com

Penn Janney Fund, Inc.
1801 Market St., 11th Fl.
Philadelphia, PA 19103
(215)665-4447
Fax: (215)557-0820

Philadelphia Ventures, Inc.
The Bellevue
200 S. Broad St.
Philadelphia, PA 19102
(215)732-4445
Fax: (215)732-4644

Birchmere Ventures Inc.
2000 Technology Dr.
Pittsburgh, PA 15219-3109
(412)803-8000
Fax: (412)687-8139
Website: http://www.birchmerevc.com

CEO Venture Fund
2000 Technology Dr., Ste. 160
Pittsburgh, PA 15219-3109

(412)687-3451
Fax: (412)687-8139
E-mail: ceofund@aol.com
Website: http://www.ceoventurefund.com

Innovation Works Inc.
2000 Technology Dr., Ste. 250
Pittsburgh, PA 15219
(412)681-1520
Fax: (412)681-2625
Website: http://www.innovationworks.org

Keystone Minority Capital Fund L.P.
1801 Centre Ave., Ste. 201
Williams Sq.
Pittsburgh, PA 15219
(412)338-2230
Fax: (412)338-2224

Mellon Ventures, Inc.
One Mellon Bank Ctr., Rm. 3500
Pittsburgh, PA 15258
(412)236-3594
Fax: (412)236-3593
Website: http://www.mellonventures.com

Pennsylvania Growth Fund
5850 Ellsworth Ave., Ste. 303
Pittsburgh, PA 15232
(412)661-1000
Fax: (412)361-0676

Point Venture Partners
The Century Bldg.
130 Seventh St., 7th Fl.
Pittsburgh, PA 15222
(412)261-1966
Fax: (412)261-1718

Cross Atlantic Capital Partners
5 Radnor Corporate Center, Ste. 555
Radnor, PA 19087
(610)995-2650
Fax: (610)971-2062
Website: http://www.xacp.com

Meridian Venture Partners (Radnor)
The Radnor Court Bldg., Ste. 140
259 Radnor-Chester Rd.
Radnor, PA 19087
(610)254-2999
Fax: (610)254-2996
E-mail: mvpart@ix.netcom.com

TDH
919 Conestoga Rd., Bldg. 1, Ste. 301
Rosemont, PA 19010
(610)526-9970
Fax: (610)526-9971

Adams Capital Management
500 Blackburn Ave.
Sewickley, PA 15143

(412)749-9454
Fax: (412)749-9459
Website: http://www.acm.com

S.R. One, Ltd.
Four Tower Bridge
200 Barr Harbor Dr., Ste. 250
W. Conshohocken, PA 19428
(610)567-1000
Fax: (610)567-1039

Greater Philadelphia Venture Capital Corp.
351 East Conestoga Rd.
Wayne, PA 19087
(610)688-6829
Fax: (610)254-8958

PA Early Stage
435 Devon Park Dr., Bldg. 500, Ste. 510
Wayne, PA 19087
(610)293-4075
Fax: (610)254-4240
Website: http://www.paearlystage.com

The Sandhurst Venture Fund, L.P.
351 E. Constoga Rd.
Wayne, PA 19087
(610)254-8900
Fax: (610)254-8958

TL Ventures
700 Bldg.
435 Devon Park Dr.
Wayne, PA 19087-1990
(610)975-3765
Fax: (610)254-4210
Website: http://www.tlventures.com

Rockhill Ventures, Inc.
100 Front St., Ste. 1350
West Conshohocken, PA 19428
(610)940-0300
Fax: (610)940-0301

Puerto Rico

Advent-Morro Equity Partners
Banco Popular Bldg.
206 Tetuan St., Ste. 903
San Juan, PR 00902
(787)725-5285
Fax: (787)721-1735

North America Investment Corp.
Mercantil Plaza, Ste. 813
PO Box 191831
San Juan, PR 00919
(787)754-6178
Fax: (787)754-6181

Rhode Island

Manchester Humphreys, Inc.
40 Westminster St., Ste. 900
Providence, RI 02903
(401)454-0400
Fax: (401)454-0403

Navis Partners
50 Kennedy Plaza, 12th Fl.
Providence, RI 02903
(401)278-6770
Fax: (401)278-6387
Website: http://www.navispartners.com

South Carolina

Capital Insights, L.L.C.
PO Box 27162
Greenville, SC 29616-2162
(864)242-6832
Fax: (864)242-6755
E-mail: jwarner@capitalinsights.com
Website: http://www.capitalinsights.com

Transamerica Mezzanine Financing
7 N. Laurens St., Ste. 603
Greenville, SC 29601
(864)232-6198
Fax: (864)241-4444

Tennessee

Valley Capital Corp.
Krystal Bldg.
100 W. Martin Luther King Blvd., Ste. 212
Chattanooga, TN 37402
(423)265-1557
Fax: (423)265-1588

Coleman Swenson Booth Inc.
237 2nd Ave. S
Franklin, TN 37064-2649
(615)791-9462
Fax: (615)791-9636
Website: http://www.colemanswenson.com

Capital Services & Resources, Inc.
5159 Wheelis Dr., Ste. 106
Memphis, TN 38117
(901)761-2156
Fax: (907)767-0060

Paradigm Capital Partners LLC
6410 Poplar Ave., Ste. 395
Memphis, TN 38119
(901)682-6060
Fax: (901)328-3061

SSM Ventures
845 Crossover Ln., Ste. 140
Memphis, TN 38117
(901)767-1131

Fax: (901)767-1135
Website: http://www.ssmventures.com

Capital Across America L.P.
501 Union St., Ste. 201
Nashville, TN 37219
(615)254-1414
Fax: (615)254-1856
Website: http://www.capitalacross
america.com

Equitas L.P.
2000 Glen Echo Rd., Ste. 101
PO Box 158838
Nashville, TN 37215-8838
(615)383-8673
Fax: (615)383-8693

Massey Burch Capital Corp.
One Burton Hills Blvd., Ste. 350
Nashville, TN 37215
(615)665-3221
Fax: (615)665-3240
E-mail: tcalton@masseyburch.com
Website: http://www.masseyburch.com

Nelson Capital Corp.
3401 West End Ave., Ste. 300
Nashville, TN 37203
(615)292-8787
Fax: (615)385-3150

Texas

Phillips-Smith Specialty Retail Group
5080 Spectrum Dr., Ste. 805 W
Addison, TX 75001
(972)387-0725
Fax: (972)458-2560
E-mail: pssrg@aol.com
Website: http://www.phillips-smith.com

Austin Ventures, L.P.
701 Brazos St., Ste. 1400
Austin, TX 78701
(512)485-1900
Fax: (512)476-3952
E-mail: info@ausven.com
Website: http://www.austinventures.com

The Capital Network
3925 West Braker Lane, Ste. 406
Austin, TX 78759-5321
(512)305-0826
Fax: (512)305-0836

Techxas Ventures LLC
5000 Plaza on the Lake
Austin, TX 78746
(512)343-0118
Fax: (512)343-1879
E-mail: bruce@techxas.com
Website: http://www.techxas.com

Alliance Financial of Houston
218 Heather Ln.
Conroe, TX 77385-9013
(936)447-3300
Fax: (936)447-4222

Amerimark Capital Corp.
1111 W. Mockingbird, Ste. 1111
Dallas, TX 75247
(214)638-7878
Fax: (214)638-7612
E-mail: amerimark@amcapital.com
Website: http://www.amcapital.com

AMT Venture Partners / AMT Capital Ltd.
5220 Spring Valley Rd., Ste. 600
Dallas, TX 75240
(214)905-9757
Fax: (214)905-9761
Website: http://www.amtcapital.com

Arkoma Venture Partners
5950 Berkshire Lane, Ste. 1400
Dallas, TX 75225
(214)739-3515
Fax: (214)739-3572
E-mail: joelf@arkomavp.com

Capital Southwest Corp.
12900 Preston Rd., Ste. 700
Dallas, TX 75230
(972)233-8242
Fax: (972)233-7362
Website: http://www.capitalsouthwest.com

Dali, Hook Partners
One Lincoln Center, Ste. 1550
5400 LBJ Freeway
Dallas, TX 75240
(972)991-5457
Fax: (972)991-5458
E-mail: dhook@hookpartners.com
Website: http://www.hookpartners.com

HO2 Partners
Two Galleria Tower
13455 Noel Rd., Ste. 1670
Dallas, TX 75240
(972)702-1144
Fax: (972)702-8234
Website: http://www.ho2.com

Interwest Partners (Dallas)
2 Galleria Tower
13455 Noel Rd., Ste. 1670
Dallas, TX 75240
(972)392-7279
Fax: (972)490-6348
Website: http://www.interwest.com

Kahala Investments, Inc.
8214 Westchester Dr., Ste. 715
Dallas, TX 75225
(214)987-0077
Fax: (214)987-2332

MESBIC Ventures Holding Co.
2435 North Central Expressway, Ste. 200
Dallas, TX 75080
(972)991-1597
Fax: (972)991-4770
Website: http://www.mvhc.com

North Texas MESBIC, Inc.
9500 Forest Lane, Ste. 430
Dallas, TX 75243
(214)221-3565
Fax: (214)221-3566

Richard Jaffe & Company, Inc,
7318 Royal Cir.
Dallas, TX 75230
(214)265-9397
Fax: (214)739-1845

Sevin Rosen Management Co.
13455 Noel Rd., Ste. 1670
Dallas, TX 75240
(972)702-1100
Fax: (972)702-1103
E-mail: info@srfunds.com
Website: http://www.srfunds.com

Stratford Capital Partners, L.P.
300 Crescent Ct., Ste. 500
Dallas, TX 75201
(214)740-7377
Fax: (214)720-7393
E-mail: stratcap@hmtf.com

Sunwestern Investment Group
12221 Merit Dr., Ste. 935
Dallas, TX 75251
(972)239-5650
Fax: (972)701-0024

Wingate Partners
750 N. St. Paul St., Ste. 1200
Dallas, TX 75201
(214)720-1313
Fax: (214)871-8799

Buena Venture Associates
201 Main St., 32nd Fl.
Fort Worth, TX 76102
(817)339-7400
Fax: (817)390-8408
Website: http://www.buenaventure.com

The Catalyst Group
3 Riverway, Ste. 770
Houston, TX 77056
(713)623-8133

Fax: (713)623-0473
E-mail: herman@thecatalystgroup.net
Website: http://www.thecatalystgroup.net

Cureton & Co., Inc.
1100 Louisiana, Ste. 3250
Houston, TX 77002
(713)658-9806
Fax: (713)658-0476

Davis, Tuttle Venture Partners (Dallas)
8 Greenway Plaza, Ste. 1020
Houston, TX 77046
(713)993-0440
Fax: (713)621-2297
Website: http://www.davistuttle.com

Houston Partners
401 Louisiana, 8th Fl.
Houston, TX 77002
(713)222-8600
Fax: (713)222-8932

Southwest Venture Group
10878 Westheimer, Ste. 178
Houston, TX 77042
(713)827-8947
(713)461-1470

AM Fund
4600 Post Oak Place, Ste. 100
Houston, TX 77027
(713)627-9111
Fax: (713)627-9119

Ventex Management, Inc.
3417 Milam St.
Houston, TX 77002-9531
(713)659-7870
Fax: (713)659-7855

MBA Venture Group
1004 Olde Town Rd., Ste. 102
Irving, TX 75061
(972)986-6703

First Capital Group Management Co.
750 East Mulberry St., Ste. 305
PO Box 15616
San Antonio, TX 78212
(210)736-4233
Fax: (210)736-5449

The Southwest Venture Partnerships
16414 San Pedro, Ste. 345
San Antonio, TX 78232
(210)402-1200
Fax: (210)402-1221
E-mail: swvp@aol.com

Medtech International Inc.
1742 Carriageway
Sugarland, TX 77478

(713)980-8474
Fax: (713)980-6343

Utah

First Security Business Investment Corp.
15 East 100 South, Ste. 100
Salt Lake City, UT 84111
(801)246-5737
Fax: (801)246-5740

Utah Ventures II, L.P.
423 Wakara Way, Ste. 206
Salt Lake City, UT 84108
(801)583-5922
Fax: (801)583-4105
Website: http://www.uven.com

Wasatch Venture Corp.
1 S. Main St., Ste. 1400
Salt Lake City, UT 84133
(801)524-8939
Fax: (801)524-8941
E-mail: mail@wasatchvc.com

Vermont

North Atlantic Capital Corp.
76 Saint Paul St., Ste. 600
Burlington, VT 05401
(802)658-7820
Fax: (802)658-5757
Website: http://www.northatlanticcapital
.com

Green Mountain Advisors Inc.
PO Box 1230
Quechee, VT 05059
(802)296-7800
Fax: (802)296-6012
Website: http://www.gmtcap.com

Virginia

Oxford Financial Services Corp.
Alexandria, VA 22314
(703)519-4900
Fax: (703)519-4910
E-mail: oxford133@aol.com

Continental SBIC
4141 N. Henderson Rd.
Arlington, VA 22203
(703)527-5200
Fax: (703)527-3700

Novak Biddle Venture Partners
1750 Tysons Blvd., Ste. 1190
McLean, VA 22102
(703)847-3770
Fax: (703)847-3771

E-mail: roger@novakbiddle.com
Website: http://www.novakbiddle.com

Spacevest
11911 Freedom Dr., Ste. 500
Reston, VA 20190
(703)904-9800
Fax: (703)904-0571
E-mail: spacevest@spacevest.com
Website: http://www.spacevest.com

Virginia Capital
1801 Libbie Ave., Ste. 201
Richmond, VA 23226
(804)648-4802
Fax: (804)648-4809
E-mail: webmaster@vacapital.com
Website: http://www.vacapital.com

Calvert Social Venture Partners
402 Maple Ave. W
Vienna, VA 22180
(703)255-4930
Fax: (703)255-4931
E-mail: calven2000@aol.com

Fairfax Partners
8000 Towers Crescent Dr., Ste. 940
Vienna, VA 22182
(703)847-9486
Fax: (703)847-0911

Global Internet Ventures
8150 Leesburg Pike, Ste. 1210
Vienna, VA 22182
(703)442-3300
Fax: (703)442-3388
Website: http://www.givinc.com

Walnut Capital Corp. (Vienna)
8000 Towers Crescent Dr., Ste. 1070
Vienna, VA 22182
(703)448-3771
Fax: (703)448-7751

Washington

Encompass Ventures
777 108th Ave. NE, Ste. 2300
Bellevue, WA 98004
(425)486-3900
Fax: (425)486-3901
E-mail: info@evpartners.com
Website: http://www.encompassventures
.com

Fluke Venture Partners
11400 SE Sixth St., Ste. 230
Bellevue, WA 98004
(425)453-4590
Fax: (425)453-4675
E-mail: gabelein@flukeventures.com
Website: http://www.flukeventures.com

Pacific Northwest Partners SBIC, L.P.
15352 SE 53rd St.
Bellevue, WA 98006
(425)455-9967
Fax: (425)455-9404

Materia Venture Associates, L.P.
3435 Carillon Pointe
Kirkland, WA 98033-7354
(425)822-4100
Fax: (425)827-4086

OVP Venture Partners (Kirkland)
2420 Carillon Pt.
Kirkland, WA 98033
(425)889-9192
Fax: (425)889-0152
E-mail: info@ovp.com
Website: http://www.ovp.com

Digital Partners
999 3rd Ave., Ste. 1610
Seattle, WA 98104
(206)405-3607
Fax: (206)405-3617
Website: http://www.digitalpartners.com

Frazier & Company
601 Union St., Ste. 3300
Seattle, WA 98101
(206)621-7200
Fax: (206)621-1848
E-mail: jon@frazierco.com

Kirlan Venture Capital, Inc.
221 First Ave. W, Ste. 108
Seattle, WA 98119-4223
(206)281-8610
Fax: (206)285-3451
Website: http://www.kirlanventure.com

Phoenix Partners
1000 2nd Ave., Ste. 3600
Seattle, WA 98104
(206)624-8968
Fax: (206)624-1907

Voyager Capital
800 5th St., Ste. 4100
Seattle, WA 98103
(206)470-1180
Fax: (206)470-1185
E-mail: info@voyagercap.com
Website: http://www.voyagercap.com

Northwest Venture Associates
221 N. Wall St., Ste. 628
Spokane, WA 99201
(509)747-0728
Fax: (509)747-0758
Website: http://www.nwva.com

Wisconsin

Venture Investors Management, L.L.C.
University Research Park
505 S. Rosa Rd.

Madison, WI 53719
(608)441-2700
Fax: (608)441-2727
E-mail: roger@ventureinvestors.com
Website: http://www.ventureinvesters.com

Capital Investments, Inc.
1009 West Glen Oaks Lane, Ste. 103
Mequon, WI 53092
(414)241-0303
Fax: (414)241-8451
Website: http://www.capitalinvestment
sinc.com

Future Value Venture, Inc.
2745 N. Martin Luther King Dr., Ste. 204
Milwaukee, WI 53212-2300
(414)264-2252
Fax: (414)264-2253
E-mail: fvvventures@aol.com
William Beckett, President

Lubar and Co., Inc.
700 N. Water St., Ste. 1200
Milwaukee, WI 53202
(414)291-9000
Fax: (414)291-9061

GCI
20875 Crossroads Cir., Ste. 100
Waukesha, WI 53186
(262)798-5080
Fax: (262)798-5087

Glossary of Small Business Terms

Absolute liability
Liability that is incurred due to product defects or negligent actions. Manufacturers or retail establishments are held responsible, even though the defect or action may not have been intentional or negligent.

ACE
See Active Corps of Executives

Accident and health benefits
Benefits offered to employees and their families in order to offset the costs associated with accidental death, accidental injury, or sickness.

Account statement
A record of transactions, including payments, new debt, and deposits, incurred during a defined period of time.

Accounting system
System capturing the costs of all employees and/or machinery included in business expenses.

Accounts payable
See Trade credit

Accounts receivable
Unpaid accounts which arise from unsettled claims and transactions from the sale of a company's products or services to its customers.

Active Corps of Executives (ACE)
A group of volunteers for a management assistance program of the U.S. Small Business Administration; volunteers provide one-on-one counseling and teach workshops and seminars for small firms.

ADA
See Americans with Disabilities Act

Adaptation
The process whereby an invention is modified to meet the needs of users.

Adaptive engineering
The process whereby an invention is modified to meet the manufacturing and commercial requirements of a targeted market.

Adverse selection
The tendency for higher-risk individuals to purchase health care and more comprehensive plans, resulting in increased costs.

Advertising
A marketing tool used to capture public attention and influence purchasing decisions for a product or service. Utilizes various forms of media to generate consumer response, such as flyers, magazines, newspapers, radio, and television.

Age discrimination
The denial of the rights and privileges of employment based solely on the age of an individual.

Agency costs
Costs incurred to insure that the lender or investor maintains control over assets while allowing the borrower or entrepreneur to use them. Monitoring and information costs are the two major types of agency costs.

Agribusiness
The production and sale of commodities and products from the commercial farming industry.

America Online
An online service which is accessible by computer modem. The service features Internet access, bulletin boards, online periodicals, electronic mail, and other services for subscribers.

Americans with Disabilities Act (ADA)
Law designed to ensure equal access and opportunity to handicapped persons.

Annual report
Yearly financial report prepared by a business that adheres to the requirements set forth by the Securities and Exchange Commission (SEC).

Antitrust immunity
Exemption from prosecution under antitrust laws. In the transportation industry, firms with antitrust immunity are permitted under certain conditions to set schedules and sometimes prices for the public benefit.

Applied research
Scientific study targeted for use in a product or process.

Asians
A minority category used by the U.S. Bureau of the Census to represent a diverse group that includes Aleuts, Eskimos, American Indians, Asian Indians, Chinese, Japanese, Koreans, Vietnamese, Filipinos, Hawaiians, and other Pacific Islanders.

Assets
Anything of value owned by a company.

Audit
The verification of accounting records and business procedures conducted by an outside accounting service.

Average cost
Total production costs divided by the quantity produced.

Balance Sheet
A financial statement listing the total assets and liabilities of a company at a given time.

Bankruptcy
The condition in which a business cannot meet its debt obligations and petitions a federal district court either for reorganization of its debts (Chapter 11) or for liquidation of its assets (Chapter 7).

Basic research
Theoretical scientific exploration not targeted to application.

Basket clause
A provision specifying the amount of public pension funds that may be placed in investments not included on a state's legal list (see separate citation).

BBS
See Bulletin Board Service

BDC
See Business development corporation

Benefit
Various services, such as health care, flextime, day care, insurance, and vacation, offered to employees as part of a hiring package. Typically subsidized in whole or in part by the business.

BIDCO
See Business and industrial development company

Billing cycle
A system designed to evenly distribute customer billing throughout the month, preventing clerical backlogs.

Birth
See Business birth

Blue chip security
A low-risk, low-yield security representing an interest in a very stable company.

Blue sky laws
A general term that denotes various states' laws regulating securities.

Bond
A written instrument executed by a bidder or contractor (the principal) and a second party (the surety or sureties) to assure fulfillment of the principal's obligations to a third party (the obligee or government) identified in the bond. If the principal's obligations are not met, the bond assures payment to the extent stipulated of any loss sustained by the obligee.

Bonding requirements
Terms contained in a bond (see separate citation).

Bonus
An amount of money paid to an employee as a reward for achieving certain business goals or objectives.

Brainstorming
A group session where employees contribute their ideas for solving a problem or meeting a company objective without fear of retribution or ridicule.

Brand name
The part of a brand, trademark, or service mark that can be spoken. It can be a word, letter, or group of words or letters.

Bridge financing
A short-term loan made in expectation of intermediateterm or long-term financing. Can be used when a company plans to go public in the near future.

Broker
One who matches resources available for innovation with those who need them.

Budget
An estimate of the spending necessary to complete a project or offer a service in comparison to cash-on-hand and expected earnings for the coming year, with an emphasis on cost control.

Bulletin Board Service (BBS)
An online service enabling users to communicate with each other about specific topics.

Business and industrial development company (BIDCO)
A private, for-profit financing corporation chartered by the state to provide both equity and long-term debt capital to small business owners (see separate citations for equity and debt capital).

Business birth
The formation of a new establishment or enterprise. The appearance of a new establishment or enterprise in the Small Business Data Base (see separate citation).

Business conditions
Outside factors that can affect the financial performance of a business.

Business contractions
The number of establishments that have decreased in employment during a specified time.

Business cycle
A period of economic recession and recovery. These cycles vary in duration.

Business death
The voluntary or involuntary closure of a firm or establishment. The disappearance of an establishment or enterprise from the Small Business Data Base (see separate citation).

Business development corporation (BDC)
A business financing agency, usually composed of the financial institutions in an area or state, organized to assist in financing businesses unable to obtain assistance through normal channels; the risk is spread among various members of the business development corporation, and interest rates may vary somewhat from those charged by member institutions. A venture capital firm in which shares of ownership are publicly held and to which the Investment Act of 1940 applies.

Business dissolution
For enumeration purposes, the absence of a business that was present in the prior time period from any current record.

Business entry
See Business birth

Business ethics
Moral values and principles espoused by members of the business community as a guide to fair and honest business practices.

Business exit
See Business death

Business expansions
The number of establishments that added employees during a specified time.

Business failure
Closure of a business causing a loss to at least one creditor.

Business format franchising
The purchase of the name, trademark, and an ongoing business plan of the parent corporation or franchisor by the franchisee.

Business license
A legal authorization issued by municipal and state governments and required for business operations.

Business name
Enterprises must register their business names with local governments usually on a "doing business as" (DBA) form. (This name is sometimes referred to as

Glossary

a "fictional name.") The procedure is part of the business licensing process and prevents any other business from using that same name for a similar business in the same locality.

Business norms
See Financial ratios

Business permit
See Business license

Business plan
A document that spells out a company's expected course of action for a specified period, usually including a detailed listing and analysis of risks and uncertainties. For the small business, it should examine the proposed products, the market, the industry, the management policies, the marketing policies, production needs, and financial needs. Frequently, it is used as a prospectus for potential investors and lenders.

Business proposal
See Business plan

Business service firm
An establishment primarily engaged in rendering services to other business organizations on a fee or contract basis.

Business start
For enumeration purposes, a business with a name or similar designation that did not exist in a prior time period.

Cafeteria plan
See Flexible benefit plan

Capacity
Level of a firm's, industry's, or nation's output corresponding to full practical utilization of available resources.

Capital
Assets less liabilities, representing the ownership interest in a business. A stock of accumulated goods, especially at a specified time and in contrast to income received during a specified time period. Accumulated goods devoted to production. Accumulated possessions calculated to bring income.

Capital expenditure
Expenses incurred by a business for improvements that will depreciate over time.

Capital gain
The monetary difference between the purchase price and the selling price of capital. Capital gains are taxed at a rate of 28% by the federal government.

Capital intensity
The relative importance of capital in the production process, usually expressed as the ratio of capital to labor but also sometimes as the ratio of capital to output.

Capital resource
The equipment, facilities and labor used to create products and services.

Caribbean Basin Initiative
An interdisciplinary program to support commerce among the businesses in the nations of the Caribbean Basin and the United States. Agencies involved include: the Agency for International Development, the U.S. Small Business Administration, the International Trade Administration of the U.S. Department of Commerce, and various private sector groups.

Catastrophic care
Medical and other services for acute and long-term illnesses that cost more than insurance coverage limits or that cost the amount most families may be expected to pay with their own resources.

CDC
See Certified development corporation

CD-ROM
Compact disc with read-only memory used to store large amounts of digitized data.

Certified development corporation (CDC)
A local area or statewide corporation or authority (for profit or nonprofit) that packages U.S. Small Business Administration (SBA), bank, state, and/or private money into financial assistance for existing business capital improvements. The SBA holds the second lien on its maximum share of 40 percent involvement. Each state has at least one certified development corporation. This program is called the SBA 504 Program.

Certified lenders
Banks that participate in the SBA guaranteed loan program (see separate citation). Such banks must have a good track record with the U.S. Small Business Administration (SBA) and must agree to certain conditions set forth by the agency. In return, the SBA agrees to process any guaranteed loan application within three business days.

Champion
An advocate for the development of an innovation.

Channel of distribution
The means used to transport merchandise from the manufacturer to the consumer.

Chapter 7 of the 1978 Bankruptcy Act
Provides for a court-appointed trustee who is responsible for liquidating a company's assets in order to settle outstanding debts.

Chapter 11 of the 1978 Bankruptcy Act
Allows the business owners to retain control of the company while working with their creditors to reorganize their finances and establish better business practices to prevent liquidation of assets.

Closely held corporation
A corporation in which the shares are held by a few persons, usually officers, employees, or others close to the management; these shares are rarely offered to the public.

Code of Federal Regulations
Codification of general and permanent rules of the federal government published in the Federal Register.

Code sharing
See Computer code sharing

Coinsurance
Upon meeting the deductible payment, health insurance participants may be required to make additional health care cost-sharing payments. Coinsurance is a payment of a fixed percentage of the cost of each service; copayment is usually a fixed amount to be paid with each service.

Collateral
Securities, evidence of deposit, or other property pledged by a borrower to secure repayment of a loan.

Collective ratemaking
The establishment of uniform charges for services by a group of businesses in the same industry.

Commercial insurance plan
See Underwriting

Commercial loans
Short-term renewable loans used to finance specific capital needs of a business.

Commercialization
The final stage of the innovation process, including production and distribution.

Common stock
The most frequently used instrument for purchasing ownership in private or public companies. Common stock generally carries the right to vote on certain corporate actions and may pay dividends, although it rarely does in venture investments. In liquidation, common stockholders are the last to share in the proceeds from the sale of a corporation's assets; bondholders and preferred shareholders have priority. Common stock is often used in firstround start-up financing.

Community development corporation
A corporation established to develop economic programs for a community and, in most cases, to provide financial support for such development.

Competitor
A business whose product or service is marketed for the same purpose/use and to the same consumer group as the product or service of another.

Computer code sharing
An arrangement whereby flights of a regional airline are identified by the two-letter code of a major carrier in the computer reservation system to help direct passengers to new regional carriers.

Consignment
A merchandising agreement, usually referring to secondhand shops, where the dealer pays the owner of an item a percentage of the profit when the item is sold.

Consortium
A coalition of organizations such as banks and corporations for ventures requiring large capital resources.

Consultant
An individual that is paid by a business to provide advice and expertise in a particular area.

Consumer price index
A measure of the fluctuation in prices between two points in time.

Consumer research
Research conducted by a business to obtain information about existing or potential consumer markets.

Continuation coverage
Health coverage offered for a specified period of time to employees who leave their jobs and to their widows, divorced spouses, or dependents.

Contractions
See Business contractions

Convertible preferred stock
A class of stock that pays a reasonable dividend and is convertible into common stock (see separate citation). Generally the convertible feature may only be exercised after being held for a stated period of time. This arrangement is usually considered second-round financing when a company needs equity to maintain its cash flow.

Convertible securities
A feature of certain bonds, debentures, or preferred stocks that allows them to be exchanged by the owner for another class of securities at a future date and in accordance with any other terms of the issue.

Copayment
See Coinsurance

Copyright
A legal form of protection available to creators and authors to safeguard their works from unlawful use or claim of ownership by others. Copyrights may be acquired for works of art, sculpture, music, and published or unpublished manuscripts. All copyrights should be registered at the Copyright Office of the Library of Congress.

Corporate financial ratios
The relationship between key figures found in a company's financial statement expressed as a numeric value. Used to evaluate risk and company performance. Also known as Financial averages, Operating ratios, and Business ratios.

Corporation
A legal entity, chartered by a state or the federal government, recognized as a separate entity having its own rights, privileges, and liabilities distinct from those of its members.

Cost containment
Actions taken by employers and insurers to curtail rising health care costs; for example, increasing employee cost sharing (see separate citation), requiring second opinions, or preadmission screening.

Cost sharing
The requirement that health care consumers contribute to their own medical care costs through deductibles and coinsurance (see separate citations). Cost sharing does not include the amounts paid in premiums. It is used to control utilization of services; for example, requiring a fixed amount to be paid with each health care service.

Cottage industry
Businesses based in the home in which the family members are the labor force and family-owned equipment is used to process the goods.

Credit Rating
A letter or number calculated by an organization (such as Dun & Bradstreet) to represent the ability and disposition of a business to meet its financial obligations.

Customer service
Various techniques used to ensure the satisfaction of a customer.

Cyclical peak
The upper turning point in a business cycle.

Cyclical trough
The lower turning point in a business cycle.

DBA
See Business name

Death
See Business death

Debenture
A certificate given as acknowledgment of a debt (see separate citation) secured by the general credit of the issuing corporation. A bond, usually without security, issued by a corporation and sometimes convertible to common stock.

Debt
Something owed by one person to another. Financing in which a company receives capital that must be repaid; no ownership is transferred.

Debt capital
Business financing that normally requires periodic interest payments and repayment of the principal within a specified time.

Debt financing
See Debt capital

Debt securities
Loans such as bonds and notes that provide a specified rate of return for a specified period of time.

Deductible
A set amount that an individual must pay before any benefits are received.

Demand shock absorbers
A term used to describe the role that some small firms play by expanding their output levels to accommodate a transient surge in demand.

Demographics
Statistics on various markets, including age, income, and education, used to target specific products or services to appropriate consumer groups.

Demonstration
Showing that a product or process has been modified sufficiently to meet the needs of users.

Deregulation
The lifting of government restrictions; for example, the lifting of government restrictions on the entry of new businesses, the expansion of services, and the setting of prices in particular industries.

Desktop Publishing
Using personal computers and specialized software to produce camera-ready copy for publications.

Disaster loans
Various types of physical and economic assistance available to individuals and businesses through the U.S. Small Business Administration (SBA). This is the only SBA loan program available for residential purposes.

Discrimination
The denial of the rights and privileges of employment based on factors such as age, race, religion, or gender.

Diseconomies of scale
The condition in which the costs of production increase faster than the volume of production.

Dissolution
See Business dissolution

Distribution
Delivering a product or process to the user.

Distributor
One who delivers merchandise to the user.

Diversified company
A company whose products and services are used by several different markets.

Doing business as (DBA)
See Business name

Dow Jones
An information services company that publishes the Wall Street Journal and other sources of financial information.

Dow Jones Industrial Average
An indicator of stock market performance.

Earned income
A tax term that refers to wages and salaries earned by the recipient, as opposed to monies earned through interest and dividends.

Economic efficiency
The use of productive resources to the fullest practical extent in the provision of the set of goods and services that is most preferred by purchasers in the economy.

Economic indicators
Statistics used to express the state of the economy. These include the length of the average work week, the rate of unemployment, and stock prices.

Economically disadvantaged
See Socially and economically disadvantaged

Economies of scale
See Scale economies

EEOC
See Equal Employment Opportunity Commission

8(a) Program
A program authorized by the Small Business Act that directs federal contracts to small businesses owned and operated by socially and economically disadvantaged individuals.

Electronic mail (e-mail)
The electronic transmission of mail via phone lines.

E-mail
See Electronic mail

Employee leasing
A contract by which employers arrange to have their workers hired by a leasing company and then leased back to them for a management fee. The leasing company typically assumes the administrative burden of payroll and provides a benefit package to the workers.

Employee tenure
The length of time an employee works for a particular employer.

Employer identification number
The business equivalent of a social security number. Assigned by the U.S. Internal Revenue Service.

Enterprise
An aggregation of all establishments owned by a parent company. An enterprise may consist of a single, independent establishment or include subsidiaries and other branches under the same ownership and control.

Enterprise zone
A designated area, usually found in inner cities and other areas with significant unemployment, where businesses receive tax credits and other incentives to entice them to establish operations there.

Entrepreneur
A person who takes the risk of organizing and operating a new business venture.

Entry
See Business entry

Equal Employment Opportunity Commission (EEOC)
A federal agency that ensures nondiscrimination in the hiring and firing practices of a business.

Equal opportunity employer
An employer who adheres to the standards set by the Equal Employment Opportunity Commission (see separate citation).

Equity
The ownership interest. Financing in which partial or total ownership of a company is surrendered in exchange for capital. An investor's financial return comes from dividend payments and from growth in the net worth of the business.

Equity capital
See Equity; Equity midrisk venture capital

Equity financing
See Equity; Equity midrisk venture capital

Equity midrisk venture capital
An unsecured investment in a company. Usually a purchase of ownership interest in a company that occurs in the later stages of a company's development.

Equity partnership
A limited partnership arrangement for providing start-up and seed capital to businesses.

Equity securities
See Equity

Equity-type
Debt financing subordinated to conventional debt.

Establishment
A single-location business unit that may be independent (a single-establishment enterprise) or owned by a parent enterprise.

Establishment and Enterprise Microdata File
See U.S. Establishment and Enterprise Microdata File

Establishment birth
See Business birth

Establishment Longitudinal Microdata File
See U.S. Establishment Longitudinal Microdata File

Ethics
See Business ethics

Evaluation
Determining the potential success of translating an invention into a product or process.

Exit
See Business exit

Experience rating
See Underwriting

Export
A product sold outside of the country.

Export license
A general or specific license granted by the U.S. Department of Commerce required of anyone wishing to export goods. Some restricted articles need approval from the U.S. Departments of State, Defense, or Energy.

Failure
See Business failure

Fair share agreement
An agreement reached between a franchisor and a minority business organization to extend business ownership to minorities by either reducing the amount of capital required or by setting aside certain marketing areas for minority business owners.

Feasibility study
A study to determine the likelihood that a proposed product or development will fulfill the objectives of a particular investor.

Federal Trade Commission (FTC)
Federal agency that promotes free enterprise and competition within the U.S.

Federal Trade Mark Act of 1946
See Lanham Act

Fictional name
See Business name

Fiduciary
An individual or group that hold assets in trust for a beneficiary.

Financial analysis
The techniques used to determine money needs in a business. Techniques include ratio analysis, calculation

of return on investment, guides for measuring profitability, and break-even analysis to determine ultimate success.

Financial intermediary
A financial institution that acts as the intermediary between borrowers and lenders. Banks, savings and loan associations, finance companies, and venture capital companies are major financial intermediaries in the United States.

Financial ratios
See Corporate financial ratios; Industry financial ratios

Financial statement
A written record of business finances, including balance sheets and profit and loss statements.

Financing
See First-stage financing; Second-stage financing; Thirdstage financing

First-stage financing
Financing provided to companies that have expended their initial capital, and require funds to start full-scale manufacturing and sales. Also known as First-round financing.

Fiscal year
Any twelve-month period used by businesses for accounting purposes.

504 Program
See Certified development corporation

Flexible benefit plan
A plan that offers a choice among cash and/or qualified benefits such as group term life insurance, accident and health insurance, group legal services, dependent care assistance, and vacations.

FOB
See Free on board

Format franchising
See Business format franchising; Franchising

401(k) plan
A financial plan where employees contribute a percentage of their earnings to a fund that is invested in stocks, bonds, or money markets for the purpose of saving money for retirement.

Glossary

Four Ps
Marketing terms referring to Product, Price, Place, and Promotion.

Franchising
A form of licensing by which the owner-the franchisor- distributes or markets a product, method, or service through affiliated dealers called franchisees. The product, method, or service being marketed is identified by a brand name, and the franchisor maintains control over the marketing methods employed. The franchisee is often given exclusive access to a defined geographic area.

Free on board (FOB)
A pricing term indicating that the quoted price includes the cost of loading goods into transport vessels at a specified place.

Frictional unemployment
See Unemployment

FTC
See Federal Trade Commission

Fulfillment
The systems necessary for accurate delivery of an ordered item, including subscriptions and direct marketing.

Full-time workers
Generally, those who work a regular schedule of more than 35 hours per week.

Garment registration number
A number that must appear on every garment sold in the U.S. to indicate the manufacturer of the garment, which may or may not be the same as the label under which the garment is sold. The U.S. Federal Trade Commission assigns and regulates garment registration numbers.

Gatekeeper
A key contact point for entry into a network.

GDP
See Gross domestic product

General obligation bond
A municipal bond secured by the taxing power of the municipality. The Tax Reform Act of 1986 limits the purposes for which such bonds may be issued and establishes volume limits on the extent of their issuance.

GNP
See Gross national product

Good Housekeeping Seal
Seal appearing on products that signifies the fulfillment of the standards set by the Good Housekeeping Institute to protect consumer interests.

Goods sector
All businesses producing tangible goods, including agriculture, mining, construction, and manufacturing businesses.

GPO
See Gross product originating

Gross domestic product (GDP)
The part of the nation's gross national product (see separate citation) generated by private business using resources from within the country.

Gross national product (GNP)
The most comprehensive single measure of aggregate economic output. Represents the market value of the total output of goods and services produced by a nation's economy.

Gross product originating (GPO)
A measure of business output estimated from the income or production side using employee compensation, profit income, net interest, capital consumption, and indirect business taxes.

HAL
See Handicapped assistance loan program

Handicapped assistance loan program (HAL)
Low-interest direct loan program through the U.S. Small Business Administration (SBA) for handicapped persons. The SBA requires that these persons demonstrate that their disability is such that it is impossible for them to secure employment, thus making it necessary to go into their own business to make a living.

Health maintenance organization (HMO)
Organization of physicians and other health care professionals that provides health services to subscribers and their dependents on a prepaid basis.

Health provider
An individual or institution that gives medical care. Under Medicare, an institutional provider is a hospital, skilled nursing facility, home health agency, or provider of certain physical therapy services.

Hispanic
A person of Cuban, Mexican, Puerto Rican, Latin American (Central or South American), European Spanish, or other Spanish-speaking origin or ancestry.

HMO
See Health maintenance organization

Home-based business
A business with an operating address that is also a residential address (usually the residential address of the proprietor).

Hub-and-spoke system
A system in which flights of an airline from many different cities (the spokes) converge at a single airport (the hub). After allowing passengers sufficient time to make connections, planes then depart for different cities.

Human Resources Management
A business program designed to oversee recruiting, pay, benefits, and other issues related to the company's work force, including planning to determine the optimal use of labor to increase production, thereby increasing profit.

Idea
An original concept for a new product or process.

Import
Products produced outside the country in which they are consumed.

Income
Money or its equivalent, earned or accrued, resulting from the sale of goods and services.

Income statement
A financial statement that lists the profits and losses of a company at a given time.

Incorporation
The filing of a certificate of incorporation with a state's secretary of state, thereby limiting the business owner's liability.

Incubator
A facility designed to encourage entrepreneurship and minimize obstacles to new business formation and growth, particularly for high-technology firms, by housing a number of fledgling enterprises that share an array of services, such as meeting areas, secretarial services, accounting, research library, on-site financial and management counseling, and word processing facilities.

Independent contractor
An individual considered self-employed (see separate citation) and responsible for paying Social Security taxes and income taxes on earnings.

Indirect health coverage
Health insurance obtained through another individual's health care plan; for example, a spouse's employersponsored plan.

Industrial development authority
The financial arm of a state or other political subdivision established for the purpose of financing economic development in an area, usually through loans to nonprofit organizations, which in turn provide facilities for manufacturing and other industrial operations.

Industry financial ratios
Corporate financial ratios averaged for a specified industry. These are used for comparison purposes and reveal industry trends and identify differences between the performance of a specific company and the performance of its industry. Also known as Industrial averages, Industry ratios, Financial averages, and Business or Industrial norms.

Inflation
Increases in volume of currency and credit, generally resulting in a sharp and continuing rise in price levels.

Informal capital
Financing from informal, unorganized sources; includes informal debt capital such as trade credit or loans from friends and relatives and equity capital from informal investors.

Initial public offering (IPO)
A corporation's first offering of stock to the public.

Innovation
The introduction of a new idea into the marketplace in the form of a new product or service or an improvement in organization or process.

Intellectual property
Any idea or work that can be considered proprietary in nature and is thus protected from infringement by others.

Internal capital
Debt or equity financing obtained from the owner or through retained business earnings.

Internet
A government-designed computer network that contains large amounts of information and is accessible through various vendors for a fee.

Intrapreneurship
The state of employing entrepreneurial principles to nonentrepreneurial situations.

Invention
The tangible form of a technological idea, which could include a laboratory prototype, drawings, formulas, etc.

IPO
See Initial public offering

Job description
The duties and responsibilities required in a particular position.

Job tenure
A period of time during which an individual is continuously employed in the same job.

Joint marketing agreements
Agreements between regional and major airlines, often involving the coordination of flight schedules, fares, and baggage transfer. These agreements help regional carriers operate at lower cost.

Joint venture
Venture in which two or more people combine efforts in a particular business enterprise, usually a single transaction or a limited activity, and agree to share the profits and losses jointly or in proportion to their contributions.

Keogh plan
Designed for self-employed persons and unincorporated businesses as a tax-deferred pension account.

Labor force
Civilians considered eligible for employment who are also willing and able to work.

Labor force participation rate
The civilian labor force as a percentage of the civilian population.

Labor intensity
The relative importance of labor in the production process, usually measured as the capital-labor ratio; i.e., the ratio of units of capital (typically, dollars of tangible assets) to the number of employees. The higher the capital-labor ratio exhibited by a firm or industry, the lower the capital intensity of that firm or industry is said to be.

Labor surplus area
An area in which there exists a high unemployment rate. In procurement (see separate citation), extra points are given to firms in counties that are designated a labor surplus area; this information is requested on procurement bid sheets.

Labor union
An organization of similarly-skilled workers who collectively bargain with management over the conditions of employment.

Laboratory prototype
See Prototype

LAN
See Local Area Network

Lanham Act
Refers to the Federal Trade Mark Act of 1946. Protects registered trademarks, trade names, and other service marks used in commerce.

Large business-dominated industry
Industry in which a minimum of 60 percent of employment or sales is in firms with more than 500 workers.

LBO
See Leveraged buy-out

Leader pricing
A reduction in the price of a good or service in order to generate more sales of that good or service.

Legal list
A list of securities selected by a state in which certain institutions and fiduciaries (such as pension funds, insurance companies, and banks) may invest. Securities not on the list are not eligible for investment. Legal lists typically restrict investments to high quality securities meeting certain specifications. Generally, investment is limited to U.S. securities and investment-grade blue chip securities (see separate citation).

Leveraged buy-out (LBO)
The purchase of a business or a division of a corporation through a highly leveraged financing package.

Liability
An obligation or duty to perform a service or an act. Also defined as money owed.

License
A legal agreement granting to another the right to use a technological innovation.

Limited partnerships
See Venture capital limited partnerships

Liquidity
The ability to convert a security into cash promptly.

Loans
See Commercial loans; Disaster loans; SBA direct loans; SBA guaranteed loans; SBA special lending institution categories Local Area Network (LAN) Computer networks contained within a single building or small area; used to facilitate the sharing of information.

Local development corporation
An organization, usually made up of local citizens of a community, designed to improve the economy of the area by inducing business and industry to locate and expand there. A local development corporation establishes a capability to finance local growth.

Long-haul rates
Rates charged by a transporter in which the distance traveled is more than 800 miles.

Long-term debt
An obligation that matures in a period that exceeds five years.

Low-grade bond
A corporate bond that is rated below investment grade by the major rating agencies (Standard and Poor's, Moody's).

Macro-efficiency
Efficiency as it pertains to the operation of markets and market systems.

Managed care
A cost-effective health care program initiated by employers whereby low-cost health care is made available to the employees in return for exclusive patronage to program doctors.

Management Assistance Programs
See SBA Management Assistance Programs

Management and technical assistance
A term used by many programs to mean business (as opposed to technological) assistance.

Mandated benefits
Specific treatments, providers, or individuals required by law to be included in commercial health plans.

Market evaluation
The use of market information to determine the sales potential of a specific product or process.

Market failure
The situation in which the workings of a competitive market do not produce the best results from the point of view of the entire society.

Market information
Data of any type that can be used for market evaluation, which could include demographic data, technology forecasting, regulatory changes, etc.

Market research
A systematic collection, analysis, and reporting of data about the market and its preferences, opinions, trends, and plans; used for corporate decision-making.

Market share
In a particular market, the percentage of sales of a specific product.

Marketing
Promotion of goods or services through various media.

Master Establishment List (MEL)
A list of firms in the United States developed by the U.S. Small Business Administration; firms can be selected by industry, region, state, standard metropolitan statistical area (see separate citation), county, and zip code.

Maturity
The date upon which the principal or stated value of a bond or other indebtedness becomes due and payable.

Medicaid (Title XIX)
A federally aided, state-operated and administered program that provides medical benefits for certain low income persons in need of health and medical care who are eligible for one of the government's welfare cash payment programs, including the aged, the blind, the disabled, and members of families with dependent children where one parent is absent, incapacitated, or unemployed.

Medicare (Title XVIII)
A nationwide health insurance program for disabled and aged persons. Health insurance is available to insured persons without regard to income. Monies from payroll taxes cover hospital insurance and monies from general revenues and beneficiary premiums pay for supplementary medical insurance.

MEL
See Master Establishment List

MESBIC
See Minority enterprise small business investment corporation

MET
See Multiple employer trust

Metropolitan statistical area (MSA)
A means used by the government to define large population centers that may transverse different governmental jurisdictions. For example, the Washington, D.C. MSA includes the District of Columbia and contiguous parts of Maryland and Virginia because all of these geopolitical areas comprise one population and economic operating unit.

Mezzanine financing
See Third-stage financing

Micro-efficiency
Efficiency as it pertains to the operation of individual firms.

Microdata
Information on the characteristics of an individual business firm.

Mid-term debt
An obligation that matures within one to five years.

Midrisk venture capital
See Equity midrisk venture capital

Minimum premium plan
A combination approach to funding an insurance plan aimed primarily at premium tax savings. The employer self-funds a fixed percentage of estimated monthly claims and the insurance company insures the excess.

Minimum wage
The lowest hourly wage allowed by the federal government.

Minority Business Development Agency
Contracts with private firms throughout the nation to sponsor Minority Business Development Centers which provide minority firms with advice and technical assistance on a fee basis.

Minority Enterprise Small Business Investment Corporation (MESBIC)
A federally funded private venture capital firm licensed by the U.S. Small Business Administration to provide capital to minority-owned businesses (see separate citation).

Minority-owned business
Businesses owned by those who are socially or economically disadvantaged (see separate citation).

Mom and Pop business
A small store or enterprise having limited capital, principally employing family members.

Moonlighter
A wage-and-salary worker with a side business.

MSA
See Metropolitan statistical area

Multi-employer plan
A health plan to which more than one employer is required to contribute and that may be maintained through a collective bargaining agreement and required to meet standards prescribed by the U.S. Department of Labor.

Multi-level marketing
A system of selling in which you sign up other people to assist you and they, in turn, recruit others to help them. Some entrepreneurs have built successful companies on this concept because the main focus of their activities is their product and product sales.

Multimedia
The use of several types of media to promote a product or service. Also, refers to the use of several different types of media (sight, sound, pictures, text) in a CD-ROM (see separate citation) product.

Multiple employer trust (MET)
A self-funded benefit plan generally geared toward small employers sharing a common interest.

NAFTA
See North American Free Trade Agreement

NASDAQ
See National Association of Securities Dealers Automated Quotations

National Association of Securities Dealers Automated Quotations
Provides price quotes on over-the-counter securities as well as securities listed on the New York Stock Exchange.

National income
Aggregate earnings of labor and property arising from the production of goods and services in a nation's economy.

Net assets
See Net worth

Net income
The amount remaining from earnings and profits after all expenses and costs have been met or deducted. Also known as Net earnings.

Net profit
Money earned after production and overhead expenses (see separate citations) have been deducted.

Net worth
The difference between a company's total assets and its total liabilities.

Network
A chain of interconnected individuals or organizations sharing information and/or services.

New York Stock Exchange (NYSE)
The oldest stock exchange in the U.S. Allows for trading in stocks, bonds, warrants, options, and rights that meet listing requirements.

Niche
A career or business for which a person is well-suited. Also, a product which fulfills one need of a particular market segment, often with little or no competition.

Nodes
One workstation in a network, either local area or wide area (see separate citations).

Nonbank bank
A bank that either accepts deposits or makes loans, but not both. Used to create many new branch banks.

Noncompetitive awards
A method of contracting whereby the federal government negotiates with only one contractor to supply a product or service.

Nonmember bank
A state-regulated bank that does not belong to the federal bank system.

Nonprofit
An organization that has no shareholders, does not distribute profits, and is without federal and state tax liabilities.

Norms
See Financial ratios

North American Free Trade Agreement (NAFTA)
Passed in 1993, NAFTA eliminates trade barriers among businesses in the U.S., Canada, and Mexico.

NYSE
See New York Stock Exchange

Occupational Safety & Health Administration (OSHA)

Federal agency that regulates health and safety standards within the workplace.

Optimal firm size

The business size at which the production cost per unit of output (average cost) is, in the long run, at its minimum.

Organizational chart

A hierarchical chart tracking the chain of command within an organization.

OSHA

See Occupational Safety & Health Administration

Overhead

Expenses, such as employee benefits and building utilities, incurred by a business that are unrelated to the actual product or service sold.

Owner's capital

Debt or equity funds provided by the owner(s) of a business; sources of owner's capital are personal savings, sales of assets, or loans from financial institutions.

P & L

See Profit and loss statement

Part-time workers

Normally, those who work less than 35 hours per week. The Tax Reform Act indicated that part-time workers who work less than 17.5 hours per week may be excluded from health plans for purposes of complying with federal nondiscrimination rules.

Part-year workers

Those who work less than 50 weeks per year.

Partnership

Two or more parties who enter into a legal relationship to conduct business for profit. Defined by the U.S. Internal Revenue Code as joint ventures, syndicates, groups, pools, and other associations of two or more persons organized for profit that are not specifically classified in the IRS code as corporations or proprietorships.

Patent

A grant made by the government assuring an inventor the sole right to make, use, and sell an invention for a period of 17 years.

PC

See Professional corporation

Peak

See Cyclical peak

Pension

A series of payments made monthly, semiannually, annually, or at other specified intervals during the lifetime of the pensioner for distribution upon retirement. The term is sometimes used to denote the portion of the retirement allowance financed by the employer's contributions.

Pension fund

A fund established to provide for the payment of pension benefits; the collective contributions made by all of the parties to the pension plan.

Performance appraisal

An established set of objective criteria, based on job description and requirements, that is used to evaluate the performance of an employee in a specific job.

Permit

See Business license

Plan

See Business plan

Pooling

An arrangement for employers to achieve efficiencies and lower health costs by joining together to purchase group health insurance or self-insurance.

PPO

See Preferred provider organization

Preferred lenders program

See SBA special lending institution categories

Preferred provider organization (PPO)

A contractual arrangement with a health care services organization that agrees to discount its health care rates in return for faster payment and/or a patient base.

Premiums

The amount of money paid to an insurer for health insurance under a policy. The premium is generally paid periodically (e.g., monthly), and often is split between the employer and the employee. Unlike deductibles and coinsurance or copayments, premiums are paid for coverage whether or not benefits are actually used.

Prime-age workers
Employees 25 to 54 years of age.

Prime contract
A contract awarded directly by the U.S. Federal Government.

Private company
See Closely held corporation

Private placement
A method of raising capital by offering for sale an investment or business to a small group of investors (generally avoiding registration with the Securities and Exchange Commission or state securities registration agencies). Also known as Private financing or Private offering.

Pro forma
The use of hypothetical figures in financial statements to represent future expenditures, debts, and other potential financial expenses.

Proactive
Taking the initiative to solve problems and anticipate future events before they happen, instead of reacting to an already existing problem or waiting for a difficult situation to occur.

Procurement
A contract from an agency of the federal government for goods or services from a small business.

Prodigy
An online service which is accessible by computer modem. The service features Internet access, bulletin boards, online periodicals, electronic mail, and other services for subscribers.

Product development
The stage of the innovation process where research is translated into a product or process through evaluation, adaptation, and demonstration.

Product franchising
An arrangement for a franchisee to use the name and to produce the product line of the franchisor or parent corporation.

Production
The manufacture of a product.

Production prototype
See Prototype

Productivity
A measurement of the number of goods produced during a specific amount of time.

Professional corporation (PC)
Organized by members of a profession such as medicine, dentistry, or law for the purpose of conducting their professional activities as a corporation. Liability of a member or shareholder is limited in the same manner as in a business corporation.

Profit and loss statement (P & L)
The summary of the incomes (total revenues) and costs of a company's operation during a specific period of time. Also known as Income and expense statement.

Proposal
See Business plan

Proprietorship
The most common legal form of business ownership; about 85 percent of all small businesses are proprietorships. The liability of the owner is unlimited in this form of ownership.

Prospective payment system
A cost-containment measure included in the Social Security Amendments of 1983 whereby Medicare payments to hospitals are based on established prices, rather than on cost reimbursement.

Prototype
A model that demonstrates the validity of the concept of an invention (laboratory prototype); a model that meets the needs of the manufacturing process and the user (production prototype).

Prudent investor rule or standard
A legal doctrine that requires fiduciaries to make investments using the prudence, diligence, and intelligence that would be used by a prudent person in making similar investments. Because fiduciaries make investments on behalf of third-party beneficiaries, the

standard results in very conservative investments. Until recently, most state regulations required the fiduciary to apply this standard to each investment. Newer, more progressive regulations permit fiduciaries to apply this standard to the portfolio taken as a whole, thereby allowing a fiduciary to balance a portfolio with higher-yield, higher-risk investments. In states with more progressive regulations, practically every type of security is eligible for inclusion in the portfolio of investments made by a fiduciary, provided that the portfolio investments, in their totality, are those of a prudent person.

Public equity markets
Organized markets for trading in equity shares such as common stocks, preferred stocks, and warrants. Includes markets for both regularly traded and nonregularly traded securities.

Public offering
General solicitation for participation in an investment opportunity. Interstate public offerings are supervised by the U.S. Securities and Exchange Commission (see separate citation).

Quality control
The process by which a product is checked and tested to ensure consistent standards of high quality.

Rate of return
The yield obtained on a security or other investment based on its purchase price or its current market price. The total rate of return is current income plus or minus capital appreciation or depreciation.

Real property
Includes the land and all that is contained on it.

Realignment
See Resource realignment

Recession
Contraction of economic activity occurring between the peak and trough (see separate citations) of a business cycle.

Regulated market
A market in which the government controls the forces of supply and demand, such as who may enter and what price may be charged.

Regulation D
A vehicle by which small businesses make small offerings and private placements of securities with limited disclosure requirements. It was designed to ease the burdens imposed on small businesses utilizing this method of capital formation.

Regulatory Flexibility Act
An act requiring federal agencies to evaluate the impact of their regulations on small businesses before the regulations are issued and to consider less burdensome alternatives.

Research
The initial stage of the innovation process, which includes idea generation and invention.

Research and development financing
A tax-advantaged partnership set up to finance product development for start-ups as well as more mature companies.

Resource mobility
The ease with which labor and capital move from firm to firm or from industry to industry.

Resource realignment
The adjustment of productive resources to interindustry changes in demand.

Resources
The sources of support or help in the innovation process, including sources of financing, technical evaluation, market evaluation, management and business assistance, etc.

Retained business earnings
Business profits that are retained by the business rather than being distributed to the shareholders as dividends.

Revolving credit
An agreement with a lending institution for an amount of money, which cannot exceed a set maximum, over a specified period of time. Each time the borrower repays a portion of the loan, the amount of the repayment may be borrowed yet again.

Risk capital
See Venture capital

Risk management
The act of identifying potential sources of financial loss and taking action to minimize their negative impact.

Routing
The sequence of steps necessary to complete a product during production.

S corporations
See Sub chapter S corporations

SBA
See Small Business Administration

SBA direct loans
Loans made directly by the U.S. Small Business Administration (SBA); monies come from funds appropriated specifically for this purpose. In general, SBA direct loans carry interest rates slightly lower than those in the private financial markets and are available only to applicants unable to secure private financing or an SBA guaranteed loan.

SBA 504 Program
See Certified development corporation

SBA guaranteed loans
Loans made by lending institutions in which the U.S. Small Business Administration (SBA) will pay a prior agreed-upon percentage of the outstanding principal in the event the borrower of the loan defaults. The terms of the loan and the interest rate are negotiated between theborrower and the lending institution, within set parameters.

SBA loans
See Disaster loans; SBA direct loans; SBA guaranteed loans; SBA special lending institution categories

SBA Management Assistance Programs
Classes, workshops, counseling, and publications offered by the U.S. Small Business Administration.

SBA special lending institution categories
U.S. Small Business Administration (SBA) loan program in which the SBA promises certified banks a 72-hour turnaround period in giving its approval for a loan, and in which preferred lenders in a pilot program are allowed to write SBA loans without seeking prior SBA approval.

SBDB
See Small Business Data Base

SBDC
See Small business development centers

SBI
See Small business institutes program

SBIC
See Small business investment corporation

SBIR Program
See Small Business Innovation Development Act of 1982

Scale economies
The decline of the production cost per unit of output (average cost) as the volume of output increases.

Scale efficiency
The reduction in unit cost available to a firm when producing at a higher output volume.

SCORE
See Service Corps of Retired Executives

SEC
See Securities and Exchange Commission

SECA
See Self-Employment Contributions Act

Second-stage financing
Working capital for the initial expansion of a company that is producing, shipping, and has growing accounts receivable and inventories. Also known as Second-round financing.

Secondary market
A market established for the purchase and sale of outstanding securities following their initial distribution.

Secondary worker
Any worker in a family other than the person who is the primary source of income for the family.

Secondhand capital
Previously used and subsequently resold capital equipment (e.g., buildings and machinery).

Securities and Exchange Commission (SEC)
Federal agency charged with regulating the trade of securities to prevent unethical practices in the investor market.

Securitized debt
A marketing technique that converts long-term loans to marketable securities.

Seed capital
Venture financing provided in the early stages of the innovation process, usually during product development.

Self-employed person
One who works for a profit or fees in his or her own business, profession, or trade, or who operates a farm.

Self-Employment Contributions Act (SECA)
Federal law that governs the self-employment tax (see separate citation).

Self-employment income
Income covered by Social Security if a business earns a net income of at least $400.00 during the year. Taxes are paid on earnings that exceed $400.00.

Self-employment retirement plan
See Keogh plan

Self-employment tax
Required tax imposed on self-employed individuals for the provision of Social Security and Medicare. The tax must be paid quarterly with estimated income tax statements.

Self-funding
A health benefit plan in which a firm uses its own funds to pay claims, rather than transferring the financial risks of paying claims to an outside insurer in exchange for premium payments.

Service Corps of Retired Executives (SCORE)
Volunteers for the SBA Management Assistance Program who provide one-on-one counseling and teach workshops and seminars for small firms.

Service firm
See Business service firm

Service sector
Broadly defined, all U.S. industries that produce intangibles, including the five major industry divisions of transportation, communications, and utilities; wholesale trade; retail trade; finance, insurance, and real estate; and services.

Set asides
See Small business set asides

Short-haul service
A type of transportation service in which the transporter supplies service between cities where the maximum distance is no more than 200 miles.

Short-term debt
An obligation that matures in one year.

SIC codes
See Standard Industrial Classification codes

Single-establishment enterprise
See Establishment

Small business
An enterprise that is independently owned and operated, is not dominant in its field, and employs fewer than 500 people. For SBA purposes, the U.S. Small Business Administration (SBA) considers various other factors (such as gross annual sales) in determining size of a business.

Small Business Administration (SBA)
An independent federal agency that provides assistance with loans, management, and advocating interests before other federal agencies.

Small Business Data Base
A collection of microdata (see separate citation) files on individual firms developed and maintained by the U.S. Small Business Administration.

Small business development centers (SBDC)
Centers that provide support services to small businesses, such as individual counseling, SBA advice, seminars and conferences, and other learning center activities. Most services are free of charge, or available at minimal cost.

Small business development corporation
See Certified development corporation

Small business-dominated industry
Industry in which a minimum of 60 percent of employment or sales is in firms with fewer than 500 employees.

Small Business Innovation Development Act of 1982
Federal statute requiring federal agencies with large extramural research and development budgets to

allocate a certain percentage of these funds to small research and development firms. The program, called the Small Business Innovation Research (SBIR) Program, is designed to stimulate technological innovation and make greater use of small businesses in meeting national innovation needs.

Small business institutes (SBI) program
Cooperative arrangements made by U.S. Small Business Administration district offices and local colleges and universities to provide small business firms with graduate students to counsel them without charge.

Small business investment corporation (SBIC)
A privately owned company licensed and funded through the U.S. Small Business Administration and private sector sources to provide equity or debt capital to small businesses.

Small business set asides
Procurement (see separate citation) opportunities required by law to be on all contracts under $10,000 or a certain percentage of an agency's total procurement expenditure.

Smaller firms
For U.S. Department of Commerce purposes, those firms not included in the Fortune 1000.

SMSA
See Metropolitan statistical area

Socially and economically disadvantaged
Individuals who have been subjected to racial or ethnic prejudice or cultural bias without regard to their qualities as individuals, and whose abilities to compete are impaired because of diminished opportunities to obtain capital and credit.

Sole proprietorship
An unincorporated, one-owner business, farm, or professional practice.

Special lending institution categories
See SBA special lending institution categories

Standard Industrial Classification (SIC) codes
Four-digit codes established by the U.S. Federal Government to categorize businesses by type of

economic activity; the first two digits correspond to major groups such as construction and manufacturing, while the last two digits correspond to subgroups such as home construction or highway construction.

Standard metropolitan statistical area (SMSA)
See Metropolitan statistical area

Start-up
A new business, at the earliest stages of development and financing.

Start-up costs
Costs incurred before a business can commence operations.

Start-up financing
Financing provided to companies that have either completed product development and initial marketing or have been in business for less than one year but have not yet sold their product commercially.

Stock
A certificate of equity ownership in a business.

Stop-loss coverage
Insurance for a self-insured plan that reimburses the company for any losses it might incur in its health claims beyond a specified amount.

Strategic planning
Projected growth and development of a business to establish a guiding direction for the future. Also used to determine which market segments to explore for optimal sales of products or services.

Structural unemployment
See Unemployment

Sub chapter S corporations
Corporations that are considered noncorporate for tax purposes but legally remain corporations.

Subcontract
A contract between a prime contractor and a subcontractor, or between subcontractors, to furnish supplies or services for performance of a prime contract (see separate citation) or a subcontract.

Surety bonds
Bonds providing reimbursement to an individual, company, or the government if a firm fails to complete

a contract. The U.S. Small Business Administration guarantees surety bonds in a program much like the SBA guaranteed loan program (see separate citation).

Swing loan
See Bridge financing

Target market
The clients or customers sought for a business' product or service.

Targeted Jobs Tax Credit
Federal legislation enacted in 1978 that provides a tax credit to an employer who hires structurally unemployed individuals.

Tax number
A number assigned to a business by a state revenue department that enables the business to buy goods without paying sales tax.

Taxable bonds
An interest-bearing certificate of public or private indebtedness. Bonds are issued by public agencies to finance economic development.

Technical assistance
See Management and technical assistance

Technical evaluation
Assessment of technological feasibility.

Technology
The method in which a firm combines and utilizes labor and capital resources to produce goods or services; the application of science for commercial or industrial purposes.

Technology transfer
The movement of information about a technology or intellectual property from one party to another for use.

Tenure
See Employee tenure

Term
The length of time for which a loan is made.

Terms of a note
The conditions or limits of a note; includes the interest rate per annum, the due date, and transferability and convertibility features, if any.

Third-party administrator
An outside company responsible for handling claims and performing administrative tasks associated with health insurance plan maintenance.

Third-stage financing
Financing provided for the major expansion of a company whose sales volume is increasing and that is breaking even or profitable. These funds are used for further plant expansion, marketing, working capital, or development of an improved product. Also known as Third-round or Mezzanine financing.

Time deposit
A bank deposit that cannot be withdrawn before a specified future time.

Time management
Skills and scheduling techniques used to maximize productivity.

Trade credit
Credit extended by suppliers of raw materials or finished products. In an accounting statement, trade credit is referred to as "accounts payable."

Trade name
The name under which a company conducts business, or by which its business, goods, or services are identified. It may or may not be registered as a trademark.

Trade periodical
A publication with a specific focus on one or more aspects of business and industry.

Trade secret
Competitive advantage gained by a business through the use of a unique manufacturing process or formula.

Trade show
An exhibition of goods or services used in a particular industry. Typically held in exhibition centers where exhibitors rent space to display their merchandise.

Trademark
A graphic symbol, device, or slogan that identifies a business. A business has property rights to its trademark from the inception of its use, but it is still prudent to register all trademarks with the Trademark Office of the U.S. Department of Commerce.

Translation
See Product development

Treasury bills
Investment tender issued by the Federal Reserve Bank in amounts of $10,000 that mature in 91 to 182 days.

Treasury bonds
Long-term notes with maturity dates of not less than seven and not more than twenty-five years.

Treasury notes
Short-term notes maturing in less than seven years.

Trend
A statistical measurement used to track changes that occur over time.

Trough
See Cyclical trough

UCC
See Uniform Commercial Code

UL
See Underwriters Laboratories

Underwriters Laboratories (UL)
One of several private firms that tests products and processes to determine their safety. Although various firms can provide this kind of testing service, many local and insurance codes specify UL certification.

Underwriting
A process by which an insurer determines whether or not and on what basis it will accept an application for insurance. In an experience-rated plan, premiums are based on a firm's or group's past claims; factors other than prior claims are used for community-rated or manually rated plans.

Unfair competition
Refers to business practices, usually unethical, such as using unlicensed products, pirating merchandise, or misleading the public through false advertising, which give the offending business an unequitable advantage over others.

Unfunded accrued liability
The excess of total liabilities, both present and prospective, over present and prospective assets.

Unemployment
The joblessness of individuals who are willing to work, who are legally and physically able to work, and who are seeking work. Unemployment may represent the temporary joblessness of a worker between jobs (frictional unemployment) or the joblessness of a worker whose skills are not suitable for jobs available in the labor market (structural unemployment).

Uniform Commercial Code (UCC)
A code of laws governing commercial transactions across the U.S., except Louisiana. Their purpose is to bring uniformity to financial transactions.

Uniform product code (UPC symbol)
A computer-readable label comprised of ten digits and stripes that encodes what a product is and how much it costs. The first five digits are assigned by the Uniform Product Code Council, and the last five digits by the individual manufacturer.

Unit cost
See Average cost

UPC symbol
See Uniform product code

U.S. Establishment and Enterprise Microdata (USEEM) File
A cross-sectional database containing information on employment, sales, and location for individual enterprises and establishments with employees that have a Dun & Bradstreet credit rating.

U.S. Establishment Longitudinal Microdata (USELM) File
A database containing longitudinally linked sample microdata on establishments drawn from the U.S. Establishment and Enterprise Microdata file (see separate citation).

U.S. Small Business Administration 504 Program
See Certified development corporation

USEEM
See U.S. Establishment and Enterprise Microdata File

USELM
See U.S. Establishment Longitudinal Microdata File

VCN
See Venture capital network

Venture capital
Money used to support new or unusual business ventures that exhibit above-average growth rates, significant potential for market expansion, and are in need of additional financing to sustain growth or further research and development; equity or equity-type financing traditionally provided at the commercialization stage, increasingly available prior to commercialization.

Venture capital company
A company organized to provide seed capital to a business in its formation stage, or in its first or second stage of expansion. Funding is obtained through public or private pension funds, commercial banks and bank holding companies, small business investment corporations licensed by the U.S. Small Business Administration, private venture capital firms, insurance companies, investment management companies, bank trust departments, industrial companies seeking to diversify their investment, and investment bankers acting as intermediaries for other investors or directly investing on their own behalf.

Venture capital limited partnerships
Designed for business development, these partnerships are an institutional mechanism for providing capital for young, technology-oriented businesses. The investors' money is pooled and invested in money market assets until venture investments have been selected. The general partners are experienced investment managers who select and invest the equity and debt securities of firms with high growth potential and the ability to go public in the near future.

Venture capital network (VCN)
A computer database that matches investors with entrepreneurs.

WAN
See Wide Area Network

Wide Area Network (WAN)
Computer networks linking systems throughout a state or around the world in order to facilitate the sharing of information.

Withholding
Federal, state, social security, and unemployment taxes withheld by the employer from employees' wages; employers are liable for these taxes and the corporate umbrella and bankruptcy will not exonerate an employer from paying back payroll withholding. Employers should escrow these funds in a separate account and disperse them quarterly to withholding authorities.

Workers' compensation
A state-mandated form of insurance covering workers injured in job-related accidents. In some states, the state is the insurer; in other states, insurance must be acquired from commercial insurance firms. Insurance rates are based on a number of factors, including salaries, firm history, and risk of occupation.

Working capital
Refers to a firm's short-term investment of current assets, including cash, short-term securities, accounts receivable, and inventories.

Yield
The rate of income returned on an investment, expressed as a percentage. Income yield is obtained by dividing the current dollar income by the current market price of the security. Net yield or yield to maturity is the current income yield minus any premium above par or plus any discount from par in purchase price, with the adjustment spread over the period from the date of purchase to the date of maturity.

Index

Listings in this index are arranged
alphabetically by business plan type,
then alphabetically by business plan
name. Users are provided with the volume
number in which the plan appears.

Index

Index

Housing Rehabilitation Company
Madison Builders, LLC, 10

Human Resources Consultant
Anders Johnson LLC, 20

Ice Cream Parlor
SonnyScoops, 16

Ice Cream Shop
Fran's Ice, 3 and 19

Image Consulting
Simply Fabulous, 27

Import Boutique
Bellisimo Imports, Inc., 1

Import/Export Company
Rotole Import Export Company,
Inc., 30

Import/Export Store
Central Import/Export, 9, 29

Indoor Playground
Kid's World, 3

Indoor Softball Practice Facility
Richmond Fieldhouse, 24

**Inflatable Amusement Rental
Business**
FunGiant Enterprises Inc., 22

Information Broker Business
InfoSource, LLC, 27

**Information Technology
Personnel Agency**
Rekve IT Staffing, 12

Infusion Therapy
Pharma Infusion Services, Inc., 22

In-Home Senior Adult Services
HANNAH'S HELPING HAND, LLC, 28

Inn/Resort
Lighthouse Inn, The, 1

Insurance Agency
Englund Insurance Agency, 29

Interactive Testing Service
Greenbrier Technology Testing LLC, 32

Interior Decorator
Lindsay Smith Interiors LLC, 19

Interior Design Company
Gable & Nash LLC, 19
Make It Your Own Space Inc., 11

Interior Painting Service
Eyecatching Interiors LLC, 11

Interior Renovation Company
Addams Interiors, 14

Internet Cafe
The Postal Cafe Inc., 33

**Internet & Network Security
Solution Provider**
Safety Net Canada, Inc., 10

Internet Bid Clearinghouse
Opexnet, LLC, 5

Internet Cafe
Surf Brew Cafe, LLC, 28
Wired Bean, 5

**Internet Communications Service
Provider**
Appian Way Communications
Network, Ltd., 9

Internet Consultant
Allen Consulting, 3
Worldwide Internet Marketing
Services, 3

Internet Loyalty Program
Tunes4You, 11

Internet Marketplace
ABC Internet Marketplace, Inc., 8

Internet Services Portal Site
Net Solutions, 11

Internet Software Company
Poggle, Inc., 9

Internet Travel Agency Business
Memory Lane Cruises, 9

**Investor Trading Software
Company**
Investor Trends, Inc., 6

iPhone App Developer
AppStar, 22

IT Network Installer
Misch Computer Network Services, 22

Jewelry Designer
Oswipi Custom Costume Jewelry
Designs, 18

Junk Removal Business
Harry's Haul-Away Service Inc., 21

Kennel
Best Friend Kennel, 2

Ladder Company
Jacks' Ladder Inc., 1

Landscaping Service
Cantalupo Landscape Services,
Inc., 28
G & D Landscaping, 20
Greenscapes Lawn Care, 25
Helping Hand, Inc., 13

Laundromat
Duds and Suds Laundry Mat, 19

Law Practice
Wehler Legal Services, 29

**Lawn and Garden Equipment
Repair Business**
Center City Repair Inc., 33

Leasing Company
Leasing Group, 8

Leather Accessory Manufacturer
Safari Leatherworks, 13

Library Systems Consultants
Library Solutions, LLC, 33

Limited Liability Company
Northern Investments, LLC, 7

Litigation Services Company
Acme Litigation Company, 10

**Low–Cost Home Decorating
Service**
Your Home Stylists, 15

Magazine Publisher
GRAPEVINE, 1

Mailing List Service
Forest Mail Service, 3

Management Consulting Service
Salmon & Salmon, 3

Manufacturing Business
Fiber Optic Automation, Inc., 3

Marble Quarry
Vomarth Marble Quarry, 9

Marina
The Bayshore Marina, 19

Marketing Communications Firm
Cornelius Marketing, 4
Meridian Consulting, 5

INDEX

Index